Nathaniel Lardner

A large Collection of ancient Jewish and Heathen Testimonies to the Truth of the Christian Religion

Vol. I

Nathaniel Lardner

A large Collection of ancient Jewish and Heathen Testimonies to the Truth of the Christian Religion
Vol. I

ISBN/EAN: 9783337147846

Printed in Europe, USA, Canada, Australia, Japan

Cover: Foto ©ninafisch / pixelio.de

More available books at **www.hansebooks.com**

A LARGE

COLLECTION

OF ANCIENT

Jewish and Heathen Testimonies

To the TRUTH of the

CHRISTIAN RELIGION,

WITH

NOTES AND OBSERVATIONS.

VOL. I.

Containing the JEWISH TESTIMONIES, and the TESTIMONIES of HEATHEN AUTHORS of the First Century.

By NATHANIEL LARDNER. *D. D.*

LONDON: M.DCC.LXIV.

Sold by J. BUCKLAND, and T. LONGMAN, in Pater Noster Rowe, and J. WAUGH in Lombard Street.

PREFACE.

IT is well known, that I have long since intended a Collection of Passages of Jewish and Heathen Authors, who bear Testimonie to the Books, or Facts of the New Testament, or the Affairs of Christians in their own Times. I have also intimated, that I had by me large materials for that purpose: at the same time expressing my doubts, whether I ever should be able to put those materials into * order. But God, in his good providence, has prolonged my life. And having compleated the Supplement to the Second Part of the Credibility of the Gospel History, I have now put my collections of Jewish and Heathen Testimonies into such order, that it has been judged not improper to begin the publication.

This part of my design has been long deferred. But I hope, it is not the worse for that.

---

* *See the Preface to the* 12th *Volume of the Second Part of the Credibility of the Gospel History, near the end, published in the year* 1755.

PREFACE.

Many others of late times have made collections of this kind.

This Argument was not omitted by Mr. *Addison*, in his *Evidences of the Christian Religion*, who has insisted, though briefly, upon the Testimonies of *Tacitus, Suetonius, Phlegon, Dion, Celsus, Macrobius*, and other Heathen Authors, and made good remarks upon them: intending likewise to add the Testimonies of Jewish Writers, but was prevented by death.

In the year 1733. was published a book with this title: *An Appeal to the genuine Records and Testimonies of Heathen and Jewish Writers, in Defense of Christianity: By Thomas Dawson. D. D. Vicar of New Windsor, some time Member of Convocation.* †

That work has a pompous title, from which a great deal might be expected: but it is little more than an angry declamation against Dr. *Sykes*, for not shewing due respect to *Phlegon*, and *Dionysius the Areopagite*. I have made no use of that work. Nor do I know, that I shall have occasion to take any farther notice of it.

An Argument in Defense of Christianity, taken from the Concessions of the most ancient Adversaries, Jews, and Pagans, Philosophers and Historians. By Gregory Sharpe, L. L. D. Fellow of the Royal Society, and of the Society of Antiquarians. ⁂ I am indebted to this learned Author, and shall quote him sometimes.

In 1725. J. A. Fabricius published a volume in Quarto concerning the *Truth of the Christian Religion*. ‖ In the 32. Chapter of which volume

---

† *It is in two parts: 201 pages for the first part, and 112 for the second, in octavo.*
⁂ *A small volume of 166 pages, published in 1755.*
‖ Delectus argumentorum, et Syllabus Scriptorum, qui veritatem Religionis Christianae adversus Atheos, Deistas, ... lucubrationibus suis asseruerunt. Hamb. 1725.

PREFACE.

volume is a Catalogue of Authors, who have supported the evidence of the Jewish and Christian Religion by Testimonies of Heathen writers. †† Where are mentioned many Authors, with whom I am unacquainted, as well as others, whom I have seen, and of whom I shall take notice presently.

Le Clerc, who in the year 1727. revised that work of Fabricius, in his *Bibliotheque Ancienne et Moderne*, observes, that †* *there are in Pagan Authors, still remaining, Testimonies and Events, which may be*

of

---

†† Cap. xxxii. Ethnicorum Testimonia, veritatis Religionis Naturalis, Judaicae, et Christianae suffragantia. *Ibid, p.* 634. ... 643.

†* Il y a dans les Auteurs Payens, qui nous restent, des temoignages et des evenemens, qui peuvent beaucoup servir à confirmer la verité de la Religion Chrétienne. C'étoit le sentiment d' Herman Conringius, qui étoit, comme l'on sait, un tres-savant homme. *Bib. A. et M. T.* 27. *P. i. p.* 71.

Le Clerc here follows the modern way of speaking. Which indeed is now in use with all learned men in general. But Heathen people were not called *Pagans*, Pagani, before the year of Christ 365. about which time, and afterwards, that denomination became common in Latin Authors, as *Prudentius, Salvian, Orosius, Augustin.* That denomination is supposed to have had it's rise from the state of things at that time. Sacrifices were prohibited by Christian Emperours in cities, but allowed of for a while in villages and countrey-places. But I do not recollect, that this way of speaking is adopted by the Greek ecclesiastical historians, Socrates, Sozomen, and Theodoret: though they wrote after this stile was common in Latin authors. To me it seems not quite proper, to call those writers *Pagans*, who lived before the times of the Christian Emperours. I therefore generally say, *Heathens, Gentils, Greeks : Heathenism, Gentilism, Hellenism.*

Haec omnia, ut in *Urbibus* primo sublata, sic permissa ad tempus in *Pagis* et vicis, ubi templa aliquamdiu Gentilibus patuére. ... Unde Paganorum nomen enatum est, primum auditum sub Imperatoribus Christianis, primaque Pagnorum mentio exstat in L. xviii. Cod. Theod. *De Episcopis*, &c. Valentiniano et Valente. A. A. Coss. *Spanhem. Hist. Christ. Sec. iv. T. i. p.* 836. *Vid. et Jac. Gothofred. in nstis in Tit. de Paganis. Et Conf. Pagi ann.* 351. *num.* v.

Praeceperas mihi, ut scriberem adversus vaniloquam pravitatem eorum, qui alieni a Civitate Dei, ex locorum agrestium compitis et pagis, Pagani vocantur, sive Gentiles. *Oros. Hist. l.* 1. *cap.* 1.

PREFACE.

of great use to confirm the Truth of the Christian Religion. The same is said by *Herman Conringius,* who, as is well known, was a very learned man.

Unquestionably, Conringius, of Brunswick, was a very learned man, Author of many valuable works, and in great esteem with divers Princes ‡ of Germanie. But I wish, that Le Clerc had quoted his words at length, or referred to the work, in which Conringius delivered his judgement upon this point, and where, possibly, he so enlarged upon it, as to afford us some instruction.

Houtteville, in his work, entitled, *The Christian Religion proved by Facts,* and in his *Historical and Critical Discourse,* prefixed to it, ‡ has alleged the testimonies of many Jewish and Heathen Writers, *Celsus, the Emperour Julian, Porphyrie, Jamblichus, the Talmud and the Rabbins.* Fabricius, in the forecited volume, has given a large account of this performance.

I may not omit *Tobias Eckhard,* who has published a learned and useful work, entitled, †* *The Testimonies of such as are not Christians, collected from ancient Monuments.* Of which there have been two editions, both in my hands: and from which I have reaped benefit. This Author also is in the forementioned catalogue of Fabricius.

The *⁎* *Christian Religion confirmed by the Testimonies of ancient Pagan*

‡ *See the Dictionarie and Supplement of Moreri.*
‡ *A large volume in Quarto, at Paris, in* 1722.
†* Non-Christianorum de Christo Testimonia, ex Antiquis Monumentis proposita et dijudicata. Quarto. 1725. et 1736.
⁎ La Religion Chrétienne autorisée par le temoignage des anciens Auteurs Payens. Par le P. Dominique de Colonia, de la Compagnie de Jesus. A Lyon. 1718.

PREFACE.

Pagan Authors, by *Dominique Colonia*, of the *Society of Jesus*. This Author likewife is in the catalogue of Fabricius, who ‡ calls him a polite and eloquent writer.

This work has a nearer refemblance with mine, than any other, which I have met with. Many Authors are here ††* quoted. And Colonia gives fome account of them, for fhewing the value of their teftimonie. I fhall often quote him, or refer to him. Whereby the character of the work, and the judgement of the Author, will be apparent to my readers. Undoubtedly, he has learning, and zeal. But fome allowances muft be made for the credulity of his Church.

However, it can little become me to pafs cenfures upon others, who am as liable to be cenfured : and may fall into miftakes, notwithftanding my beft care to avoid them.

One fault in my work may be reckoned to be very obvious, which is the prolixity of it. In regard to which, I beg leave to fay beforehand, that I aim to be diftinct and particular. Thefe things have been already flightly touched upon by many. I propofe to enlarge, and fet them in a fuller light. I allege paffages of ancient authors at length. I fettle their time: I diftinguifh their works, and endeavour to fhew the value of their teftimonies. I intend likewife to allege

‡ ... elegans ac difertus fcriptor. *Fabr. ubi fupra. p.* 635.

††* Tom. 1. ch. I. Phlegon, et Thallus. ch. II. Ammianus Marcellinus. III. Mark Antonin. Dion. Capitolinus. Claudian. Themiftius. IV. Plutarch. *Where comes in the pilot Thamus.* Strabo. Lucan. Juvenal. V. Claudian. *again.* VI. Chalcidius. Amelius, and Macrobius. VII. Cornelius Tacitus. VIII. Celfus, the Epicurean. IX. The Philofopher Porphyrie.... Tom. 2. ch. I. Lampridius. II. The Younger Pliny. III. The Sophift Libanius. IV. The Emperour Julian, the Apoftate. V. Lucian, of Samofata. VI. Rutilius Claudius Numatianus. VII. The Emperour Antonin the Pious. VIII. The Emperour Mark Antonin. *again.* IX. The falfe Prophet Mahomet. X. Jofephus the Hiftorian. XI. The true Acts of Pilate.

PREFACE.

allege the judgements of divers learned moderns who have gone before me in this service. All the persecutions of this time are a part of my subject, as they were appointed by Edicts of Heathen Emperours, and were carried on by Heathen Governours of provinces, and officers under them. I shall have an opportunity to shew the patience and fortitude of the primitive Christians: and the state of Judaism, Gentilism, and Christianity, in the first four centuries. As most of the Authors to be quoted by me are men of great distinction in the Republick of Letters, some occasions will offer for critical observations, which cannot be all declined. But nice and intricate questions will be carefully avoided, that the whole may be upon the level with the capacities of all, who are inquisitive, and disposed to read with attention.

In the first volume are the Jewish Testimonies, and the Testimonies of Heathen Authors, who lived in the first centurie.

In the second Volume are Heathen writings of the second centurie. Among which are the Letter, of the Younger Pliny to Trajan, and that Emperour's Rescript: which will give occasion for many observations concerning the sufferings of the Christians at that time, and afterwards: and the remains of the work of Celsus against the Christians, preserved in Origen. Which afford an early, and very valuable testimonie to the genuinnesse of the books of the New Testament, and to the truth of the evangelical historie.

In the third Volume will be Ulpian, Dion Cassius, Porphyrie, Hierocles, and other Heathen Writers, and a historie of the several persecutions of the Christians in the third centurie, concluding with that of the Emperour Diocletian.

PREFACE.

The fourth and laſt Volume, (not †† yet finiſhed,) in which will be the Emperour Julian, Ammianus Marcellinus, Libanius, and other Heathen Writers of the fourth and fifth centuries, may be as entertaining, as any of the reſt. But it cannot be ſo important. Julian, in his work againſt the Chriſtians, may mention the names of the Evangeliſts, and of the other writers of the New Teſtament, and quote the books more diſtinctly than Celſus. But his teſtimonie to the Scriptures in the fourth centurie, cannot be ſo valuable, as that of Celſus in the ſecond. However, theſe alſo deſerve to be collected, and put together in their proper order. We ſhall there ſee the laſt ſtruggles of expiring Gentiliſm, and ſome attempts to reſtore it, after it had been for a while exploded with ſcorn and diſdain. And we may meet with more than a few men of great learning, and fine abilities, who were ſtill tenacious of the ancient rites, and fond of all the fables, upon which they were founded, and by which they had been long upheld and encouraged.

The Author profeſſes great impartiality. For which reaſon he is not without hopes, that his work, notwithſtanding ſome imperfections, may be approved by the candid of every denomination. If it ſhall be of ſome uſe to promote good learning, and true religion, he will have great reaſon to be well pleaſed.

†† Divers chapters of the fourth volume are compoſed. But ſome others are ſtill wanting.

CONTENTS
OF THE
FIRST VOLUME.

Jewish Testimonies.

CHAP. I.

Page

THE Faith of many Jewish Believers in early Times, a valuable Testimonie to the Truth of the Christian Religion. 3

CHAP. II.

Of the Treatment given to the primitive Christians by the unbelieving Jews. 24

CHAP. III.

Josephus, with his Testimonie at large to the Fulfilment of our Saviour's Predictions concerning the Destruction of the City and Temple of Jerusalem, and the Miseries coming upon the Jewish People. 30

CHAP.

CONTENTS.

CHAP. IV.
Three Paragraphs in the Works of Josephus, concerning John the Baptist, our Saviour, and James the Lord's Brother, and Observations upon his Writings, and Testimony. 142

CHAP. V.
The Mishnical and Talmudical Writers. 175

CHAP. VI.
Joseph Ben Gorion, or Josippon. 209

CHAP. VII.
A Recollection of the preceding Articles, and Reflexions upon them. 247

Testimonies of ancient Heathen Authors.

CHAP. I.
The Epistle of Abgarus, King of Edessa, to Jesus, and the Rescript of Jesus to Abgarus. 297

CHAP. II.
Of the Knowledge, which the Emperour Tiberius had of our Saviour Jesus Christ. 310

CHAP. III.
A monumental Inscription concerning the Christians, in the Time of Nero. 335

CONTENTS.

CHAP. IV.
Pliny the Elder. 339

CHAP. V.
Tacitus. 341

CHAP. VI.
Martial. 354

CHAP. VII.
Juvenal. 358

CHAP. VIII.
Suetonius. 363

To be corrected.

P. 54. l. 5. from the bottom, for his r. this
P. 73. l. 8. from the bottom, after Scopos put .
P. 155. l. 2. from the bottom, for Peroea r. Peraca
P. 193. l. 8. for not r. nor
P. 273. l. 17. for Ezra iii. 18. r. 10.
 and l. 20. for *ordinarie* r. *ordinance*
P. 278. l. 15. after may strike out the comma

In the Notes.

P. 56. note (p) r. *Reimari annot.*
P. 57. l. 6. from the bottom, for *Sem.* r. *Sen.*
P. 239. l. 4. for *p.* 472. r. 452.
P. 241. l. 1. for Chronologia r. Chorographia; and for *p.* 474. r. 454.

JEWISH

JEWISH

TESTIMONIES.

CHAP. I.

The Faith of many Jewish Believers in early Times, a valuable Testimonie to the Truth of the Christian Religion.

I. *That many of the Jewish People believed in Jesus as the Christ, shewn from the Books of the New Testament.* II. *From other ancient Writings.* III. *Their Faith a valuable Testimonie.*

I.  HE Lord JESUS was born at Bethlehem, and brought up at Nazareth, and in Judea, (understanding thereby the land of Israel,) he fulfilled his ministrie. At Jerusalem he was crucified. There he arose from the dead, and thence he ascended to heaven.

That many Jews believed in Jesus as the Christ, shewn from N. T.

A short time before his appearance in the world, John, called the Baptist, a man of an austere character, and acknowledged by all to be a Prophet, who acted with a divine commission, preached to the people, saying: *Repent, for the kingdom of heaven is at hand.* " Be persuaded by me, to reform your lives, and break off every evil course

course by repentance. For the kingdom of God by the Messiah, long since promised by God, and foretold by the Prophets, is now about to be erected among you, which is a dispensation of the greatest purity and perfection, the privileges of which are appropriated to sincere penitents only, and really good men." He also pointed to Jesus, as the person, who was to set up that kingdom, and was much greater than himself.

Soon after which Jesus also appeared preaching the like doctrine in the name of God: recommending the practise of strict and sublime virtue in heart and life, with a view, not to honour from men, or any other worldly advantages: but with an eye to the favour and approbation of God, who knows all things. These were the general terms proposed by him: forgiveness of past sins upon repentance, and eternal life to perseverance in the profession of the truth, and the practise of virtue: without any assurances of worldly riches, honour or preferment, and with frequent intimations of many difficulties, and external discouragements.

As he went about preaching that doctrine, he wrought many miracles, healing all men who came to him, of the diseases they labored under: and raising to life, some who had died. And twice he miraculously fed in desert places with a few loaves and small fishes great numbers of men, who had long attended upon his discourses. At the begining of his ministrie, and during the time of it, there were some extraordinarie manifestations from heaven, bearing testimonie to him, as the *beloved Son of God*, or the Messiah, the great and extraordinarie person, who had been long since foretold, and promised, as the *seed of the woman, that should bruise the head of the serpent, the seed of Abraham, in whom all the families of the earth should be blessed*, and *the Son of David*, in whom the promise of an extensive and everlasting kingdom was to be fulfilled. Of all which things the blessed Jesus sometimes, in the later part of his ministrie, reminded the Jewish people, his hearers, to induce them to act according to evidence, and to emprove the present opportunity, and accept

Ch. I.   *a valuable Testimony.*   5

accept the blessings offered to them, least they should expose themselves to the divine displeasure and resentment. But, as before hinted, he never invited any with assurances of worldly advantages from him. And all were at liberty to act according to their own judgement, and to *go away,* or stay with him. John vi. 66...71.

   Wherever he went, preaching that excellent and heavenly doctrine, he was attended by many : who plainly discerned it to be superior to that of their ordinarie teachers, the scribes and pharisees, and that he spoke and acted, as a Prophet, with divine illumination and authority. The people in general were so well satisfied of his great character, that they could not help wondring, that their scribes and rulers, for whom they had a great respect, did not publicly acknowledge him to be the Messiah. *And many of the people believed on him, and said : When the Christ cometh, will he do more miracles, than these which this man has done?* Again. *And many resorted unto him, and said : John did no miracle. But all things that John spake of this man were true. And many believed on him there.* John vii. 31. and see ch. ix. 20. 34. John x. 40. . 42.

   Nevertheless *among the chief rulers also many believed on him : but because of the Pharisees they did not confess him, least they should be put out of the synagogue. For they loved the praise of men more than the praise of God.* But *Nicodemus,* a Pharisee, and a Ruler, and in the very early part of our Lord's ministrie, came to him of his own accord, and acknowledged him to be a *teacher come from God.* And it is very likely, that he went away fully convinced, that he was the Christ. And when the Jewish Council reproved their officers for not having apprehended Jesus, and brought him before them, *Nicodemus, being one of them,* pleaded his cause, saying : *Doth our law judge any man, before it hear him, and knows what he doeth?* For which he was reviled, as very ignorant, and greatly mistaken. However, he afterwards attended the burial of Jesus, together with *Joseph of Arimathea,* another *disciple of Jesus, but secretly, for fear of the Jews.* He *was a rich man, and an honourable Counsellor.* Who John xii. 42, 43. John iii. ch. vii. 45..51. John xix. 38. 42.

went

went to Pilate, and begged the body of Jesus, and wrapt it in a clean linen cloth, and laid it in his own new tomb, hewen out of a rock.

Matth. xxvi. xxvii.
Mark xv.
Lu. xviii.

Beside them, *Jairus*, ruler of a synagogue, and a *Nobleman* of Capernaum, were disciples of some distinction. And there may have been some others in like stations, who paid their respects to Jesus, though they are not named. The centurion at Capernaum had such faith in Jesus, as to believe him able to heal his sick servant at a distance, by speaking a word only. He was a Gentil, but he was in esteem with *the Elders of the Jews*, who lived in that city. And they also joyned with him in the request to Jesus to heal his sick servant, *saying, that he was worthy, for whom he should do this.* So that they also were persuaded in their minds, that Jesus had power to perform so great a miracle. Not now to take any notice of our Saviour's female disciples, though they also were, some of them, respectable for their outward condition, as well as for their eminent virtue.

Mat. ix.
Mark v.
Luk. viii.
John iv.
Mat. viii.
Luke vii.

Luke viii.

Out of the number of his disciples Jesus chose twelve, to be generally with him, and to be employed by him, whom he named *Apostles*. Who, notwithstanding some imperfections, and failings, owing to the prevailing prejudices of the Jewish people, all continued faithfull to him, excepting only Judas the traitor, a man of a worldly and covetous disposition. And though the miscarriage and losse of Judas could not but be a great grief and discouragement to them, the other eleven kept together, even after the death of their Lord.

When he was risen from the dead, he came again among them, and shewed himself to them. And though they were not to be persuaded without good proof, in the end they were all satisfied, that it was he.

Acts i.

Having in the space of forty days been often seen by them, and having frequently conversed with them, *speaking of the things pertaining to the kingdom of God*, he was in their sight taken up into heaven.

Soon

Ch. I. *a valuable Testimony.* 7

Soon after which, when they were assembled together, to the number of *about one hundred and twenty*, another, named *Matthias*, was chosen in the room of Judas, to be a witness with the rest of the things concerning the Lord Jesus, and particularly his resurrection from the dead.

At the next following Pentecost the Holy Ghost in a remarkable manner came down upon the Apostles and their companie, agreeably the promise, which Jesus had made to them. And hence forward the Apostles, being fully qualified, preached to all men in the name of Christ, exhorting them to repentance, with the promise of the remission of sins, and everlasting salvation. *Acts ii.*

Such was the effect of St. Peter's first discourse at Jerusalem, after our Lord's ascension, that *there were added to them about three thousand souls*. And afterwards such accessions were made, that their number was *about five thousand*. *Acts ii. 41. Acts iv 4.*

But though many miracles were done by the hands of the Apostles, and the whole company of the believers behaved in a very becoming manner: insomuch that it is said, *they had favour with all the people*, and again, that *the whole multitude of them that believed, was of one heart, and of one soul: neither said any of them, that aught of the things which he possessed was his own, but they had all things common*: yet they met with many difficulties, and were ill-treated by the Jewish rulers. Peter and John were apprehended and brought before the Council, and examined, and were then commanded, *not to speak at all, nor teach in the name of Jesus:* And they were farther threatened, if they transgressed that order. But they, nevertheless, thinking themselves obliged to persist in their work, and *to obey God, rather than men*; in a short time afterwards, all the Apostles were taken up, and put *in the common prison*, and then brought before the Council. And having been *beaten*, and again *commanded, not to speak in the name of Jesus*, they were dismissed. Soon after this, *Stephen*, a man of great eminence, and usefulnesse, among the disciples, was stoned. And *James*, brother of John, one of the chief Apostles *Acts ii. 49. .. iv. 32. Acts iv. ch. v. ch. vi. vii.*

Acts xii. Apostles of Jesus, was beheaded by order of Herod Agrippa, then King in the land of Judea. *And because he saw it pleased the Jews, he proceeded farther to take Peter also, and put him in prison, intending after Easter to bring him forth to the people.* But now Divine Providence interposed: *Peter* was miraculously delivered out of prison. And Herod died under tokens of divine displeasure. What is added is well worthie of observation. *But the word of God grew, and multiplied.*

And gradually the Apostles and their fellow-laborers, with divine approbation and encouragement, enlarged their views, and preached the Gospel to *Samaritans,* and then to *Gentils.* But wherever they went, they first addressed themselves to the Jewish inhabitants, and particularly, in their synagogues, which there were at that time in many cities of Greece, and elsewhere, and usually had some converts among them. The evidences of the Christian religion were fairly and openly proposed, and to many they appeared sufficient, and satisfactorie. The whole argument is briefly summed up in those words of St. Paul before the Governour Festus, and King Agrippa, and the rest of that great audience. *Having therefore obtained help of God, I continue to this day, witnessing both to small and great, saying none other things, than those which the prophets and Moses did say should come: That the Christ should be liable to sufferings, and that being the first who rose from the dead,* to dye no more, *he should shew light unto the People, and to the Gentils.* Acts xxvi. 22, 23. Thus, at Antioch in Pisidia, it is said of Paul and Barnabas, *Acts xiii. they went into the synagogue on the sabbath day.* Where Paul made a
14.
ver. 43. long discourse. . . . *Now when the congregation was broken up, many of the Jews, and religious,* or worshiping *proselytes, followed Paul and Barnabas, who speaking to them, persuaded them to continue in the grace*
. . xiv. 1, *of God.* Afterwards, at Iconium, *they went both into the synagogue,*
2. *and so spake, that a great multitude of the Jews, and also of the Greeks believed.* And in like manner at other places. And particularly, at Thessalonica. Acts xvii. 1. and at Beroea. ver. 10. At Athens, ver.

Ch. I.   *a valuable Testimony.*   9

ver. 17. At Corinth. xviii. 4. At Ephesus. xviii. 19. and 26. When Paul came to Rome, he was a prisoner. He therefore could not go to any Jewish synagogue. But being *suffered to dwell by him-* *self, with a soldier that kept him, he called the chief of the Jews toge-* *ther...And when they had appointed him a day, there came many to* *him into his lodging: to whom he expounded and testified the kingdom of* *God, persuading them concerning Jesus, both out of the law and the* *prophets, from morning to evening. And some believed, and some be-* *lieved not.*   *Acts xxviii. 16..24.*

As for the Jews at Jerusalem, we know from the historie of the Council held there in the year of Christ 50. about the terms, upon which the Gentiles should be received, that the believers were then numerous there, and greatly concerned for the establishment and propagation of the gospel. And when St. Paul came thither again, at the Pentecost of the year 58. as we compute, the believers there were still steady and numerous. And St. *James*, the Apostle who presided there, and the Elders, reminded him, saying: *Thou seest, brother, how many thousands of Jews there are that believe.* By which I suppose to be intended chiefly the church at Jerusalem: though some others may be included, who were come up thither upon occasion of the feast. And about four years after this, near the end of his imprisonment at Rome, or soon after it, Paul wrote his epistle to *the* Hebrews, or the believers at Jerusalem, and in Judea, not excluding such as lived elsewhere, to confirm and strengthen them, and fortify them against discouragements.   *Acts xv.*   *ch. xxi. 20.*

Indeed, it should be particularly observed by us, that there were societies of believers in other parts of Judea, beside Jerusalem. For in the account of things about the year of Christ 40. it is said: *Then had the churches rest throughout all Judea, and Galilee, and Samaria, and were edified: and walking in the fear of the Lord, and in the comfort of the Holy Ghost, were multiplied.* And St. Paul, in his epistle to the Galatians, speaks of his being *unknown by face unto the churches of Judea, which are in Christ.* See likewise 1 Thess. ii. 14.   *Acts ix. 31.*   *Gal. i.22.*

C   Nor

Nor were all thefe men of the loweft rank and condition. For in the general account of the early progreffe of the gofpel, we are told:

Acts vi. 7. *And the word of God encreafed, and the number of the difciples multiplied in Jerufalem greatly. And a great companie of the priefts were obedient to the faith.* And we can reckon up fome by name, who upon feveral accounts were men of eminence. Nicolas, a profelyte of Antioch, then refiding at Jerufalem, who generoufly undertook a fhare in providing for the poor of the church: a man of fubftance, undoubtedly, and probably a man of good underftanding, and great probity. *Barnabas,* a Levite: a native of Cyprus, where he had an eftate in land, which he fold for the relief of thofe believers in Jefus, who were poor and indigent. *Paul,* a Pharifee, fon of a Pharifee, a native of Tarfus in Cilicia, educated in Jewifh learning at Jerufalem, under *Gamaliel, a doctor of the law, and had in reputation among all the people,* and not unacquainted with Greek literature, and a perfon of uncommon acutenefle, who of a violent perfecutor, became a fincere convert to the faith, and a zealous preacher of the gofpel. In which fervice he labored as fervently, and as fuccefsfully, as any other of the Apoftles: fhewing therein great fidelity, and felf-denial. Whofe difintereftedneffe had been fo confpicuous, that he could openly appeal to the world, and fay: *Though I be free from all men, yet have I made myfelf fervant to all, that I might gain the more.*

ch. iv. 36, 37.
ch. v. 34. and xxii. 3.

1 Cor. ix. 19.

The character of this perfon is fo extraordinarie, that I muft enlarge fomewhat in his hiftorie: notwithftanding the brevity, which I have prefcribed to myfelf in this article. By the fpecial choice and defignation of Jefus Chrift, after his refurrection from the dead, he was added to the other twelve Apoftles, *that he might bear his name before the Gentiles, and kings, and the children of Ifrael:* though it was forefeen, that he would *fuffer many things* in that fervice. In the courfe of his miniftrie he preached, and afferted the Chriftian doctrine to the Jewifh people in general, and before the Jewifh Council at Jerufalem. He pleaded alfo, and preached the doctrine of Chrift before *Felix* and *Feftus,* Roman Governours of Judea, and before King

Acts ix. 15, 16. and xxvi. 16. .. 20.

Acts xxii. xxiii. xxiv. xxv. xxvi.

Ch. I.   *a valuable Testimony.*

King *Agrippa*, and his sisters *Drusilla*, and *Bernice*, who were Jews by religion, and in the presence of many other personages of great distinction at Cesarea, the residence of the Roman Governour. He also pleaded *(a)* before the Emperour *Nero* himself at Rome: by whom was signed the order of his confinement in that city, which was a kind of free custodie. *Where he dwelt two whole years in his own hired house, and received all that came in unto him, preaching the kingdom of God, and teaching those things, which concern the Lord Jesus Christ, with all confidence, and with great successe, no man forbidding him.* At the end of which period he was discharged, and set at liberty, by the same authority by which he had been confined. And then he went abroad again, preaching the gospel as he had done before, and visiting and confirming the Christian Churches in several places. Afterwards, as we have reason to believe, he came to *Rome* again. And there, in the year 64. or 65. in the persecution of the christians ordered by the same Emperour, he suffered martyrdom, being beheaded, as a Roman citizen: so bearing his final testimonie to the truth of that doctrine, which he had long preached with great zeal and diligence: I now proceed.

Acts xxviii. 30, 31.

   The Chamberlain and Treasurer of Candace, queen of the Ethiopians, a Jewish proselyte, *who had come up to Jerusalem to worship*. His high station, and the great trust reposed in him, are arguments of his ability and fidelity. His journey to Jerusalem indicates his zeal for the religion, which he had embraced. And his reading the Jewish sacred scriptures, as he was returning in his chariot, shews his studiousnesse to understand them. His discourse with Philip, a disciple of Jesus, who drew near to him, manifests inquisitivenesse, and opennesse to conviction, which are laudable dispositions. And his conversion to the faith of Jesus is therefore a testimonie to the truth of the Christian Religion, which cannot be slighted.

Acts viii. 36..40.

C 2   *Judas*

(a). See the second vol. of the Supplement to the Credibility, &c. p. 250. &c.

The Faith of the early Jewish Believers Ch. 1.

Acts xv. 22. xvi. 37. xviii. 2. xvi 2 Tim. i.

Judas and *Silas,* chief men among the brethren at Jerusalem: and the later of them, as it seems, a Roman Citizen. *Aquila* and *Priscilla,* Jews of Pontus, persons of good understanding, and uncommon piety. *Timothie,* a young man of good understanding at Lystra, who from his childhood had been instructed in the scriptures of the Old Testament, being the son of a Jewesse. His mother *Eunice,*

Acts xii. 12. Col. iv. 10.

and his grandmother *Lois* also were believers. *John Mark,* an Evangelist, son of *Marie,* a woman of great zeal and courage in the profession of the Christian religion, an inhabitant of Jerusalem, and nephew to Barnabas. *Luke,* another Evangelist, by some thought to be the same as *Lucius of Cyrene.* Acts xiii. 1. If so, he was a Jew by birth. If he was not that *Lucius,* yet very probably he was a Jewish proselyte, before he became a Christian. With that Lucius of Cyrene is mentioned, in the place just referred to, *Manaen, who had been brought up with Herod the Tetrarch.* A *(b)* person, undoubtedly, of a liberal education.

Acts xviii. 24. ch. xviii. 8. ... 17. 1 Cor. i. 1. and 24. Tit. iii. 13.

Apollos, a Jew of Alexandria, an *eloquent,* or learned *man,* and *mighty in the Scriptures,* of the old Testament. *Crispus,* and *Sosthenes,* rulers in the Jewish synagogue at Corinth: and *Zenas,* a Jewish Lawyer.

All these I have reckoned up briefly, and imperfectly, (*) among the

---

(*b*) Μαναήντι Ἡρώδου τῦ τετράρχυ σύντροφος. *Herodis Tetrarchae collactaneus.* Vulg. "At vocabulum συντρόφου latius patet, significatque *eum, qui a prima aetate cum altero educatus est. Grot. in loc.*

(*) I say *imperfectly.* For I have not rehearsed all the Jewish believers, who are expressly mentioned, and by name. I have omitted several: as *Jason,* who was so friendly to St. *Paul,* at *Thessalonica,* as related, Acts xvii. 5. ... 9. *Sopater* of *Berea.* Acts xx. 4. These two seem to be the same, who are mentioned again. Rom. xvi. 21. where they appear to have been the Apostle's *kinsmen.* And therefore must have been Jews. *Aristarchus* a *Thessalonian.* Acts xx. 4. who is mentioned again in the epistle to the Colossians. iv. 10. 11. writ during the Apostle's imprisonment at Rome, or near the end of it, in the year 62. Where St. Paul calls him *his fellow-prisoner.* And reckons him among those *of the circumcision, who had been his fellow-workers unto the*

the Jewish believers: designedly omitting converts from among the Gentiles. All these Jews by their faith and profession bore a testimonie to Jesus, well deserving our regard. For they must have acted under as great discouragements, as can be conceived. They underwent the keenest reproaches from the unbelieving Jews their neighbours: for receiving a person as the Messiah, who instead of working out a great deliverance for their nation, as was generally expected, and earnestly desired, had himself undergone an ignominious death. For my own part, I always think of these early Jewish believers with peculiar respect. I am not able to celebrate all the virtues of their willing and steady faith under the many difficulties which they met with. But I am persuaded, that when the Lord Jesus shall come again, he will bestow marks of distinction upon those who extricated themselves out of the snares, in which their close connexions with others had involved them. And as *they were not ashamed of him, and his words, but confessed his name in the midst of an adulterous and sinful generation: he will not be ashamed of them, but will confess them*, and own them for his, *when he shall come in the glorie of his Father, with the holy angels*.

Mark viii. 38. Mat. x. 32.

For certain, I apprehend, that the faith of the Jewish believers is of greater importance, than the unbelief of other Jews in the time of Jesus, and his Apostles.

II. What has been hitherto alleged, we know from the books of the New Testament. It will be worth while to attend also to the informations of Ecclesiastical Historie.

The same shewn from other ancient writers.

There is good reason to believe, that no Christians were involved in the miseries of the last siege of Jerusalem. They are supposed to have left it, before the siege began. Some went to Pella, as mentioned

---

the kingdom of God. *Mnason of Cyprus, an old disciple*. Acts xxi. 16. And there are divers others, who may be observed by attentive readers of the Acts, and St. Paul's Epistles.

tioned by Eusebius, *(c)* a city on the other side Jordan. Others might go elsewhere, into *(d)* Asia, or *(e)* other remote countreys, where they could get a settlement. St. *John*, *(f)* as I suppose, left Judea, and went to Ephesus in the year 66. or thereabout, a short time, before the war commenced. Some Jews of Jerusalem, and other parts of Judea, might go with him, or follow him afterwards. And under his direction and assistance, they might procure a comfortable settlement in some places not far from him.

After the war was over in Judea, it is supposed, that the believers, who had retired into the countrey beyond Jordan, returned to Jerusalem, and formed a church there.

James, the Lord's brother, who had presided in the church of Jerusalem, died, as we suppose, in the year of Christ 62. who was succeeded by *Simeon*. In his ecclesiastical Historie *(g)* Eusebius placeth his election after the destruction of Jerusalem. But in his Chronicle *(h)* it is so expressed, as if it had been done immediatly after the death of James. That is no very material circumstance. Nor are we able to determine, which is right, for want of sufficient evidence. By Hegesippus he is *(i)* said to have been son of Cleophas, brother of Joseph: and therefore was our Lord's cousin-german. But Eusebius mentions that in a doubtfull manner. We should therefore, as I apprehend, be cautious of being too particular in our decisions about

---

(c) H. E. l. 3. cap. 5. p. 75. A. Vid. et Epiph. H. 29. vii. H. 30. n. ii.

(d) See the Supplement, Vol. i. p. 346. 347. Ch. ix. §. iii. and Vol. iii. Ch. xx. p. 311. 312.

(e) Credibile est, Judaeae Christianos, non tantum Pellae, ad ortum Jordanis, commoratos esse, sed et per vicinas, immo et remotiores Romani Imperii provincias, in quibus tutiores esse poterant, sparsos esse : &c. Cleric. H. E. Ann. 71. num. i.

(f) See the Supplement to the Credib. Vol. i. p. 346... 349.

(g) H. E. L. 3. cap. xi.

(h) Jacobus frater Domini, quem omnes Justum appellabant, a Judaeis lapidibus opprimitur : in cujus thronum Symeon, qui et Simon, secundus assumitur. Chr. p. 161.

(i) ... Ἀνεψιον ὥς γε φασὶ γεγονότα τῦ σωτῆρος. Τὸν γὰρ ἐν Κλωπᾶν, ἀδελφὸν τε Ἰωσὴφ ὑπάρχειν Ἡγήσιππος ἱστορεῖ. H. E. l. 3. c. xi. p. 87. Conf. l. 4. cap. 22. p. 142. C.

Ch. I.   *a valuable Testimony.*   15

about it. However, Eusebius *(k)* justly reckons him among the eye and ear-witnesses of the Lord. And according *(l)* to Hegesippus, whose Ecclesiastical Historie Eusebius had before him, he suffered martyrdom in Trajan's persecution. We therefore without hesitation place his death at the year of our Lord 107, where also it is placed by Eusebius in *(m)* his Chronicle. *Simeon* was then 120 years old. By order of Atticus, President of Syria, he was crucified. He must therefore have been born several years before our Lord. And supposing him chosen Bishop of Jerusalem in the year 62. he presided in that church more than 40 years.

He was succeded by *Justus*, a Jew. And, as Eusebius adds, " there *(n)* were then many believers of the circumcision." " The *(o)* times of the ensuing successions of Bishops at Jerusalem, Eusebius says, he could never learn. But it was said they had sat in the See for a short time only. This he had learned from ancient writers, that to the war in Adrian's time, (about the year 132.) there had been fifteen successions, who were all Hebrews by birth, and had held the genuine doctrine of Christ." Whose names are all put down by him. In this catalogue of fifteen Eusebius reckons *James* the first, *Simeon* the second: after which there follow thirteen more. Why their times were so short, we cannot say. There is no reason to think, that any of them were taken off by persecution. But possibly they were all in years, seniority being esteemed a ground of preference. After *(p)* their defeat by Adrian, the Jews were forbid

to

(k) Λογισμῷ δ' ἂν ᾗ τὸν Συμεῶνα τῶν αὐτοπτῶν ᾗ αὐτηκόων ἔσωι ἄντις γεγονέναι τῷ κυρίῳ. L. 3. c. 32. p. 104. B.

(l) Apud Euseb. H. E. l. 3. c. 32. p. 104. C.

(m) Trajano advertus Christianos persecutionem movente, Simon filius Cleopae, qui in Jerosolymis episcopatum tenebat, crucifigitur. Cui successit Justus. Ignatius quoque Antiochenae ecclesiae

episcopus Romam perductus bestiis traditur. Chr. p. 165.

(n) . . Τῆς ἐν Ἱεροσολύμοις ἐπισκοπῆς τὸν θρόνον Ἰουδαῖος τις ὄνομα Ἰοῦστος, μυρίων ὅσων ἐκ περιτομῆς εἰς τὸν χριστὸν τηνικαῦτα πεπιστευκότων εἷς ᾗ αὐτὸς ᾖ, διαδέχεται. l. 3. c. 35. p. 106.

(o) L. 4. cap. v.

(p) Ib. l, 4. cap. 6. Vid. et Chron. p. 167.

to come to Jerusalem. From that time the church there consisted of Gentiles, whose first Bishop was named *Mark*.

That there were Jews who believed in Jesus, we are assured even by *Celsus*, the Epicurean, who wrote against the Christians about the midle of the second centurie. In divers parts of his work he personates a Jew. It is likely, that he had conversed with divers unbelievers of that nation. He consulted them, that they might assist him in his argument against the Christians, and likewise furnish him with scandal against them, if they could. " In (*q*) this manner, says Origen, this personated Jew addresseth those who had believed from among the Jews. What ailed you, fellow-citizens, that you forsook the law of your countrey, to follow him, whom we mentioned just now, by whom you have been miserably deceived, leaving us, and going over to another name, and another way of living?"

And Origen, in his books against Celsus, says, " that (*r*) the " Messiah had been foretold so long, and by so many, that the whole " nation of the Jews were in earnest expectation of his coming. But " since the birth of Jesus, they have been divided in their opinion. " For many of them have believed, that Jesus is the person, whom " the Prophets foretold. But others rejected him, despising him, be- " cause of the meannesse of his outward character."

Irenaeus says, " there (*s*) were many of the circumcision, who believed in Jesus, who rose from the dead, hearkening to Moses and the Prophets, who before hand preached the coming of the Son of God."

Among

(*q*) *Contr. Cels. l.* 2. §. 1. *p.* 57. *Conf.* §. 3. *p.* 58. 59.

(*r*) .. " Ὅτε τὸ Ἰουδαίων ὅλον ἔθνος ἠρτημένον τῆς περὶ τοῦ ἐλπιζομένε ἐπιδημήσειν προσδοκίας, εἰς τὴν πρὸς ἀλλήλους ζήτησιν ἐληλυθέναι, τῷ Ἰησοῦ ἐπιδημήσαντος· καὶ πολὺ μὲν πλῆθος αὐτῶν ὁμολογηκέναι χριστόν, καὶ πεπιστευκέναι αὐτὸν εἶναι τὸν προφητευόμενον· τὸς

δὲ μὴ πιστεύοντας, κ. λ. *Contr. Cels. l.* 3. *n.* 28. *p.* 127.

(*s*) —— etiam ipsum Dominum, qui resurrexit a mortuis, in quem et credunt multi, qui sunt ex circumcisione, qui et Moysem et Prophetas audiunt praedicantes adventum Filii Dei. *Iren. l.* 4. *cap.* ii. §. 4.

Ch. I.   *a valuable Testimony.*

Among these Jewish believers there were different sentiments. Origen says, " there (*t*) were two sorts of Ebionites: some, " who believed Jesus to have been born of a virgin, as we do. Some, " who supposed Jesus to be born, as other men are." Origen speaks of both sorts of these men, as fond of the Jewish observances. Afterwards, (*u*) in the same book against Celsus, he says, that both sorts of the Ebionites, like the Encratites, rejected St. Paul's Epistles. Nor did they consider him, as a wife, or good man.

Eusebius, in his Ecclesiastical Historie, in a chapter, entitled *Of the Heresie of the Ebionites*, speaks to the like purpose. " Some, (*x*) " says he, who are not to be moved by any means from their respect " for the Christ of God, are in some respects very infirm. They " are called by the ancients Ebionites, because they have but a low " opinion of Christ, thinking him to be a mere man, born of Joseph " and Marie, honoured for his advancement in virtue: and esteem- " ing the ritual ordinances of the law necessarie to be observed by them, " as if they could not be justified by faith in Christ only. Others " of them do not deny, that Jesus was born of a virgin by the Holy " Ghost. Nevertheless they do not acknowledge his pre-existence " as God the Word. And like the others, they are fond of the " external observances of the law of Moses. They also reject Paul's " epistles, and call him an apostate from the law."

(*t*) ... ἔτι δὲ κ̀ τὸν Ἰεδαίων νόμον ὡς τὰ Ἰεδαίων πλήθη βιῶν ἐθέλοντες. Οὖτοι δ᾽ εἰσὶν οἱ διττοὶ Ἐβιωναῖοι, ἤτοι ἐκ παρθένε ὁμολογοῦντες ὁμοίως ἡμῖν τὸν Ἰησοῦν, ἢ οὐχ οὕτω γεγενῆσθαι ἀλλ᾽ ὡς τὸς λοιπὸς, ἀνθρώπες. *Contr. Cels. l.* 5. §. 61. *p.* 272.

(*u*) Εἰσὶ γάρ τινες αἱρέσεις, τὰς Παύλε ἐπιστολὰς τῶ ἀποςόλε μὴ προσιέμεναι, ὥσπερ Ἐβιωναῖοι ἀμφότεροι, κ̀ οἱ καλέμενοι Ἐγκρατηταί. Οὐκ ἂν ἄν οἱ μὴ χρώμενοι τῷ ἀποστόλῳ, ὡς μακαρίῳ τινὶ κ̀ σοφῷ. *Ib. n.* 65. *p.* 274.

(*x*) Ἄλλες δὲ ὁ πονηρὸς δαίμων τῆς περὶ τὸν χριςὸν τοῦ Θεῖ διαθέσεως ἀδυνατῶν ἐκσεῖσαι,

θατεραλήπτες εὑρὼν, ἐσφετερίζετο. Ἐβιωνάες τέτες εἰκείως ἐπεφήμιζον οἱ πρῶτοι, πτωχῶς κ̀ ταπεινῶς τὰ περὶ τοῦ χριςοῦ δοξάζοντας· λιτὸν μὲν γὰρ αὐτὸν κ̀ κοινὸν ἡγοῦντο, κατὰ προκοπὴν ἤθες αὐτὸ μόνον ἄνθρωπον δεδικαιωμένον, ἐξ ἀνδρός τε κοινωνίας κ̀ τῆς Μαρίας γεγεννημένον ... Ἄλλοι δὲ παρὰ τέτοις τῆς αὐτῆς ὄντες προσηγορίας, ἐκ παρθένε κ̀ τοῦ ἁγίε πνεύματος μὴ ἀρνέμενοι γεγονέναι τὸν κύριον, ὁ μὴν ἐθ᾽ ὁμοίως κ̀ ἔτοι προϋπάρχειν αὐτὸν Θεὸν Λόγον ὄντα κ̀ σοφίαν ὁμολογῶντες. κ. λ. *L.* 3. *cap.* 27. *p.* 99.

These

These two learned ancient authors speak of two sorts of *Ebionites*, therein, as (y) may be supposed, including those who are sometimes called *Nazareans*, and were the descendents of the Jewish believers at Jerusalem.

It may be also here observed by us, that many learned men are now of opinion, that there never was any man named *Ebion*, the leader of a sect: but that the Ebionites were so called from their low opinion concerning the person of Christ, and their attachment to the external rites of the law of Moses. And that opinion, as I apprehend, is much countenanced by the passages, which have been just quoted.

We cannot deny, that there were some believers, who supposed Jesus to have been born, as other men. But I apprehend, that the number of these was very small. Nor do I recollect any Christian writing now exstant, where that opinion is maintained.

We must also allow, that there were some, who (z) rejected the Apostle Paul, whilst they received the other Apostles. These likewise I suppose to have been few in number. I know no work of any ancient author now remaining, who speaks disrespectfully of him, excepting only (a) the *Recognitions*, or *Clementin Homilies*, of which we formerly took particular notice.

As for the other *Ebionites*, called also *Nazareans*, it is allowed, as we have just seen, that they believed Jesus to be born of a Virgin, by an especial Interposition of the power of God, or by the Holy Ghost. These also received the Apostle Paul. The Testaments of the Twelve Patriarchs were writ by a Jewish believer of this character

---

(y) Et Origines, cum duplices facit Ebionaeos in disputatione contra Celsum, Ebionaeorum nomine abutens, sub priore illa nota Nazaraeos, ut credibile est, describat. *Grot. Prol. in Matt. p. 5.*

(z) Nota, quod primi Apostoli Salvatoris literam Sabbathi destruunt adversus

Ebionitas, qui quum ceteros recipiant Apostolos, Paulum quasi transgressorem legis repudiant. *Hieron. in Matt. xii. 2. T. 4. P. i. p. 46.*

(a) *See the Credib. P. ii. Vol. ii. p.* 787. 788. *and p.* 794... 796.

Ch. I. *a valuable Testimony.*

character in the second centurie. He plainly received Paul, and his Epistles, and the Acts of the Apostles, as was shewn (*b*) formerly. It is a very curious work. When it came in my way, I enlarged in my extracts of it. Nor do I now repent of that labour.

That the *Nazareans*, called also believers from among the Hebrews, received Paul, is apparent from Jerome's commentarie upon If. ix. 1. . . 3. quoted Matt. iv. 15, 16. "The (*c*) Nazareans, says " he, whom I before mentioned, endeavor to explain this text after " this manner. When Christ came, and began to enlighten the " world with his doctrine, the land of Zabulon and Naphtali was " first delivered from the errours of the Scribes and Pharisees, and " shook off from their necks the heavie yoke of Jewish traditions. " Afterwards by the preaching of the Apostle Paul, who was the " last of all the Apostles, the preaching was encreased, and even " multiplied : and the gospel of Christ shone out among the Gen-" tils, and by *the way of the sea*. At length the whole world, that " had walked, or *sat in darknesse*, and had been held in the chains " of idolatrie and death, saw the clear light of the gospel." So, he says, that text was explained by the *Nazareans*, whom just before he called *the Hebrews that believed in Christ*.

That the Nazareans received all Christ's Apostles, is evident from the passage just transcribed. It is also manifest from Jerome's commentarie upon If. xxxi. 6. . . 9. "The (*d*) Nazareans, says he, un-
D 2 derstand

(*b*) See *the Credib.* P. 2. Vol. 2. p. 760. . . . 764.

(*c*) Hebraei credentes in Christum hunc locum ita edisserunt. . . Nazaraei, quorum opinionem supra posui, hunc locum ita explicare conantur. Adveniente Christo, ac praedicatione illius coruscante, prima terra Zabulon et terra Nephtali Scribarum et Pharisaeorum est erroribus liberata, et gravissimam traditionum Judaicarum jugum excussit de cervicibus suis. Postea autem per evangelium apostoli Pauli, qui novissimus omnium apostolorum omnium fuit, ingravata est, id est, multiplicata praedicatio : et in terminos gentium, et viam universi maris Christi evangelium splenduit. Denique omnis orbis, qui ante ambulabat, vel sedebat in tenebris, et idolatriae ac mortis vinculis tenebatur, claram evangelii lucem aspexit. *In If. cap. ix.* T. 3. . p. 83.

(*d*) Nazaraei locum istum sic intelligunt.

"derstand this place after this manner. O ye children of Israel, "who under the worst direction denied the Son of God, return to "him, and to his Apostles. For, if you do that, you will then "cast away your idols, which have been a sin to you: and the de- "vil shall fall before you, not by your own power, but by the mer- "cy of God: and his young men, who before fought for him, "shall be tributary to the church, and all his strength and power "shall be subdued."

The Ebionites (*e*) are said to have adhered to the injunctions of the law of Moses, after they had received the gospel of Christ. "Some of them, as (*f*) Jerome intimates, were for imposing the "legal observances upon all men, as necessarie to salvation. But the "other Ebionites, (or *Nazareans*) as the same ancient and learned "writer owns, observed those appointments themselves, as being of "the seed of Israel, without imposing them upon others." These were evidently of the same opinion with the believers in the church of Jerusalem. See the Acts of the Apostles, ch. xxi. And divers learned moderns (*g*) are now convinced of this, and readily allow, that the Jewish believers, who were called *Nazareans*, did not impose

---

gunt. O filii Israel, qui consilio pessimo Dei Filium denegastis, revertimini ad eum, et ad Apostolos ejus. Si enim hoc feceritis, omnia abjicietis idola, quae vobis prius fuerant in peccatum: et cadet vobis diabolus, non vestris viribus, sed misericordia Dei, et juvenes ejus, qui quondam pro illo pugnaverant, erunt Ecclesiae vectigales, omnisque fortitudo et petra illius pertransibit. *In If. cap. xxxi. T.* 3. *p.* 267.

(*e*) Simul arat in bove et asino Ebion, dignus pro humilitate sensu paupertate nominis sui, qui sic recipit evangelium, ut Judaicarum superstitionum, quae in umbra et imagine praecesserunt, caeremonias non relinquat. *Hieron. in If. cap. i. T.* 3. *p.* 9.

(*f*) Audiant Ebionaei, qui post passionem abolitam legem putant esse servandam. Audiant Ebionitarum socii, qui Judaeis tantum, et de stirpe Israelitici generis haec custodienda decernunt. *Id. in If. cap. i. T.* 3. *p.* 15.

(*g*) Ego ad eos accedere non vereor, qui statuunt, Nazaraeos, nullos Christianorum, nisi Judaeos, et Abrahae posteros, legi Mosaicae allegare voluisse, &c. *Moshem. de Reb. Chrift. ante C. M. p.* 330.

Ch. I.   *a valuable Testimony.*

pose the ordinances of the law upon others, though they observed them, as descendents of Israel, and Abraham.

The Ebionites, or some, who went under that denomination, must have received the Acts of the Apostles. " For, as (h) we learn " from Epiphanius, they said, they were called Ebionites, or poor, " because in the times of the Apostles they *sold their goods, and laid* " *them at the Apostles feet :* and by that means they had voluntarily " reduced themselves to poverty. For that reason men called them " poor, but they gloried in the name." Manifestly referring to the historie in the fourth and fifth chapters of the Acts. They who received that book, must have received Paul, and all the Apostles of Jesus, and, very probably, all their writings, which were received by other christians.

I suppose likewise, that all the Jewish believers in general received the gospel of St. Matthew entire, with the genealogie, at the begining. The testimonie of Irenaeus, as seems to me, without searching for any other authority, is sufficient to put it out of question.

" The *(i)* gospel according to Matthew, he says, was writ to the " Jews. For they earnestly desired a Messiah of the seed of David. " And Matthew having the same desire to a yet greater degree, " strove by all means to give them full satisfaction, that Christ was " of the seed of David. Wherefore he began with his genealo- " gie." (A)

Eusebius,

(*h*) Αυτοὶ δὲ ὅτι δὲν σεμνύνονται, ἑαυτὰς φάσκοντες πτωχὸς διὰ τὸ φάσιν ἐν χρόνοις τῶν ἀποστόλων πωλεῖν τὰ αὐτῶν ὑπάρχοντα, ἡ τιθέναι παρὰ τὴς πόδας τῶν ἀποστόλων, ἡ εἰς πτωχείαν ἡ ἀποταξίαν μεταληλυθέναι· ἡ διὰ τοῦτο καλεῖσθαι ὑπὸ πάντων, φασὶ, πτωχοί. H. 30. n. xiii. p. 141. A.

(*i*) *Iren.* p. 347. *Mass. and see the Credib.* P. 2. *Vol. i.* p. 356.

(A) As many mistakes have been entertained about *the Gospel according to the Hebrews*, it may not be unseasonable to observe here, that probably it was an Hebrew translation of St. Matthew's original Greek Gospel, with additions from the other Gospels. To which, possibly, might be added, some few particulars received by tradition from the early Jewish Believers. *See Credibility.* P. 2. *ch. v. Vol. i.* p. 185. *and Vol.* 2. *ch. xxix.* p. 804. 805.

Eusebius, in a place above cited, says, *that even those Ebionites,* (or Nazareans,) *who believed Jesus to be born of a virgin by the Holy Ghost, did not acknowledge his pre-existence, as God the Word.* Nevertheless, I presume, they did believe Jesus Christ to be *the Word, and Wisdom, and Power of God.* But they did not believe the pre-existence of the Word, as a distinct person, and separate from God the Father: as Eusebius, and some Arianizing Christians of his time did. That I take to be the truth, and the ground and reason, why Eusebius expresseth himself, as he does. And it might be easily shewn, that (k) the Nazarean Christians did not reject St. John's Gospel, nor held any principles, that obliged them to reject or dislike it.

Finally, we are assured by St. Jerome, " that (l) in his time, there " were many all over the East, called *Nazareans,* upon whom the " Jews pronounced their curses, as heretics. They profess, says Je-" rome, that they believe in Christ, the Son of God, born of the vir-" gin Marie, who suffered under Pontius Pilate, and rose again from " the dead, the same, in whom we also believe."

I shall proceed no farther, in this argument, nor go any lower. There were, for the first four centuries, many Jews, who professed faith in Jesus as the Christ, notwithstanding the difficulties and discouragements, to which they were exposed. For they were in

an

---

805. Epiphanius therefore says, *that the Hebrew Gospel of Matthew, used by the Nazareans, was a full Gospel.* Ἔχουσι δὲ τὸ κατὰ Ματθαῖον εὐαγγέλιον πληρέστατον ἑβραϊστί. *H.* 29. *num. ix. p.* 124. The Nazareans therefore did not reject the authority of the other Evangelists, but owned, and acknowledged it. That St. Matthew wrote in Greek, see the *Supplement, Vol.* i. *p.* 118. 119. 120. Says Lampe. *Synops. H. E. p.* 73. Graeca vero lingua omnes, ne Matthaeo quidem excepto, usi sunt, ut a Judaeis et Gentibus uterentur.

(k) Vid. Lampe *Prolegom. in Joh. Evang. l.* 2. *cap.* i. §. 1. 2. 3. *et cap. iii. num.* 38. ... 43.

(l) Usque hodie per totas Orientis synagogas, inter Judaeos haeresis est, quae dicitur minaeonem, et a Pharisaeis nunc usque damnatur: quos vulgo Nazaraeos nuncupant, qui credunt in Christum Filium Dei, natum ex virgine Maria, et eum dicunt esse, qui sub Pontio Pilato passus est, et resurrexit, in quem et nos credimus. &c. *Hieron. ad August. ep.* 74. *al.* 89. *Tom.* 4. *p.* 623.

Ch. I. *a valuable Testimony.*

an especial manner the object of the spight and enmity of the unbelieving part of their nation: and besides, they *(m)* were too much slighted and disregarded by the Gentil Christians.

III. I now leave it to my readers to judge, whether the faith of so many Jewish believers, in the early days of the gospel, be not a valuable testimonie to the truth of the Christian Religion. *Their Faith a valuable Testimonie.*

Some Jews have all along, in every age since, embraced the Christian Religion, who have joyned themselves to the Gentil believers, and have been incorporated with them. These are not now the subjects of my historie.

(m) See *W. Wall* in the *Preface* to his *Notes upon the O. T. p. xi. xii.*

CHAP.

CHAP. II.

Of the Treatment given to the primitive Christians by the unbelieving Jews.

JUSTIN, in his Dialogue with *Trypho,* (a) speaks to this purpose. " For ye have killed the Just, and his Prophets before
" Him. And now you despise, and as much as in you lyes, disparage
" them who hope in Him, and in God Almighty, Lord of the
" whole world, who sent Him, cursing in your synagogues those who
" believe in Christ. For it is not now in your power to lay hands
" upon us, being hindred by them, who have the chief government
" of things. But whenever you have had it in your power, you
" have done that also.... For no other people are so averse to us, and
" Christ, as you: who are the authors of all the prejudices, which
" others have against Him, and us. For after that you had crucified
" Him, that one unblamable and righteous man, *by whose stripes they*
" *are healed,* who come to the Father through Him: and, when
" ye knew, that he was risen from the dead, and was ascended into
" heaven, as the Prophets had foretold, you not only did not repent
" of the evil that you had done, but you sent out chosen men from
" Jerusalem into all the earth, saying, that an atheistical sect, called
" Christians, had arisen among you: thus spreading abroad all those
" evil reports concerning us, which all who are ignorant of us, now
" believe. So that you have been the causes not only of your own
" wickednesse, but likewise of the wickednesse of others."

1 Pet ii. 24.

Eusebius (b) rehearsing the works of Justin, has transcribed this passage from his Dialogue with Trypho.

And

(a) *Justin. M. Dialog.* p. 234. 235. *Parif.* §. 16. *et* 17. p. 117. *Bened.*
(b) *H. E. l.* 4. *cap.* 18.

Ch. II.   *by the unbelieving Jews.*

And afterwards, in the same Dialogue, or the second part of it:
"Notwithstanding *(c)* all that Christ said to you, you did not repent.
So far from it, that after he was risen from the dead, you sent forth
chosen men into all the world, giving out, that a wicked and atheistical sect was arisen, the author of which was one Jesus of Galilee, an impostor: whom, when you had crucified, his disciples
stole out of the sepulchre by night, where he had been laid after
his crucifixion: and that they deceived men, saying, that he was
risen from the dead, and ascended into heaven. Moreover you
gave out, that he taught those wicked and impure and abominable
things, which you every where charge upon all those who confess
Him to be the Christ, and their master, and the Son of God. And
though your city has been taken, and your countrey laid waste, you
do not repent: but still pronounce curses upon Him, and upon all
who believe in Him."

He has somewhat to the like purpose, once more afterwards, in
the same *(d)* Dialogue: where he chargeth them with hating all
who believed in God through Christ, and killing them, when they
had power, and still continually devoting Him and them to destruction.

Tertullian does not expressly say all this. But *(e)* he often intimates,

---

(c) Dial. p. 335. Par. §. 108. p. 202. Bened.

(d) Dial. p. 363. Parif. §. 133. p. 225. Bened

(e) Novo jam de Deo nostro fama suggissit. Adeo nuper quidam perditissimus in ista civitate, etiam suae religionis defertor, solo detrimento cutis, Judaeus ... picturam in nos proposuit sub ista proscriptione, Onochoëtes. Is erat auribus canteriorum, et in togâ, cum libro, altero pede ungulato. Et credidit vulgus Judaeo. Quod enim aliud genus seminari-um est infamiae nostrae? Itaque in tota civitate Onochoëtes praedicatur. *Adv. Nat. l. i. cap.* 14. *p.* 59. *l'id. et Ap. cap.* 16. *p.* 17. *D. et conf. Minuc. Fel. cap.* ix. *et* xxviii.

Dehinc, cum ex perseverantia furoris, et nomen Domini per ipsos blasphemaretur, sicut scriptum est: *Propter vos blasphematur nomen meum in nationibus:* (ab illis enim coepit infamia:) et tempus medium a Tiberio usque ad Vespasianum, non poenitentiam intellexissent, facta est terra eorum deserta, civitates eorum exustae

26 Of the Treatment given to the first Christians Ch. II.

mates, that the Jews were the principal authors of the reproaches cast upon the Christians. And he speaks of one calumnie in particular, which had been then lately forged by them, in his own time.

Origen says much the same that Justin does. Having taken notice of some things in Celsus, he says, " that (e) therein he acted much " like the Jews of old, who at the rise of the Christian religion, " spread abroad calumnies against it: as if the Christians killed a " child, and ate it, and putting out the lights practised promiscuous " lewdnesse. Which calumnies, though very absurd, were in for- " mer times believed by many."

And Eusebius, in his commentarie upon Is. xviii. 1. 2. " We (f) " find in the writings of the ancients, says he, that the Priests and " Elders of the Jewish nation, who dwelt at Jerusalem, wrote let- " ters which they sent to the Jews abroad in all countreys, tradu- " cing the doctrine of Christ, as a new and strange heresie, and ex- " horting them not to embrace it."

Whether the Jews did send out men in this manner, before the destruction of Jerusalem, to asperse the followers of Jesus, is not quite certain. The question is particularly considered by the Benedictins (g) in their Preface to Justin Martyr. The origin of the early calumnies upon the Christians is somewhat doubtfull. Some have supposed them to have been occasioned by the absurd doctrines, and vicious lives of those called heretics. However, I formerly

---

ustae igni, regionem eorum sub corum conspectu extranei devorant. *Adv. Marcion. l. iii. cap.* 23. *p.* 498. B.

(e) Καὶ δοκεῖ μοι παραπλήσιον Ἰουδαίοις πεποιηκέναι, τοῖς κατὰ τὴν ἀρχὴν τῆς τῇ χρισιανισμῦ διδασκαλίας κατασκεδάσασι δυσφημίαν τῷ λόγῳ· ὡς ἄρα καταθύσαντες παιδίον, μεταλαμβάνοσι αὐτῦ τῶν σαρκῶν· κ᾽ πάλιν, ὅτι οἱ ἀπὸ τῦ λόγυ τὰ τῦ σκότυ πράττειν βυλόμενοι, σβεννύυσι μὲν τὸ φῶς, ἕκαστος δὲ τῇ παρατυχέσῃ μίγνυται. *Contr. Cels. l.* 6. *num.* 27. *p.* 293.

(f) Εὕρομεν ἐν τοῖς παλαιῶν συγγράμμασιν, ὡς οἱ τὴν Ἱερυσαλὴμ οἰκᾶντες τῶν τῶν Ἰουδαίων ἔθνους ἱερεῖς κ᾽ πρεσβύτεροι γράμματα διαχαράξαντες εἰς πάντα διεπέμψαντο τὰ ἔθνη τοῖς ὁπανταχῦ Ἰουδαίοις διαβάλλοντες τὴν χρισῦ διδασκαλίαν, ὡς αἵρεσιν καινὴν κ᾽ ἀλλοτρίαν τῦ Θεῦ, παραγγέλλοντες δι᾽ ἐπιστολῶν μὴ παραδέξασθαι αὐτήν. *Euseb. in Es. cap.* xviii. *p.* 424.

(g) *Pr. Part* 3. *cap. iv. p.* 76. &c.

Ch. II.   *by the unbelieving Jews.*

merly *(h)* propofed fome obfervations, tending to fhew, that they are not to be accounted for in that way.

It is certain, that the Chriftians were very early afperfed with crimes, of which they were not guilty. When St. Paul was come a prifoner to Rome, he fent for the chief of the Jews of that city to come to him, who fay to him: *As for this sect, we know, that every where it is spoken against.* Acts xxviii. 22. Thofe words might be fpoken in the year of Chrift 61. and not far from the begining of it. And Tacitus giving an account of Nero's perfecution of the Chriftians, which feems to have begun in the year 64. intimates, " that *(i)* the Chriftians were generally hated for the crimes imputed to them."

Whether the Jewifh Rulers did before the deftruction of Jerufalem fend abroad meffengers and letters on purpofe to defame the doctrine of Chrift and his followers, or not: it muft be allowed to be true, which Juftin fays, *that no other people were so averse to Christ and his followers, as the Jews*. It muft alfo be allowed to be very true, which he likewife fays of them, that *they continued to anathematize Jesus Christ, and his followers*.

In the authentic account of the martyrdom of *Polycarp* at Smyrna, when he was condemned to be burnt, it is faid, " that *(k)* pre-
" fently the people brought together dried wood, and branches of
" trees from their fhops, and from the baths: in which the Jews
" efpecially, as is ufual with them, readily affifted."

We are affured by Jerome that the Jews anathematized the Chriftians under the name of Nazareans in their fynagogues, thrice every day. So he writes in *(l)* his commentarie upon *If.* v. 18. 19.

And

(h) Credib. P. 2. *ch. xxix. p.* 712, 713.

(i) Ergo abolendo rumori Nero fubdidit reos, et quaefitiffimis poenis affecit, quos per flagitia invifos, vulgus Chriftia-

nos appellabat. *Tac. Ann. l.* 15. *cap.* 44.

(k) ... μάλιστα Ἰουδαίων προθύμως, ὡς ἔθος αὐτοῖς, εἰς τοῦτο ὑπεργόντων. *Ap. Euseb. H. E. l.* 4. *cap.* 15. *p.* 133. *A.*

(l) Dicuntur autem haec ad principes Ju-

And again *(m)* in like manner upon If. xlix. 7. and *(n)* upon the firſt chapter of the prophecie of Amos.

Epiphanius ſays, "that *(o)* the Jews three times every day ana-"thematized the Nazareans in their ſynagogues. For they were "more eſpecially diſpleaſed with them, becauſe though they were "Jews, they believed in Jeſus as the Chriſt."

All which may be very true. The Jews, as Jerome ſays, anathematized in their ſynagogues all Chriſtians under the denomination of Nazareans: and yet, as Epiphanius ſays, they were more eſpecially diſpleaſed with thoſe believers, who were of the ſeed of Iſrael.

Theſe paſſages of ancient Chriſtian writers do ſufficiently atteſt the early, and continued enmity of the unbelieving Jews, to all Chriſtians of every denomination.

There are ſtill ſome other things to be here taken notice of. For ſome time after our Saviour's aſcenſion, they aſperſed the character of Marie, our Lord's mother, and reproached Him with a ſpurious nativity. When theſe aſperſions were firſt given out, we cannot ſay exactly. But they are in *(p)* Celſus, who wrote againſt the Chriſtians about the midle of the ſecond centurie. And doubtleſs he had them

---

Judaeorum, qui ſupra arguti ſunt in avaritia et luxuria: quod provocati a Domino ad poenitentiam, et poſtea ab Apoſtolis ejus uſque hodie perſeverant in blaſphemiis: et ter per ſingulos dies in omnibus ſynagogis ſub nomine Nazarenorum anathematizant vocabulum Chriſtianum. *In If. cap. v. T.* 3. *p.* 53.

(m) Ipſe enim bonus paſtor poſuit animam ſuam pro ovibus ſuis, et contemſit eam: qui abominationi eſt genti Judaeorum, cui ter per ſingulos dies ſub nomine Nazarenorum maledicunt in ſynagogis ſuis. *Id. in If. cap. xlix, T.* 3. *p.* 353.

(n) ———— antiquumque furorem et iracundiam tenentes, uſque hodie in ſyna-

gogis ſuis ſub nomine Nazarenorum blaſphemant populum Chriſtianum, et dummodo nos interficiant, volunt igne comburi. *In Amos. cap. i.* p. 1378. *fin.*

(o) Ὃν μίνοι γὰρ δι τῶν Ἰουδαίων παῖδες πρὸς τούτοις κέκτηνται μῖσος, ἀλλὰ ἀνιστάμενοι ἕωθεν, κ᾽ μέσης ἡμέρας, κ᾽ περὶ ἑσπέραν, τρὶς τῆς ἡμέρας ὅτε εὐχὰς ἐπιτελοῦσιν ἐν ταῖς αὐτῶν συναγωγαῖς, ἐπαρῶνται αὐτοῖς, κ᾽ ἀναθεματίζουσι, φάσκοντες, ὅτι ἐπικαταράσαι ὁ Θεὸς τοὺς Ναζωραίους. Καὶ γὰρ τούτοις περισσότερον ἐνέχουσι, διὰ τὸ ἀπὸ Ἰουδαίων αὐτοὺς εἶναι, Ἰησοῦν κηρύσσειν εἶναι χριστόν. κ. λ. *Epiph. H.* 29. §. *ix. p.* 124.

(p) Vid. Orig. Contr. Celſ. l. i, num. 28. *et* 32. *p.* 22. *et* 26.

Ch. II.   *by the unbelieving Jews.*

them from the Jews. They are also in the Talmudical writings, as we shall see hereafter.

In order to disparage our Lord's miracles, they gave out, that they were performed by magical arts, such as he had learned in Egypt. This Calumnie also is in *(q)* Celsus. And doubtless he had it from the Jews. It is also in the Talmudical writers, as we shall see hereafter.

In the time of the Emperour Adrian, about the year of Christ 132. the Jews rebelled under the conduct of the impostor *Barchochebas*, who set up himself for the Messiah, "who *(r)* inflicted heavie penalties upon the Christians, to induce them to deny and blaspheme Jesus Christ. And if they did not, he ordered them to be put to death." So writes Justin Martyr, who lived at that time. Some have censured Justin for saying that Barchochebas tortured Christians only. But without reason, as seems to me. For certain, the Christians were above all men objects of his, and his followers enmity. Nor could any be called upon to deny Jesus Christ, but such as had received him for the Messiah. Of the sufferings of the Christians at that time Eusebius speaks in *(s)* his Chronicle, and in *(t)* his Ecclesiastical Historie: not now to refer to any *(u)* others.

(*q*) *Vid. Orig. Contr. Celf. l. i. §. 28. p. 22.*

(*r*) Καὶ γὰρ ἐν τῷ νῦν γεγενημένῳ Ἰουδαϊκῷ πολέμῳ, βαρχοχέβας ὁ τῆς Ἰουδαίων ἀποστάσεως ἀρχηγέτης, χριστιανοὺς μόνους εἰς τιμωρίας δεινὰς, εἰ μὴ ἀρνοῖντο Ἰησοῦν τὸν χριστὸν κ̓ βλασφημοῖεν, ἐκελεύσατο ἀπάγεσθαι. *Ap. i. p. 72. E. Par. p. 62. Bened.*

(*s*) Cochebas dux Judaicae factionis nolentes Christianos adversum Romanum militem ferre subsidium omnimodis cruciatibus necat. *Chron. p. 167.*

(*t*) *H. E. l. 4. cap. 6.*

(*u*) *Vid. Moshem. de Reb. Christianor. ante Const. p. 238. 239.*

CHAP.

CHAP. III.

JOSEPHUS, with his Testimonie at large to the Fulfilment of our Saviour's Predictions concerning the Destruction of the Temple, and the City of Jerusalem, and the Miseries coming upon the Jewish People.

I. *His Time, Works, and Character.* II. *The State of Things in Judea, in the Time of our Saviour, and some while before.* III. *Our Lord's Predictions concerning the Destruction of the Temple, and the City of Jerusalem, and the Miseries to be endured by the Jewish People: with the several Signs, preceding those Calamities, as recorded in the Gospels.* IV. *The Dates of several Events:* vid. *the Commencement, and the Duration of the War, and the Siege of Jerusalem: when the Temple was burnt, and the City taken.* V. *Of the Abomination of Desolation standing in the holy Place.* VI. *The actual Accomplishment of our Saviour's Predictions concerning divers Events, that should precede the great Calamities coming upon the Jewish People: the Gospel preached all over the World: the Disciples of Christ persecuted in many places: Declensions among his Followers: Famines, Pestilences, and Earthquakes, in divers Places: Wars and Commotions.*
VII.

VII. *The Occasion of the Jewish War with the Romans, as represented by Josephus.* VIII. *The Historie of the Jewish War from Josephus, with his Account of the Siege of Jerusalem, and the Miseries endured therein, and the Demolition of the Temple, and City of Jerusalem, and the Desolation of the Land of Judea, being his Testimonie to the Fulfilment of our Lord's Predictions of those Events.* IX. *Reflexions upon the preceding Historie, and the Value of the Testimonie of Josephus.* X. *Other ancient Writers, who have born Witnesse to the Accomplishment of our Lord's Predictions in the Conquest of Judea by Vespasian and Titus: Justus of Tiberias: Pausanias: Antonius Julianus: Suetonius: Tacitus: Dion Cassius: Philostratus: The Arch of Titus.*

I. JOSEPHUS, son of *Matthias*, of the race of the Jewish Priests, and of the first course of the four and twenty, by his mother descended from the Asmonean familie, which for a considerable time had the supreme government of the Jewish nation, was born in the first year of the reign of *Caligula*, of our Lord (*a*) 37.

His Time, Works, and Character.

He was educated together (*b*) with *Matthias*, who was his own brother by father and mother, and made such proficience in knowledge, that when (*c*) he was about fourteen years of age, the High-Priests, and some of the principal men of the city came frequently to him to consult him about the right interpretation of things in the law. In the sixteenth year of his age, he retired into the wildernesse,

---

(*a*) *Joseph. in Vita sua. cap. i.*
(*b*) *Cap. 2.*
(*c*) Ἔτι δὲ παῖς ὢν, περὶ τεσσαρεσκαιδέ- κατον ἔτος... συνιόντων ἀεὶ τῶν ἀρχιερέων ᾗ τῶν τῆς πόλεως πρώτων ὑπὲρ τῇ παρ' ἐμᾶ περὶ τῶν νομίμων ἀκριβέστερόν τι γνῶναι. *Cap. 2.*

nesse, where he lived three years an abstemious course of life in the companie of *Banus*. Having fully acquainted himself with the principles of the three sects, the Pharisees, the Sadducees, and the Essens, he determined to follow the rule of the Pharisees. And being now nineteen years of age, he began to act in public life.

Felix, when Procurator of Judea, sent some Priests of his acquaintance for a trifling offense to Rome, to be tried before Cesar. Josephus, hearing that they behaved well, resolved to go to Rome, to plead their cause. But he had a bad voyage. The ship was wrecked. And out of 600 persons, not more than eighty were saved. Soon after his arrival at Rome, he became acquainted with Aliturius, a Jew by birth, but a stage-player, in favour with Nero. By him he was introduced to Poppèa, the Emperour's wife: by whose interest he procured, that the priests should be set at liberty. Josephus, who never omits what may be to his own honour, adds, that (*d*) beside that favour, he also received from Poppèa many valuable presents. And then he returned home. This voyage was made, as (*e*) he says, in the 26. year of his age, which must have been in the 62. or 63. year of (*f*) Christ.

Upon his return to Judea he found things in great confusion, many (*g*) being elevated with hopes of advantage by a revolt from the Romans. He says, he did what lay in his power to prevent it, though in vain.

Soon after the begining of the war, in the year of Christ 66. (when he must have been himself about thirty years of age,) he was

sent

(*d*) ... μεγάλων δὲ δωρεῶν πρὸς τῇ ἐνεργεσίᾳ ταύτῃ τυχὼν παρὰ Ποππαίας. *Cap*. 3.

(*e*) Μετ' εἰκοστὸν κ̣̀ ἕκτον ἐνιαυτὸν εἰς Ῥώμην μοι συνέπεσεν ἀναβῆναι. *Ib*.

(*f*) Felix must have been removed from his government some while before that. Which may be thought to create a difficulty in this account. But it may be observed, that Josephus had heard of the good behaviour of those Priests at Rome, before he left Judea. Consequently, they had been some while at Rome, before he set out on his journey.

(*g*) ... κ̣̀ πολλοὺς ἐπὶ τῇ Ῥωμαίων ἀποστάσει μέγα φρονοῦντας. *Vit*. c. 4.

Ch. III.   *His Life, and Works.*   33

sent from Jerusalem, to command in *(h)* Galilee. Where, having ordered matters as well as he could, and made the best preparations for war by fortifying the cities, in case of an attack from the Romans, he was at length shut up in the city of *Jotapata*: which, after a vigorous defense, and a siege of seven and forty days, was taken by Vespasian, *(i)* on the first day of July, in the 13. year of Nero, and the 67. of our Lord.

When that city was taken, by Vespasian's order, strict search was made for *Josephus*. For, if *(k)* that General was once taken, he reckoned, that the greatest part of the war would be over. However, he had hid himself in a deep cavern, the opening of which was not easily discerned above ground. Here he met with forty persons of eminence, who had concealed themselves, and had with them provisions enough for several days. On the third day the Roman soldiers seised a woman, that had been with them. She made a discoverie of the place, where they were. Whereupon Vespasian sent two tribunes, inviting him to come up, with assurances, that his life should be preserved. Josephus however refused. Vespasian therefore sent a third tribune, named Nicanor, well known to Josephus, with the like assurances. Josephus, after some hesitation, was then willing to surrender himself. But the men, who were with him, exclaimed against it, and were for killing him and themselves, rather than come alive into the hands of the Romans. Hereupon he made a long speech to them, shewing, that it was not lawful for men to kill themselves, and that it was rather a proof of pusillanimity, than courage. But all without effect. He then proposed an expedient, which was, that they should cast lots, two by two, who should die first. He who had the second lot, should kill the first, and the next him, and so on, and the last should kill himself. It happened, that Josephus and another were preserved to the last lot.

(*h*) *Vit. cap.* 7. 8. *De B. J. l.* 2. *c.* 20.   (*k*) μεγίϛη γὰϱ ἦν μοῖϱα τȣ̃ πολέμȣ ληϕ-
(*i*) *De B. J. l.* 3. *cap.* 7. *Conf. cap.* 8.   θεὶς. *De B. J. l.* 3. *c.* 8. *in.*
§. 9.
              F   When

When all the reſt were killed, he without much difficulty perſuaded that other perſon to yield up himſelf to the Romans. So they they two eſcaped with their *(l)* lives.

This *(m)* has been judged to be a remarkable providence, by which Joſephus was preſerved to write the hiſtorie, of which we are now able to make ſo good uſe.

When *(n)* Joſephus had ſurrendered, Veſpaſian gave ſtrict orders, that he ſhould be kept carefully, as if he had intended to ſend him to Nero. Joſephus then preſented a requeſt, that he might ſpeak to Veſpaſian in private. Which was granted. When all were diſmiſſed, except Titus, and two friends; he ſpoke to Veſpaſian after this manner. " You *(o)* think, Veſpaſian, that you have in Jo-
" ſephus a mere priſoner. But I am come to you as a meſſenger of
" great tidings. Had I not been ſent to you by God, I *(p)* know
" what the law of the Jews is, and how it becomes a General to
" dye. Do you intend to ſend me to Nero? Are they, who are to
" ſucceed Nero before you, to continue? You, Veſpaſian, will be
" Ceſar: You will be Emperour. So will likewiſe this your Son.
" Bind me therefore ſtill faſter, and reſerve me for yourſelf. For
" you are Lord not of me only, but of the earth, and the ſea, and
" all mankind. And I for puniſhment deſerve a cloſer confinement,
" if I ſpeak falſhood to you in the name of *(q)* God." Veſpaſian,
as he ſays, at firſt paid little regard to all this. But afterwards his expectations of empire were raiſed. " Beſides, as he goes on to ſay,
" he

(l) De B. J. l. 3. c. 8. §. 1. ... 7.
(m) See Tillotſon's Serm. numb. 186. vol. 2. p. 564.
(n) De B. l. 3. c. 8. §. 8.
(o) Ibid. §. 9.
(p) That is, that a Jewiſh General ſhould make away with himſelf, rather than be taken priſoner alive by heathen people. We know not of any ſuch law in the books of the Old Teſtament. And it ſeems to be a manifeſt contradiction to what he ſays in the ſpeech before referred to.

(q) Joſephus's addreſſe to Veſpaſian is very preciſe and formal, predicting things then future. Poſſibly, this ſpeech was emproved afterwards, and at the time of writing this hiſtorie made more clear, and expreſs, and more agreeable to the events, than when firſt ſpoken.

Ch. III. His Life, and Works.

"he found Josephus to have spoken truth upon other occasions. For when one of his friends, who were admitted to be present at that interview, said, It appeared strange to him, that Josephus should not have foretold to the people of Jotapata, the event of the siege, nor have foreseen his own captivity, if all he now said, was not invention to save his own life: Josephus answered, that he had foretold to the people of Jotapata, that the place would be taken upon the forty-seventh day of the siege, and that himself should be taken alive by the Romans. Vespasian having privately inquired of the prisoners concerning these predictions, found the truth of (r) them."

All these things I have inserted here for shewing the character of this writer: though the prolixity of my narration be thereby encreased.

It is very likely, that he (s) often thought of *Joseph* in Egypt, and of *Daniel* at Babylon: and was in hopes of making a like figure at the court of Rome. But I suppose, it may be no disparagement to Josephus, to say, that he was not equal to them in wisdom, or in virtue and integrity. And the circumstances of things were much altered. The promised Messiah was come. And the Jewish people were no longer entitled to such special regard, as had been shewn them in times past. Nor was it then a day of favour and mercie for them, but the day of the Lord's vengeance against them, as Josephus himself saw. And they were entering into a long captivity, of which they have not yet seen the end, after a period of almost seventeen hundred years, though they are still wonderfully preserved.

Josephus

(r) Among other presages of Vespasian's Empire *Suetonius* has mentioned this of Josephus. Et unus ex nobilibus captivis Josephus, cum conjiceretur in vincula, constantissime asseveravit, fore, ut ab eodem brevi solveretur, verum jam Imperatore. *Sueton. Vespas. cap.* 5.

(s) Josephus has several times spoken of his having had prophetic dreams; and of his ability to interpret dreams that were ambiguous. *Vid. De B. J. l.* 3. *viii.* 3. *et* 9. *et de Vit.* §. 42.

Jofephus was ftill a prifoner. But, when Vefpafian had been proclaimed Emperour, he ordered his iron chain to be cut *(t)* afunder. When Vefpafian went to Rome, Jofephus continued to be with Titus, and was prefent at the fiege of Jerufalem, and faw the ruin of his city and countrey.

After the war was over, when Titus went to Rome, he went with him. And Vefpafian allotted him an apartment in the fame houfe, in which himfelf had lived, before he came to the empire. He alfo made him a Citizen of Rome, and gave him an annual penfion, and continued to fhew him great refpect, fo long as he lived. His fon Titus, who fucceded him, fhewed him the like regard. And afterwards Domitian, and his wife Domitia, did him many kind *(u)* offices.

Jofephus, however, does not deny, that *(x)* he had many enemies. But the Emperours, in whofe times he lived, protected him. Indeed, it is very likely, that the Jews fhould have little regard for a man, who was with the Romans in their camp, during the fiege of their city. He particularly fays, that *(y)* upon the firft tidings of the taking of Jotapata, the people at Jerufalem made great and public lamentations for him, fuppofing, that he had been killed in the fiege. But when they heard, that he had efcaped, and was with the Romans, and was well ufed by them, they loaded him with all manner of reproaches, not excepting treacherie itfelf. Nor do we find, that *(z)* the Jewifh people ever had any great refpect for his writings: though they have been much efteemed, and often quoted by Chriftian, and *(a)* other writers in early and later times.

Of

(*t*) *De B. J. l.* 4. *cap. x.* §. 7.
(*u*) *Vit. cap.* 76.
(*x*) *Ibid.*
(*y*) *De B. J. l.* 3. *cap. ix.* §. 7.
(*z*) Quamvis enim ejus fcripta apud Judaeos in nullo pretio fuerint... Gentiles tamen pariter et Chriftiani Jofephum, licet Judaeum, ejufque opera, magni aeftimarunt. *Ittig. Proleg. pag.* 88. *ap. Havercamp.*
(*a*) Jofephus is quoted by *Porphyrie*, not in his books againft the Chriftians, but elfewhere. See the Teftimonies prefixed to the works of Jofephus.

Ch. III.   *His Life, and Works.*   37

Of them *(b)* we are now to take some Notice.

The *first* is *the Historie of the Jewish War*, and the taking of Jerusalem, in seven books. In which work he goes back to the times of Antiochus Epiphanes, and the Maccabees. In the preface he says, that he *(c)* first wrote it in the language of his own countrey, for the sake of such as lived in Parthia, Babylonia, Arabia, and other parts, and afterwards published it in Greek for the benefit of others: which is what we have. It is generally supposed to have been published by him in the 75. year of Christ, and the 38. year of his own age. He professeth to have writ with great *(d)* fidelity. And for the truth of his historie appeals to Vespasian, and Titus, and King Agrippa, then *(e)* living. He *(f)* presented it to Vespasian and Titus. Which last *(g)* not only desired the publication of it, but with his own hand signed the book, that should be reckoned authentic.

2. *The Jewish Antiquities*, in twenty books, or the Historie of the Jews from the creation of the world to the twelfth year of Nero, in which the war began. This work was finished by him *(h)* in the 56. year of his own life, in the third year of the reign of Domitian, and the year of Christ 93.

3. To this work is subjoyned, as a part of it, or an appendix to it, *His Life*, writ by himself some while afterwards.

4. After the several above-mentioned works, he published another work, in two books, entitled Of *the Antiquity of the Jews, against Apion*: being a vindication of the Jewish People against the calumnies of that Egyptian author.

5. To

(b) *Particular accounts of them are to be seen in Cav. Hist. Lit. Fabric. Bib. Gr. l. 4. cap. 6. Tom. 3. p. 228. &c. Tillemont La Ruine des Juifs. art. 79. &c. Hist. des Emp. Tom. i.*

(c) De B. J. l. i. in Pro. §. 2.

(d) In Pr. §. 5. &c. et l. 7. cap. ult. fin.

(e) In Vit. cap. 65. Adv. Ap. l. i. c. 9.

(f) Αλλ' αυτοῖς ἀπέδωκα τοῖς αυτοκράτορσι τὰ βιβλία. *Vit. §. 65. Conf. Adv. Ap. ut supr.*

(g) ὥστε χαράξας τῇ ἑαυτῦ χερὶ τὰ βιβλία δημοσιεύεσθαι προέταξεν. *Vit. §. 65.*

(h) Ant. l. 20. cap. ult. fin.

5. To Josephus likewise is generally ascribed a book, entitled *A Discourse of the Maccabees*. But, as (*i*) *Cave* says, there is good reason to doubt of it's genuinness. And (*k*) Mr. *Whiston*, who made an English Translation of all the above named works of this writer, declined to translate this, and would not publish it among the rest.

The works of Josephus, notwithstanding many things in them liable to exception, which may be observed by careful and impartial readers, are very valuable. In his larger work, the *Jewish Antiquities*, he confirms the truth of the historie of the Old Testament. And, as in several of the last books of that work he has brought down the Jewish historie from the ceasing of prophecie among them to the twelfth of Nero, he has let us know the state of affairs in Judea, during the time of the evangelical historie. And he had before done the like in the first two books of the *Jewish War*. What he has therein said of Herod, and his Sons, of the Roman Governours in Judea, the Jewish sects, and their principles, the manners of the Jewish people, and likewise concerning the Samaritans, greatly confirms, and illustrates the historie of our Evangelists. As was formerly shewn in the first part of this work, the *Credibility of the Gospel-Historie:* the design of which was to confirm the facts *occasionally* mentioned in the New Testament by passages of ancient (*l*) authors.

We are now to consider, whether there is any thing in the works this Jewish author more directly confirming the *principal* facts of the of New Testament: particularly, whether he affords any evidences of the fulfilment of our Lord's predictions concerning the destruction of the temple and city of Jerusalem, and the great calamities coming upon the Jewish people: and whether he has said any thing of *John*

the

(*i*) Nihilominus an genuinum sit Josephi opus, justa est dubitandi ratio. *Cav. H. L. de Josepho. p. 35.*

(*k*) *See his note at the end of his translation of Josephus.*

(*l*) Quam in multis capitibus Evangelistarum narrationi suffragetur Josephus, erudite nuper demonstravit Nathanael Lardnerus in opere Anglice edito, de Fide Historiae Evangelicae. *Lond.* 1727. 8vo. 2 volum. *J. A. Fabric. Lux Evangelii. p.* 16. *not.* (*a*).

Ch. III. *The State of Judea in our Saviour's Time.*

the Baptist, our Lord's fore-runner, or of our Lord himſelf, or of any of his Apoſtles.

A. D. 76.

I ſhall begin with the firſt article. For it is very likely, that in his *hiſtorie of the Jewiſh war*, we ſhould find many things giving credit to the fulfilment of our Lord's predictions concerning the Jewiſh people.

II. Judea was firſt brought into ſubjection to the Romans by Pompey. Who after a ſiege of three months took Jeruſalem in the year 63. before the Chriſtian aera, about the time of our (*m*) midſummer. Joſephus always dates (*n*) the loſſe of their liberty at that time. The ſame is ſaid by (*o*) Tacitus.

The State of Judea, in our Saviour's Time, and before.

But though the Jewiſh People then became ſubject to the Romans: and it may be ſaid, that from that time forward the rod of heaven hung over them; they enjoyed many privileges, and the freedom of their worſhip, under the mild government of thoſe maſters: as appears both from Joſephus, and from the hiſtorical books of the New Teſtament.

When Pompey became maſter of Jeruſalem, he *(p)* and ſome of his officers entred into the temple, and the moſt holy places of it. But he took nothing away. There were then in it the table, the candleſtick, with it's lamps, the pouring veſſels, and the cenſers, all of gold, and great quantities of ſpices, and two thouſand talents in money. All which he left untouched. And the day after he gave orders, that they who had the charge of the temple ſhould

cleanſe

(*m*) See *Prideaux, in the year before Chriſt*. 63. *p.* 439. *And Joſeph. Antiq. l.* 14. *cap. iv.* 4. *De B. J. l. i. cap. vii.* §. 6.

(*n*) Τότε τῇ πάθης τοῖς Ἱεροσολύμοις αἴτιοι κατέστησαν Ὑρκανὸς κ̀ Ἀριςόβολος πρὸς ἀλλήλους ςασιάζοντες. Τὴν τε γὰρ ἐλευθερίαν ἀπεβάλομεν, κ̀ ὑπήκοοι Ῥωμαίων κατέσημεν. *An-*

tiq. l. 14. *iv.* 5. And compare what A-grippa ſays to the Jews at Jeruſalem. *De B. J. l.* 2. *cap. xvi.* 4. *p.* 187.

(*o*) Romanorum primus Cn. Pompeius Judaeos domuit, templumque jure victoriae ingreſſus eſt. *Tacit. H. E.* 5. *c.* 9.

(*p*) *De B. J. l.* 1. *cap. vii.* 6. *Conf. Antiq. l.* 14. *cap. iv.*

A. D. 76. cleanse it, and perform the accustomed sacrifices. And he restored the priesthood to Hyrcanus.

And that after this the Jewish People were, sometimes at least, in a flourishing condition, appears from many considerations. It was during this period, that *(q)* Herod repaired the temple. Excepting the cloud of glorie, with which the first temple had been favoured: that erected by Herod may be reckoned to have been equal to it in the splendour and magnificence of the building, and in rich and costly presents, and other ornaments.

When the Jewish People, after their return from the Babylonish captivity, laid the foundation of the new house, *many of the Priests, and Levites, and chief of the fathers, who were ancient men, wept with a loud voice.* Ezr. iii. 12. But God encouraged them by the Prophet Haggai, in this manner. ch. ii. 3. *Who is left among you, that saw this house in it's first glorie? And how do ye see it now? Is it not in your eyes, in comparison of it, as nothing? Yet now be strong, o Zerubbabel, saith the Lord.... and be strong all ye people of the land, and work: for I am with you, saith the Lord of hosts... For thus saith the Lord of hosts, .. I will shake all nations. And the desire of all nations shall come. And I will fill this house with glorie, saith the Lord of hosts. The silver is mine, and the gold is mine, saith the Lord of hosts. The glorie of this later house shall be greater than that of the former, saith the Lord of hosts. And in this place will I give peace, saith the Lord of hosts.*

Here is, undoubtedly, a renewal of the great promise concerning the coming of the Messiah, the true *Shechinah*, whose presence would make this second temple more glorious than the first. But here is also a gracious assurance of external grandeur and splendour. "Sil-
" ver and gold, and all the riches of the world, says God, are mine,
" to bestow on whom I please. And notwithstanding the present
" mean and despicable appearance of the building before your eyes;
" I will

(q) Vid. Antiq. l. 15. cap. xi. De B. J. l. 1. cap. xxi. et l. 5. cap. v.

Ch. III. *The State of the Jews in our Saviour's Time.*

" I will fill it with glorie, and will cause it to equal, or even fur- A. D.
" pass the former in splendour and magnificence... *For in this place* 76.
" will I give peace. My purpose is to bless you abundantly, and to
" give you great prosperity." Which gracious declaration was fulfilled.

That they were in flourishing circumstances at the time of our
Lord's preaching among them, is apparent: though they were un-
easie under subjection to the Romans. Josephus continually speaks
of the temple, as very grand and magnificent. And it appears to be
so from his large and particular description of it in the fifth chapter
of the fifth book of his Jewish War, just before it's final ruin. And
when Titus, upon the fire having seised the temple, entred it, with
some of his officers, he says, " that (r) Titus saw it to be far supe-
" rior to the report of strangers, and not inferior to our boastings
" concerning it." And having related, how it was burnt, he says,
it might be justly lamented: " since (s) it was the most admirable
" of all the works, which we have seen, or heard of, for it's curi-
" ous structure, and magnitude, and for all the wealth bestowed up-
" on it, as well as for the reputation of it's sanctity." And he expressly calls it (t) the temple, that was built, or begun to be built,
in the second year of Cyrus, under the direction of the prophet
Haggai. And our Lord's disciples bear witnesse to the same in some
passages, that will come before us in reciting his predictions, of
which we are now to take notice, and then observe the fulfillment of
them.

III. We find our Lord's disciples speaking of the magnificence of Our
the temple with admiration. So in Mark xiii... 10. *And as he* predicti-

(r) ... παρελθὼν μετὰ τῶν ἡγεμόνων ἔν-
δον ἐθεάσατο τό ναὸν τὸ ἅγιον, κỳ τὰ ἐν αὐτῷ
πολὺ μὲν τῆς παρὰ τοῖς ἀλλοφύλοις φήμης ἀ-
μείνω, τῆ δὲ κόμπῳ κỳ τῆς παρὰ οἰκείοις δόξης
ὑπελάττω. *De B. J. l. 6. cap. iv. 7.*

(s) *L. 6. iv. 8. Conf. l. 6. x. fin.*
(t) ἀπὸ δὲ τῆς ὑστερον, ἣν ἔτει δευτέρῳ Κύ-
ρυ βασιλεύοντος ἐποιήσατο Ἀγγαῖος. *L. 0.
c. iv. 8.*

went

A. D. 76.

ons concerning the calamities coming upon the Jewish People.

went out of the temple, one of his disciples saith unto him: Master, see what manner of stones, and what buildings are here! And Jesus answering said unto him: seest thou these great buildings? There shall not be left one stone upon another, that shall not be thrown down. And as he sat upon the Mount of Olives over against the temple, Peter, and James, and John, and Andrew, asked him privatly: Tell us, when shall these things be? and what shall be the sign, when all these things shall be fulfilled? And Jesus answering them began to say: Take heed, least any man deceive you. For many will come in my name, and say: I am Christ. And will deceive many. And when ye shall hear of wars, and rumours of wars, be ye not troubled. For such things must needs be. But the end shall not be yet. For nation shall rise against nation, and kingdom against kingdom. And there shall be earthquakes in divers places. And there shall be famines and troubles. These are the beginings of sorrows.... And the gospel must first be published among all nations. And ver. 14...20. *But when ye shall see the abomination of desolation spoken of by Daniel the Prophet, standing where it ought not, (let him that readeth understand:) then let them that be in Judea flee to the mountains. And let him that is on the house-top, not go down into the house, neither enter therein, to take any thing out of his house. And let him that is in the field, not turn back again for to take up his garment. But woe to them that are with child, and to them that give suck in those days. And pray ye, that your flight be not in the winter. For in those days shall be affliction, such as was not from the beginning of the creation, which God created, unto this time. Neither shall be.*

The like things are in St. Matthew xxiv. 1...35. *And Jesus went out, and departed from the temple. And his disciples came to him, for to shew him the buildings of the temple. And Jesus said unto them: See ye not all these things? Verily I say unto you, there shall not be left here one stone upon another, that shall not be thrown down. And as he sat upon the Mount of Olives, the disciples came unto him privatly, saying: Tell us, when these things shall be, and what will be the sign*

of

Ch. III. *Our Lord's Predictions of the Jewish Calamities.*

of thy coming, and of the end of the world? And Jesus answered, and said unto them: Take heed, that no man deceive you. For many will come in my name, saying, I am Christ. And will deceive many. And ye will hear of wars and rumours of wars. See that ye be not troubled. For all these things must come to pass. But the end is not yet. For nation will rise against nation, and kingdom against kingdom. And there will be famines, and pestilences, and earthquakes in divers places. All these are the beginings of sorrows. Then shall they deliver you up to be afflicted, and shall kill you. And ye will be hated of all nations for my name sake. And then will many be offended, and will betray one another, and will hate one another. And many false prophets will arise, and will deceive many. And because iniquity shall abound, the love of many will wax cold. But he that shall endure to the end, shall be saved. And this gospel of the kingdom shall be preached in all the world, for a witnesse unto all nations. And then shall the end come. When ye therefore shall see the abomination of desolation, spoken of by Daniel the prophet, stand in the holy place, (whoso readeth, let him understand:) then let them which are in Judea, flee to the mountains. Let him which is on the house-top, not come down to take any thing out of his house. Neither let him that is in the field return back, to take his cloths. And woe unto them which are with child, and to them that give suck in those days. But pray ye, that your flight be not in the winter, neither on the sabbath-day. For then shall be great tribulation, such as was not from the begining of the world to this time: no, nor ever shall be. And except those days should be shortened there should no flesh be saved. But for the elects sake those days shall be shortened. Then, if any say unto you: Lo, here is Christ, or there: believe it not. For there will arise false Christs, and false Prophets, and shall shew great signs and wonders, insomuch that (if it were possible,) they should deceive the very elect. Behold, I have told you before. Wherefore, if they shall say unto you, Behold he is in the desert, go not forth: Behold, he is in the secret chambers, believe it not. For as the lightening cometh out of the east, and shineth even unto the west, so shall also the com-

A. D. 76.

ing of the son of man be. For wheresoever the carcase is, there will the eagles be gathered together.... Verily, I say unto you, This generation shall not pass, till all these things be fulfilled. Heaven and earth shall pass away. But my words shall not pass away.

Those inquiries of the disciples, and our Lord's answers to them, are made in private. But they plainly refer to things said by our Lord publicly in the courts of the temple. We may do well therefore to look back to what precedes, as related in St. Matthew's Gospel, especially. Where are recorded the many woes pronounced by our Lord upon the Scribes and Pharisees, and the people in general, who were under their influence and direction. Matt. xxiii. 29...39. *Woe unto you, Scribes and Pharisees, hypocrites: because ye build the tombs of the Prophets, and garnish the sepulchres of the righteous. And ye say, if we had been in the days of our fathers, we would not have* Compare Luke xi. 47..51. *been partakers with them in the bloud of the Prophets. Wherefore ye be witnesses unto yourselves, that ye are the children of them that killed the Prophets. Fill ye up then the measure of your fathers. Ye serpents, ye generation of vipers, how can ye escape the damnation of hell! Wherefore behold I send unto you prophets, and wise men, and scribes. And some of them ye will kill and crucify: and some of them ye will scourge in your synagogues, and persecute from city to city: that upon you may come all the righteous bloud, shed upon the earth, from the bloud of righteous Abel, unto the bloud of Zacharias, son of Barachias, whom ye slew between the temple and the altar. Verily I say unto you, All these things shall come upon this generation. O Jerusalem, Jerusalem, thou that killest the Prophets, and stonest them that are sent unto thee: how often would I have gathered thy children together, even as a hen gathereth her chickens under her wings! And ye would not! Behold, your house is left unto you desolate. For I say unto you, ye shall not see me henceforth, till ye shall say: Blessed is he that cometh in the name of the Lord.*

The like things are recorded by St. Luke, ch. xxi. 5...28. A part of which I shall also transcribe here. *And as some spake of the temple, how*

Ch. III. *Our Lord's Predictions of the Jewish Calamities.* 45

how it was adorned with goodly stones, and gifts, he said: As for these things, which ye behold, the days will come, in the which shall not be left one stone upon another, that shall not be thrown down. And they asked him, saying, Master, but when shall these things be? and what signs will there be when these things shall come to pass? And he said: Take heed, that ye be not deceived. For many will come in my name, saying, I am Christ, and the time draws near. Go ye not therefore after them. But when ye shall hear of wars and commotions, be not terrified. For these things must first come to pass. But the end is not by and by. Then said he unto them: Nation shall rise against nation, and kingdom against kingdom. And great earthquakes shall be in divers places, and famines, and pestilences, and fearfull sights, and great signs shall there be from heaven. But before all these things they shall lay their hands upon you, and persecute you, delivering you up to the synagogues, and into prisons, being brought before Kings and Rulers for my name sake. And it shall turn to you for a testimonie. . . . And ye shall be betrayed both by parents, and brethren, and kinsfolke, and friends. And some of you shall they cause to be put to death. And ye shall be hated of all men for my name sake. But there shall not an hair of your head perish. In your patience possess ye your souls. And when ye shall see Jerusalem compassed with armies; then know, that the desolation thereof is nigh. Then let them which are in Judea flee to the mountains: and let them which are in the midst of it, depart out. And let not them that are in the countrey, enter thereinto. For these are the days of vengeance, that all things which are written may be fulfilled. But woe unto them that are with child, and to them that give suck in those days. For there will be great distresse in the land, and wrath upon this people. And they shall fall by the edge of the sword, and shall be led away captive into all nations. And Jerusalem shall be trodden down of the Gentils, untill the times of the Gentils be fulfilled.

A. D. 76.

And before this, when he was making his public entrance into Jerusalem. Says St. Luke xix. 41. . . . 44. *And when he was come near, he beheld the city, and wept over it, saying: If thou hadst known,*

even

even thou, at left in this thy day the things, which belong to thy peace! But now they are hid from thy eyes! For the days will come upon thee, that thy enemies shall cast a trench about thee, and compass thee round, and keep thee in on every side, and will lay thee even with the ground, and thy children within thee. And they will not leave in thee one stone upon another, because thou knewest not the time of thy visitation.

And afterwards, when they were leading him away to be crucified. Luke xxiii. 25. ... 31. *And there followed him a great companie of people, and of women : which also bewailed, and lamented him. But Jesus turning unto them said : Daughters of Jerusalem, weep not for me, but weep for yourselves, and for your children. For behold the days are coming, in the which they will say : Blessed are the barren, and the wombs that never bare, and the paps which never gave suck. Then shall they begin to say to the mountains, Fall on us, and to the hills, Cover us. For if they do such things in a green tree, what shall be done in the dry!*

Our Lord delivers these predictions, of which he had the foresight, with marks of great and undissembled compassion and tenderness. If all these desolations and calamities had been now present, and before his eyes : and if they had been the calamities of his best friends, he could not have been more affected. He is particularly touched with the foresight of the difficulties of such as are most helpless, the distresses of women with child, or who have infants at their breasts. This is true compassion, the effect of the sensibility of the human nature : which he is not ashamed of, and does not dissemble. And that the apprehension of these calamities impending on the Jewish people, lay much upon his mind, is manifest from his so often speaking of them.

And there are references likewise to the calamities coming upon the Jewish People in divers parables. Luke xiii. 6. . . 9. Matt. xxii. 1. . . 7. Luke xiv. 17. . . 24. . . Matt. xxi. 33. . . 46. Mark xii. 1. . . 12. Luke xx. 9 . . 19. . . . Luke xix. 11 . . 27. Compare Matt. xxv. 14. . . 30. and also in the miracle upon the barren fig-tree. Matt. xxi. 18. 19. Mark xi. 12. 13. and 20. 21.

In

Ch. III. *Our Lord's Predictions of the Jewish Calamities.* 47

A. D. 76.

In what has been just transcribed from the Evangelists, are observable these several things.

1. Our Lord foretells the destruction of the temple and city of Jerusalem.

2. He speaks of great and extraordinarie afflictions and distresses, which the Jewish people would suffer at that time.

3. He says, that the doctrine of the gospel should be preached in all the world, or all over the Roman Empire, before the final ruin and overthrow of the Jewish Nation.

4. He foretells, that his disciples and followers would be brought before Kings and Governours for his name sake, and would suffer many hardships, and that some of them would be put to death.

5. He intimates, that among his followers there would be great declensions, and that they would betray each other.

6. He foretells, that there would be famines, and pestilences, and earthquakes in divers places.

7. He speaks of wars and tumults in many places, preceding the final ruin of the Jewish nation, and as preludes of it.

8. He likewise says, that at that time, and before it, would appear many false-prophets, and impostors, by whom many would be deceived, and he warns men against hearkening to them.

9. He declares, that all these things would come to pass, before the end of that age, or generation of men.

10. He forewarns and advises those who regarded their own welfare, to flee out of Judea and Jerusalem, when they perceived the near approach of the calamities, which had been spoken of by him. Which they might know, when they should see the Roman armies with their idolatrous ensigns, standing where they ought not, that is, near Jerusalem, or in the land of Judea.

Of all these several things I propose to shew the fulfillment: though not exactly in the order, in which they have been just now mentioned.

IV. Be-

A. D. 76.

The Dates of some Events, vid. the Commencement and Duration of the War, and of the Siege of Jerusalem, &c.

IV. Before I enter upon the historie of the fulfillment of these predictions, it may be of use to observe, in general, the dates of some events.

The war began, as (*u*) Josephus says, in the second year of the government of *Gessius Florus*, who succeeded *Albinus*, successor of *Porcius Festus*, mentioned in the Acts of the Apostles, in the month of May, in the twelfth year of the Emperour *Nero*, and the seventeenth year of the reign of *Agrippa*, mentioned Acts xxv. and xxvii. that is, in the month of May, in the year of our Lord 66.

" The (*x*) Temple was burnt on the tenth day of the month of " August, [in the year of Christ 70.] the same day and month, on " which it had been burnt by the King of Babylon." Which *(y)* Josephus repeats again afterwards.

The (*z*) City was taken on the eighth day of September, in the second year of the reign of Vespasian, or the year of Christ 70.

That was the end of the siege of Jerusalem, which began, as the same author (*a*) observes several times, about the fourteenth day of the month Nisan, or our April.

The war therefore lasted four years and four months, computing from May 66. to September in the year 70. And the siege lasted about five months, computing from the 14. day of April to the eighth of

---

(*u*) Καὶ δὴ τὴν ἀρχὴν ἔλαβεν ὁ πόλεμος δευτέρῳ μὲν ἔτει τῆς ἐπιτροπῆς Φλώρε, δωδεκάτῳ δὲ τῆς Νέρωνος ἀρχῆς. *Ant. l.* 20. *xi.* 1.

Καὶ περιελάμβατε τὴν ἀρχὴν ὁ πόλεμος δωδεκάτῳ μὲν ἔτει τῆς Νέρωνος ἡγεμονίας, ἑπτακαιδεκάτῳ δὲ τῆς Ἀγρίππα βασιλείας, Ἀρτεμισίῳ μηνός. *De B. J. l.* 2. *cap. xiv.* 4.

(*x*) Παρῆν δ' ἡ εἱμαρμένη χρόνων περίοδος ἡμέρᾳ δεκάτη Λώε μηνός, καθ' ἣν κὶ τὸ πρότερον ὑπὸ τῶν Βαβυλωνίων βασιλέως ἐνεπρήσθη. *De B. J. l.* 6. *iv.* 5.

(*y*) Θαυμάσαι δ' ἄν τις ἐν αὐτῇ τῆς περιόδου τὴν ἀκρίβειαν κὶ μῆνα γοῦν, ὡς ἔφην, κὶ ἡμέραν ἐπετήρησε τὴν αὐτὴν, ἐν ᾗ πρότερον ὑπὸ Βαβυλωνίων ὁ ναὸς ἐνεπρήσθη. . . . ἡ γέγονεν ἔτει δευτέρῳ τῆς Οὐεσπασιανοῦ ἡγεμονίας. *Ib.* §. 8.

(*z*) Ἑαλῶ μὲν ἔτος Ἱεροσόλυμα ἔτει δευτέρῳ τῆς Οὐεσπασιανοῦ ἡγεμονίας, Γορπιαίῳ μηνὸς ὀγδόῃ. *Ib. l.* 6. *cap. x. in.*

(*a*) *De B. J. l.* 5. *cap. iii.* 1. *cap. xiii.* 7. *L.* 6. *cap. ix.* 3.

Ch. III. *The Time of the Siege, and other Events.*

of September, in the year 70. If we carry on our computation to the taking of the castle of *Massada,* which happened in the year 73. (as we shall see hereafter:) the war lasted seven years.

V. I think it proper here also to take notice of our Lord's expressions concerning the sign, whereby the approach of these calamities might be discerned. Matt. xxiv. 15. 16. *When ye therefore shall see the abomination of desolation, . . . stand in the holy place; then let them which be in Judea flee to the mountains.* Mark xiii. 14. *When ye shall see the abomination of desolation standing where it ought not . . . then let them which are in Judea flee to the mountains.* Luke xxi. 20. *And when ye shall see Jerusalem compassed with armies, then know, that the desolation thereof is nigh.*

By *the abomination of desolation, or the abomination that maketh desolate,* therefore is intended the Roman Armies, with their ensigns. As the Roman ensigns, especially the eagle, which was carried at the head of every legion, were objects of worship; they are, according to the usual stile of scripture, called *an abomination.*

By *standing in the holy place,* or *where it ought not,* needs not to be understood the temple only, but Jerusalem also, and any part of the land of Israel.

There are several things in Josephus, which will confirm this interpretation. " *Pilate (y)* says he, the prefect of Judea, sending his
" armie from Cesarea, and putting them into winter-quarters at Je-
" rusalem, brought the carved images of Cesar, which are in the en-
" signs, into the city, in violation of the Jewish laws: since our
" law forbids the making of images. For which reason the former
" governours were wont to come into the city with ensigns destitute
" of these ornaments. Pilate was the first, who set up images in
" Jerusalem. And he did it privately, the armie making their en-
" trance in the night-time. But as soon as the people knew it, they
" went

A. D. 76.

The Abomination of desolation standing in the holy place.

(y) *Antiq. l.* 18. *cap. iii.* §. 1.

H

"went in a large body to Cesarea, making earnest supplications, "that the images might be removed.... And at length Pilate gave "orders, for bringing back the images from Jerusalem to Cesarea."

And not long after that, *Vitellius*, President of Syria, received orders from Tiberius to attack Aretas, King of Petra. Whereupon he was going to march through Judea. "But (z) some of their chief "men waited on him, and entreated him, not to lead his armie "through their country, because it was contrarie to their laws, that "any images should be brought into it, whereas there were a great "many in his armie. And he hearkened to them, altered his inten-"tion, and marched his troops another way."

Our Lord's disciples and followers therefore might well be alarmed, as soon as they saw Roman armies, with their idolatrous ensigns, appear in an hostile manner in any part of the land of Israel: But as they approached to Jerusalem, the danger would be more imminent and pressing.

And as men unwillingly leave their native countrey, and their accustomed habitations: and removals are always attended with dangers and difficulties: our Lord recommends flight in very urgent terms, least any of those who loved him, and respected his doctrine, should partake in the dreadful calamities of the siege.

How the several Events, foretold to precede the Destruction of Jerusalem, came to pass. The Gospel preached all over the world.

VI. We now observe some events spoken of by our Lord, which would precede the great calamity coming upon the Jewish nation.

1. One is, that the *doctrine of the gospel* should be preached throughout the Roman Empire, and in other places adjoyning to it.

And this gospel of the kingdom, says he, *shall be preached in all the world, for a witnesse to all nations. And then shall the end come.* Matt. xxiv. 14. *And the gospel must first be published to all nations.* Mark xiii. 10.

And however unlikely that might seem, when those words were spoken by our Lord, they were verified. The Epistles of the New Testament,

(z) *Ant. l.* 18. *cap. v.* 3.

Ch. III. *Christ's Disciples persecuted in many Places.* A. D. 76.

Testament, still exstant, and writ to Christians in divers cities and countreys, are a standing monument of it. For they are sent to believers at *Rome, Corinth, Galatia, Ephesus, Philippi, Colosse, Thessalonica,* and the *Hebrews.* All writ by St. Paul. And the epistles of the Apostle Peter are directed to Christians, residing in *Pontus, Galatia, Cappadocia, Asia* and *Bithynia.* And the four Gospels, and the Acts of the Apostles afford evidence, that there were numerous converts to the faith of Jesus. For they were writ for the use of such. St. Paul says Rom. xv. 19. that *from Jerusalem, and round about unto Illyricum, he had fully preached the gospel of Christ.* He reminds the Romans, i. 18. *that their faith was spoken of throughout the whole world.* To the Colossians he observes, *that the gospel had been preached to every creature under heaven.* ch. i. 23. and see ver. 6. The prediction therefore of that great event had been accomplished within the limits of the time assigned for it.

And *Tacitus* (*a*) bears witnesse, that the Christian Religion, which had it's rise in Judea, had spread into many parts, and had reached *Rome* itself, where the professors of it were numerous, and many of them underwent grievous torments in the reign of Nero, about the year of our Lord 64. and afterwards.

2. Our Lord also says to his disciples in his prophetical discourses concerning the coming calamities upon Judea: *Before all these things they will lay their hands upon you, and persecute you; delivering you up to the synagogues, and into prisons, being brought before kings and rulers for my name sake.* .... *And some of you shall they cause to be put to death. And ye will be hated of all men for my name sake.* Luke xxi. 12. and 16. 17. And to the like purpose in the other Evangelists.

Christ's Disciples persecuted in many Places.

The full accomplishment of these things is well known to Christians from the book of the Acts, and the Epistles of the New Testament. The Apostles of Jesus met with great difficulties in preaching the gospel. And the converts made by them were exposed to

H 2   many

(*a*) *Ann. l.* 15. *cap.* 44.

many sufferings. *Peter* and *John*, and *all the Apostles*, were brought before the Jewish Council, and were imprisoned, and beaten, and farther threatened. Acts iv. Stephen, an eminent disciple, and Evangelist, suffered death by stoning. vi. vii. *James*, the brother of John, was beheaded by king *Agrippa*. Who also shut up *Peter* in prison, with intention to put him to death also. But he was miraculously delivered. ch. xii. Paul was kept in prison two years in Judea, and afterwards as long at Rome. He pleaded before Felix and Festus, Roman Governours in Judea, and king Agrippa the younger, as well as before the Jewish Council at Jerusalem. xxi... xxviii. And there is good reason to believe, that *(b)* he was brought before Nero himself. Many of his sufferings and dangers are enumerated in 2 Cor. xi. 23...33.

They who received the doctrine taught by the Apostles, had also their share of afflictions and trials. Paul, whilst he was their enemie, *made havock of the Church, entering into every house, and haling men and women committed them to prison. And when they were put to death, he gave his voice against them:.. he punished them in every synagogue, and persecuted them even into strange cities.* Acts viii. 3. and xxvi. 10. 11. And in his epistle to the Hebrews he observes to them, that *they had endured a great fight of afflictions, partly whilst they were made a gazing stock both by reproaches and afflictions: and partly whilst they became companions of those who were so used: and that they had joyfully taken the spoiling of their goods.* ch. x. 32...34. And Agrippa before-mentioned began with *laying his hands upon certain of the church.* Acts xii. 1. And that the believers suffered afflictions in other places beside Judea, is manifest from 2 Thess. i. 3.....6. James ii. 5...7. 2 Pet. iv. 12...19. And the Jews at Rome, whom Paul sent for to come to him, say: *As concerning this sect, we know that every where it is spoken against.*

Tacitus

(b) See that fully proved in the second volume of the Supplement to the Credibility, &c. p. 250. &c.

Ch. III. *Christ's Disciples persecuted in many Places.*

Tacitus confirms the truth of these predictions of our Lord. He has given a particular account of the sufferings of many Christians at Rome, before the desolations of Judea. In the tenth year of Nero, the 64. of our Lord, there happened a great fire at Rome. Nero was suspected to have set it on fire himself. "For (c) suppres- "sing that common rumour, Nero procured others to be accused, "and inflicted exquisite punishments upon those people, who were "in abhorrence for their crimes, and were commonly known by the "name of Christians." And he says, "that they were condemned, "not so much for the crime of burning the city, as for their enmity "to mankind." Thus Tacitus bears witnesse, not only to their undeserved sufferings, but also to the reproaches they underwent, agreeably to what our blessed Lord had said, that *they would be hated of all men for his name sake.* However, these innocent sufferers had their supports. For their unerring Master, all whose words were true, has said: *Blessed are ye, when men shall revile you, and persecute you, and shall say all manner of evil against you falsly for my sake.*

3. Farther, our Lord intimates, that before the full accomplishment of his predictions concerning the miseries coming upon the Jewish nation, there would be *declensions* of zeal among his own professed disciples and followers.

Declensions among his Followers.

And then shall many be offended, and shall betray one another.... and because iniquity will abound, the love of many will wax cold. Matt. xxiv. 10. 12. And see Mark xiii. 12. 13. and Luke xxi. 16.

What is said of this matter in the Gospels may be verified from the epistles of the New Testament. The whole epistle to the Hebrews is an argument to stedfastnesse, implying the great danger of apostasie from the faith, or of abatements of zeal for it: *Let us*, says he, *hold fast the profession of our faith without wavering...And let us*

A. D. 76.

(c), Ergo abolendo rumori Nero subdidit reos, et exquisitissimis poenis affecit quos per flagitia invisos, vulgus Christianos appellabat.... Igitur primo correpti qui fatebantur, deinde indicio eorum multitudo ingens, haud perinde crimine incendii, quam odio humani generis convicti sunt. &c. *Ann.* 15. c. 44.

us consider one another, to provoke unto love and good works, not forsaking the assembling of ourselves together, as the manner of some is. Heb. x. 23...25. and onwards to ver. 39. And ch. xii. 12. *Wherefore lift up the hands, which hang down, and the feeble knees.* In ch. vi. 4...9. he shews the great guilt, and the deplorable condition of such as apostatize. In his second epistle to Timothie ch. i. 15. *This thou knowest,* says he, *that all they which are of Asia* [probably meaning such as were then at Rome] *are turned away from me: of whom are Phygellus and Hermogenes.* And afterwards ch iv. 16. he complains of other Christians at Rome, who deserted him, when he made his appearance there before Nero. *At my first answer,* or apologie, *no man stood with me: but all men forsook me.* And again, in the same epistle, ch. ii. 17. he speaks of Hymeneus and Philetus: *who concerning the truth have erred, saying that the resurrection is past, and overthrow the faith of some.* And see 1 Tim. i. 19. 20. I allege nothing more from the books of the New Testament.

Tacitus, in his account of Nero's persecution of the Christians, already quoted more than once, does also confirm the truth of this prediction of our Lord. Who says, " that *(d)* at first they only were " apprehended, who confessed themselves to be of that sect. After-" wards, many more were taken up, whom they discovered to be " of their number."

Nor ought this to be thought exceeding strange, notwithstanding the perfection of the christian doctrine, and the evidences of it's truth. For in a great number of men it is very likely, that some should be overcome by the difficulties and dangers attending the profession of it. So says the chief sower of his heavenly doctrine. *Some seed fell in stony places. The same is he that heareth the word, and anon with joy receiveth it. Yet hath he not root in himself, but endureth for a while. For when tribulation or persecution ariseth because of the word, by and by he is offended.*

4. Our

(*d*) Igitur primo correpti, qui fatebantur: deinde indicio eorum multitudo ingens, &c. *Ann.* 15. c. 44.

Ch. III. Famines in divers Places.

4. Our blessed Lord said, that before the great calamity predicted by him, there would be *famines, and pestilences, and earthquakes in divers places.*

We know from the historie in the Acts of the Apostles, that there was a famine in Judea, in the time of the Emperour Claudius. Ch. xi. 25...30. It was not an accidental scarcity at Jerusalem only, but it was a famine all over that countrey. It began in the fourth year of that Emperour, and lasted several years. We have a particular account of it in (e) Josephus. He also says, it was a very severe (f) famine. And in another place (g) he mentions the high price of corn at that season: and says, that this famine happened in the reign of Claudius, not long before the war.

That famine is also taken notice of by Eusebius in (h) his Chronicle, and (i) in his Historie, and by (k) Orosius.

There was also a famine at Rome, and in Italie, mentioned (l) by Dion Cassius, which began in the first year of Claudius, and continued in the next year.

There was another famine in the same reign, mentioned (m) by Tacitus, and (n) Eusebius. Which seems to have been chiefly in the tenth or eleventh year of that Emperour.

To all these (o) Suetonius seems to refer, though he does not mention the years, in which they happened.

Con-

(e) *Ant. l.* 20. ii. 6.

(f) Ἐπὶ τότοις δὴ κ̓ μέγαν λιμὸν κατὰ τὴν Ἰουδαίαν συνέβη γενέσθαι. *Ib. cap. v.* 2.

(g) ... ὃ μὲν ἀλλὰ κ̓ τῷ δὲ τῷ πολέμῳ μικρὸν ἔμπροσθεν, Κλαυδίου Ῥωμαίων ἀρχοντος, κ̓ λιμοῦ τὴν χώραν ἡμῶν καταλαβόντος, ὡς τεσσάρων δραχμῶν πωλεῖσθαι τὸν ἀσσάρων. *Ant. l.* 3. xv. 3.

(h) *Chr. p.* 160.

(i) *H. E. l.* 2. *cap. xii.*

(k) *Or. l.* 7. *cap.* 6.

(l) *Dio. l.* 60. *p.* 671. *al.* 949.

(m) Frugum quoque egestas, et orta ex eo fames, in prodigium accipiebatur. *Tac. Ann. l.* 12. *c.* 43.

(n) Fames facta in Graecia. Modius sex drachmis venundatus est.... Magna fames Romae. *Chr. p.* 160. *infr. m.*

(o) Arctiore autem annona propter assiduas sterilitates, &c. *Suet. Claud. cap.* 18. *Vid. it cap.* 19. *et* 20.

56   *JOSEPHUS.*   Ch. III.

A. D. 76.

Pestilences.

Concerning the famines in the reign of the Emperour Claudius, some *(p)* modern hiftorians and chronologers might be confulted.

Our Lord fpeaks alfo of *pestilences*. By Jofephus we are informed, that about the year of Chrift 40. there was *(q)* a peftilence at Babylon, in which the Jews fuffered.

In the *(r)* 65. year of the Chriftian aera there was a great mortality at Rome. At the fame time there were other calamities in divers parts of the Roman Empire, as we learn from *(s)* Tacitus, and *(t)* Suetonius, as well as from *(u)* Orofius, who might tranfcribe from them.

Earthquakes.

... and *earthquakes*.

Tacitus *(x)* fpeaks of an earthquake at Rome in the time of Claudius, and of another *(y)* at Apamea in the fame reign.

In the reign of Nero there was an earthquake at Laodicea, mentioned

(*p*) *Vid.* Pagi. A. D. 72. n. vii. Reimariann. ad Dion Caff. p. 948. See alfo Credib. P. i. B. i. ch. x.

(*q*) ... ἐφρα ἐν Βαβυλῶνι ἐγένετο αὐτῶν. Ant. l. 18. ix. 8.

(*r*) *Vid.* Pagi. A. D. 67. n. iii.

(*s*) Tot facinoribus foedum annum etiam Dii tempeftatibus et morbis infignivere. Vaftata Campania turbine ventorum, qui villas, arbufta, fruges paffim disjecit, pertulitque violentiam ad vicina Urbi. In qua omne mortalium genus, vis peftilentiae depopulabatur, nulla coeli intemperie, quae occurreret oculis. Sed domus corporibus exanimis, itinera funeribus compilebantur. Non fexus, non aetas periculo vacua. Servitia perinde ac ingenua plebes raptim exftingui, inter conjugum et liberorum lamenta: qui domo affident, dum deflent, faepe eodem rogo cremabantur. Equitum, Senatorumque interitus, quamvis promifcui, minus fle-

biles erant, tanquam communi mortalitate faevitiam principis praevenirent. Tacit. Ann. 16. cap. 13.

(*t*) Accefferunt tantis ex principe malis, probrifque, quaedam et fortuita: peftilentia unius autumni, quo triginta funerum millia in rationem Libitinae venerunt: clades Britannica, qua duo praecipua oppida, magna civium fociorumque caede direpta funt: ignominia ad Orientem, legionibus in Armenia fub jugum miffis, aegreque fyria retenta. Sueton. Nero. cap. 39.

(*u*) Orof. l. 7. cap. vii.

(*x*) Multa eo anno prodigia evenere. Infeffum diris avibus Capitolium: crebris terrae motibus prorutae domus. Ann. 12. cap. 43.

(*y*) Tributumque Apamienfibus terrae motu convulfis, in quinquennium remiffum. Id. l. 12. cap. 58.

Ch. III.   *Earthquakes in divers Places.*   57

tioned by (z) Tacitus: and likewise by (a) Eusebius in his Chronicle: who says, that in Asia three cities, namely Laodicea, Hierapolis, and Colosse, were overturned by an earthquake. And in like manner (b) Orosius. Possibly, the earthquake, which was most violent at Laodicea, was felt in the other cities likewise.

A. D. 76.

In the same reign there was an earthquake in Campania, mentioned by (c) Tacitus, and (d) Seneca. By the former it seems to be placed in the year of Christ 62, by the later in the year 63.

And there may have been other earthquakes in the time of the just mentioned Emperours.

5. Our Lord foretells *wars and commotions*, preceding the final ruin. Matt. xxiv. 6. Mark xiii. 7. Luke xxi. 9.

Wars, and Rumours of Wars.

Josephus (e) has a long storie of a disturbance in Mesopotamia, occasioned by the ambition and indiscretion of two Jews, who were brothers. It seems to have happened (f) about the year of Christ 40. Josephus says, it (g) was not inferior to any calamity, which
                                                                                                 the

---

(z) Eodem anno ex illustribus Asiae urbibus Laodicea, tremore prolapsa, nullo a nobis remedio, propriis viribus revaluit. *Ib. l. 14. c. 27.*

(a) In Asia tres urbes terrae motu conciderunt. Laodicea, Hierapolis, Colossae. *Eus. Chr. p. 161.*

(b) *Oros. l. 7. cap. vii.*

(c) Iisdemque Consulibus gymnasium ictu fulminis conflagravit, effigiesque in eo Neronis ad informe aes liquefacta. Et motu terrae celebre Campaniae oppidum Pompeii magna ex parte proruit. *Ann. l. 15. c. 22.*

(d) Pompeios, celebrem Campaniae urbem ... desedisse terrae motu, vexatis quacumque adjacentibus regionibus, Lucili virorum optime, audivimus: et quidem diebus hibernis, quos vacare a tali periculo majores nostri solebant promittere.

Nonis Febr. fuit motus hic, Regulo et Virginio Consulibus, qui Campaniam nunquam securam hujus mali, indemnem tamen, et totiens defunctam motu, magna strage vastavit. Nam et Herculensis oppidi pars ruit, dubieque stant etiam quae relicta sunt. Et Nucirinorum colonia, ut sine clade, ita non sine querela est. Neapolis quoque privatim multa, publice nihil amisit, leviter ingenti malo perstricta. Villae vero praeruptae passim sine injuria tremuere. Adjiciunt his sexcentarum ovium gregem exanimatum, et divisas statuas, &c. *Sen. Nat. Qu. l. 6. c. 1.*

(e) *Antiq. l. 18. cap. ix.*

(f) *Vid. Usser. A. P. J. 4753 p. 864. Basnag. ann. 40. n. xiii. Tillem. Ruine des Juifs. art. xxviii.*

(g) Γίνεται δὲ ᾧ περὶ τοὺς ἐν τῇ Μεσοποταμίᾳ

the Jews had suffered hitherto: and that *(h)* it occasioned the death of more than fifty thousand people.

When *Cuspius Fadus* came Procurator into Judea, in the reign of Claudius, in the year of Christ 44. or 45. as (*i*) Josephus says, " he " found the Jews in Perèa in a riot, fighting with the Philadelphi- " ans about the limits of the village Mia. And indeed the people of " Perèa had taken up arms without the consent of their chief men, " and had killed a good number of the Philadelphians. When *Fa-* " *dus* heard of it, he was much displeased, that they had taken up " arms, and had not left the decision of the dispute to him, if they " thought the Philadelphians had done them any injurie. Three of " the principal men, who were the causes of the sedition, were appre- " hended, and put in prison: one of whom was afterwards put to " death, and the two others banished."

Afterwards, in the year of our Lord 49. whilst *Cumanus* was Procurator of Judea, there *(k)* happened a tumult at Jerusalem, at the time of Passover. The number of Jews that perished in it, was not less than twenty thousand: as it is in his Antiquities: but in the Jewish War the number is *more than ten thousand.*

Whilst *Cumanus* was yet in Judea, there *(l)* happened a disturbance between the Jews and the Samaritans, in which many were killed on both sides.

Josephus also says, that *(m)* under *Cumanus* the troubles of the Jewish people began, and that in his time they suffered very much.

These disturbances went on encreasing. At Cesarea there had long been contentions between the Jewish people and the other inhabitants.

μία κỳ μάλιςα τὴν Βαβυλᾶνα οἰκοῦντας Ἰυδάιυς σύμφερα ἐτι, κỳ οδεμιᾶς ἧς τίνος ἐλάσσων, φόνος τε αὐτῶν πολὺς, κỳ ὁπόσος ἐχ ἱςορημένος πρότερον. *Ib.* §. 1.

(*h*) *Ib.* §. 9.
(*i*) *Ant. l.* 20. *cap. i.* 1.

(*k*) *Antiq. l.* 20. *cap. v.* 3. *De B. J. l.* 2. *cap. xii.* 1.
(*l*) *Antiq. l.* 20. *vi.* 1. *De B. J. l.* 2. *xii.* 3.
(*m*) ... ἐφ' ὃ θορυβοί τε ἤρξαντο, κỳ φθορά σάλις Ἰυδάιων ἐγένετο. *De B. J. l.* 2. *c. xii.* 1.

Ch. III. Wars and Commotions.

habitants. "And, as (n) Josephus says, in one hour's time more "than twenty thousand Jews were destroyed, and all Cesarea was "at once emptied of it's Jewish inhabitants. Some fled, whom Flo-"rus caught, and sent them bound to the galleys. At which the "whole nation was enraged. They therefore divided themselves "into several parties, and laid waste the villages of the Syrians, and "their neighboring cities, Philadelphia, Sebonitis, Gerasa, Pella, and "Scythopolis: and after them Gadara and Hippos. And falling "upon Gaulanitis, some cities they demolished there, others they set "on fire. Then they went to Kedasa, belonging to the Syrians, and "to Ptolemais, and Gaba, and Cesarea. Nor was Sebaste, or Ash-"kalon able to withstand the violence, with which they were at-"tacked. When they had burnt these to the ground, they demo-"lished Anthedon and Gaza. Many also of the villages round a-"bout these cities were plundered. And an immense slaughter was "made of the men found in them."

"The (o) Syrians destroyed not a less number of the Jews.... So "that the disorders all over Syria were terrible. For every city was "divided into parties, armed against each other. And the safety "of the one, depended upon the destruction of the other. The "days were spent in slaughter, and the nights in terrours, which were "the worst of the two... It was common to see cities filled with "dead bodies, lying unburied, those of old men mixed with in-"fants, all dead, and scattered about promiscuously, and women "without covering for their nakedneffe."

"At (p) Scythopolis the contention was carried so far, that above "thirteen thousand Jews were killed."

"After that (q) other cities also rose up against the Jews that were

I 2 " among

A. D. 76.

(n) Τῆς δὲ αὐτῆς ἡμέρας καὶ ὥρας, ὥσπερ ἐκ δαιμονίου προνοίας, ἀνῄρουν οἱ Καισαρεῖς τοὺς παρ᾽ αὐτοῖς Ἰουδαίους ὡς ὑπὸ μίαν ὥραν ἀποσφαγῆναι μὲν ὑπὲρ δισμυρίους, κενωθῆναι δὲ πᾶσαν τὴν Ἰουδαίων Καισάρειαν. De B. J. l. 2. cap. xviii. 1.
(o) Ibid. §. 2.
(p) Ib. §. 3.
(q) Ib. §. 5.

A. D. 76.

"among them. They of Aſhkalon ſlew two thouſand, and five hundred, they of Ptolemais two thouſand, and put many others into priſon. The Tyrians acted in the like manner: as did alſo Hippos and Gadara, and divers other cities of Syria."

"At (r) Alexandria fifty thouſand lay dead in heaps. Nor would the remainder have been ſpared, if they had not petitioned for mercie."

Not long after that, the (s) men of Damaſcus having got the Jewiſh inhabitants into the place of exerciſe, ἐν τῷ γυμνασίῳ, they came upon them unarmed and ſlew ten thouſand in an hour's time.

Theſe are what our Lord calls *the begining of ſorrows*: when there were *wars and rumours of wars, one people and nation riſing up againſt another. The end was not yet.* Jeruſalem was not yet beſieged, nor the people in it ſhut up, for univerſal deſtruction. But that period was nigh. See Matt. xxiv. 6... 8. Mark xiii. 7. 8. Luke xxi. 9. 10.

The Occaſion of the Jewiſh War, from Joſephus.

VII. And now I think, it may not be improper for us to take notice of Joſephus's accounts of the occaſion of the war.

Giving an account of the contentions between the Jews and Greeks, or Syrians, at Ceſarea, where the later obtained a decree from Nero, that the government of the city belonged to them, he ſays: "And (t) this occaſioned the war, which began in the twelfth year of Nero." Soon after which, the Jews at Ceſarea were treated very contemptuouſly, and injuriouſly, till they were all deſtroyed, as he there proceeds to relate: and we have already, in part, tranſcribed from him.

In the laſt chapter of the Jewiſh Antiquities he complains much of *Albinus*, and ſtill more of *Florus*, who ſucceeded him, and exceeded him in avarice and cruelty: inſomuch, that the Jews were

ready

(r) Ibid. §. 7. 8.
(s) De B. J. l. 2. cap. xx. §. 2.
(t) Ἐν δὲ τούτῳ κỳ οἱ Καισαρέων Ἕλληνες νικήσαντες παρὰ Νέρωνι τῆς πόλεως ἀρχὴν, τὰ τῆς κρίσεως ἐκέμισαν γράμματα. Καὶ προσελάμβανε τὴν ἀρχὴν ὁ πόλεμος δωδεκάτῳ μὲν ἔτει τῆς Νέρωνος ἡγεμονίας. De B. J. l. 2. c. xiv. 4.

Ch. III.   *The Occasion of the War, from Josephus.*

ready to consider Albinus, as a benefactor. "Finally (*u*) says he,   A. D. 76.
" without adding any thing more, it was *Florus*, who compelled us
" to take up arms against the Romans, thinking it better to be de-
" stroyed all at once, than by little and little."

In his own Life he says: " I (*x*) have mentioned all these things
" to shew, that the Jews war with the Romans was not their own
" choice, but rather that they were compelled by necessity."

In another place he says: " And *(y)* at the temple Eleazar, son of
" Ananias the High-Priest, a young man of a daring temper, and
" then Governour, persuaded those who officiated in the divine
" service, not to accept of the gift or sacrifice of a foreigner. That
" was the origin of the war with the Romans. For thus they re-
" jected the sacrifice of Cesar for them. [*That is, as I apprehend,*
" *they refused to offer prayers and sacrifices, as subjects ought to do, for*
" *the Emperour, and for the prosperity of the Roman Empire.*] And
" though many of the High-Priests, and of the principal men of
" the nation earnestly entreated them, not to omit the customarie re-
" spect for their Governours, they could not prevail."

Afterwards, near the conclusion of his historie of the Jewish War,
when the city was actually taken, he says: " But (*z*) that which
" principally encouraged them to the war, was an ambiguous oracle,
" found also in their sacred writings, that about this time some one
" from their countrey should obtain the empire of the world. This
" they understood to belong to themselves. And many of the wise
" men were mistaken in their judgement about it. For the oracle
" intended the government of Vespasian, who was proclaimed Em-
" rour in Judea."

That

(*u*) Καὶ τί δ᾿ ἂν πλέω λέγοις; Τὸν γὰρ πρὸς Ῥωμαίους πόλεμον ὁ καταναγκάσας ἡμᾶς ἄρασθαι, Φλῶρος ἦν, κρεῖττον ἡγουμένους ἀθρόως, ἢ κατ᾿ ὀλίγον ἀπολίσθαι. *Antiq.* l. 20. xi. 1.

(*x*) ... ὅτι ὁ πρυκείμενος ἐγένετο τῦ πολέμου πρὸς Ῥωμαίους Ἰουδαίοις, ἀλλὰ τὸ πλέον ἀνάγκη. *Vit.* §. 6.

(*y*) ... ἀνατέθη, μηδενὸς ἀλλοφύλου δῶρον ἢ θυσίαν προσδέχεσθαι. Τῦτο δὲ ἦν τῦ πρὸς Ῥωμαίους πολέμου καταβολή. Τὴν γὰρ ὑπὲρ τούτων θυσίαν Καίσαρος ἀπέρριψαν. *De B.* l. 2. xvii. 2.

(*z*) *De B. J.* l. 6. cap. v. 4.

A. D. 76.

That is very a remarkable paſſage. Some farther notice ſhall be taken of it by and by.

That the Jewiſh people were uneaſie under ſubjection to the Romans, even in our Saviour's time, long before the war broke out, appears from many things recorded in the Goſpels: as their great averſion to the Publicans, though Jews, who were employed in collecting the Roman tribute: from the queſtion brought to our Saviour, *whether it was lawful to give tribute to Ceſar or not.* Matt. xxii. 15...22. Mark xiii. 13...17. Luke xx. 19...26. from the attempt of ſome, who followed our Lord for a time, to make him a King. John vi. 15. from their frequent and importunate demands, that he would *ſhew them a ſign from heaven,* meaning ſome token, that he intended to work out for them a temporal deliverance, *that they might believe in him,* and have full aſſurance of his being the Chriſt. Matt. xii. 38. xvi. 1...4. and elſewhere: and from divers other things, which muſt be obvious to all, who have read the Goſpels with attention.

This uneaſineſſe under the Roman yoke continued and encreaſed. Obſervable here is the anſwer, which was made by Titus, after the temple was burnt, to the petition of Simon and John, the two great leaders of the factions in Jeruſalem. "You (a) have never ceaſed
" rebelling, ſince Pompey firſt made a conqueſt of your countrey.
" And at length you have declared open war againſt the Romans.
" ... Our kindneſſe to you has encouraged your enmity againſt us:
" who have let you live in your countrey in peace and quietneſſe. In
" the firſt place we gave you your own countrey to live in, and ſet
" over you kings of your own nation, and farther we preſerved to you
" your own laws: and withall we have permitted you to live either
" by yourſelves, or among others, as you liked beſt. And which is
" the greateſt favour of all, we have given you leave to gather up
" that tribute, which you pay to God, together with all ſuch other
" gifts

(a) *De B. J. l. 6. cap. vi. 2.*

"gifts as are dedicated to him. Nor have we called those to account, who carried such donations, nor given them any obstruction: till at length you became richer than ourselves, even when you were our enemies, and you have made preparations for the war against us with our own money."

There are other things likewise in Josephus, which deserve to be taken notice of in this place. Giving an account of the assessment made in Judea after the removal of Archelaus, he says: "At (b) the persuasion of Joazar the High-Priest, the Jews did generally acquiesce. However, Judas the Gaulanite, of the town called Gamala, associating to himself Sadduc a Pharisee, excited the people to rebellion, telling them, that an assessment would bring in downright slaverie, and exhorting the whole nation to assert their liberty. The whole nation heard their discourses with incredible pleasure. And it is impossible to represent the evils the nation has suffered, which were owing to these men... For Judas and Sadduc brought in among us this fourth sect. And there being many, who embraced their sentiments, they not only caused disturbances in the government at that time, but laid the foundation of those evils that followed. Which indeed are owing to this principle, till then unknown among us."

He then delivers the character and principles of the three chief and more ancient sects of the Jews, as he calls them. And after that returns again to the men, of whom he had been speaking before. "Judas (c) the Galilean, was the leader of the fourth sect. In all other points they hold the same sentiments with the Pharisees, but they have an invincible affection for liberty, and acknowledge God alone their Lord and Governour... From that time the nation became infected with this principle. And Florus, by abusing his power when he was Governour, threw them into despair, and provoked them to rebel against the Romans."

Those

(b) *Antiq. l.* 18. *cap.* i. §. 1.   (c) *Ibid.* §. 6.

A. D. 76.

Those two passages were cited by me *(d)* formerly. And divers observations were made upon them. Which still appear to me not impertinent. But I am unwilling to repeat them here. And I think, that in the connexion, in which they are now cited by me, it must be apparent from them, without farther remarks, that the nation in general was infected with the doctrine of Judas of Galilee. They had an invincible zeal for liberty, scorned subjection to the Romans, their masters, and took up arms against them. As Cappellus says, " Florus *(e)* by his exactions forced them against their consent, or " rather drove them who were already disposed to it, and wanted " no incitement to rebel against the Romans."

I would now take farther notice of the passage above cited, wherein our Jewish historian says, *what principally encouraged them to the war was an ambiguous oracle, found in their sacred writings, that about that time some one from their own countrey should obtain the empire of the world.*

False Prophets and false Christians in Judea, as our Lord had foretold.

The truth and importance of that observation, as I apprehend, may be confirmed and illustrated by the accounts, which Josephus has given of numerous impostors, or false-prophets, which arose among them about this time, agreeably to our Lord's predictions, as I shall now shew.

" Whilst *(f)* Fadus was Procurator of Judea, a certain impostor,
" called (*) *Theudas*, persuaded a very great multitude, taking their ef-
" fects with them, to follow him to the river Jordan: assuring them,
" that he was a Prophet, and that causing the river to divide at his
" command, he would give them an easie passage over: By such
" speeches

(d) Credibility. Part i. B. i. ch. 9. p. 486. &c.

(e) Florus, pessimus homo, qui modis omnibus Judaeos cum vexaret et opprimeret, cogit vel invitos, aut potius ultro ruentes impulit, adversus Romanos rebellare. L. Capp. Hist. Jud. p. 121.

(f) Ant. l. 20. cap. v. 1.

(*) *That Theudas is different from him, mentioned by Gamaliel, Acts v. 36. as was shewn formerly. Credib. P. i. B. 2. ch. vii. p. 921. &c.*

Ch. III.   *False Prophets, and false Christs in Judea.*

"speeches he deceived many. But Fadus was far from suffering
"them to go on in their madnesse. For he sent out a troop of horse,
"who coming upon them unexpectedly, slew many, and took ma-
"ny prisoners. *Theudas* himself was among the last mentioned.
"They cut off his head, and brought it to Jerusalem. These things
"happened in Judea, whilst Cuspius Fadus was Procurator."

Fadus was sent into Judea by the Emperour Claudius, after the death of Herod Agrippa. This affair of Theudas therefore must be rightly placed in the year of Christ 45. or 46.

That is transcribed from the 20. and last book of the Antiquities. In the same book, afterwards, in another chapter, in the historie of transactions in the time of Nero, Josephus says. "But (g) affairs in
"Judea went on continually growing worse and worse. The countrey
"was again filled with robbers and impostors, who deceived the peo-
"ple. But *Felix* time after time apprehended, and put to death many
"of them." A little lower. "And (h) indeed by means of the crimes
"committed by the robbers, the city was filled with all sorts of im-
"piety. And impostors and deceivers perswaded the people to follow
"them into the wildernesse: where, as they said, they should see ma-
"nifest wonders and signs, performed by the providence of God.
"And many hearkening unto them at length suffered the punishment
"of their folly. For Felix fetched them back, and punished them.
"About the same time there came a man out of Egypt to Jerusalem,
"who said, he was a Prophet: and having perswaded a good number
"of the meaner sort of people to follow him to the mount of Olives,
"he told them, that thence they should see the walls of Jerusalem
"fall down at his command, and promised through them to give
"them entrance into the city. But Felix being informed of these
"things, ordered his soldiers to their arms. And marching out of
"Jerusalem with a large body of horse and foot, he fell upon the
"Egyptian: and killed four hundred of them, and took two hun-

---

(g) *Antiq.* l. 20. cap. viii. 5.   (h) *Ib.* §. 6.

"dred

"dred prisoners. But the Egyptian getting out of the fight escaped."

This same storie is also in the War, with some differences in the numbers, which were considered (*i*, formerly).

There the account concludes in this manner. "When *(k)* they "came to engage, the *Egyptian* fled, followed by a few only. A "large part of those who were with him, were either slain, or ta- "ken prisoners. The rest of the multitude being scattered, shifted "for themselves, as they could."

This is supposed to have happened in the year of Christ 55.

In the War, in the paragraph preceding his account of the Egyptian impostor, having just before related, how Judea then abounded with robbers, called Sicarii, he says: "Beside *(l)* them, there was "another body of wicked men, whose hands indeed were cleaner, "but their intentions were as impious: who disturbed the happy "state of the city no less than those murderers. For deceivers and "impostors, under a pretense of divine inspiration, aiming at changes "and innovations, made the people mad. And induced them to "follow them into the wildernesse, pretending, that God would "there give them signs and wonders. Felix judging these proceed- "ings to be no less than the begining of a revolt, sent out his sol- "diers, both horse and foot, and destroyed great numbers of them."

In the forecited chapter of the 20. book of the Antiquities, speaking of the Robbers in the time of *Porcius Festus*, about the year of Christ 60. he says, " that *(m)* he also sent out both horse and foot "to fall upon those, who had been seduced by a certain impostor, "who had promised them deliverance, and freedom from the mi- "series, under which they labored, if they would but follow him "into the wildernesse. The forces destroyed both him that had de- "ceived them, and those that followed him."

Josephus speaks of six thousand, who perished in the outer courts

(*i*) *Credib*. Part i. B. 2. ch. viii.
(*k*) *De B. J.* l. 2. c. xiii. 5.
(*l*) *Ibid*. §. 4.
(*m*) *Ant*. l. 20. cap. viii. §. 10.

Ch. III.   *Falſe Prophets, and falſe Chriſts.*   67

courts of the temple, after it had been ſet on fire. "The (*n*) ſoldi-
" ers, ſays he, ſet fire to the portico. Whereupon ſome threw them-
" ſelves headlong down the precipice, others periſhed in the flames.
" And not one out of ſo great a number eſcaped. A falſe Prophet
" was the occaſion of the ruin of thoſe people, who on that very
" day had made proclamation in the city, aſſuring them, that God
" commanded them to go up to the temple, where they would re-
" ceive ſigns of deliverance. And indeed there were then many
" prophets, ſuborned by the tyrants, to impoſe upon the people, and
" telling them, that they ought to wait for help from God."

And preſently after, proceeding to relate the omens and prodigies foreſignifying the calamities coming upon the Jewiſh people,
and the city of Jeruſalem, which ſhall be recited by and by, he
ſays: " Impoſtors (*o*) who ſpake lies in the name of God, deceived
" this miſerable people. They neither attended to, nor believed
" the manifeſt ſigns, foreſignifying the coming deſolation. But like
" infatuated men, who have neither eyes to ſee, nor minds to per-
" ceive, they neglected the divine denunciations."

So truly did our Lord ſay: *I am come in my Father's name. And
ye receive me not. If another ſhall come in his own name, him ye will
receive.* John v. 43.

Our bleſſed Lord ſays, Matt. xxiv. 24. *For there will ariſe falſe
Chriſts, and falſe prophets, and will ſhew great ſigns and wonders, inſomuch that, (if it were poſſible) they will deceive the very elect.* But
our Lord does not intend to ſay, that any of thoſe falſe prophets
would exhibit or perform great wonders. The original word is δώσυσι
they will give: the ſame word that is in the ſeptuagint verſion of
Deut. xiii. 1. *If there ariſe among you a prophet, or a dreamer of
dreams, and he giveth thee a ſign, or a wonder.* καὶ δῶ σοι σημεῖον ἢ
τέρας, that is, ſhall propoſe, or promiſe ſome ſign or wonder, as the
ſequel ſhews. Parallel with the text juſt cited from St. Matthew
is

(*n*) *De B. J. l.* 6. *cap. v.* §. 2.   (*o*) *Ibid.* §. 3.

A. D. 76.

is Mark xiii. 22. *For falſe Chriſts and falſe prophets will ariſe, and will ſhew ſigns and wonders,* the ſame word again, καὶ δώσουσι σημεῖα καὶ τέρατα, *in order to ſeduce, if it were poſſible, even the elect.*

The accounts, which Joſephus has given of the impoſtors in his time, ſhew the exact accompliſhment of theſe predictions of our Lord. *They perſuaded the people to follow them, into the wilderneſſe, where, as they ſaid, they would ſee manifeſt ſigns and wonders performed by the power of God :* or, aſſuring them, *that God would there give them ſigns, and wonders :* or, that *they ſhould there receive ſigns of deliverance,* and the like.

The paſſages of Joſephus bear witneſſe to the fulfillment of our Lord's prediction, *that many falſe prophets would ariſe, and deceive many.* Matt. xxiv. 11.

Our Lord does alſo ſay there, at ver. 5. *And many will come in my name, ſaying, I am Chriſt. And will deceive many.* And it is eaſie to believe, that *(p)* ſome of the many falſe-prophets did expreſsly take to themſelves that title, though Joſephus does not ſay it. But whether they did, or not, our Saviour's predictions are verified in the appearance of thoſe falſe-prophets. " Joſephus, ſays *(q)* ABp. *Til-*
" *lotſon,* mentions ſeveral of theſe : of whom, though he does not
" expreſsly ſay, that they called themſelves the Meſſias : yet he ſays
" that, which is equivalent : that they undertook to reſcue the peo-
" ple from the Roman yoke. Which was the thing, which the
" Jews expected the Meſſias would do for them. And therefore we
" find, that the diſciples who were going to Emmaus, and knew
" not that Chriſt was riſen, and were doubtful what to think of him,
" ſay : *We hoped, this had been he that ſhould have redeemed Iſrael :*
" that is, they hoped, this had been the Meſſias, that being, it ſeems,
" a common periphraſis of the Meſſias, that he was *he that was to*
" *deliver Iſrael.*" Which is agreeable to a note of *(r)* Grotius, upon

---

(p) See *Tillemont Ruine des Juifs, art.* 36. *A. D.* 52.

(q) Vol. 3. *p.* 552.

(r) Chriſti nomine populus Judaicus intel-

on the place. All they therefore, who pretended, that they were inspired, and sent by God to deliver the Jewish people, were indeed *false-chrifts*. They took upon themselves the character of the Messiah.

We may now readily admit the truth of what Josephus says in the passage transcribed not long ago. "That what principally excited the Jewish people, the wise men, as he calls them, as well as others, to the war with the Romans was the expectation of a great deliverer to arise among them, who should obtain the empire of the world." This great deliverer was the Messiah. The numerous *false-prophets* and *false-chrifts*, of whom Josephus speaks so frequently, and so distinctly, are full proofs of it.

The expectation of the coming of the Messiah, about the time of the appearance of Jesus, was universal, and had been so for some (s) while. But with the idea of a prophet, or extraordinarie teacher of religion, they had joyned also that of a worldly king and conquerour, who should deliver the Jewish People from the burdens under which they laboured, raise them to a state of independence, and bring the nations of the earth into subjection to them, to be ruled and tyrannised over by them. And because our Lord did not perform, nor attempt this, they rejected and crucified him. If he would but have assumed the state and character of an earthly prince, Scribes and Pharisees, Priests and People, would all have joyned themselves to him, and have put themselves under his banner. Of this we see many proofs in the Gospels. This disposition prevailed to the last. The people therefore, though they had already met with many disappointments, when our Lord entred into Jerusalem, in no

greater

---

intelligebat vindicem libertatis. Nam illud, ἡμεῖς δὲ ἠλπίζομεν, ὅτι αὐτός ἐςιν ὁ μέλλων λυτρέεσθαι τὸν Ἰσραὴλ, descriptio est nominis Christi. Quare quicumque se missos divinitus liberatores populi Judaici dicebant, eo ipso Christos se profitebantur, et erant ψευδόχρισοι. &c. *Grot. in Matt. xxiv.* 5.

(s) *Proofs of this, together with divers remarks, may be seen in Credib. Part* i. B. i. *ch. v. p.* 289. *&c.*

greater state than riding upon an asse, accompanied him with loud acclamations, and other tokens of respect, saying: *Hosanna to the Son of David. Blessed is the King, that cometh in the name of the Lord.* And Jesus, our Lord, not assuming then the character of an earthly prince was a fresh disappointment, and left deep resentments. Which rendered them susceptible of the worst impressions from the chief priests, and their other rulers. And at their instigation they desired Pilate the Roman Governour, to set Barabbas at liberty, and crucify Jesus. With which clamorous, and importunate demand, he at length complied, still bearing testimonie to the innocence of him, whom he unwillingly condemned. The account of St. Matthew alone, without any other, will suffice for shewing this amazing transaction. *Pilate saith unto them: What shall I do then with Jesus, who is called Christ? They all say unto him: Let him be crucified. The Governour said: Why! what evil has he done? But they cried out the more, saying: Let him be crucified. When Pilate saw, that he prevailed nothing, and that rather a tumult was made, he took water and washed his hands before the multitude, saying: I am innocent from the bloud of this just person. See ye to it. Then answered all the people: His bloud be upon us, and upon our children. Then released he Barabbas unto them. And when he had scourged Jesus, he delivered him to be crucified.* Matt. xxvii. 22... 26.

The continued expectation of the Messiah, as a worldly King and Conquerour, as we have just seen in Josephus, and their uneasinesse under the Roman yoke, were the immediate occasions of their rebelling against the authority, to which they were then subject. And the same principles, that induced them to reject, and crucify Jesus, brought upon them their utter and final ruin.

As the sin of the Jewish People in rejecting and crucifying Jesus, after a life of perfect innocence, and consummate virtue, after speaking as no man had done before, and doing works, which no other man had done, at Jerusalem, and in every part of the land of Israel, after such preparations as had been made for his reception by the Pro-

Ch. III. *The Occasion of the War.*

Prophets, and by the testimonie of John the Baptist, his forerunner, was (*) very great and aggravated. And as they rejected the renewed offers of mercie, and repeated and earnest calls to repentance, made by Christ's Apostles, and went on encreasing in wickednesse: God at length suffered the Romans to come upon them with an armed force, demolished their temple, and made desolate their city, and their whole countrey, with many circumstances of uncommon and even unparalleled distresse. All which having been foreseen, and often foretold, by the Lord Jesus, in his public discourses: the accomplishment of these predictions, in the event, is an argument of great force in favour of his divine mission, and of his being indeed the Messiah, additional to the excellent doctrine, and wonderfull works of his ministrie.

VIII. Having shewn the occasion and causes of the war, and having also observed the several things foretold by the Lord Jesus, as preceding it. I now proceed to the historie of the war itself, collecting it from Josephus, and making my extracts in his own words.

The disturbances still encreasing at Jerusalem, and the animosity against Florus being very great, " *Cestius Gallus* (*t*) President of Sy-
" ria, judged it not proper for him to lie still any longer. He there-
" fore determined to march into Judea. Whereupon he took out
" of Antioch the twelfth legion entire, and out of the rest two thou-
" sand chosen men, with six cohorts of foot, and four troops of
" horse, beside the auxiliaries, which were sent by the Kings. Of
" which *Antiochus* sent two thousand horse, and three thousand foot,
" all archers. *Agrippa* sent a thousand horse, and two thousand
foot.

A. D. 76.

The Historie of the Jewish War, and of the Siege of Jerusalem, from Josephus.

(*) *If ye were blind, ye should have no sin. But now you say, we see: therefore your sin remaineth.* John ix. 41. *If I had not come and spoken to them, they had not had sin. But now they have no cloake for their sin. If I had not done among them the works, which no other man did, they had not had sin. But now have they both seen, and hated, both me and my Father.* John xv. 22...24.

(*t*) *De B. J. l. 2. cap. xviii. §. 9.*

A. D. 76.

"foot. *Sohemus* followed with four thousand. He then marched
" to Ptolemais. Agrippa accompanied Cestius, as a guide in the
" journey, and as capable of being usefull to him in other respects.
" After he was come thither, Cestius took a part of his armie, and
" marched hastily to Zabulon, a strong city of Galilee, which sepa-
" rates the countrey of Ptolemais from our nation. That he found
" destitute of it's men, the multitude having fled to the mountains,
" but full of all good things, which he allowed the soldiers to seize
" as plunder. And he set fire to the city, though it's buildings were
" very beautiful, resembling those of Tyre, and Sidon, and Berytus.
" After that he overran the neighboring countrey, seising whatever
" came in his way, and setting fire to the villages. And then re-
" turned to Ptolemais." At this very time, as Josephus adds in the
same paragraph, the Jews found means to destroy about two thousand Syrians at Berytus, and near it, Cestius being at a distance.

" Now (*u*) Cestius himself marched from Ptolemais, and came to
" Cesarea. And then sent part of his armie before him to *Joppa*.
" Who coming suddenly upon that people, who were prepared nei-
" ther for flight, nor for their own defense, slew them all with their
" families, and then plundered, and burnt the city. The number
" of the slain were eight thousand and four hundred. In like manner
" he sent a number of horse into the toparchie of *Narbata*, not far
" from Cesarea, who slew many of the inhabitants, plundered their
" goods, and set fire to the villages."

" Now (*x*) also Cestius sent Gallus, commander of the twelfth
legion into Galilee, where he slew more than two thousand."

" Gallus (*y*) then returned to Cesarea, and Cestius moved with
" his whole armie, and came to *Antipatris*. Thence he set forward
" to *Lydda*, where he found the place empty of men, the people
" being gone up to Jerusalem upon account of the feast of Taberna-
" cles. However, he found there fifty men, whom he slew, and
" burnt

(*u*) §. 10.   (*x*) *Ib*. §. 11.   (*y*) *Ib. cap. xix*. §. 1.

"burnt the city. And then marched onward. and going up by
"Bethoron, he pitched his camp at Gaba, fifty furlongs from Jeru-
"salem."

"The (z) Jews seeing the war approaching to their metropolis,
"relying upon their numbers, went out to fight in a hastie and dis-
"orderly manner, even in the time of the festival. But the rage,
"which made them forget their religion, did also make them su-
"perior to their enemies. Cestius with his whole armie was in
"danger. Five hundred and fifteen of the Romans were slain,
"whilst the Jews lost only two and twenty. The most valiant of
"the Jews were Monobazus, and Kenedaeus, related to Monobazus
"King of the Adiabenes. Next to them were Niger of Peréa,
"and Silas of Babylon, who had deserted from King Agrippa to the
"Jews, and Simon son of Gioras, to be hereafter often mentioned.
"After that the Jews retired into the city. Cestius stayed there
"three days."

"At (a) this time Agrippa with the consent of Cestius sent to the
"Jews two ambassadours, *Borcaeus* and *Phoebus*, men well known
"to them, with assurances of plenarie forgivenesse from Cestius, if
"they would lay down their arms, and submit. But the Jews would
"not so much as receive the ambassadours. *Phoebus* they fell upon,
"and slew him, before he had spoken a word. *Borcaeus* too was
"wounded. But he retreated, and escaped."

"Soon (b) after that Cestius moved forward with his whole ar-
"mie, and encamped upon an elevated spot of ground called Scopos
"[signifying the Prospect, or Watch-tower.] Here he rested three
"days. On the fourth day, which was the thirtieth of October, he
"brought his armie into the city. The seditious, as Josephus calls
"them, were much terrified, and retired from the suburbs to the
"inner part of the city, and the temple. Cestius soon set fire to the
"place called Bezetha, or the new city, and to the wood-market.
"After which he came forward to the upper part of the city, and

(z) *Ib.* §. 2.   (a) *Ib.* §. 3.   (b) *Ib.* §. 4.

"pitched

A. D. 76. "pitched his camp over againſt the Royal Palace. And if at that
"time he had attempted to make his way within the walls by force,
"he would have won the city preſently, and put an end to the war
"at once. But Tyrannus Priſcus, a General in the armie, and ma-
"ny officers of the horſe, who had been corrupted by Florus, di-
"verted him from that deſign. Which was the occaſion, that this
"war laſted ſo long, and the Jews were involved in ſuch grievous
"calamities."

N. B. So writes Joſephus. And afterwards he ſays: "If (c) Ceſtius had
"continued the ſiege a little longer, he had certainly taken the city.
"But God, as I think, for the wickedneſſe of the people, abhorring
"his own ſolemnities, ſuffered not the war to come to an end at
"that time."

"Ceſtius (d) then withdrew from the city. The Jews reſumed
"courage, and went after him. And coming upon his rear, de-
"ſtroyed a good number both of horſe and foot. That night Ceſti-
"us lay at his former camp, Scopos. As he went farther off the
"the next day, he even invited his enemies to purſue him. The
"Romans ſuffered greatly. Among the ſlain were Priſcus, com-
"mander of the ſixth legion, Longinus a tribune, and Aemilius
"Secundus, commander of a troop of horſe. It was not without
"a great deal of difficulty that they got to Gabao, their former
"camp, and leaving behind their baggage. There Ceſtius ſtayed two
"days, and was in great perplexity, how to proceed. On the third
"day he judged it expedient to move."

"That (e) he might march on with the greater expedition, he
"threw away every thing that might retard his march. He killed
"the mules, and the other beaſts, excepting only ſuch as carried
"weapons of war: which the Romans kept for their own uſe, and
"that they might not fall into the hands of the Jews, to be after-
"wards employed againſt them. In that march they met with ſuch
"difficul-

(c) §. 6.   (d) §. 7.   (e) §. 8.

Ch. III.   Transactions in the Year of Christ 66.

"difficulties, that the Jews were near taking the whole armie of Cestius prisoners. And would have effected it, if night had not come on."

"In (f) their flight they left behind them many engines for sieges, and for throwing stones, and a great part of their other instruments of war. The Jews pursued them, as far as Antipatris, and then returned, taking up the engines, spoiling the dead bodies, and gathering up the prey, which the Romans had left behind them. So they came back to their metropolis with great rejoycings. They lost but a few men themselves. But they had slain of the Romans and their auxiliaries five thousand and three hundred foot, and three hundred and eighty horse. These things happened on the eighth day of November, in the twelfth year of the reign of Nero."

"After (g) that calamity had befallen Cestius, says Josephus, many of the most considerable of the Jewish people forsook the city as men do a sinking ship."

And it is very likely, that at this time many of the Christians also withdrew from Jerusalem, and Judea. Eusebius says, that (h) before the war began, the Christians left Jerusalem, and went to a place beyond Jordan, called Pella. Epiphanius (i) speaks to the like purpose. Eusebius does not quote any ancient author for what he says. But it might be founded upon tradition, and such as could be relied upon. As he resided near the place, he might have satisfactorie information of it, and receive the account from the descendents of those Jewish believers.

However, some of them may have gone abroad into the other countreys. St. John, as is well known, lived for some time in A-
sia.

(f) Ib. §. 9.
(g) Μετὰ δὲ τὴν Κεςίε συμφοράν, πολλοὶ τῶν ἐπιφανῶν Ἰεδαίων, ὥσπερ βαπτιζομένης νεὼς, ἀπενήχοντο τῆς πόλεως.   De. B. J. l. 2. c. xx. §. 1.

(h) ... πρὸ τȣ πολέμȣ, μετασῆναι τῆς πόλεως, ᾗ τίνα τῆς Περαίας πόλιν οἰκεῖν.... Πέλλαν αὐτὴν ὀνομάζȣσιν.   H. E. l. 3. cap. v. p. 75. A.
(i) H. 29. §. vii.

sia. When he came thither, we cannot say exactly: but probably, in the year of Christ 66. or sooner. Some of the Jewish believers might go with him out of Judea, or come to him into Asia afterwards. St. John in his third epistle, ver. 6. speaks of *strangers*, who were under difficulties. Some learned men have supposed, that *(k)* thereby are meant Jewish believers, who had been driven out of Palestine, or had fled from it, induced thereto by the necessity of the times, and their fidelity to Christ, and had left their substance behind them.

I think, we may reckon it to be certain, or at least highly probable, that none of the faithful disciples of Jesus were shut up in Jerusalem at the siege: and that most of them left it some while before it began, in the year of Christ 66. or thereabout, or sooner.

Our blessed Lord speaking of the difficulties of these times, and of the declensions of some of his followers, encourages faithfulness in strong terms. Mark xiii. 13... *And ye shall be hated of all men for my name sake. But he that shall endure unto the end, shall be saved.* And Luke xxi. 17... 19. *And ye shall be hated of all men for my name sake. But there shall not an hair of your head perish. In your patience possess ye your souls.* And compare Matt. x. 21. 22. These gracious assurances were now fulfilled. The difficulties, which the followers of Jesus met with, were very great. And the *love of many waxed cold*, and some apostatized to Judaism, to avoid sufferings. Neverthelesse they gained nothing by it. They joyned themselves to the unbelieving part of the nation, and had part with them in the heavie calamities, which befell them. But the faithfull followers of Jesus, who were steadie to their profession, and attended to his predictions concerning coming calamities, and observed the signs of their near approach, escaped, and obtained safety, with only the lesser difficulties of a flight, which was necessarie in the time of a general calamity.

(*k*) See the *Supplement to the Credib. vol.* 3. *p.* 311.

Ch. III. *Transactions in the Year of Christ* 66.

The *(l)* Jews who had defeated Cestius, upon their return to Jerusalem appointed governours and commanders for several places. *Joseph son of Gorion*, and *Ananus* the High-Priest, were chosen to govern the city, and to repair the walls. *Josephus son of Matthias*, our historian, was made governour of both the *Galilees*. Others were sent to other places.

Cestius *(m)* sent messengers to Nero in Achaia, to give him an account of what had happened, and of the state of affairs in Judea, and to lay the blame of all the disturbances upon Florus.

Nero *(n)* as Josephus says, was not a little moved at these things, though he dissembled his concern. However, he chose for a General a man of known valour, and experience in war, several of whose important services are here mentioned by Josephus, agreeably to the testimonie of the *(o)* Roman authors. Who represent Vespasian

A. D. 76.

(l) Ib. cap. xx. §. 3. 4.
(m) Ib. cap. xx. §. 1.
(n) De B. J. l. 3. cap. i. §. 1, 2.
(o) Missu Neronis, Vespasianus fortuna, fama ue, et egregiis ministris, &c. *Tacit. Hist. L. v. cap.* 10.
Claudio principe, Narcissi gratia legatus legionis in Germania missus est. Inde in Britanniam translatus, tricies cum hoste conflixit.... Peregrinatione Achaica inter comites Neronis, cum cantante eo discederet saepius, aut praesens obdormisceret, gravissimam contraxit offensam. Prohibitusque non contubernio modo, sed etiam publica salutatione, secessit in parvam ac deviam civitatem, quoad latenti, etiamque extrema metuenti, provincia cum exercitu oblata est. Percrebuerat Oriente toto vetus et constans opinio, esse in fatis, ut eo tempore Judaeâ profecti rerum potirentur. Id de Imperatore Romano, quantum eventu postea praedictum patuit. Judaei ad se trahentes rebellarunt: caesoque Praeposito, Legatum insuper Syriae consularem suppetias ferentem, raptâ Aquilâ fugaverunt. Ad hunc motum comprimendum cum exercitu ampliore, et non instrenuo duce, cui tamen tuto tanta res committeretur, opus esset, ipse potissimum delectus est: et ut industriae expertae, nec metuendus ullo modo ob humilitatem generis ac nominis. Additis igitur ad copias duabus legionibus, octo alis, cohortibus decem, atque inter Legatos majore filio assumto, ut primum provinciam attigit, proximas quoque convertit in se. Correctâ statim castrorum disciplina: uno quoque et altero proelio tam constanter inito, ut in oppugnatione castelli lapidis ictum genu scuto sagittas aliquot exceperit. *Sueton. Vespasian. cap. iv.*

A. D. 76.

sian to have been chosen for this service out of regard to his merit, when upon some accounts he was disagreeable to Nero.

Vespasian *(p)* sent his own son Titus from Achaia, where he then was, to Alexandria, to fetch thence the fifth and tenth legions. Himself, having crossed the Hellespont, went by land into Syria, where he gathered together the Roman forces, and a good number of auxiliaries from the neighboring princes.

The *(q)* Jews elevated by the advantages, which they had gained over Cestius, determined to carry the war to a greater distance. Accordingly they marched to Ashkalon, a city always at enmity with them, distant from Jerusalem 550 furlongs. [*more than* 60 *miles.*] Here the Jewish people were defeated in two attacks, losing more than eighteen thousand men, and two of their Generals, *John the Essen*, and *Silas* the Babylonian. *Niger* the Peraite the third General, narrowly escaped with his life.

Vespasian (*r*) when he arrived at Antioch, the metropolis of Syria, reckoned the third city of the Roman Empire for magnitude and dignity, found there Agrippa waiting for him. And taking the whole armie with him, he soon marched forward to Ptolemais.

Titus (*s*) making great expedition than could have been expected, especially in the winter season, came to his father at Ptolemais, bringing with him the fifth and tenth legions. To which were added the fifteenth legion, and eighteen cohorts. There were also five cohorts from Cesarea, with one troop of horse, and also five other troops from Syria. There was also a considerable number of auxiliaries from the Kings *Antiochus* [of Comagene] and *Agrippa*, and *Seleucus*, and *Malchus* the Arabian. So that the whole armie of Romans and auxiliaries, horse and foot, amounted to about sixty thousand men, beside servants, whom Josephus represents as far from being useless, according to the Roman discipline.

Thus we have pursued the historie to the end of the year 66. and into the begining of the year 67.

Ves-

(*p*) *De B. J. l.* 3. *cap. i.* §. 3.
(*q*) *Ib. cap. ii.* §. 1. 2. 3.
(*r*) *Ibid.* §. 4.
(*s*) *Ib. cap. iv. n.* 2.

Ch. III. *Transactions in the Year of Christ* 67.

Vespasian (*t*) stayed some while at Ptolemais. However Placidus, who was before sent into Galilee, destroyed many, whom he met with in the open countreys. He also made an attack upon Jotapata, but was repulsed.

Vespasian (*u*) leaves Ptolemais, and marcheth with his armie in great order into Galilee.

The (*x*) first place taken by Vespasian was *Gadara*, which at that time had in it few men of a militarie age. But he slew all the young people: the Romans, from hatred of the Jews, and resenting the defeat of Cestius, having no mercie on any age. He also set fire to the city, and burnt all the villages, and smaller towns, round about: making some totally desolate, in others taking some captives.

Josephus (*y*) leaves Tiberias, and enters *Jotapata* on the 21. day of May.

The (*z*) next day Vespasian marches to Jotapata, at (*a*) the siege of which he received a slight wound in one of his feet.

" Whilst (*b*) Vespasian lay with his armie before Jotapata, he
" sent Trajan, commander of the tenth legion, to *Japha*, not far
" off. The place was strong, and surrounded by a double wall. A
" large number made a salley upon the Romans. Being beaten back
" they retired within the outer wall. But when they came to the
" inner wall, their fellow-citizens refused to admit them, least the
" Romans should also force their way in with them. And (*c*) now,
" says Josephus, it might be seen, that God had given up the Ga-
" lileans to the Romans, to be destroyed by their cruel enemies.
" The number of the slain in the distresse between the two walls
" was twelve thousand. Of this Trajan gave information to Vespa-
" sian,

A.D. 76.

N. B.

(*t*) *L*. 3. *cap. vi*. 1.
(*u*) *Ib. n*. 2. 3.
(*x*) *Cap. vii*. 1.
(*y*) §. 3.
(*z*) *Ib*. 4.

(*a*) *Ib*. §. 22.
(*b*) *Ib*. §. 31.
(*c*) Θεὸς δ' ἦν ἄρα, ὁ Ῥωμαίοις τὰ Γαλιλαίων πάθη χαριζόμενος. κ. λ. *Ibid*.

"sian, desiring him to send his son Titus thither, that he might have the honour of compleating the conquest."

"Vespasian suspecting there might still be some difficulty, sent Titus with five hundred horse, and a thousand foot. When the place was taken, all the people, young and old, were destroyed. None were saved, excepting the male infants, and the women, who were made slaves. The number of those, who were slain now, and in the former attack, were fifteen thousand. The prisoners were two thousand a hundred and thirty. This calamity befell the Galileans on the five and twentieth day of May."

At (d) the same time the *Samaritans* got together in a riotous manner at mount Garizim. Whereupon Vespasian sent against them Cerealis, commander of the fifth legion, with six hundred horse, and three thousand foot. Who slew them all, to the number of eleven thousand and six hundred. This happened on the 25 day of the month of June.

Now (e) the final attack was made upon Jotapata, which was taken after a siege of forty seven days. All of every age were slain, except infants and women. The captives were a thousand and two hundred. The number of slain in the last attack, and in the former encounters was forty thousand. Vespasian ordered the city to be demolished, and set fire to all the castles. Thus Jotapata was taken on the first day of July, in the thirteenth year of the reign of Nero.

I think it may be worth the while to observe here, for shewing the violent and desperate disposition of the Jewish people at this time: "that (f) in the distresse of the last attack, when the Romans were got within the walls of Jotapata, many of the people made away with themselves, rather than come into the hands of the Romans. Josephus calls them chosen men, who were near his person. They could

---

(d) *Ibid.* p. 32.
(e) §. 33 . . . . 35.
(f) Τίτο πολλὰς ᾗ περὶ τὸν Ἰάσηπον ἐπιλέκτων, ἐπ' αὐτοχειρίαν παρέξενε. Κατι-
δόντες γὰρ, ὡς ἐδένα τῶν Ῥωμαίων ἀνελεῖν δύναιντο, τόγε μὴ πεσεῖν αὐτοὶ ὑπὸ Ῥωμαίων προέλαβον, ᾗ συναθροισθέντες ἐπὶ τὰ καταλήγοντα τῆς πόλεως σφᾶς αὐτοὺς ἀνεῖλον. §. 34.

"could not kill the Romans. And they resolved not to be killed by them."

Undoubtedly, my readers recollect here what was taken notice of *(g)* formerly, which happened presently afterwards, in the cave, where *(h)* Josephus and forty other persons of distinction had hid themselves. And several other like instances may appear hereafter, as we proceed in this historie, which ought not to pass unnoticed.

Josephus *(i)* now came into the hands of the Roman General. He was still a prisoner, and carried a chain. But he had change of apparel given him, and was otherwise well used.

The *(k)* siege of Jotapata being over, on the fourth of July Vespasian returned to Ptolemais. Thence he went to Cesarea by the sea-side. Here he put two legions, for some while, for their refreshment: but sent the tenth and fifth to Scythopolis, that Cesarea might not be overburdened.

"In *(l)* the mean time he sent some of his soldiers, both horse and foot, to *Joppa*. Which though it had been demolished not long since by Cestius, was repeopled by men who had escaped from other cities. Here they built many ships, and exercised a kind of piracie. Upon the approach of the Romans they betook themselves to their ships, which met with a violent storm, and were cast away. The number that perished was computed to be four thousand and two hundred. Here *(m)* also some rather than be drowned, or be cast on the shore, and then be killed by the Romans, put an end to their own lives. The place was now entirely demolished. However, by Vespasian's direction, a number of horse and foot were left here, with orders to destroy the neighboring villages. So those troops overrun the countrey, as they were ordered, and laid waste the whole region."

(g) See p. 33.
(h) ... ἔνθα τισσαρακοντα μὲν τὸν ἐπισήμων ἄνδρας καταλαμβάνει λανθάνοντες. *Ib. cap. viii. 1.*
(i) Ib. §. 9.
(k) Ibid. cap. 9. §. 1.
(l) §. 2. 3. 4.
(m) Τινὲς δὲ ὡς κυρστίρω τὴν θάλασσαν ἔσθανον, τῷ σιδήρῳ σφᾶς αὐτὸς ἀναιροῦντες. *Ib. §. 3.*

In (n) a short time Vespasian went from Cesarea before mentioned to Cesarea Philippi, to pay a compliment to King Agrippa, by whom he had been invited, and by whom he was now entertained twenty days.

Hearing (o) of the revolt of *Taricheas* Vespasian sent thither his son Titus. Taricheas (p) was a strong place, and had been fortified by Josephus. The number of people who perished in the several attacks, and in taking the city, was six thousand and five hundred.

After (q) which Vespasian sat upon his tribunal, to consider what should be done with the people that remained. And at length by his order all the old men and other useless people, to the number of twelve hundred, were slain. Out of the young men he chose six thousand of the strongest, whom he sent to Nero to work at the Isthmus. The rest he sold for slaves, who were in number thirty thousand and four hundred. This was done on the eighth day of September.

The place (r) to which Vespasian went next was *Gamala*. Where he met with great difficulties, and many of the Romans were slain. It was taken at last on the 23. day of October. When there was no way of escaping left, many Jews threw their children, their wives, and themselves from the hill on which the citadel was built into the deep valley below. The number of those who thus precipitated themselves was computed to be five thousand. The rest amounted to four thousand. For here the Romans spared none, not even infants. None escaped, except two women.

To *Gischala* (s) Vespasian sent Titus. Here about six thousand were slain. But *John*, son of Levi, who had commanded in the place, escaped, and got to Jerusalem, with some others. Which

as

(n) Ibid. §. 7.
(o) Ib. §. 7.
(p) ... Cap. x. 1. ... 10.
(q) §. 10.
(r) De B. J. l. 4. cap. 1. §. 1. ... 10.
(s) Ibid. cap. ii. n. 1. ... 5.

Ch. III.   *Transactions in the Year of Christ* 67.

(*t*) as our historian says, was the work of God, who saved John for the destruction of Jerusalem.

"Thus says (*u*) Josephus, was all *Galilee* subdued, after it had cost the Romans much labour."

The (*x*) next chapter of our Author contains an account of the state of things in Jerusalem, after John came into it. Where he likewise says: "At (*y*) the same time there were disturbances, and civil wars in every city. And all they who were quiet from the Romans, turned their hands one against another. At this time Robbers, and others of the worst characters, came into the city, where it had been long usual to receive all who came. But their numbers consumed those provisions, which might have been of use in a siege."

They (*z*) now exercised tyrannie over the most considerable men. *Antipas*, a man of royal linage, the most potent man in the city, to whom the care of the public treasure had been committed, they laid hold of, and sent to prison: and after him *Levias*, a man of great distinction, and *Sophas*, son of Raguel, a man of like eminence, and both of royal linage. And (*a*) not thinking themselves safe, whilst they were living, they sent some men of desperate characters, to put them to death in the prison.

Dissensions (*b*) encreasing, there were slain (*c*) in one night eight thousand and five hundred, and afterwards (*d*) twelve thousand of the better sort, beside many others. Here also are mentioned by name, as put to death by the zealots, or others, divers men of great eminence, whose deaths our historian laments in pathetic terms: *Ana-*
nus

(*t*) Θεῦ δὲ ἦν τὸ ἔργον, ὅρα τὸ σώζοντος τὸν Ἰωάννην ἐπὶ τὴν τῶν Ἱεροσολύμων ὄλεθρον. §. 3.
(*u*) Γαλιλαῖα μὲν οὖν ἕως ἐάλω πᾶσα, πολλοῖς ἱδρῶσι προγυμνάσασα Ῥωμαίους. §. 5.
(*x*) *Ib. cap.* 3.
(*y*) *Ib.* §. 2. 3.
(*z*) §. 4.
(*a*) §. 5.
(*b*) *L.* 4. *cap. v. Et Conf. cap. iii.* §. 7.
(*c*) *Cap. v.* §. 1.
(*d*) Μύριοι δὲ ᾗ δισχίλιοι τῶν εὐγενῶν οὕτω διεφθάρησαν. §. 3.

mus (e) the most ancient of the High-Priests, *Jesus* also High-Priest, inferior to Ananus, but yet a person of great eminence, and *Zacharias* son of Baruch, different from *Zacharias*, mentioned in Matt. xxiii. 35. and Luke xi. 51. as was shewn in another (f) place.

Soon (g) after this was put to death by the zealots *Gorion*, a man of great eminence for his own virtues, as well as upon account of his familie. Nor did *Niger* the Peraite escape their hands, though he had been so serviceable to them in this war. "When (h) they "were killing him, he uttered this imprecation upon them, that "beside the war, they might undergo famine and pestilence, and "after that come to the mutual slaughter of each other. All which "imprecations God ratified against those wicked men. And most "justly did they soon after reap the fruit of their madnesse in their "mutual dissensions."

These (i) things being heard of in the Roman camp, the commanders were for hastening the attack upon the city. But Vespasian, as Josephus says, answered them, that the Jews were not now making armour, nor building walls: but they are every day tearing themselves to pieces by intestin wars and dissensions: and suffer greater miseries, than could be inflicted upon them by us, if they were in our hands. And it was the best way to let the Jews destroy one another.

These things we suppose to have happened at the end of the year 67. and the begining of 68.

" However, Vespasian was not inattentive to affairs, and took care " to reduce other places, before he went to Jerusalem. He then left " Cesarea for a while, and marched to *Gadara*, the metropolis of " Perea, as Josephus says, and entred it on the fourth day of March.

" After which he returned to Cesarea, and left Placidus to carry " on the war in those parts. Who (k) took *Abila*, *Julias*, and Be-
"*semoth*,

(e) §. 2. et 4.   (h) Ib. §. 1.
(f) See *Credibility*. P. i. B. 2. ch. 6. p. (i) Ib. §. 2.
903. &c.   (g) Ib. cap. vi. §. 1.   (k) L. 4. cap. vii.

Ch. III. *Transactions in the Year of Christ* 68.

"*Jemoth*, and other smaller cities and villages, as far as the lake As-
"phaltites. Insomuch that now all *Perea* was in the hands of the
"Romans, excepting *Macherus*. This expedition was very fatal to
"the Jews. Many of the Jewish people were slain by the sword,
"others were driven into the river Jordan. The number of the
"slain was not less than fifteen thousand, beside two thousand and
"two hundred, which were made captives. And Placidus had a
"rich booty of asses, and sheep, camels, and oxen. This disaster
"was equal to any that had yet befallen the Jews."

In the mean time (*l*) Vespasian with a part of his armie went from Cesarea to *Antipatris*: where he spent two days in settling the affairs of that city. On the third day he marched on, laying waste and burning all the villages. And when he had laid waste all the places about the toparchie of *Thamnas*, he passed on to *Lydda* and *Jamnia*. And then came to *Ammaus*. Thence he went to the toparchie of *Bethleptephon*. And destroying that and other neighboring places, he slew more than ten thousand, and made captives more than a thousand. And on the second day of the month of July he pitched his camp at *Corea*, not far from *Neapolis*, called by the people of the countrey *Mabortha*. And then went to *Jericho*.

Not long afterwards he returned to Cesarea. And (*m*) now, when he was getting ready all his forces for the siege of Jerusalem, he hears of the death of Nero, which happened on the tenth of June, in the year of our Lord 68. Wherefore Vespasian for a while put off his intended expedition against Jerusalem: waiting to see to whom this Empire would be transferred, and expecting to receive orders from him.

During the remaining part of the year 68. and the year 69. little (*n*) was done by the Romans in the war against the Jews. They kept garrisons in the places already conquered, and fortified some places. But
they

A. D. 76.

N. B.

(*l*) *Ib. Cap. viii.* 1.
(*m*) *Ib. cap. ix.* 1. 2.

(*n*) Nihil hoc anno alicujus momenti in Judaea gestum. *Pagi ann.* 69. *n. xiii.*

A. D. 76.

they made little progresse, and the siege of Jerusalem was deferred. This delay was a favourable opportunity for the Jewish people to consider and relent, and make peace with the Romans their enemies, having first repented of their sins, and humbled themselves before God. But nothing of that kind came to passe. They went on in their old way, quarrelling among themselves, and forming parties, weakening themselves by divisions and contentions, and thereby hastening their ruin.

Our Lord foresaw this, as appears from the terms of all his predictions concerning them. He foresaw, that nothing would reclaim them, after his own teachings had failed of the effect. *When he was come near, he beheld the city, and wept over it, saying: If thou hadst known, even thou, in this thy day the things that belong to thy peace. But now they are hid from thy eyes. For the days will come upon thee, that thy enemies shall compass thee round, and lay thee even with the ground, and thy children within thee, because thou knewest not the time of thy visitation.* Luke xix. 41...44. He would still send among them prophets, wise men, and scribes, his Apostles and Evangelists. But they would not hearken to them. They would reject their message, and abuse them. Matt. xxiii. 34.

At *(d)* this time, says Josephus, a new war began at Jerusalem. And *Simon, son of Gioras*, who for a while had been troublesome to the people there by his furious attacks upon the place, was admitted *(e)* into the city, in the month of April, near the end of the third year of the war.

On the third day of July in the year of our Lord 69. Vespasian was proclaimed Emperour *(f)* by the Roman armie in Judea: as *(g)* he

---

(d) Ἐπανίσταται δὲ ἄλλος τοῖς Ἱεροσολύμοις πόλεμος. L. 4. c. ix. §. 3. in.

(e) Cap. ix. §. 12.

(f) Ib. cap. x.

(g) Initium ferendi ad Vespasianum Imperii Alexandriae coeptum, festinante Tiberio Alexandro, qui Kal Jul. sacramento ejus legiones adegit. Isque primus principatus dies in posterum celebratus, quamvis Judaicus exercitus v. nonas Jul. apud ipsum jurasset, eo ardore, ut ne Titus quidem filius exspectaretur, Syriâ remeans,

he had been proclaimed on the first day of the same month at Alexandria, which day was reckoned the begining of his reign. A. D. 76.

And may we not be allowed to suppose, that *Vespasian* and *Titus* were thus advanced by way of recompense for their services, as instruments in the hand of providence for inflicting that punishment upon the Jewish people, which their crying sins deserved, and thus accomplishing the predictions concerning it. We cannot say, that they were truly virtuous. But they were persons of great eminence, and many abilities. And they had a more social and benevolent disposition, than many others. Titus in particular is represented by Roman authors, as a man of a very amiable *(h)* character. And Josephus, who was present with him in the war, often says, that he unwillingly treated the Jewish people so severely, as he did, and that he often made them offers of mercie, if they would lay down their arms, and accept of reasonable terms.

Vespasian *(i)* not long after this, went to Alexandria, and thence to Rome, leaving his son Titus, to carry on the war in Judea.

Vespasian stayed some months at Alexandria, waiting for a fair wind, and good weather, or upon account of some political views and considerations. Several extraordinarie things are related to have happened, during his stay there: Which are related very briefly by *(k) Dion Cassius*, more particularly by *(l) Suetonius*, and still more prolixly by *(m) Tacitus.* " Two

et consiliorum inter Municianum et patrem nuntius. *Tacit. Hist.* 2. *cap.* 79. *Conf. Sueton. Vespasian. cap.* 6. *Vid. et Pagi ann.* 69. *n. vii. et Basnag. ann.* 69. *n. xxi.*

(*h*) Titus, cognomento paterno, amor ac deliciae humani generis. *Sueton. Tit. cap. i.*

(*i*) *Jos. De B. J. l.* 4. *cap. xi.*

(*k*) *Dio. l.* 66. *n.* 8. *p.* 1082.

(*l*) Auctoritas et quasi majestas quaedam, ut scilicet inopinato et adhuc novo Principi, deerat: haec quoque accessit. E

plebe quidam luminibus orbatus, item alius debili crure, sedentem pro tribunali pariter adierunt, orantes opem valetudinis, demonstratam a Serapide per quietem: restiturum oculos, si inspuisset: confirmaturum crus, si dignaretur calce contingere. Cum vix fides esset rem ullo modo successuram, ideoque ne experiri quidem auderet: extremo hortantibus amicis, palam pro concione utrumque tentavit, nec eventus defuit. *Sueton. Vespasi. cap. vii.*

(*m*) Per eos menses, qui Vespasianus Alex-

A. D. 76.

"Two men of low rank at Alexandria, one of them blind, the other lame in one of his hands, came both together to him in a humble manner, saying, that they had been in dream admonish- ed by the god Serapis to apply to him for cure of their disor- ders. Which they were assured might be done for the one, if he would be pleased to anoint his eyes and face with his spittle, and for the other, if he would vouchsafe to tread upon his hand. Ves- pasian, as is said, hesitated for a while. However, the Physicians having been consulted, they gave their opinion, that the organs of sight were not destroyed in the blind man, and that sight might be restored, if obstacles were removed: and that the other's hand was only disjointed, and with proper remedies might be set right again. At length, moved by the entreaties of the distempered persons, and encouraged by the flatteries of those about him, Ves- pasian performed what had been desired. And the effect was an- swerable. One of them presently recovered the use of his hands, and the other his sight."

I do not see reason to believe, that any miracle was now wrought. It was a contrivance between Vespasian and his friends and favorites.

Nor

Alexandriae statos aestivis flatibus dies, et certa maris opperiebatur, multa miracula evenere quis coelestis favor et quaedam in Vespasianum inclinatio numinum os- tenderetur. Ex plebe Alexandrina qui- dam oculorum tabe notus, genua ejus ad- volvitur, remedium coccitatis expostens gemitu: monitu Serapidis dei, quem de- dita superstitionibus gens ante alios colit. Precabaturque principem, ut genas et ocu- lorum orbes dignaretur respergere oris excremento. Alius manu aeger, eo- dem deo auctore, ut pede ac vestigio Caesaris calcaretur, orabat. Vespasianus primo irridere, aspernari: atque illis instantibus, modo famam vanitatis me- tuere, obsecratione ipsorum, et vocibus a-

dulantium, in spem induci: postremo aestimari a medicis jubet, an talis caeci- tas ac debilitas ope humana superabiles fo- rent. Medici varie disserere: Huic non exesam vim luminis, et redituram, si pel- lerentur obstantia: illi illapsos in pravum artus, si salubris vis adhibeatur, posse in- tegrari.. Igitur Vespasianus cuncta for- tunae suae parere ratus, nec quidquam ul- tra incredibile, laeto ipse vultu, erecta quae astabat multitudine, jussa exsequitur. Statim conversa ad usum manus, ac coeco reluxit dies. Utrumque qui interfuere nunc quoque memorant, postquam nul- lum mendacio pretium. *Tacit. Hist.* 4. *cap.* 81.

Ch. III. *Transactions in the Year of Christ* 69.

Nor (*n*) could it be safe for any to examine and make remarks upon an event, which an Emperour and his favorites recommended to public belief.

Suetonius has accounted for these stories in the introduction to his narration, saying, that *somewhat was wanting to give dignity and authority to a new chosen Emperour*. And at the begining of his life of Vespasian, he observes, " that (*o*) the Flavian familie was not renowned for it's antiquity." And it is easie for any to discern from several things said by Suetonius and Tacitus, that Vespasian was very willing to encourage the belief of extraordinarie things concerning himself.

I think, that what Spartian *(p)* writes of some miracles ascribed to Adrian, may illustrate this historie. And therefore I have transcribed him below very largely. Spartian lets us know, that *Marius Maximus*, who before him had writ the Life of Adrian, and some other Emperours, said, those miracles were mere fictions. And says the learned and judicious *Reimar* in his notes upon Dion Cassius: " Nor *(q)* ought we to form any other judgement of the miracles ascribed to Vespasian." And perhaps it may deserve notice, that

(*n*) Ad rei ipsius veritatem quod adtinet, non facile adfirmantibus credere licet, cum vix tutum esset id negare, quo Imperatori obsequentiores Aegyptii, et quod proinde intererat Imperatoris, verum videri. Fraudes ejus retegere, qui fallere vult, et omnibus Reipublicae copiis instructus est, numquam tutum fuit. &c. *Cleric. Ann.* 138. *n. iii.*

(*o*) Imperium suscepit, firmavitque tandem gens Flavia: obscura illa quidem, ac sine majorum imaginibus. *Vespasian. cap. i.*

(*p*) Ea tempestate supervenit quaedam mulier, quae diceret, somnio se monitam, ut insinuaret Adriano, ne se occideret, quod esset bene valiturus: quod cum non fecisset esse caecatam: Jussam tamen iterum Adriano eadem diceret, atque genua ejus oscularetur, receptura visum, si id fecisset. Quod cum insomnium implesset, oculos recepit, quum aqua quae in fano erat, ex quo venerat, oculos abluisset. Venit et de Pannonia quidam natus caecus ad febrientem Adrianum, eumque contigit: quo facto et ipse oculos recepit, et Adrianum febris reliquit: quamvis Marius Maximus haec per simulationem facta commemoret. *Spartian. Hadrian. cap.* 25.

(*q*) Sed Marius Maximus haec per simulationem facta commemorat. Ita diserte Spartianus Hadr. c. 25. Nec aliter de Vespasiani miraculis existimandum. *Reimar. in Dion Cass. l.* 66. §. 50. *p.* 1083.

notwithstanding such fine things were ascribed to Vespasian, Dion presently afterwards says, " he (r) was not at all acceptable to the Alexandrians, but they hated him, and ridiculed and reproached him both in public and private."

However *Crevier's* observation is to this effect. " At (s) the same " time, we ought carefully to observe, that these disorders, which " Vespasian cured, were not of an incurable nature. And conse- " quently, we are at liberty to think, that the healing them did not " exceed the power of the demon." And, indeed, Popish saints and Heathen demons are much alike. Nor is there any great difference between Heathen and Popish credulity.

I cannot forbear to take notice of one remarkable historie in this (t) reign. *Sabinus* (u) in Gaul, engaged with some others in a revolt from the Romans, but was soon defeated. He might then have escaped into Germanie. But affection for his wife, the best of women, whom he could not carry with him, led him into another scheme, which he communicated to two only of his freedmen, in whom he could confide. His countrey-house was burnt down, and he was supposed to have perished in the flames. But really he retired into a large subterraneous cavern, which he had near it. It was universally believed, that he had made away with himself. And his wife *Epponnina* abandoned herself to all the excesses of grief, and for three days and three nights refused to take any sustenance. Sabinus, hearing of it, and dreading the consequences, sent one of his freedmen to her, to assure her of his life, and to advise her to

keep

(r) Τὸ μὲν ὅσον τούτοις αὐτὸν ἐσεμνυνεν. Οὐ μέντοι κὶ Ἀλεξανδρεῖς ἔχαιρον αὐτῷ, ἀλλὰ κὶ πάνυ ἤχθοντο. κ. λ. *Dio. p.* 1082.

(s) *Hist. of the Rom. Emp. Vol.* 6. p. 32.

(t) *See Tillem. Vespasian. art. vi. et xvii. Crevier's Hist. of the Roman Emperours, Vol. vi. p.* 103. 104.

(u) Fusi Lingones. Sabinus festina- tum temere proelium pari formidine deseruit. Utque famam exitii sui faceret, villam, in quam perfugerat, cremavit. Illic voluntaria morte interiisse creditus. Sed quibus artibus latebrisque vitam per novem annos traduxerit, simul amicorum ejus constantiam, insigne Epponninae uxoris exemplum, suo loco reddemus. *Tacit. Hist.* 4. *cap.* 67.

Ch. III. *Transactions in the Year of Christ* 69.

keep up the appearance of a mourner, still avoiding extremities. Afterwards she had access to him, and bore two children, of which she delivered herself in the cavern. By various artfull pretenses and the faithfulnesse of friends, the truth was kept secret, and Sabinus lay concealed nine years. In which interval there were once some hopes of obtaining the Emperour's pardon, and Epponnina had Sabinus to Rome, so disguised, that none knew him. But being disappointed in those expectations, they returned to the place of their retreat. At (*w*) length Sabinus was discovered. He, and Epponnina, and their two sons were brought before Vespasian. She behaved with becoming firmnesse, yet endeavoured to move the Emperour's pity. Presenting her two sons to him: " These, says she, Cesar, I have brought forth, and nursed in the cavern, that I might encrease the number of your supplicants." And, as is said, neither the Emperour himself, nor any others with him, could refrain from tears. However, perceiving, that he did not yield, she then upbraided him, and told him, she had lived more happily in the darknesse of a cave, than he upon his throne. Sabinus and his wife were condemned, but the children were spared. Plutarch says, " that (*x*) thereby Vespasian provoked the vengeance of heaven, and brought upon himself the exstinction of his familie. It was, says he, the most tragical action of that reign, a thing which neither gods nor demons could bear the sight of." Indeed, not only he, but Tacitus and Dion, shew a dislike of that action. But we have not Tacitus's conclusion of the storie, he having deferred it to a following book, which is now wanting. It must appear not a little strange, that a General and his wife, should be put to death nine years after a disturbance had been suppressed, and which had no bad consequences. When likewise, of the two miscreant rebels and tyrants at Jerusalem, one only was condemned to death, and the other to perpetual imprisonment. Vespasian did not live long after this. We now proceed in our historie.

About

(*w*) *Dio. l.* 66. *p.* 1090.   (*x*) *Erot. sub fin.*

About (y) this time the Jews became divided into three parties or factions: the leaders of which were *John, Eleazar*, and *Simon*: by whom the city, and every part of it, and the temple itself, were filled with slaughter and bloudshed. This happened, as (z) Josephus expressly says, whilst Titus was with his father at Alexandria: and must therefore be rightly placed by us in the year 69: and perhaps, not far from the end of it. "So, as the same writer says, one fac-
" tion fought against the other. Which (a) partition in evil cases
" may be said to be a good thing, and the effect of divine justice."

Eleazar (b) had the temple, *John* was below him in the city, *Simon* had the upper part of the city. *Simon* (c) had with him ten thousand, beside the Idumeans. His own men had fifty commanders, of which he was supreme. The Idumeans, that joyned with him, were five thousand, and had ten commanders. With *Eleazar* were two thousand and five hundred of the zealots. John had six thousand armed men under twenty commanders. But soon after the begining of the siege, these two parties united into one: after which there were but two factions, *John's* and *Simon's*.

" But before that union, whilst they were in three parties, out of
" spight to each other, as it seems, they set fire (d) to several store-
" houses, that were full of corn, and other provisions: as if they
" had done it on purpose to serve the Romans: destroying what
" would have been sufficient for a siege of many years. So they
" were taken with the famine. Which could not have been, if they
" had not by this means brought it upon themselves." So says our Jewish historian.

Titus

(y) *L.* 5. *cap.* i. §. 1.
(z) Ibid.
(a) ὅπερ ἄν τις ὡς ἐν κακοῖς ἀγαθὸν εἴποι, ἢ δίκης ἔργον. Ibid.
(b) Ib. §. 2. 3.
(c) *L.* 5. *cap.* vi. 1. *Vid. et cap.* iii. 1.
(d) ... ὑπεμπίπρα τὰς οἰκίας σίτυ μεςὰς,

ἢ παντοδαπῶν ἐπιτηδείων ... κατακαῆναι δὲ πλὴν ὀλίγε πάντα τὸν σῖτον, ὃς ἂν αὐτοῖς ἐκ ἐπ' ὀλίγα διήρκισεν ἔτη πολιορκυμένοις. Λιμῷ γεν ἑάλωσαν· ὅπερ ἥκιϛα δυνατὸν ἦν, εἰ μὴ τοῦτον ἑαυτοῖς προπαρεσκεύασαν. *L.* 5. *cap.* i. §. 4.

Ch. III. Of the Siege of Jerusalem in the Year 70.

Titus (e) now leaves Alexandria, and comes to Cesarea, designing to move forward to Jerusalem, and lay siege to it: having with him an armie of about sixty thousand men, Romans and auxiliaries. He (f) pitcheth his camp at the place called Scopus, making however two other encampments at a small distance, one of which was on the mount of Olives. He (g) presented himself before the city about the time of Passover, which was on the fourteenth day of the month of April, in the year of Christ 70. Here he met with difficulties at the first, as the Jews made furious sallies upon his armie. Some of his soldiers were put by them into disorder, and suffered very considerably.

The (h) city of Jerusalem was surrounded by three walls, excepting in such parts where were deep vallies, which rendred the place inaccessible. There it had but one wall. On (i) the fifteenth day of the siege, which was the seventh day of May, the Romans got possession of the first wall, and demolished a great part of it. Titus (k) then encamped within the city, in a place called *the Assyrians camp*. On (l) the fifth day after that he got possession of the second wall, but was repulsed, and beat out of it again. "Whereupon those Jews, who were armed, and were the fighting men, as our historian says, were much elevated, persuading themselves, that the Romans could never conquer the city. For (m) God had blinded their minds for the transgressions, which they had been guilty of, so that they did not consider the superior force of the Romans, nor discern how the famine was creeping in upon them. For hitherto they had fed themselves out of the public distresses, and drunk the bloud of the city. But poverty was now become the lot of many good men, and a great many had already perish-
" ed

A. D. 76.

N. B.

(e) *De B. J. l. 4. cap. xi. n. 5. L. 5. cap. i. et cap. ii. 1.*
(f) *Cap. ii. §. 3.*
(g) *Cap. iii. 1.*
(h) *L. 5. cap. iv.*
(i) ... *cap. vii. §. 2.*
(k) ... *ib. §. 3.*
(l) *cap viii. §. 1. 2.*
(m) Επισκότει γὰρ αὐτῶν ταῖς γνώμαις διὰ τὰς παρανομίας ὁ Θεὸς κ. λ. *Ib. §. 2.*

ed for want of neceffaries. But they fuppofed the deftruction of "the meaner people to be a benefit to them." However Titus renewed the attack. The Jews defended themfelves refolutly for three days. But on the fourth day he again became mafter of that wall. And then he demolifhed all that part, which lay to the north, and fortified the fouth fide with towers, and placing foldiers in them. And then confidered how he might attack the third and inmoft wall.

Now (n) Titus thought fit to relax the fiege for a while, in order to eafe the foldiers, and to pay them fubfiftence-money, as alfo to fee whether the Jews would relent, and make fome propofals for furrendring, that he might fhew them mercie.

Moreover, Jofephus (o) by order of Titus, took this opportunity, to addrefs the Jews in a pathetic difcourfe: having fought out a place to ftand in, where he might be heard, and be in fafety. In that fpeech he entreats the Jews to fave themfelves, their temple, and their countrey, and tells them, that they were fighting againft God.

" Moreover, fays he, as for Titus, thofe fprings, which were al-
" moft dried up, when they were in your power, fince his coming,
" they run more plentifully, than they did before. Accordingly, you
" know, that Siloam, as well as all the other fprings about the city, did
" fo far fail, that water was fold in pitchers: whereas they now have
" fuch a quantity for your enemies, as is fufficient for themfelves,
" and for their cattle, and for watering gardens. The fame won-
" derfull fign you had experience of formerly, when the afore-
" mentioned King of Babylon, made war againft us, who took this
" city, and burnt the temple: though (p) the men of that time, I
" believe, were far from being fuch tranfgreffors, as you are."

With regard to that particular, the flowing of the fprings without the city in the time of the King of Babylon, Mr. *Whiston* fays in a mar-

---

(n) *L.* 5. *cap. ix.* §. 1.
(o) §. 3. 4.
(p) ... ἐδὲν δίμαι τῶν τότε ἠσεβηκότων

τηλικούτων ἡλίκα ὑμεῖς. *Ib.* §. 4. *p.* 350.
Haverc.

Ch. III. *Of the Siege of Jerusalem in the Year 70.*

marginal note upon the place. "The history of this is now wanting elsewhere."

Four days were spent in that relaxation. On the fifth day, when no offers of peace came from the Jews, Titus began to raise new banks at several places.

"The *(q)* famine now began to be very severe. And with the
" famine encreased also the madnesse of the seditious, [*as Josephus*
" *calls them, meaning John and Simon, and the officers under them.*]
" There could no corn appear publicly any where, but those rob-
" bers came running for it. They also searched private houses. If
" they found any corn, they tormented the people, because they had
" denied it. If they found none, they tormented them neverthelefs,
" because they supposed, the people had concealed it."

Here *(r)* Josephus enlargeth upon the miseries of the people, and the great wickednesse of their present governours. "But, says he, N. B.
" it is impossible to enumerate every instance of the iniquity of those
" men. But, in a word, never did any city suffer so great calami-
" ties. Nor was there ever from the begining of the world any
" time more fruitfull of wickednesse, than that... These were the
" men, who overthrew the city, and compelled the Romans un-
" willingly, to gain a disagreeable victorie. They did little less than
" throw fire upon the temple, and seemed to think it came too
" slowly."

"At *(s)* this time many came out of the city, to seek for food,
" or with a view of making an escape, who were apprehended by
" the Romans, and crucified before the walls. And many of them
" were scourged, before they were crucified. This seemed to Titus
" very grievous. For five hundred Jews were taken in a day, and
" sometimes more. Neverthelefs he allowed of it. To dismiss them,
" and let them go off, would not have been safe. Nor could he
" spare men enough to keep guard upon so many. Moreover, he
                                                    " hoped,

(q) L. 5. cap. x. §. 1. 2.   *(r)* cap x. §. 4. 5.   *(s)* cap. xi. §. 1.

"hoped, that the fight of thefe miferable objects might difpofe them in the city to think of furrendring. The foldiers out of anger, and hatred of the Jews, hung them upon the croffes, fome one way, fome another, as it were in jeft. And fo great was the number, that room was wanting for croffes, and croffes were wanting for bodies."

"Now (t) alfo Titus ordered the hands of fome of them, who had come out of the city to be cut off. And then he fent them back, to let the people within the city know, that henceforward he fhould carry on the fiege with vigour: however ftill wifhing them to repent, and not compell him to deftroy their city, and their admired temple. But they who ftood upon the wall returned reproaches upon him, and upon his father Vefpafian, telling him, that death was better than flaverie, and that fo long as they had breath, they would do the Romans all the harm, they could. As for the temple, they believed it would be preferved by him who inhabited it. Having him for their helper, they defpifed all his threatenings. For the event depended upon God only."

The (u) Romans were employed in raifing batteries. But though they had begun to raife them on the 12. day of May, they had much ado to finifh them by the 29. day of the fame month, after having labored hard for feventeen days fucceffively. In which time, however, four batteries were compleated.

But John found means to undermine them, fo that they fell down all at once, caufing great confufion among the Romans. And after that Simon and his men made a furious fally upon the Romans.

The Roman armie was greatly difcouraged, to fee their batteries ruined in one hour, which had coft them fo much labour. And many defpaired, thinking it impoffible to take the city with the ufual engines of war.

Titus

(t) Ib. §. 5.   (u) §. 4.

Ch. III. *Of the Siege of Jerusalem in the Year* 70.

A. D. 75.

Titus (*x*) confulted with his officers what might be fit to be done. At length it was determined to encompafs the city with a wall. Which was compleated in three days, with towers at proper diftances, to place foldiers in as garrifons.

Our bleffed Lord fays, Luke xix. 43. *For the days will come upon thee, that thy enemies fhall caft a trench about thee, and compafs thee round, and keep thee in on every fide.* Some think, that this prophecie was now particularly fulfilled in the building of the wall, here mentioned by Jofephus. Others may fuppofe, that it had it's accomplifhment, when the Romans laid fiege to the city of Jerufalem, and encompafled it with an armie.

"The (*y*) famine now encreafing, it devoured whole houfes. For " a while, they who had no relations to take care of them, were " buried at the public expenfe. Afterwards the dead were thrown " over the wall into the ditch.

N. B.

"When (*z*) Titus, in going his rounds, near the valleys, below " the walls, faw the dead bodies, and the putrefaction iffuing from " them, he fetched a deep figh, and lifting up his hands to heaven; " called God to witneffe, that this was not his doing." However, he propofed erecting new platforms: which was a difficult work, as all the timber near the city was already confumed, and it was now to be fetched from a great diftance.

In the next chapter (*a*) Jofephus relates the death of *Matthias*, fon of *Bëthus*, one of the High-Priefts, and feveral other perfons of eminence, and divers others, who were flaughtered by order of Simon in a moft fhamefull manner. *Matthias* was the perfon, who had advifed the admitting of Simon into the city, contrarie to the inclinations of many others. Matthias had four fons, one of which had faved himfelf by getting away to Titus. The other three were all put to death together with their father: but with this exprefs

(*x*) *cap. xii.* §. 1. 2.
(*y*) §. 3.

(*z*) §. 4.
(*a*) *cap. xiii.* §. 1.

order from Simon, that the sons should be first slain before the eyes of their father. Nor was burial allowed to them. The execution was committed by Simon to *Ananus*, son of *Bamadus*, the most barbarous man of his guards. After them were slain *Ananias* a Priest, and *Aristeas*, scribe of the Sanhedrim, and fifteen other men of eminence among the people. They also slew such as made lamentation for these persons, without farther examination.

"Many *(b)* did still find means to get out of the city. Some leaped down from the wall. Others went out of the city with stones in their hands, as if they were going to fight with the Romans. But most of them died miserably. Some perished by excessive eating upon empty stomachs. Moreover some of them had swallowed gold, and were detected afterwards in searching for it in their excrements. This having been observed in a few instances excited the avarice of the soldiers, who concluded that all the deserters were full of gold. They therefore cut up their bellies, and searched their entrails. In this way, as Josephus says, there perished two thousand in one night. Nor does it seem to me, that any miserie befell the Jews more terrible than this."

"When Titus heard of it, he was greatly displeased, especially when he found, that not only the *Syrians* and *Arabians* had practised this cruelty, but the *Romans* likewise. He therefore gave orders, that all who for the future acted in that manner should be put to death. But the love of money prevailed against the dread of punishment. And indeed it was God who had condemned the whole nation, and defeated every method taken for their preservation."

About *(c)* this time John melted down many of the sacred utensils, in the temple, to make use of them as instruments of war. He also distributed the sacred wine and oyl for common use to persons, who

(b) §. 4. 5.   *(c)* §. 6.

Ch. III. *Of the Siege of Jerusalem in the Year 70.*

who in drinking, and anointing themselves, wasted them in a profuse manner.

"But *(d)* why do I stay to relate particularly these several cala‑
"mities? For at this time *Mannaeus*, son of *Lazarus*, fled out of
"the city, and came to Titus, and told him, that through the one
"gate, which had been entrusted to his care, there had been carried
"out no fewer than a hundred and fifteen thousand eight hundred
"and eighty dead bodies, from the day that the Romans encamped
"near the city, the fourteenth day of the month of April to the first
"day of July. That was a prodigious number. The man was not
"a governour at the gate. But he was appointed to pay the pub‑
"lic allowance for carrying the bodies out. And therefore was o‑
"bliged to number them. Others were buried by their relations:
"though their burial was no other than to bring them, and cast
"them out of the city. After that man there came to Titus seve‑
"ral other deserters of good condition, who told him, that the
"whole number of the poor, who had been thrown out at the gates
"was not less than six hundred thousand. The number of the rest
"could not be exactly known. They farther told him, that when
"they were no longer able to carry out the dead bodies of the
"poor, they laid them in heaps in large houses, and then shut them
"up. They likewise said, that a measure of wheat had been sold
"for a talent. And that afterwards, when it had been impossible to
"come out to gather herbs, because the city was encompassed with
"a wall, some were driven to such distresse, as to search the com‑
"mon shores and old dunghills of cattle, and to eat the dung which
"they found there: and that what they could not before endure to
"see, they now made use of for food. When the Romans heard of
"these things, they commiserated their case. But the seditious,
"who saw them, did not repent, till the same distresse reached
them‑

(d) §. 7.

A. D. 76. N. B.
"themselves. For *(e)* they were blinded by that fate, which was coming upon the city and themselves."

There ends the fifth book of our Author's historie of the Jewish War. The sixth book contains the progresse of the siege, and the miseries of the people, till the city was taken by Titus.

The *(f)* Roman batteries are now raised at the end of one and twenty days hard labour, and the miseries of the city encrease. The Romans begin to batter upon the walls of the tower called *Antonia*. The Jews make a vigorous defense. But the Romans gained possession of it about the midle of July.

N. B.
" Titus *(g)* thereupon ordered his soldiers to dig up the founda-
" tions of the tower Antonia, to make way for him to come up
" with his whole armie. And being informed, that on that very
" day, the seventeenth of July, the daily sacrifice had failed, and
" that it had not been offered up for want of men, and that the
" people were greatly concerned at it, he sent for Josephus, and
" commanded him to say to John the same things that had been said
" before. Accordingly Josephus sought for a proper place to stand
" in, and in the name of Titus himself, earnestly exhorted John,
" and those that were with him, to spare their own countrey, and to
" prevent that fire which was ready to seize upon the temple, and
" to offer to God therein their usual sacrifices." But John cast ma-
" ny reproaches upon Josephus, with imprecations, adding withall,
" that *(h)* he did not fear the city should ever be taken, which was
" God's own city: After which Josephus went on with a pathetic
" speech. Which though it did not persuade John, and his adhe-
" rents, was not altogether without effect."

And *(i)* some watching for an opportunity, fled to the Romans.

Of

(*e*) Πεπήρωτο γὰρ ὑπὸ τοῦ χρεὼν, ὁ τῆτε πόλει κ᾽ αὐτοῖς ἤδη παρῆν.
(*f*) L. 6. cap. i. §. 1. ... 8.
(*g*) cap. ii. §. 1.
(*h*) ... ὡς ὐκ ἄνποτε δ᾽ἐάσειεν ἅλωσιν, Θιῦ γὰρ ὑπάρχειν τὴν πόλιν.
(*i*) Ibid. cap. ii. §. 2.

Ch. III. *Of the Siege of Jerusalem in the Year* 70.

Of whom were the High-Priests *Joseph,* and *Jesus,* and of sons of High-Priests three, and four sons of *Matthias,* as well as one son of the other *Matthias,* formerly mentioned, who with three of his sons had been killed by order of Simon, son of Gioras. And many others of the nobility. All whom Titus received very kindly, and sent them to *Gophna,* a small city, where they might live quietly, following their own customs. Which offer they chearfully accepted. But as they did not appear, the seditious within the city gave out, that those men had been slain by the Romans. It was in vain therefore, they said, for any to go over to the Romans, unless they were willing to be put to death.

Titus *(k)* therefore sent for those men from Gophna, and let them go round near the wall, with Josephus, to assure people, that they might come over to him with safety.

If all this be true, as Josephus writes, it is a proof of the good temper of Titus. Moreover, the Romans were now pushing their conquests upon the Temple itself, which Titus seems unwilling to have destroyed.

" And *(l)* as Josephus adds, Titus was much affected with the
" present state of things, and reproached John and those with him.
" Reminding them of the regard, which had been shewn to the tem-
" ple by the Romans, who had allowed them to erect in the courts
" of it a partition wall, with inscriptions in Greek, forbidding all
" foreigners to enter within those limits, and allowing them to kill
" such as did so, though they were Romans. I call to witnesse, says
" he, the Gods of the countrey, and every God, who ever had a
" regard to this place: (for I do not now suppose it to be regarded by
" any of them:) I also call to witnesse my own armie, and the Jews
" who are with me, and your own selves, that I do not compell you
" to pollute your sanctuarie. And if you will change the place of
" combat, no Roman shall come near it. For I will endeavour to
" preserve your temple, whether you will or not."

Such

A. D. 76.

N. B.

(k) Ib. §. 3.   *(l)* §. 4.

Such (*m*) things were spoken by Titus, and by Josephus after him in Hebrew, to John and the rest with him. But they perverted it, as if all these fine offers proceeded from fearfulnesse, and not from any good will to them.

Titus (*n*) therefore proceeded in his attacks. His soldiers fought with the Jews at the temple, whilst he continued on the higher ground in Antonia, to observe their conduct.

They (*o*) had now made a broad way from the tower Antonia to the Temple, and began to play on the temple with their battering engines.

The (*p*) fight was very desperate. A cloyster near Antonia was set on fire. On the 24. day of July the Romans set fire to another cloyster, when the fire proceeded fifteen cubits farther.

" Whilst (*q*) the Jews and Romans were thus fighting at the tem-
" ple, the famine prevailed in the city, till at length, they did not ab-
" stain from girdles and shoes. The very leather that belonged to
" shields, they took off, and gnawed. Wisps of old straw became
" food to them."

At (*r*) this time, a woman named *Marie*, of a good familie, beyond Jordan, who had fled from her native place to Jerusalem, to avoid the inconveniences of the war in the open countrey, when all she had brought with her was consumed, or taken from her by the rapaciousnesse of the tyrants, and their adherents, was reduced to such extremity, that she killed her sucking child, and dressed it for food.

On (*s*) the eighth day of the month of August the Roman batteries were compleated, and Titus ordered the batteries to play upon the Temple. The battle between the Jews and Romans was very desperate..

" Titus

(*m*) §. 5.
(*n*) §. 5. 6.
(*o*) §. 7.
(*p*) §. 8. 9.

(*q*) cap. iii. §. 3.
(*r*) §. 4.
(*s*) cap. iv. §. 1.

Ch. III. *Of the Siege of Jerusalem in the Year 70.*

"Titus *(t)* retired to the tower of Antonia. And resolved the next day early in the morning to storm the temple with his whole armie, and to encamp about it. But certainly the divine sentence had long since condemned it to the fire. And now the fatal day was come, according to the revolution of ages. It was the tenth day of the month August, the same day, upon which it had been formerly burnt by the King of Babylon."

A. D. 76.

N. B.

"The *(u)* temple was now on fire. Nevertheless Titus still desirous to save it, if possible, came near, and went into the sanctuarie of the temple with his commanders, and saw it, with what was in it. Which he found to be far superior to the accounts of foreigners, and not inferior to our boastings and persuasion concerning it."

As *(x)* the fire had not yet reached the inner parts of the temple, Titus gave fresh orders for extinguishing the fire, and preserving the temple. But to no purpose. Such was the enmity of the soldiers against the Jews, filled also with the hopes of plunder, and now animated with the rage of war.

"Nor *(y)* can we forbear to wonder at the accuracie of the period. For this happened, as before said, in the same month, and day of the month, in which the temple had been burnt by the Babylonians. And the number of years from it's first foundation by King Solomon, to this it's destruction in the second year of Vespasian, are collected to be one thousand and thirty, and seven months, and fifteen days. And from it's second building by Haggai in the second year of King Cyrus, to it's destruction by Vespasian, there were six hundred, and thirty nine years, and forty five days."

Whilst *(z)* the temple was burning, every thing was plundered that came to hand, and ten thousand of those who were caught, were slain. Nor was there any regard had to age, or condition. But children

(*t*) §. 5.
(*u*) §. 7.
(*x*) Ibid.

(*y*) §. 8.
(*z*) cap. v. §. 1.

A. D. 76.

dren and old men, profane perfons and priefts, were all flain in the fame manner.

"At *(a)* this time the treafurie-chambers were burnt, where was an immenfe quantity of money, and an immenfe number of garments, with other precious things. For there it was, that the riches of the Jews were heaped up... The foldiers alfo came to the reft of the cloyfters in the outer court, where were women, and children, and a mixed multitude of people, to the number of fix thoufand. And before Cefar had given any orders about it, the foldiers in a rage fet fire to the cloyfter. Nor did any one of that multitude efcape with his life. A falfe-prophet was the occafion of their deftruction. Who that very day had made proclamation in the city, that God commanded them to go up to the temple, where they would receive figns of deliverance. And indeed there was then a great number of falfe-prophets fuborned by the leaders of the factions to impofe upon the people, who told them, that they fhould wait for deliverance from God."

N. B.

"Thus *(b)* as our Author goes on, in the words next following, was this miferable people deceived by impoftors, who fpoke lies in the name of God. But they did not attend, nor give credit to thofe prodigies, which evidently foretold their future defolation. But like men infatuated, who have neither eyes to fee, nor minds to confider, they difregarded the divine denunciations. There *(c)* was a ftar, a comet, refembling a fword, which ftood over the city, and continued for a year. And before the rebellion, and before the war broke out, when the people were come together in

"great

(a) §. 2.
(b) ib. §. 3.
(c) Τοῦτο μὲν ὅτι ὑπὲρ τὴν πόλιν ἄστρον ἔστη ῥομφαίᾳ παραπλήσιον, καὶ παρατείνας ἐπὶ ἐνιαυτὸν κομήτης.

Mr. Whifton's tranflation is: *Thus there was a ftar, refembling a fword, which ftood over the city: and a comet that continued a whole year.* And he has a note to this purpofe. "Whether Jofephus means, that this ftar was different from that comet, which lafted a whole year, I cannot certainly determine. His words moft favor their being different one from another."

Ch. III. Of the Siege of Jerusalem in the Year 70.

A. D. 76.

"great multitudes, to the feast of unleavened bread, on the eighth
" day of the month of April, at the ninth hour of the night, so
" great a light shone round the altar, and the temple, that it seemed
" to be bright day. Which light continued for half an hour. This
" to the unskilfull seemed to be a good sign: but by the sacred scribes
" it was judged to portend what has since happened. And at the
" same festival a heifer, as she was led by the High-Priest to be sacri-
" ficed, brought forth a lamb in the midst of the temple. More-
" over the eastern gate of the inner court of the temple, which was
" of brasse, and very heavie, which was not without difficulty shut
" in the evening by twenty men, and rested upon a basis armed with
" iron, and was fastened with bolts that went deep into the floor,
" which was made of one entire stone, was seen to open of it's own
" accord at the sixth hour of the night. Whereupon they who kept
" watch at the temple, went to the captain, and told him of it. He
" then came up thither, and not without difficulty had it shut again.
" This also appeared to the vulgar a good sign: as if thereby God
" thereby opened to them the gate of happinesse. But the wiser
" men concluded, that the security of the temple was gone, and that
" the gate was opened for the advantage of their enemies. And they
" said, it was a signal of the desolation that was coming upon them.
" Beside these, a few days after that festival, on the one and twenti-
" eth day of the month of May, there appeared a wonderfull pheno-
" menon almost exceeding belief. And the account of it might seem
" fabulous, if it had not been related by those who saw it, and if the
" following events had not been answerable to such signs. For be-
" fore sun-set chariots and troops in armour were seen carried upon
" the clouds, and surrounding cities. And at the festival, which
" we call the Pentecost, as the priests were going by night into the
" inner court of the temple, as the custom was, to perform their mi-
" nistrations, they first felt, as they said, a shaking, accompanied
" with a noise, and after that a sound, as of a multitude, saying:
" Let us remove hence. But, which is still more awfull, there was

P

" one

"one *Jesus*, son of *Ananus*, of a low condition, and a countreyman, who four years before the war began, when the city enjoyed profound peace, and flowing prosperity, came up to the festival, in which it is the custom for us all to make tabernacles, who on a sudden began to cry out in the temple: *A voice from the east, a voice from the west, a voice from the four winds, a voice against Jerusalem, and the temple, a voice against the bridegrooms and the brides, a voice against the whole people.* This was his cry, as he went about, both by day and by night, in all the lanes of the city. Some of the chief men were offended at this ill-boding sound, and taking him up, laid many stripes upon him, and had him beaten severely. Yet he said not a word for himself, nor made any peculiar complaint to them that beat him: but went on repeating the same words that he had said before. Hereupon the magistrates, thinking it to be somewhat more than ordinarie, as indeed it was, bring him before the Roman Governour: where he was whipped, till his bones were laid bare. All which he bore, without shedding any tears, or making any supplications. But with a mournfull voice, at every stripe, cried out: *Woe to Jerusalem.* Albinus, the Governour, asked him, Who he was, and whence he came, and why he uttered those words. To all which he made no answer, but continued making his mournfull denunciations to the city. Albinus, thinking him to be mad, dismissed him. And thence forward, to the time of the war, he did not go to any of the citizens: nor was he seen speaking to any: but only went on with his mournfull denunciation, as if it had been his premeditated vow: *Woe, woe to Jerusalem.* He did not give ill language to those who beat him, as many did frequently. Nor did he thank those, who gave him food: but went on repeating to all the dolefull presage. But especially at festivals his cry was the loudest. And so it continued for seven years and five months, without his growing hoarse, or being tired therewith, till he saw his presage fulfilled in the siege. Then he ceased. For going round upon
"the

Ch. III. *Of the Siege of Jerusalem in the Year* 70.

A. D. 76.

"the wall, with his utmost force he cried out: *Woe, woe, once more,*
"*to the city, and to the people, and to the temple.* And then at last
"he added: *Woe, woe to my-self also.* At which instant, there came
"a stone out of one of the engines, that smote him, and killed him
"immediatly. And whilst he was uttering these mournfull presa-
"ges, he gave up the ghost."

"If *(d)* any one considers these things, adds Josephus, he will
"be convinced, that God takes care of mankind, and by all ways
"possible foreshews to our race what is for their benefit: and that
"men perish by those miseries, which they madly and voluntarily
"bring upon themselves."

Thus I have transcribed this whole article of Josephus at length, and in the place and order, in which it stands in his own work. I must be so candid as to take notice of the reflexions, which some learned men have made upon it.

To this purpose speaks Dr. *Willes*, in his first *(e)* discourse upon Josephus: "The prodigies, that he saith happened before the de-
"struction of Jerusalem, would agree better to Livy or Tacitus,
"than to a Jewish historian.... The flying open of the great brazen
"gate of the temple, is the same as happened at Thebes just before
"the great battle of the Lacedemonians at Leuctra, when the great
"gates of the temple of Hercules opened of themselves, without any
"one's touching them. I omit many other things of the like na-
"ture: whence it is evident, that Josephus endeavored to Grecise
"and shape the historie of the Jews, as like as he could to those of
"the Greeks and Romans." So Dr. *Willes*. And I shall transcribe below the passage of *Cicero de Divinatione*, *(f)* to which he refers.

(d) §. 4.
(e) Prefixed to L'estrange's edition of Josephus. p. 3. 4. 8vo.
(f) Quid? Lacedaemoniis paullo ante Leuctricam calamitatem, quae significatio facta est, cum in Herculis fano arma sonuerunt, Herculisque simulachrum multo sudore manavit? At eodem tempore Thebis,

A. D. 76.

Basnage (g) in his Historie of the Jews speaks after this manner. "Besides, deception was easie in many of the things related by him. The bright light round the altar in the night-time: the cow that brought forth a lamb, as she was led to the altar: the chariots of fire that were seen in the air, and passed over the city with a frightfull noise are very liable to suspicion: The opening of the temple seems to be rather better attested than the others, because it is said, that the magistrate came to shut it. But the meaning was doubtfull. To some it seemed to be an assurance, that God had opened the treasures of his benediction: whilst others concluded, that he had abandoned the protection of his temple. But it is not easie to deny the truth of the historie of the man, that cried, *A voice from the East, a voice from the West*, and every day predicted the ruin of the city. For this man was brought before Albinus, who examined him. He was severely scourged, and he was often beaten by the people, who could not endure so dismal a noise, but he was all along unmoved. His cry continued for the space of seven years. At length he was killed upon the walls of the city, at the begining of the siege. This is not a thing, about which men might be deceived. Josephus, who relates it, was at Jerusalem, when this preacher, who was treated as a mad man, denounced it's desolation. And he might inform himself concerning his death. So that, if there are any things, to which we ought to attend, it is this, in which we must acknowledge somewhat extraordinarie." So says *Basnage*.

I am inclined to go over, and examine every one of these prodigies.

There (h) was a *star*, a *comet*, *resembling a sword*, *which stood over the city*, *and continued for a year*.

How

bis, ut ait Callisthenes, in templo Herculis valvae clausae repagulis, subito se ipsae aperuerunt: armaque, quae fixa in parietibus fuerant, ea sunt humi inventa. *De Divin. l.* 1. *cap.* 24. *n.* 74.

(g) *L. i. ch. viii.* §. 3. *p.* 224.
(h) Τῦτο μὲν ὅτε ὑπὲρ τὴν πόλιν ἄςρον ἕςη ῥομφαίᾳ παραπλήσιον, κỳ παρατείνας ἐπ᾽ ἐνιαυτὸν κομήτης.

Ch. III. *Of the Siege of Jerusalem in the Year 70.*   A. D. 76.

How Mr. *Whiston* understood this, has been seen already. L'E-strange translates thus: *What shall we say to the comet, that hung over Jerusalem, for one whole year together, in the figure of a sword?* Archbp. Tillotson (*i*) in this manner. *A little before their destruction,* he tells us, *there hung over their city a fiery sword, which continued for a year together. A little before their rebellion against the Romans, there appeared a comet, which shined so clear in the temple, and about the altar, as if it had been day.* It must be confessed, that is not exact. Tillemont: *There (k) was also a comet which appeared for a year, and over Jerusalem an extraordinarie star, which seemed to be a sword. But Josephus does not say the time.* Neither is this very exact. However, I have also transcribed below the words of Josephus himself.

This is the first prodigie. And indeed it is a wonderfull, and very awfull thing. A star, resembling a sword, hanging over a city, for a whole year... Upon this we cannot forbear to observe, that Josephus has not told us the time, when this star, or comet appeared. He says, *it continued for a year.* But does not say when. A very strange omission. I must take the liberty, to add, that, if about the time of the siege of Jerusalem, or some period, within a few years before; there had been a star, resembling a sword, which hung over that city for a year together: I should expect to find it in some author, beside Josephus, and an author, that does not depend upon him, or borrow from him.

Tacitus (*l*) has mentioned several of the prodigies preceding the ruin

---

(*i*) *As before. p.* 554.

(*k*) Il parut aussi une comete pendant un an, et sur Jerusalem un astre extraordinaire, qui sembloit être une epée. Joseph n'en marque pas le temps. *Ruine des Juifs. art.* 41.

(*l*) Evenerunt prodigia, quæ neque hostiis, neque votis piare fas habet gens superstitioni obnoxia, religionibus adversa. Visae per coelum concurrere acies, rutilantia arma, et subito nubium igne collucere templum. Expassae repente templi fores, et audita major humanâ vox, *Excedere Deos:* simul ingens motus excedentium. *Tacit. Hist. l.* 5. *cap.* 13.

ruin of the Jewish people. But he does not mention this. However, it must be owned, that his omitting it is of no great importance, as he does not appear to have been carefull to put down every thing of this kind.

2. It follows. *And before the rebellion, and before the war broke out, when the people were come together in great multitudes to the feast of unleavened bread, on the eighth day of the month of April at the ninth hour of the night,* [or three hours after midnight,] *so great a light shone round the altar, and the temple, that it seemed to be bright day. Which light continued for half an hour.* This prodigie is related by Josephus, so particularly, and circumstantially, as happening too at the time of Passover, when Jerusalem was full of people, and in the year 65. as it seems, that I am not at all disposed to contest the truth of it. I think it must have so happened. But the design of this appearance is ambiguous. And, as Josephus says, some thought it to portend good, others bad things. But that does not affect the truth of the fact.

3. *And at the same festival, a heifer, as she was led by the High-Priest to be sacrificed, brought forth a lamb in the midst of the temple.* Here again, I hesitate. I am surprized to see so trifling a storie in a grave writer. I think, Josephus inserted this to gratify his Greek readers.

4. The next prodigie is the opening of the *eastern gate of the inner court of the temple at midnight:* which, as before observed by Dr. *Willes*, has such a resemblance with like stories, told by credulous heathen people, that it seems to be only an imitation of them, and has therefore the appearance of a fiction, by way of accommodation to the judgement of Heathen readers.

5. *Beside these, a few days after that festival, on the one and twentieth day of the month of May there appeared a wonderful phenomenon, almost exceeding belief. And the account of it might seem fabulous, if it had not been related by those who saw it, and if the following events had not been answerable to such signs. For before sun-set, chariots and troops*

Ch. III. *Of the Siege of Jerusalem in the Year 70.*

A. D. 76.

troops of soldiers in armour, were seen carried upon the clouds, and surrounding cities.

Such seeming appearances have often been the effect only of imagination, without any reality. But this is related by Josephus so particularly, and with so much solemnity, that it is hard to contest the truth. And if it be true, this, and the *light surrounding the altar and the temple,* before mentioned, may be some of those things intended by our Saviour, when he said: *And fearfull sights, and great signs shall there be from heaven.* Luke xxi. 11. Of this (*m*) Crevier speaks in this manner. "I say nothing of the armed "chariots and troops of warriors, that were seen fighting in the air. "That might be the natural effect of a phenomenon, then not un- "derstood, but which we are now well acquainted with, and call "the *Aurora Borealis,* or northern light." A wise observation truly! Who ever before saw, or heard of an *Aurora borealis* in the day time? Josephus expressly says, that these chariots and warriors were seen *before sun-setting.*

6. *And at the festival, which we call the Pentecost, as the Priests were going by night into the inner court of the temple, as the custom was, to perform their ministrations, they first felt, as they said, a shaking, accompanied with a noise, and then a sound, as of a multitude, saying,* Let us remove hence.

This passage is quoted by (*n*) Eusebius, and this particular is taken notice of by (*o*) divers ancient Christian writers. But they do not always quote so accuratly, as might be wished.

I beg

(*m*) *History of the Rom. Emp. vol. vi.* p. 240.

(*n*) *H. E. l.* 3. *cap. viii. et Dem. Ev. l.* 8. p. 402. *And see the Credib. vol.* 8. p. 60.

(*o*) Καὶ Ἰάσηπες δὲ μετὰ βραχὺν γινόμενος χρόνον, ἔφη, τινὰς ἀγγέλες τε ἐπιταραμένοντας, εἰ μὴ βυληθεῖεν ἐκεῖνοι μεταςῆ- ναι, καταλιπεῖν αὐτές. *Chr. in Jo. Hom.* 64. *al.* 65. p. 390. T. 8.

Josephus quoque refert, virtutes angelicas, praesides quondam templi, tunc pariter conclamasse: Transi̅mus ex his sedibus. *Hieron. in Matt.* xxvii. 51. T. 4. p. 139. *Conf. ep. ad Itedib.* §. *viii.* T. 4. P. i. p. 176.

I beg leave to observe upon it, *first of all*, this is said to have happened in the *night-time*, and therefore deserves the less regard. *Secondly*, I do not know what ministrations the Priests had to perform in the inner temple, in the night. Doubtless they kept watch at the temple by night as well as by day. But, so far as I can recollect, the ministrations at the temple, which were of divine appointment, were performed by day-light. *Thirdly, the sound of a multitude, saying, Let us go hence*, has much of an Heathenish air.

All these signs, or prodigies, just mentioned, (excepting *the star like a sword*, of which before,) seem to be placed by Josephus in the year of Christ 65. the year before the war commenced.

7. The seventh and last is that of *Jesus, son of Ananus, who four years before the war began, came up to the festival, which we call the Feast of Tabernacles, and on a sudden began to cry out: A voice from the East .. a voice against Jerusalem and the temple. ... And so it continued for seven years and five months, till he saw his presage fulfilled in the siege.* He therefore began this cry near the end of the year 62. This last Josephus calls *more awful than the rest*, τὸ δὲ τύτων Φοβερώτατον. And as Le Clerc *(p)* observes, " if it be true, Josephus rightly says, it was somewhat divine." I hope, we may depend upon the truth of this historie, which is related with so many particulars and circumstances.

All these things Josephus has recorded, as affecting signs, warnings, and presages of great calamities coming upon the Jewish nation: omitting, entirely, the warnings, and predictions, and admonitions of Jesus Christ, and of his Apostles after him, and also the three-hours darknesse over the whole land of Judea, and the rending

Unde et Josephus in sua narrat historia, quod postquam Dominus crucifixus est, et velum templi scissum est, sive liminare templi fractum corruit, audita sit vox in adytis Templi Virtutum coelestium, Transeamus ex his sedibus. *Id. in Ezech. cap.* 47. *p.* 1058.

(p) Quae si vera sunt, non immerito Josephus rem divinitus contigisse censuit. *Cleric. H. E. An.* 62. *n. v.*

Ch. III. *Of the Siege of Jerusalem in the Year 70.*

ing the veil of the temple, and the earthquake near Jerusalem, at the time of our Saviour's crucifixion. And though all these signs and warnings related by himself, are considered by him as very affecting, he acknowledgeth, that they made not any great impression upon his nation. And says: *But they did not attend, or give credit to those prodigies, which evidently foretold their desolation. But like men infatuated, who have neither eyes to see, nor minds to consider, they disregarded the divine denunciations.* And his historie verifies the truth and justnesse of this observation.

" Now *(q)* the Romans brought their ensigns to the temple, and
" set them over against the eastern gate. There they offered sacrifi-
" ces to them, and there they made Titus Emperour, with the great-
" est acclamations of joy. And all the soldiers had such vast quan-
" tities of spoils, which they got by plunder, that in Syria a pound
" weight of gold was sold for half it's former value."

There *(r)* were some priests as Josephus says, sitting upon the wall of the temple, who continued there, till they were pined with hunger. Then they came down, and surrendered themselves. When they were brought by the guards to Titus, they begged for their lives. But Titus answered: That the time of pardon was over, as to them, that being destroyed, for the sake of which alone he should have saved them: And that it was very fit, that priests should perish with their temple. Whereupon he ordered them to be put to death.

Now *(s) Simon* and *John*, and they that were with them, desire a conference with Titus. Which he granted. He placed himself on the western side of the outer court of the temple, and there was a bridge, that parted them. There were great numbers of Jews waiting with those two tyrants, and there were also many Romans on the side of Titus. He ordered the soldiers to refrain their rage, and

Q   appointed

(q) L. 6. cap. vi. §. 1.   *(r) Ibid.*   *(s) §. 2.*

appointed an interpreter. And being conquerour, he spoke first. He then reproached them in very bitter terms, and very justly. And then concluded. However, I will not imitate your madnesse. "If "you will throw down your arms, and deliver up your bodies to "me, I grant you your lives. I will act like a mild father of a fa- "milie. What cannot be healed shall be destroyed. The rest I "will reserve for my own use."

"They answered, they could not consent to that, because they "had sworn never to do it. They asked leave to go through the "wall that surrounded them, with their wives and children. So "they would go into the desert, and leave the city to him. At which "Titus was greatly provoked, that when they were now already in "the case of men taken captives, they should pretend to make their "own terms with him, as if they were conquerours. He then gave "orders, that proclamation should be made to them, that hencefor- "ward none should be allowed to come over to him, as deserters, "nor hope for security. For that now he would spare no body, "but fight them with his whole armie. He therefore gave orders "to the soldiers both to burn and to plunder the city. On that day "however they did nothing. But the day following they set fire to "the repositorie of the archives, to the council-houses, to *Acra*, "and to the place called *Ophilas*: at which time the fire proceeded "as far as to the palace of Queen *Helena*, which was in the mid- "dle of *Acra*. The lanes also were burnt down, as were all the "houses that were full of the dead bodies of such as had died by "the famine."

"On (*t*) the same day the sons and brothers of King *Izates*, "and (*u*) with them many other eminent men, of the city, got "together, and besought Titus to give them his right hand for their "security. Whereupon, though he was now very angrie, and much
"dis-

(*t*) §. 4.   μοτῶν ἐκεῖ συνελθόντες, ἱκέτευσαν Καίσαρα,
(*u*) ... πρὸς οἷς πολλοὶ τῶν ἐπισήμων δὴ, κ. λ.

"displeased with all who were still remaining, he did not depart from his wonted moderation, but received them. However, he kept them all in custodie. And having bound the King's sons and kinsmen, he took them with him to Rome, to be kept there as hostages for the fidelity of their countrey."

Here, as I apprehend, we see a proof of the zeal of the Jewish proselytes at this time. For such were the relations of King *Izates*. These persons had chosen to reside much in the holy city of Jerusalem. Or they had come up thither to the feast of the Passover this year, notwithstanding the danger it was in from the approaches of the Roman armie. And it was, as seems to me, a remarkable instance of the moderation of this Prince, that he now shewed mercie to these persons, who might have come over to him long before, and did not surrender themselves till matters were brought to the utmost extremity, and after he had publicly declared, that he would spare none.

Titus (*x*) still had difficulties remaining in taking the rest of the city.

"Some (*y*) there were who deserted to Titus, notwithstanding the care of the tyrants to prevent it. These were all received by the Romans, because Titus grew negligent as to his former orders, and because the soldiers were wearie of killing, and because they hoped to gain money by sparing them. They therefore sold them with their wives and children, though at a very low price. For there were many to be sold, and but a few purchasers. Indeed the number of those who were sold was prodigious. And (*z*) yet there were forty thousand of the people saved, whom Titus permitted to go where they pleased."

(*x*) Cap. vii. et viii.
(*y*) Cap. viii. §. 2.
(*z*) Ὁι δημοτικοὶ δὲ διεσώθησαν ὑπὲρ τε τρακισμυρίους, οὓς διαφῆκε Καῖσαρ, ἦ φίλον ἦν ἑκάσῳ. Ibid.

A. D. 76.

And now were fulfilled thofe words of Mofes. *And ye fhall be fold for bond-men, and bond-women. And no man fhall buy you.* Deut. xxviii. 68. And likewife thofe words of our Lord, Luke xxi. 24. *And they fhall fall by the edge of the fword, and fhall be led away captive into all nations. And Jerufalem fhall be trodden down by the Gentils, untill the times of the Gentils be fulfilled.*

" At (a) this time one of the priefts, fon of *Thebuthus*, whofe
" name was *Jofhua*, upon his having fecurity given him by the oath
" of Cefar, that he fhould be preferved, upon condition that he fhould
" deliver to him certain of the precious things, depofited in the tem-
" ple, came out, and delivered to him from the wall of the temple
" two candlefticks, like to thofe that lay in the temple, together
" with tables, and cifterns, and vials, all of folid gold, and very hea-
" vie. He alfo delivered to him the veils, and the garments of the
" High-Priefts, with the precious ftones, and many other veffels be-
" longing to the facred miniftrations. And now was feized the trea-
" furer of the temple, whofe name was *Phincas*, who difcovered to
" him the coats and girdles of the priefts, with a great quantity of
" purple and fcarlet, which were repofited for the ufe of the veil:
" as alfo a great deal of cinnamon and caffia, and other fweet fpices,
" which ufed to be mixed, and offered to God as incenfe, every day.
" A great many other precious things and ornaments of the temple
" were delivered by the fame perfon. Which things fo delivered to
" Titus, obtained for that man the fame pardon that was allowed to
" fuch as deferted of their own accord."

" At (b) length after great labour, and againft a furious oppofiti-
" on, the Romans became mafters of the reft of the city, and fet
" their enfigns upon the walls in triumph, and with great joy. They
" then plundered the houfes, and killed every one whom they met
" with in the ftreets. They fet fire to the city, and made the ftreets
" run with bloud, to fuch a degree, that the fire of many houfes
" was

(a) viii. §. 3.   (b) §. 4. 5.

Ch. III. *Of the Siege of Jerusalem in the Year 70.*

" was quenched with mens bloud. However it so happened, that when
" the slayers had left off in the evening, the fire greatly prevailed
" in the night. As all was burning, came on to Jerusalem the eighth
" day of the month of September, a city, which had suffered so
" many calamities during the siege, of which it was upon no other
" account so deserving, as upon account of it's producing such a
" generation of men, as occasioned it's overthrow.

" When (c) Titus was come into this upper city, he admired
" some places of strength in it, and particularly those strong tow-
" ers, which the tyrants in their madnesse had relinquished. And
" he expressed himself in the following manner. We (d) have cer-
" tainly had God for our helper in this war. It is God, who has
" ejected the Jews out of these fortifications. For what could the
" hands of men, or any machines do, toward throwing down such
" (*) fortifications? At which time he had many like discourses
" with

A. D.
76.

N. B.

(c) *Cap. ix.* §. 1.

(d) Σὺν Θεῷ γ' ἐπολεμήσαμεν ... κ. λ. *ib.*

(*) Undoubtedly Titus, upon entering into that part of the city, which was now taken, and so becoming master of the whole city of Jerusalem, had some discourses with his Generals, suitable to the occasion. But Josephus, in imitation of the Greek and Roman historians, who made speeches for their Generals, embellisheth here. And he makes Titus say some things, which he did not say. The tyrants, as Josephus calls them, were guilty of mad conduct in their divisions, in destroying, as they had done, many stores proper for sieges, and in other respects. But Titus could not charge them with folly and madnesse in relinquishing

the three towers here referred to. Josephus has given a particular description of them. *De B. J. l.* 5. *cap. iv.* §. 3. They were strong and lofty buildings, raised upon the north wall of the city. Herod had displayed his magnificence in them. But they were not fit for garrisons, or to be made places of defense. They were rather summer-palaces, fitted for diversion and entertainment, with splendid apartments and sumptuous furniture. The Jews did not relinquish any places of defense. They vigorously defended their several walls, and the tower Antonia, and the Temple. They had fully exercised all the militarie skill and courage of Titus, and his many Generals, and tired his soldiers: and induced them more than once to despair of victorie, as our historian himself

JOSEPHUS. Ch. III.

A. D. 76.
" with his friends. He alſo ſet at liberty ſuch as had been bound by the tyrants, and were ſtill in the priſons. And when he entirely demoliſhed the reſt of the city, and overthrew it's (e) walls, he left thoſe towers to be monuments of his fortune, which had fought with him, and had enabled him to take what otherwiſe would have been impregnable."

" The (f) ſoldiers were wearie of killing. But there were many ſtill alive. Titus therefore gave orders, that none ſhould be killed, but ſuch as were in arms, or made reſiſtance, and to take the reſt captive. Neverthelefs the ſoldiers ſlew the aged and the infirm. But for thoſe who were in their flouriſhing age, and might be uſefull to them, they drove them together into the temple, and ſhut them up within the walls of the court of the women. Over whom Titus ſet one of his freed-men, and *Fronto*, one of his friends, who was to determine the fate of each one according to his deſert. Many were ordered to be ſlain. But of the young men he choſe out the talleſt, and the moſt beautifull, and reſerved them for the triumph. Such as were above ſeventeen years of age, he bound, and ſent them to work in the mines in Egypt. Titus alſo ſent a great many into the provinces, as preſents to them, that they might be deſtroyed in their theatres, either by the ſword, or by wild-beaſts. They who were under ſeventeen years of age, were ſold for ſlaves. And during the time that *Fronto* was determining the fate of theſe men, there periſhed eleven thouſand for want of food. Some of them had no food, through the ill-will of thoſe who guarded them. Others would not take what was given them. And indeed there were ſo many, that there was not food for them."

Joſe-

himſelf has informed us. It appears however from Juſephus, that *Simon* made uſe of the tower *Phaſaelus* for his own habitation, during a good part of the ſiege. Τηνικαῦτα γεμὴν τυραννεῖοι ἀπεδείχθη τῦ Σίμωνος. Ib. §. 3. p. 330. in.

(e) Αὖθις δὲ τὴν ἄλλην ἀφανίζων πόλιν, ᾗ τείχη κατασκάπτων, τότυς τὸς πύργυς κατέλιπε μνημεῖον ἔναι τῆς αὐτῦ τυχῆς, ᾗ συςρατιώτιδι χρησάμενος ἐκράτησε τῶν ἀλώναι μὴ δυναμένων. L. 7. cap. ix. §. 1.

(f) Cap. ix. §. 2.

Ch. III. *Of the Siege of Jerusalem in the Year* 70.

Josephus does not here speak of any Jews being crucified at this time. Nevertheless, I apprehend, that many now suffered in that manner. For in *(g)* one of the last sections of his Life, giving an account of things, presently after the city was taken, he says, he was sent by Titus, with *Cerealis*, one of his Generals, and a thousand horse, to a village called *Thekoa*, to see whether it was a place fit for a camp. " As I came back, says he, I saw many of the cap-
" tives crucified. Among them I discerned three of my former ac-
" quaintance, which gave me great concern. I thereupon went to
" Titus with tears in my eyes, and spoke to him. Who immediatly
" gave orders to have them taken down, and that the best care should
" be taken of them for their recoverie. However two of them di-
" ed under cure. The third survived."

" The *(h)* number of those who were taken captive, during the
" whole war, was computed to be ninety and seven thousand. And
" the number of those who perished during the siege eleven hundred
" thousand. The greater part of them were indeed of the same na-
" tion, but not inhabitants of the city. For they were come up
" from all the countrey to the festival of unleavened bread, and were
" on a sudden shut in by the armie. Which *(i)* occasioned so great
" a straitnesse, that there came on a pestilential disorder, and then a
" famine, which was more severe."

And presently afterwards, " This *(k)* great multitude was collected
" from other places. The whole nation was shut up as in a prison.
" And the Roman armie encompassed the city, when it was croud-   N. B.
" ed with inhabitants. Accordingly *(l)* the multitude of those who
" perished therein exceeded all the destructions, that men or God
" ever brought on the world."

," As

(g) *De Vit.* §. 75.
(h) §. 3.
(i) ὥϛε τὸ πρῶτον αὐτοῖς τὴν ϛενοχωρίαν γενέσθαι λοιμώδη φθορὰν, αὖθις δ᾽ ᾗ λιμὸν ὀξύτερον. *Ib.*

(k) §. 4.
(l) Πᾶσαν γοῦν ἀνθρωπίνην κ᾽ δαιμόνιον φθορὰν ὑπερβάλλει τὸ πλῆθος τῶν ἀπολωλότων. *Ib.*

"As *(m)* many were hid in caverns, the Romans made searches
"after them. If any were found alive, they were presently slain.
"But beside them they found there more than two thousand,
"some killed by themselves, and by one another, and more destroy-
"ed by famine. The ill favour of the dead bodies was offensive.
"Nevertheless for the sake of gain many of the soldiers ventured
"into the caverns, where was found much treasure."

"*John (n)* and his brethren, who were with him in a cavern,
"wanted food. Now therefore he begged, that the Romans would
"give him the right hand for security, which he had often rejected
"before. But *Simon* struggled hard with the distresse he was in,
"'till he was forced to surrender himself, as we shall relate hereaf-
"ter. So he was reserved for the triumph, and to be then slain.
"*John* was condemned to perpetual imprisonment. And *(o)* now
"the Romans set fire to the extreme parts of the city, and burnt
"them down, and demolished the walls to the foundation."

"Thus *(p)* was Jerusalem taken in the second year of the reign
"of Vespasian, on the eighth day of the month of September. It
"had been taken five times before. This is the second time of it's
"desolation." Josephus then enumerates these several times, and
computes how many years it was from the time of it's being first
built. And then adds. "But neither it's antiquity, nor it's im-
"mense riches, nor the reputation of the nation, celebrated through-
"out the whole world, nor the great glorie of it's religion, has been
"sufficient to preserve it from destruction. Such was the end of
"the siege of Jerusalem."

These are the last words of his sixth book of the Jewish War.

Then, at the begining of the seventh book, he says:

"And

(m) §. 4.
(n) Ibid. §. 4.

(o) Ρωμαῖοι τάς τε ἐσχατιὰς τῆ ἄςεος ἐνέ-
πρησαν, ᾗ τὰ τείχη κατέσκαψαν. *Ibid.*
(p) Cap. x. ibid.

Ch. III.   Of the Siege of Jerusalem in the Year 70.

"And (q) now, when no more were left to be slain, nor any more plunder remained for the soldiers; Cesar gave orders, that they should demolish to the foundation the whole city, and the temple: leaving only the fore-mentioned towers *Phasaelus, Hippicus*, and *Mariamne*, and so much of the wall, as was on the west side of the city. That was spared, in order to afford a camp for those who were to lye in garrison. But (r) as for all the rest of the whole circumference of the city, it was so thoroughly laid even with the ground, by those who dug it up to the foundation, that there was nothing left to make those who came thither to believe, it had ever been inhabited."

A. D. 76.

N. B.

So said our Lord. Luke xix. 44. *And they shall lay thee even with the ground, and thy children within thee. And they shall not leave in thee one stone upon another, because thou knewest not the time of thy visitation.*

The soldiers who were left in garrison near the city, must have been instruments in digging up every part of it to the foundation. For Josephus afterwards describing the journey of Titus through Palestine to Alexandria, and observing how Titus was affected at the sight of the deplorable condition of the place, has these expressions. "And (s) no small part of it's riches had been found in it's ruins. This the Romans dug up. They found a great deal of gold and silver, and other precious things, which the owners had treasured up under ground, against the uncertain fortunes of war. And they were assisted by the captives in the discoverie of such things."

And *Eleazar*, in one of his speeches at *Massada*, to be farther taken notice of hereafter, where he persuades the people with him to consent to be put to death, has these expressions. "Where (t) is now that great city, the metropolis of the whole Jewish nation? ... Where is that city, which we believed to have God inhabiting in

---

(q) *L.* 7. *cap.* i. §. 1.
(r) Αλλον άπαντα της πολεως περιβολον ο-
τως εξωμάλισαν οι κατασκάπτοντες. . . . κ. λ.
ib.

(s) *L.* 7. *cap. v.* §. 2. *p.* 412. *Hav. Et Conf. l.* 6. *cap. ix.* §. 4.
(t) *L.* 7. *cap. viii.* §. 7. *p.* 430. *Hav.*

"it?

A. D. 76.
N. B.

" it? It (*u*) is rooted up to the foundation, and has no other monument left, but the armie of thofe who have deftroyed it, encamping upon it's ruins... Who can confider thefe things, and not be forry, that he is ftill alive? I cannot but wifh, that we had all died, before we had feen that holy city overthrown by it's enemies, and (*x*) the holy temple fo profanely dug up to the foundation."

And *Whitby* in his notes upon Matt. xxiv. 2. fays: "The Jewifh Talmud and Maimonides add, that Turnus [*i. e. Terentius Rufus*] captain of the armie of Titus, did with a plow-fhare tear up the foundations of the temple, and thereby fignally fulfill thofe words in Micah iii. 12. *Therefore fhall Zion for your fakes be plowed as a field, and Jerufalem become heaps, and the mountain of the houfe as the high places of the foreft*."

Grotius has well obferved upon Matt. xxiv. 1. " that the temple, which had been repaired, or rebuilt by *Herod*, was rightly efteemed to be the fame temple that had been built by *Zorubabel*. So therefore Jofephus fays, that the temple had been twice deftroyed, once by the Chaldeans, a fecond time by Titus. And the Jewifh Mafters call the deftruction made by Titus, *the deftruction of the fecond temple*. Whilft this temple ftood, the Meffiah was to be expected, not only according to the prophecie of Daniel, but likewife of Haggai. ch. ii. 8. and Malachi ch. iii. 1.

" Cefar (*y*) determined to leave there as a guard the tenth legion, with fome troops of horfe and companies of foot. Having now compleated the war, he returned thanks to his whole armie, and diftributed rewards among them. For this purpofe he had a large tribunal erected for him in the place, where he formerly encamped. That was a work of three days"

" The (*z*) reft of the armie was fent away to feveral places. But he permitted the tenth legion to ftay as a guard upon Jerufalem.
" Then

(*u*) Πρόρριζος ἐκ βάθρων ἀνήρπασαι..
(*x*) ... πρὶν τὸν ναὸν τὸν ἅγιον ὕτως ἀνοσίως ἐξορωρυγμένον. Ibid.

(*y*) L. 7. cap. i. §. 1.
(*z*) §. 2.

Ch. III. *Of the Siege of Jerusalem in the Year 70.*

A. D. 76.

"Then he went to Cefarea by the fea-fide, taking with him two
"legions, the fifth and the fifteenth, to attend him, 'till he fhould
"go to Egypt. At Cefarea he laid-up the fpoils in great quantities,
"and gave orders, that the captives fhould be kept there."

"From (a) that *Cefarea* Titus went to *Cefarea Philippi*, where he
"ftayed fome while, and exhibited all forts of fhews. Here many
"of the captives were deftroyed. Some were thrown to wild-beafts.
"Others in great numbers, were compelled to fight with each other.
"Whilft he was there, he heard of the feizure of *Simon fon of Gio-*
"*ras*, who during the fiege had commanded in the upper city, and
"who had concealed himfelf under ground as long as he could.
"But now fell into the hands of *Terentius Rufus*, who had been
"left to keep guard at the ruins of Jerufalem. When Titus was
"returned to Cefarea by the fea-fide, Simon was brought bound be-
"fore him, who ordered him to be kept for the triumph at Rome."

"At (b) Cefarea Titus folemnized the birth-day of his brother
"*Domitian*, on (c) the 24. day of October, in a fplendid manner,
"doing honour to him in the punifhment of the Jews. For the
"number of thofe who were now flain, in fighting with beafts, or
"were burnt to death, or fought with one another, exceeded two
"thoufand and five hundred. Yet did all this feem to the Romans,
"though they were deftroyed ten thoufand ways, beneath their de-
"ferts. Afterwards Titus went to *Berytus*, a city in Phenicia, and
"a Roman colonie. There he ftayed a longer time, and exhibited
"a more pompous folemnity, on his Father's birth-day. [Nov. 17.]
"Here a great number of the captives were deftroyed in the like
"manner as before."

"Having (d) ftaid fome while at *Berytus*, he fet forward to *An-*
"*tioch*. And as he went, exhibited magnificent fhews in all the
"cities

(a) cap. ii. §. 1.
(b) cap. iii. §. 1.
(c) *Vid.* Pagi ann. 70. n. iii. et Bofnag.
ann. 70. n. xviii.
(d) cap. v. §. 1.

A. D. 76.

"cities of Syria, making use of the captives, as public instances of the overthrow of the Jewish nation."

At (e) *Antioch* he was received with loud acclamations. Thence he went to *Zeugma*, which lies upon the Euphrates. Whither came to him messengers from *Vologesus*, King of Parthia, who brought him a crown of gold, congratulating him upon his victorie over the Jews, which he accepted. There he feasted the King's messengers, and then returned to Antioch.

It does not appear, that Titus celebrated any shews there. And when the people of that place requested him to expell the Jews out of their city, he refused to comply with them, and confirmed to them all the privileges, which they had hitherto enjoyed there.

Having (f) sent away the two before mentioned legions, by which he had been attended, one to *Mysia*, the other to *Pannonia*: and having given orders for sending *Simon* and *John*, and seven hundred of the tallest and handsomest of the captives, to appear in the triumph at Rome, he went to Alexandria, and thence to Rome. And passing through *Palestine*, in his way to Egypt, he was much moved as Josephus says, at the sight of the desolations of that countrey.

When (g) Titus came near Rome, he was received with great rejoycings by the people, who came out to meet him, as also by his father Vespasian. And though the senate had decreed to them two several triumphs, they chose to have but one. Josephus has not informed us exactly concerning the time of it. And learned critics are now of different opinions. Some (h) place it near the end of the month of April, in 71. Others (i) argue, that it must have been later.

"Many (k) other spoils, says Josephus, were carried in great a-
"bundance. But the most considerable of all were those taken out
" of the temple at *Jerusalem*. There was the golden table, of many
" talents.

(e) .. §. 2.
(f) §. 2. 3.
(g) §. 3. 4.

(h) *Vid. Pagi ann.* 70. n. vi.
(i) *Basnag.* 71. n. iii.
(k) §. 5.

"talents. And the candlestick, likewise of gold, with it's seven
"lamps, a number much respected by the Jews. The last of all
"the spoils was the Law of the Jews. After which were carried
"images of Victorie, made of gold, or ivorie. After which came
"*Vespasian* first, on horse-back, then *Titus*. *Domitian* also was there,
"splendidly attired, and riding upon a beautifull horse."

"The (*l*) end of this pompous shew was at the temple of *Jupi-*
"*ter Capitolinus*. When they came thither, they stood still. For
"it was the ancient custom of the Romans, to stay, till word was
"brought, that the General of the enemie was slain. This was *Si-*
"*mon the son of Gioras*, who had been led in the triumph among
"the captives. A rope was put about his neck, and he was led to a
"proper place in the Forum, where malefactors were put to death.
"When tidings of his death were brought, all the people set up the
"shout of Joy. And sacrifices were offered up, with the accustom-
"ed prayers. The Emperour then went to his palace, and feast-
"ings were made every where."

"And (*m*) now Vespasian determined to build a temple to Peace,
"which was finished in a short time, and in a splendid manner.
"Here he laid up those golden vessels and instruments, that were
"taken out of the Jewish temple, as ensigns of his glorie. But their
"law, and the purple veils of the holy place he ordered to be de-
"posited in his palace."

"That (*n*) temple was adorned with paintings and statues. In
"it were collected and reposited all such curiosities, as men are wont
"to wander all over the world to obtain a sight of."

The book of the Law does not now appear in what is called the triumphal arch of Titus, though the Table and the candlestick are very visible.

Josephus in his Life says, that when the city was taken, Titus gave him leave to ask what he pleased. One (*o*) of his requests was to

(*l*) §. 6.
(*m*) §. 7.
(*n*) Ib. §. 7.

(*o*) ... ϰὶ βιϐλίων ἱερῶν ἔλαϐον χαρισαμέ-
νε Τίτε. *Vit.* §. 75.

to have the sacred books, which were granted to him. Here, in the hiftorie of the war, he feems to fay, they *(p)* were depofited in the Emperour's palace. Poffibly, they were placed there. But Jofephus was allowed to have the ufe of them, when he defired it.

The temple of Peace according to the defcription which Jofephus has given of it, appears to have refembled our *Britifh Mufeum*, and other like rich cabinets of Princes in feveral parts of Europe.

The temple of Peace was burnt down in the reign of Commodus. But it is likely, that many of the curiofities depofited in it, were preferved from the flames. And the Jewifh fpoils were in being in the fifth centurie, and afterwards, though not at Rome, as we learn from *(q) Adrian Reland*.

We have feen the overthrow of the city and temple of Jerufalem. But there ftill remained fome ftrong places in Judea, not yet taken by the Romans. Of which Jofephus has given an account. And it is fit we fhould trace him to the end of his hiftorie of the Jewifh War. For, as our Lord faid, *Wherefoever the carcafe is, there will the eagles be gathered together.* Matt. xxiv. 28. And fee Luke xvii. 37.

Lucilius Baffus (r) was fent into Judea by Vefpafian as Lieutenant, where he received a fufficient armie from *Cerealis Vitellianus*. He foon took *Herodion*, and made the garrifon prifoners.

He *(s)* then determined to go to *Machaerus*. By means of an accident, well emproved, he became mafter of it, without much loffe on either fide.

" Having *(t)* fettled affairs there, he marched haftily to the fo-
" reft

(p) Τὸν δὲ νόμον αὐτῶν, . . . προσέταξεν ἐν τοῖς βασιλείοις ἀποθεμένους φυλάττειν. *L.* 7. *c. v. §. 7.*

(q) Imperante Commodo deflagravit hoc templum Pacis, tefte Herodiano *I.* 1. cap. 14. fed cum eo non periiffe fpolia Hierofolymitana certum eft, quoniam feculo quinto a Chrifto nato ea in Africam delata funt, ut mox videbimus. &c. *Reland. De Spoliis Templ. Hieros. cap.* 13. *p.* 133.

(r) L. 7. *cap. vi.* 1.
(s) Ib. §. 1, . . 4.
(t) Ib. §. 5.

Ch. III. *How other Places in Judea were reduced.*

"rest of *Jardes*. Where, as he was informed, many were gather-
"ed together, who during the siege had escaped from *Jerusalem*,
"and *Macherus*. When they engaged, the battle was fierce and
"obstinate on both sides. Nevertheless of the Romans there were
"not more than twelve killed, and not many wounded. But of the
"Jews not one escaped out of the battle, but they were all killed,
"being not fewer in number than three thousand, and with them
"their General, *Judas*, the son of *Jaïrus*, who had been captain of
"a band in the siege of Jerusalem, and by getting out through a
"vault under ground had privatly escaped."

"About (*u*) this time the Emperour sent orders to *Lucilius Bassus*, and *Liberius Maximus*, that all Judea should be exposed to sale. For he founded not any city there, but reserved the countrey to himself. However he assigned a place for eight hundred men, whom he dismissed from the armie, which he gave them for their habitation. It is called *Ammaus*, and is distant from Jerusalem sixty furlongs. He also laid a tribute upon the Jews wherever they were, requiring that every one of them should bring two drachmas [*half a shekel*] every year to the Capitol, the same that they had been used to pay to the temple at Jerusalem."

Bassus (*x*) having died in Judea, *Flavius Silva* was sent to succeed him in the government of that countrey. Who soon made an expedition against *Massada*, the only remaining fortresse. It was in the possession of *Eleazar* a commander of the Sicarii. He was a descendent of *Judas*, who had persuaded many of the Jews, as formerly related, not to submit to the assessment made by Cyrenius, when he came into Judea after the removal of Archelaus.

When (*a*) there was no room left for escaping, *Eleazar* called together the principal persons, and consulted with them what might be best to be done. At which time he made an oration to them,
to

A. D. 76.

(*u*) §. 6.   (*x*) *Cap.* viii. §. 1.   (*a*) §. 6.

to induce them to kill themselves, rather than fall into the hands of the Romans.

That (b) oration had great effect upon many. Some however there were, who hesitated. He therefore went on, and made another oration to the like purpose. All now were persuaded.

"They (c) then chose ten men of the number by lot, to slay all the
"rest. When these ten men had without fear slain all the rest, men,
"women, and children, as determined, they cast lots upon them-
"selves. And he who had the first lot killed the other nine, and
"then himself. These people so died, with the intention, that they
"might not leave so much as one man among them to be subject
"to the Romans. However, there was one ancient woman, and
"another woman, related to *Eleazar*, who exceeded most women
"in knowledge and prudence, and five children, who had hid them-
"selves in a cavern under ground. They had carried water with
"them for their drink, and lay quiet there, whilst the rest were in-
"tent upon the slaughter of each other. The whole number of
"these people, including the just mentioned women and children,
"was nine hundred and sixty. This slaughter was made on the
"fifteenth day of the month of April in the year 73. as may be
"computed."

When the Romans entred the place the next morning their surprise was very great, as may be well supposed.

Soon (d) after this some turbulent Jews were the occasion of disturbances at *Alexandria*, where six hundred were slain, and after that in *Cyrene*, where more than three thousand suffered. The disturbance there was occasioned by the imposture of *Jonathan*, a weaver, who (e) persuaded many people of the meaner sort to follow

---

(b) Ib. §. 7.
(c) Cap. ix. §. 1. 2.
(d) Cap. x. et xi.
(e) ... ἐκ ὀλίγων τῶν ἀπόρων εἰσέπεισε πρι-

σίχεν αὐτῷ, ᾗ προήγαγεν εἰς τὴν ἔρημον, σημεῖα ᾗ φάσματα, δείξειν ὑποσχομενος. cap. xi. §. 1.

Ch. III. *How other Places in Judea were reduced.*

A. D. 76.

low him into the wildernesse, where he promised to shew them signs and wonders. Moreover Vespasian sent expres orders, that the Jewish temple of *Onias*, as it was called, built in the prefecture of *Heliopolis* in *Egypt*, should be demolished. Which was done in the year of Christ 74. about two hundred and twenty four years after it had been first built, as *(f) Prideaux* computes.

We before saw, what was the number of those, who were computed to have perished in the siege of Jerusalem. But *taking in also those who had suffered in other places out of Jerusalem, these, added to the eleven hundred thousand that perished in the siege, make the whole number thirteen hundred and thirty seven thousand four hundred and ninety, an innumerable companie still being omitted, that perished through famine, banishment, and other (g) miseries.* Which I think to be no aggravation at all.

IX. Let us now reflect.

1. All these things have we seen in Josephus, who at the beginning of his work says: "I *(h)* Josephus son of Matthias, by birth a
" Hebrew of Jerusalem, and a Priest, who my-self at first fought
" against the Romans, and was afterwards forced to be present at
" the things that were done, have writ this historie."

Reflexions upon the preceding Historie.

The conclusion of the whole work, at the end of the seventh and last book of the Jewish War, is to this effect. " Here *(i)* we put
" an end to our historie, which we promised to deliver with all ac-
" curacie to those who are desirous to know, how this war of the
" Romans with the Jews was managed. Concerning the stile, let
" the readers judge. Concerning the truth, I may boldly say, that
" only has been aimed at throughout the whole work."

(f) See his *Connexion, &c. year before Christ* 149. p. 266.
(g) See *Usher's Annals*, p. 907. *in English*, Lond. 1658.
(h) *De B. Jud. in Pr.* §. 1.
(i) L. 7. cap. xi. §. 5.

S

Per-

Perhaps likewise it may not be amiss to observe what he says of this work in his first book against Appion, writ long afterwards, near the period of his life.

"As *(k)* for my-self I have composed a true historie of that war, and of all the particulars that occurred therein: as having been concerned in all it's transactions. For I acted as General among those among us, who are called *Galileans*, as long as it was possible for us to make any opposition. And when I was taken captive by the Romans, Vespasian and Titus had me kept under a guard. But obliged me to attend them continually. At first I was in bonds, afterwards I was set at liberty, and was sent to accompany Titus, when he came from Alexandria to the siege of Jerusalem. During which time nothing was done, which escaped my knowledge. What happened in the Roman camp I saw, and wrote it down carefully. What information the deserters brought out of the city, I was the only man that understood it. Afterwards I got leisure at Rome. And when all my materials were prepared, I procured the help of one to assist me in writing Greek. Thus I composed the historie of those transactions. And I was so well assured of the truth of what I related, that I first appealed to those who had the supreme command in that war, *Vespasian* and *Titus*, as witnesses for me. For to them I first presented those books, and after them to many of the Romans, who had been in the war. I also communicated them to many of our own men, who understood the Greek philosophy: among whom were *Julius Archelaus*, and *Herod*, a person of great gravity, and King *Agrippa* himself, who deserved the greatest admiration. All these bore testimonie to me, that I had the strictest regard to truth. Who would not have dissembled the matter, nor have been silent, if through ignorance, or out of favour to either side I had altered, or omitted any thing."

2. Jo-

(k) Contr. Ap. l. i. §. 9.

Ch. III.   *Reflexions upon the foregoing Historie.*

2. Josephus's historie of the Jewish War is an ample testimonie to the fulfilment of all the predictions of our Lord, concerning the demolition of the temple and city of Jerusalem, and the miseries to be endured by the nation, during the siege, which were such as had never before happened to any people, nor were likely to happen again.

3. The sufferers in these calamities were, generally, men of the worst characters, Robbers and Sicarii, and others too much resembling them. 'It is reasonable to believe, that no Christians were then shut up in the city, nor many other good men, to partake in the miseries of that long and grievous siege. As St. Peter says, having instanced in the preservation of *Noah the eighth person, when God brought in the flood upon the world of the ungodly, and then delivering just Lot, when the cities of Sodom and Gomarrhah were turned into ashes,* adds, with a view to other like cases, and probably to the destruction of Jerusalem itself, *The Lord knoweth how to deliver the godly out of temptations, and to reserve the unjust unto the day of judgement to be punished.* 2 Pet. ii. 5 . . . 9.

4. I think it ought to be observed by us, that there was not now any pestilence at Jerusalem, but the Jews perished by the calamities of war. It might have been expected, that the bad food, which they were forced to make use of in the streightnesse of the siege, and the noisome smell of so many dead bodies, lying in heaps, in the city itself, and in the valleys or ditches without the walls, should have produced a plague. But nothing of that kind appears (*) in the historie, which must have been owing to the special interposition of Divine Providence. Josephus *(l)* in some of the places, where he

speaks

(*) Il est difficile que tant de peuples renformez dans une ville durant les chaleurs de l' été, de si mechants nourritures, et surtout la puanteur de tant de corps morts, n'aient joint la peste à la famine. Joseph n'en parle neanmoins qu'en un endroit, en passant. Ce qui marque qu'elle ne fut pas considerable. *Till. Ruine des Juifs. art.* 67. *p.* 960.

(l) Vid. De B. Jud. l. 5. *cap. xii.* §. 4.

speaks of the putrefaction of the dead bodies, may use expressions, equivalent to *pestilential*. But he never shews, that there was an infection. If there had, it would have equally affected the Romans and the Jews, and the siege of the place must have been broke up, and the Romans would have gone off, as fast as they could.

5. None can forbear to observe the time, when all these things came to pass. Our Lord says, Matt. xxiii. 36. *Verily, I say unto you, all these things shall come upon this generation.* And xxiv. 34. *Verily I say unto you: This generation shall not pass, till all these things shall be fulfilled.* So likewise Mark xiii. 30. and Luke xxi. 32. So it was. All these things foretold by our Lord came to pass, before the end of that generation of men. Jerusalem and the temple were no more, before the end of the year 70. of the christian epoch, and within forty years after his crucifixion.

Concerning the time also our Lord said: *And this gospel of the kingdom shall be preached in all the world, for a witnesse to all nations.* Matt. xxiv. 14. Comp. Mark xiii. 10.

This we know from Christian writings, particularly the books of the New Testament, most of which were writ before the destruction of Jerusalem. They bear witnesse, that the gospel had been preached to Jews and Gentiles, in *Judea, Syria, Asia, Greece, Macedonia, and Rome*, and other places, and with great successe. And the preaching of the gospel throughout the world was a *testimonie to all nations*, that the calamities inflicted upon the Jewish people were just and fit. They bear witnesse, that the Jewish nation had been called upon to repent, and were faithfully, and affectionatly, and earnestly warned and admonished, but they refused to hearken. See the Acts of the Apostles, and Mark xvi. 20. Rom. x. 18. Col. i. 6. and 23.

Says Archbishop *Tillotson*. "We (*m*) have this matter related, not
"by a Christian, (who might be suspected of partiality, and a de-
"sign

(*m*) *Vol.* 2. *p.* 563. *serm.* 186. *the seventh sermon upon* 2 *Cor.* iv. 3. 4.

Ch. III.   *The Value of his Testimonie.*

"sign to have paralleled the event with our Saviour's prediction:) but by a Jew, both by nation and religion, who seems designedly to have avoided, as much as possibly he could, the very mention of the Christian name, and all particulars relating to our Saviour, though no historian was ever more punctual in other things."

Says Mr. *Tillemont* (n) "God has been pleased to choose for our information in this historie, not an Apostle, nor any of the chief men of the Church, but an obstinate Jew, whom neither the view of the virtue and miracles of the Christians, nor the knowledge of the Law, nor the ruin of his religion and countrey, could induce to believe in and love the Messiah, who was all the expectation of the nation. God has permitted it so to be, that the testimonie, which this historian gave to an event, of which he did not comprehend the mysterie, might not be rejected, neither by Jews, nor Heathens, and that none might be able to say, that he had altered the truth of things to favour Jesus Christ and his disciples."

Dr. W. *Wotton* says of Josephus: "He (o) is certainly an Author very justly to be valued, notwithstanding all his faults. *His Historie of the Jewish War* is a noble demonstration of the truth of the Christian Religion, by shewing in the most lively manner, how the prophecies of our blessed Lord concerning the destruction of Jerusalem were literally fulfilled in their fullest extent."

And Dr. *Doddridge* in his notes upon the xxiv chapter of St. *Matthew's* Gospel, says: "Christian (p) writers have always with great reason represented *Josephus's History of the Jewish War*, as the best commentarie upon this chapter. And many have justly remarked it, as a wonderful instance of the care of Providence for the Christian Church, that he, an eye-witnesse, and in these things, of so "great

---

(n) *Ruine des Juifs*, art. i. p. 722.
(o) *Preface to his Miscellaneous Discourses relating to the Traditions and Usages of the Scribes and Pharisees.* p. xlix. The

faults, which he observes in Josephus, may be seen at p xxxiii &c.
(p) *The Family Expositor.* §. 160. Vol. 2. p. 373.

"great credit, should, (especially in so extraordinarie a manner,) be "preserved, to transmit to us a collection of important facts, which "so exactly illustrate this noble prophecie, in almost every particu- "lar circumstance. But as it would swell my notes too much to en- "ter into a particular detail of those circumstances, I must content "my-self with referring to Dr. *Whitby*'s excellent notes upon the "xxiv. of Matthew, and to Archbishop *Tillotson*'s large and accurate "discourse on the same subject in the second volume of his postu- "mous works. Serm. 183. . . . 187."

Isidore of Pelusium, who flourished about the year 412. in one of his epistles, has these expressions: "If *(q)* you have a mind to "know, what punishment the wicked Jews underwent, who ill- "treated the Christ, read the historie of their destruction, writ by "*Josephus*, a Jew indeed, but a lover of truth, that you may see the "wonderfull storie, such as no time ever saw before since the begin- "ing of the world, nor ever shall be. For that none might refuse "to give credit to the historie of their incredible and unparalleled "sufferings, truth found out not a stranger, but a native, and a man "fond of their institutions, to relate them, in a dolefull strain."

Eusebius often quotes Josephus, and in his Ecclesiastical Historie, has transcribed from him several articles at large. Having rehearsed from the Gospels divers of our Lord's predictions of the evils then coming upon Jerusalem, and the Jewish people, he adds: "Who- "soever *(r)* shall compare these words of our Saviour with the hi- "storie of the whole war, published by the above mentioned wri- "ter, must admire our Lord's great wisdom, and acknowledge that "his foresight was divine."

In his Chronicle, as we have it from Jerome in Latin, Eusebius says: "In *(s)* subduing Judea, and overthrowing Jerusalem, Titus
"slew

(*q*) Lib. 4. *ep.* 75. *vid. et ep.* 74.
(*r*) H. E. *l.* 3. *cap.* 8. *p.* 81. D.
(*s*) Titus Judaeâ captâ, et Jerosolymis

subversis, DC millia virorum interfecit. Josephus vero scribit undecies centena millia fame et gladio periisse, et alia centum millia

"slew six hundred thousand people. But Josephus writes, that ele-
"ven hundred thousand perished by famine and the sword, and that
"another hundred thousand were publicly sold and carried captives.
"And he says, that the occasion of there being so great a multitude
"of people at Jerusalem was this, that it was the time of Passover.
"For which reason the Jews having come up from all parts to wor-
"ship at the temple, they were shut up, in the city, as in a prison.
"And indeed, it was fit they should be slain at the same time, in
"which they crucified our Saviour."

It is certainly very fit, that Christians should attend to the fulfilment of our Lord's predictions, relating to the Jewish people: which are so frequent, so solemn, and affectionate. The testimonie of Josephus is the most considerable of all. It is the most full, and particular, and exact of any we have, or have the knowledge of. And he was an eye-witnesse. And he was manifestly zealous for the honour of his countrey. He had a great respect for the temple, and it's worship, and for all the peculiarities of the Mosaic law. And he continued to have the same to the last, as appears from his own life, and his books against Apion.

X. Josephus, in the preface to his own work, intimates, that some histories of the war had been before written by others. But he represents them as partial, and defective, and composed by men, who were not well informed. Undoubtedly none of these remain now. They have been lost long since.

Justus of Tiberias, contemporarie with Josephus, between whom there were many differences, also wrote a historie of the war. Josephus in his Life chargeth him with falshood, and blames him for

not

Other ancient Writers bearing Witnesse to the same Events.

---

millia captivorum publice venundata. Ut autem tanta multitudo Jerosolymis reperirentur, caussam Azymorum fuisse refert: ob quam ex omni genere Judaei ad templum confluentes urbe quasi carcere sunt reclusi. Oportuit enim in iisdem diebus eos interfici, in quibus salvatorem crucifixerant. *Chron p.* 162.

not publishing his work untill after the death of *Vespasian and Titus and King Agrippa*. Josephus owns (*t*) that Justus was well skilled in Greek learning. And he plainly says, that he wrote of the war.

I do not clearly perceive *Eusebius* (*u*) to have known any thing of Justus, but what he learned from the testimonies of Josephus above referred to by me.

Justus (*x*) is in *Jerome's* catalogue of Ecclesiastical writers. He seems to ascribe to him two books.

Photius (*y*) I think, speaks of but one work of this author, which he calls *a Chronicle*. He says, it began with Moses, and ended at the death of Agrippa. He also takes notice of Josephus's censures both of the author himself and his work.

Stephanus Byzantinus, in his article of Tiberias, says: " Of (*z*) " this city was *Justus*, who wrote of the Jewish War in the time " of Vespasian."

Diogenes Laertius (*a*) in his Life of Socrates, quotes a passage from Justus of Tiberias: and seems to quote the same book that was read by Photius.

Several learned moderns (*b*) are of opinion, that Justus like Josephus, wrote two books, one of the Jewish War, another of the Jewish Antiquities. *Menage* (*c*) in his notes upon Diogenes Laertius,

(*t*) Καὶ γὰρ ἐδ' ἄπειρος ἦν παιδείας τῆς παρ' Ἕλλησιν, ᾗ θαῤῥῶν ἐπεχείρησεν ᾧ τὴν ἱστορίαν τῶν πραγμάτων τούτων ἀναγράφειν. κ. λ. *Joseph. Vit.* §. 9. *Vid. et* § 65.

(*u*) H. E. *l*. 3. *cap. x. p*. 86. B.

(*x*) Justus Tiberiensis de provincia Galilaea, conatus est et ipse Judaicarum rerum historiam texere, et quosdam commentariolos de Scripturis componere: &c. *De V. I. cap*. 14.

(*y*) Ἀνεγνώσθη Ἰέστου Τιβεριέως χρονικὸν. κ. λ. *Cod*. 33. *p*. 20.

(*z*) Ἐκ ταύτης ἦν Ἰέστος, ὁ τὸν Ἰουδαϊκὸν πόλεμον τὸν κατὰ Οὐεσπασιανὸν ἱστορήσας. *Steph. Byz*.

(*a*) Φησὶν Ἰέστος ὁ Τιβερεὺς ἐν τῷ στέμματι. *Diog. La. l*. 2. §. 41.

(*b*) Unde colligo (*ex Hieronymi Catalogo*,) ut Josephus, ita et Justum, non modo de Antiquitatibus Judaicis, sed seorsum etiam de Bello Judaico scripsisse. *Voss. de H. Gr. Vid. et Valess. Ann. in Euseb. l*. 3. *cap. x. Tillem. Ruine de Juifs. art*. 82.

(*c*) Scripsit ille Historiam Judaicam, eodem

Ch. III. *The Testimony of other Writers.*

us, ascribes to Justus three books, that is, Memoirs, beside the two before mentioned. I rather think, there was but one: and that what Justus wrote of the war was comprised in the Chronicle. Menage's argument from Suidas is of no value. For Suidas expresseth himself inaccuratly. Nor does he mention more than two works. The Memoirs, ὑπομνήματα, are the same with Jerome's *Commentarioli de Scripturis.* Indeed, Suidas only transcribes Jerome, or his interpreter Sophronius, and has done it inaccuratly.

Some *(d)* learned men lament the losse of this work. Others *(e)* think it was of little value. I cannot but wish, that the work, which was in being in the time of Photius, had also reached us. It must have been of some use. Perhaps the censure passed upon it by Josephus, who was in great credit, has been a prejudice to it.

I have allowed my-self to enlarge in my notice of this writer, who lived at the time, and was an actor in the Jewish war with the Romans. Though his work is not exstant, he is a witnesse to that important transaction.

Pausanias, who *(f)* lived in the second centurie, and wrote after the year of our Lord 180. speaks *(g)* of a monument of Queen Helena at Jerusalem, which *(city)* an Emperour of the Romans had destroyed to the foundation.

---

dem tempore quo Josephus, a quo mendacii arguitur. Scripsit praeterea ὑπομνήματα, quorum meminit Suidas. Scripsit et Chronicon Regum Judaeorum, qui coronati fuere: Ut est apud Photium. Quod opus signat hic Laertius. *Menag. in loc.* p. 94.

(d) Josephus, in Vitâ suâ, et alibi, quasi parum fido scriptori convitiatur. Sed de inimico, non magis ei crediderim, quam Justo de Josepho crederem, si historia ejus exstaret, atque in ea aemulo ab eo detractum viderem. Utinam vero, quaecumque fuerit, ad nos usque pervenisset. *Cleric. H. E. A. C. C. cap. vii.*

(e) Tillem. as above, art. 80.

(f) See Tillem. L'Emp. Marc. Aurele. art. xxxii.

(g) Ἑβραίοις δὲ Ἑλένης γυναικὸς ἐπιχωρίας τάφος ἐςὶν ἐν πόλει Σολύμοις, ἣν ἐς ἔδαφος κατέβαλεν ὁ Ῥωμαίων βασιλεύς. *Pausan. l. 8. cap. 16. p. 633.*

"Minucius Felix refers *(h)* the Heathen people, not only to Josephus, but also to *Antonie Julian*, a Roman author, from whom they might learn, that the Jews had not been ruined, nor abandoned of God, till they had first abandoned him: and that their present low condition was owing to their wickednesse, and obstinacie therein, and that nothing had happened to them, but what had been foretold."

Who that *Julian* was, cannot be said. There have been several of that name, one *(i)* of whom was Procurator of Judea, and was present with Titus at the siege of Jerusalem, as we know from Josephus. Tillemont says, that *(k)* possibly he wrote a historie of the siege of Jerusalem. G. Vossius *(l)* upon the ground of this passage of Minucius, puts *Antonie Julian* among Latin Historians, who had writ a historie of the Jews.

Minucius reckons *Josephus* among Roman writers. Dr. Davis suspects it to be an interpolation, and assigns not improbable reasons, in his notes upon the place.

Suetonius *(m)* has mentioned the occasion of the war, the appointment of Vespasian to be General, his, and his son's triumph at *(n)* Rome, and several other material things, which have been already observed, or will in time be observed by us from him.

What

(h) Scripta eorum relege. Vel si Romanis magis gaudes, ut transeamus veteres, Flavii Josephi, vel Antonii Juliani, de Judaicis require. Jam scies, nequitia suâ, hanc eos meruisse fortunam: nec quidquam accidisse, quod non sit his, si in contumaciâ perseverarent, ante praedictum. Ita prius eos deseruisse comprehendes, quam esse desertos: nec, ut impie loqueris, cum Deo suo esse captos, sed a Deo, ut disciplinae transfugas deditos. *Minuc. cap.* 33. *Conf. cap.* 10.

(i) Καὶ Μᾶρκος Ἀντώνιος, ὁ τῆς Ἰουδαίας ἐπίτροπος. *Jos. de B. J. l.* 6. *cap. iv.* 3.

(k) Ruine des Juifs, art. 72.

(l) Antonius Julianus Judaicam videtur historiam consignasse. &c. *De Hist. Lat. l.* 3. *De Historicis incertae aetatis.*

(m) Sueton. Vespas. cap. 4. 5.

(n) ——— ac triumphum utriusque Judaicum, equo albo comitatus est. *Denuit. cap.* 2.

Ch. III.   *The Testimony of other Writers.*   139

What (o) *Tacitus* has writ upon this subject, so far as it remains, may be taken notice of hereafter.

A. D. 76.

Dion Cassius (p) is another witnesse, whose testimonie also may be taken more at large hereafter.

Philostratus says, "that *(q)* when Titus had taken Jerusalem, and "filled all about it with dead bodies, and the neighboring nations of- "fered him crowns, he said, he was not worthie of such an honour, "nor had he himself, he said, done that great work. He had only "lent his hand in the service of God, when he was pleased to shew "his displeasure." Philostratus says, that *Apollonius* was much pleased with that token of wisdom and humanity. He likewise says, that *Apollonius* wrote a letter to Titus, and sent it by Damis, to this pur- pose. "*Apollonius* sendeth greeting to Titus Emperour of the Ro- "mans. Since you refuse to be applauded for bloud-shed and vic- "torie in war, I send you the crown of moderation. You know, for "what things crowns are due."

Hence divers learned men have argued, that Titus refused to be crowned for his victorie over the Jews. *Basnage (r)* and other learn- ed men on the contrarie are of opinion, that we may relye upon the authority of Josephus, who tells us, "that he went from Antioch "to the Zeugma, whither came to him messengers from Vologe- "sus King of Parthia, and brought him a crown of gold, upon the "victorie obtained by him over the Jews: which he accepted of, "and feasted the King's messengers, and then returned to Antioch." Moreover he accepted of a triumph for his victorie over the Jews,

T 2   and

(o) *Vid. Tac. Hist. Lib. v.*
(p) *Dio. l. 66. sub in.*
(q) Ἐπεὶ δὲ Τίτος ᾑρήκει τὰ Σόλυμα, κ̀ νεκρῶν πλέα ἦν πάντα, τὰ ὅμορά τε ἐθνῶν ἔσε φαίων αὐτὸν. Ὁ δὲ οὐκ ἀξίν ἑαυτὸν τούτ' μὴ γὰρ αὐτὸν ταῦτα εἰργάσθαι, θεῷ δὲ ὀργὴν φαίνοντι ἐπιδεδωκέναι τὰς ἑαυτοῦ χεῖρας. κ. λ. *Philos. de Vit. Apol. l. 6. cap. 29.*

(r) Modestiam Titi laudibus effert Baronius, quod *oblatâ sibi coronâ aureâ a provinciis, noluit coronari, testatus se prorsus indignum.* Usserius, aliique eruditi, illud et ipsum tradunt, freti auctoritate Philostrati.... *Basnag. Ann.* 70. *n. xvi.*

and all other honours cuſtomarie upon the like occaſions. Nevertheleſs *Olearius*, in his notes upon the place, argues, that (*s*) Philoſtratus needs not to be underſtood to ſay, that Titus refuſed the crowns
offered him, but only ſaid, that he was unworthie of that honour,
he having been only an inſtrument in the hand of God for diſplay-
ing his juſt vengeance againſt guilty men.

And it muſt be owned, that Olearius expreſſeth himſelf with great
judgement and moderation. Either way, thoſe learned men are to
be reckoned miſtaken, who have maintained that Titus refuſed to
be crowned for his victorie over the Jews.

However, we are ſtill to reckon Philoſtratus, at the begining of
the third centurie, a good witneſſe to the overthrow of Jeruſalem by
Titus.

Theſe are early Heathen authors, who have related the deſtruction of Jeruſalem, and thereby bore teſtimonie to the accompliſhment of our Lord's predictions concerning it.

Nor can any forget the triumphal arch of Titus, ſtill ſtanding at
Rome, of which we before took notice.

There

(*s*) Quem tamen Joſephi locum immerito Philoſtrato opponi putem. ... Neque
enim Philoſtratus *repudiaſſe coronam* Titum
ait, atque eâ non acceptâ legatos dimiſſiſ-
ſe, quod viro docto interpretes perſuaſere,
ſed hoc tantum, quod eo honore ſe indignum dixerit: juſtitiae Dei vindicatricis
inſtrumentum, cujus nullae fuerint in iſtis
patrandis propriae vires, ſeſe exſtitiſſe ag-
noſcens, &c. *Olear. in loc.*

Ch. III.   *The Testimony of other Writers.*

There (*t*) is also an ancient inscription to the honour of Titus, *who by his Father's directions and counsels had subdued the Jewish nation, and destroyed Jerusalem, which had never been destroyed by any princes, or people before.*

A. D. 76.

Which has occasioned some learned men to say, that even inscriptions are not free from flatterie. But then it must be owned, that (*u*) the genuinnesse and antiquity of this inscription have been called in question. And there are some reasons to doubt, whether this comes from the Senate of Rome itself, as is pretended.

(*t*)   Imp. Tito. Caesari. Divi. Vespasiani. F.
Vespasiano. Aug. Pontifici. Maximo
Trib. Pot. x. Imp. xvii. Cos. viii. P. P.
Principi. suo.   S. P. Q. R.
Quod. Praeceptis. Patris. Consiliisque. et
Auspiciis. Gentem. Judaeorum. Domuit. Et
Urbem. Hierosolymam. Omnibus. Ante. Se
Ducibus. Regibus. Gentibusque. aut. Frustra
Petitam. aut. omnino. Intentatam. Delevit
Ap. Gruter. p. 244.

(*u*) Ubi steterit, ignoratur. Scaliger vult ab Onufrio fictum. *Ap. Gruter. Ib.*

CHAP. IV.

Three Paragraphs in the Works of Josephus, concerning John the Baptist, our Saviour, and James, the Lord's Brother, and observations upon the writings of Josephus.

I. *Of John the Baptist.* II. *Concerning the Lord Jesus Christ.* III. *Concerning James, the Lord's Brother.* IV. *Concluding Observations upon the Writings, and Testimonie of Josephus.*

Of John the Baptist.

I. "ABOUT this time, says (a) Josephus, there happened a
"difference between Aretas King of Petraea, and He-
"rod upon this occasion. Herod the Tetrarch had married the
"daughter of Aretas, and lived a considerable time with her. But
"in a journey he took to Rome, he made a visit to (*) Herod his
"brother, though not by the same mother... Here falling in love
"with Herodias, wife of the same Herod, daughter of their brother
"Aristobulus, and sister of Agrippa the Great, he ventured to make
"to her proposals of marriage. She not disliking them, they agreed
"together at that time, that when he was returned from Rome, she
"should go and live with him. And it was one part of the con-
"tract,

(a) *Antiq. l.* 18. *cap.* v. §. 1.

(*) Our Evangelists call him *Philip.* Matt. xiv. 3. and elsewhere. That difficulty was considered formerly. Josephus and the Evangelists mean the same person: though they call him by different names. *See the Credibility, &c. Part i. B.* 2. *ch.* v. *p.* 884. *&c.*

Ch. IV. Of John the Baptist.

" tract, that Aretas's daughter should be put away... This (b) was
" the begining of the difference, and there being also some disputes
" about the limits of their territories, a war arose between Aretas,
" and Herod. And in a battle fought by them Herod's whole ar-
" mie was defeated."

" But, says (c) Josephus, some of the Jews were of opinion, that
" God had suffered Herod's armie to be destroyed, as a just punish-
" ment upon him, for the death of John, called the Baptist. For He-
" rod had killed him, who was a just man, and had called upon the
" Jews to be baptised, and to practise virtue, exercising both justice
" toward men and piety toward God. For so would baptism be ac-
" ceptable to God, if they made use of it, nor for the expiation of
" their sins, but for the purity of the body, the mind being first pu-
" rified by righteousnesse. And many coming to him, (for they were
" wonderfully taken with his discourses:) Herod was seised with ap-
" prehensions, least by his authority they should be led into sedition
" against him. For they seemed capable of undertaking any thing
" by his direction. Herod therefore thought it better to take him
" off, before any disturbance happened, than to run the risk of a
" change of affairs, and of repenting, when it should be too late to
" remedy disorders. Being taken up upon this suspicion of Herod,
                                                        " and

(b) Ὁ δὲ ἀρχὴν ἔχθρας ταύτην ποιησάμενος, περί τε ὅρων ἐν τῇ γῇ τῇ Γαμαλίτιδι, ἢ δυνάμεως ἑκατέρω συλλεγείσης, εἰς πόλεμον καθίστανται· ἢ μάχης γενομένης, διεφθάρη πᾶς ὁ Ἡρώδε στρατὸς κ. λ. ib. §. 1.

(c) Τισὶ δὲ Ἰουδαίων ἐδόκει, ὀλωλέναι τὸν Ἡρώδε στρατὸν ὑπὸ τοῦ Θεοῦ, ἢ μάλα δικαίως τιννυμένω κατὰ ποινὴν Ἰωάννε τοῦ ἐπικαλεμένε βαπτιστ. Κτείνει γὰρ τοῦτον Ἡρώδης, ἀγαθὸν ἄνδρα, ἢ τὸς Ἰεδαίες ελεύοντα, ἀρετὴν ἐπασκοῦντας, ἢ τῇ πρὸς ἀλλήλες δικαιοσύνῃ ἢ πρὸς τὸν Θεὸν εὐσεβείᾳ χρωμένες, βαπτισμῷ συνιέναι· ἕτω γὰρ τὴν βάπτισιν ἀποδεκτὴν αὐτῷ φανεῖσθαι, μὴ ἐπί τινων ἁμαρτάδων παραιτήσει χρωμένων, ἀλλ' ἐφ' ἁγνείᾳ τοῦ σώματος, ἅτε δὴ ἢ τῆς ψυ-

χῆς δικαιοσύνῃ προεκκεκαθαρμένης. Καὶ τῶν ἄλλων συρρεζομένων· ἢ γὰρ ἤρθησαν ἐπὶ πλεῖσον τῇ ἀκροάσει τῶν λόγων δείσας Ἡρώδης τὸ ἐπὶ τοσόνδε πιθανὸν αὐτῷ τοῖς ἀνθρώποις μὴ ἐπὶ ἀποστάσει τινὶ φέρει, πάντα γὰρ ἐώκεσαν συμβουλῇ τῇ ἐκείνου πράξοντες. πολὺ κρεῖττον ἡγεῖται, πρίν τι νεώτερον ἐξ αὐτοῦ γενέσθαι, προλαβὼν διαιρεῖν, ἢ μεταβολῆς γενομένης, εἰς τὰ πράγματα ἐμπεσὼν μετανοεῖν. Καὶ ὁ μὲν ὑποψίᾳ τῇ Ἡρώδε δέσμιος εἰς τὸν Μακαιροῦντα πεμφθεὶς, τὸ προειρημένον φρέριον, ταύτῃ κτίννυται. Τοῖς δὲ Ἰουδαίοις δόξαν, ἐπὶ τιμωρίᾳ τῇ ἐκείνου τὸν ὄλεθρον ἐπὶ τῷ στρατεύματι γενέσθαι, τοῦ Θεοῦ κακῶς Ἡρώδῃ θέλοντος. Ib. §. 2.

A. D. 76.

"and being sent bound to the castle of Machaerus just mentioned, he was slain there. The Jews were of opinion, that the destruction of Herod's armie was a punishment upon him for that action, God being displeased with him."

The genuinness of this passage is generally admitted by learned men: though *(d)* Blondell hesitated about it. Tanaquil Faber *(e)* received it very readily.

The genuinness of this paragraph may be argued in the following manner.

It is quoted, or referred to, by Origen in his books against Celsus. " Besides *(f)* says that ancient writer, I would have Celsus, who personates a Jew, who after a sort admits John the Baptist, and that he baptized Jesus, to consider, that an author, who wrote not long after the time of John and Jesus, says, that John was a Baptist, and that he baptised for the remission of sins. For in the eighteenth book of his Jewish Antiquities Josephus bears witnesse to John, that he was a Baptist, and promised purification to those who were baptised."

Here it may be objected, that Origen supposes Josephus to say, that *John promised purification,* or forgivenesse of sins, to those who were baptized: whereas Josephus says of John, that he *taught the people to make use of baptism, not for the expiation of their sins, but for the purity of the body.*

But I do not think that a sufficient reason, why we should hesitate to allow, that Origen refers to the passage, which we now have in Josephus. Certainly, Origen did not design to say, or intimate, that John promised to men the forgivenesse of their sins, barely up-on

---

(d) *Des Sibylles. l.* 1. *ch.* vii. *p.* 28. 29.
(e) *Fab. ap. Haverc.* p. 269. 270.
(f) Ἐβυλόμην δ᾽ ἂν Κέλσῳ, προσωποιή-σαντι τὸν Ἰουδαῖον παραδεξάμενον πῶς Ἰωάννην ὡς βαπτιστὴν, βαπτίζοντα τὸν Ἰησοῦν, εἰπεῖν· ὅτι τὲ Ἰωάννην γεγονέναι βαπτιστὴν, εἰς ἄφεσιν ἁμαρτημάτων βαπτίζοντα, ἀνέγραψέ τις τῶν

μετ᾽ ὀ πολὺ τῦ Ἰωάννη κὴ τῦ Ἰησῦ γεγενημένων. Εν γὰρ τῷ ὀκτωκαιδεκάτῳ τῆς Ἰουδαϊκῆς ἀρχαιολογίας ὁ Ἰώσηπος μαρτυρεῖ τῷ Ἰωάννῃ ὡς βαπτιστῇ γεγενομένῳ, κὴ καθάρσιον τοῖς βαπτισαμένοις ἐπαγγελλομένῳ. *Contr. Cels. l.* 1. §. 47. *p.* 35.

Ch. IV. *Of John the Baptist.*

on their being baptized: but only upon the condition that they repented, or, as the phrase is in the Gospels, that *they brought forth fruits meet for repentance:* or, as in Josephus, *the mind being first purified by righteousnesse.* I therefore proceed.

This passage of Josephus is distinctly, and largely quoted by (g) Eusebius in his Ecclesiastical Historie.

Jerome (h) also must be allowed to refer to the same in his book of Illustrious Men: though he does it very inaccuratly.

This passage was read in Josephus by (i) Photius, as is apparent.

I do not think it needfull for me to refer to any more ancient authors. But I shall consider some difficulties.

Obj. 1. In the first place it has been said, that this passage interrupts the course of the narration.

In answer to which I must say, that I do not perceive it. The connexion is very good, in my opinion.

Obj. 2. Secondly, it is objected, that in the preceding section *Machaerus* is spoken of as subject to Aretas. Therefore John the Baptist could not be sent prisoner thither by Herod the Tetrarch.

To which I answer. It is there said to be *subject to Aretas, father of Herod's wife.* τότε πατρὶ αὐτῆς ὑποτελῆ. But it is also there said, *to be in the borders of the government of Aretas and Herod:* μεθόριον δὲ ἔςι τῆς τε Ἀρέτα καὶ Ἡρώδε ἀρχῆς.

The historie in that very section does not lead us to think, that Machaerus was in the possession of Aretas, but of Herod. It is thus. "Herod's wife, daughter of Aretas, having discovered the agree-

---

(g) *H. E. l.* 1. *cap. xi.*
(h) Hic in decimo octavo Antiquitatum libro manifestissime confitetur, propter magnitudinem signorum Christum a Pharisaeis interfectum: et Johannem Baptistam vere prophetam fuisse. *De V. I. cap. xiii.*
(i) *Cod.* 238. *p.* 972.

"ment

"ment he had made with Herodias, to come and live with him, and having difcovered it before he had notice of her knowledge of the defign: fhe defired him to fend her to Machaerus, a place in the borders of the dominions of Aretas and Herod: without inform-ing him of her intentions. Accordingly Herod fent her thither, as thinking his wife had not perceived any thing of the affair."

By that means fhe got to her father. But hence, I think, it may be collected, that Machaerus was not then a part of her father's dominions. For, if it had, her requeft to be fent thither, would have occafioned fufpicions in Herod's mind. Moreover it may be argued from many things in Jofephus, that Machaerus was now in the poffeffion of Herod the Tetrarch. It belonged to his father Herod the Great, who had both adorned it, and fortified it. And it was in the hands of the Jewifh people during the time of the war, and was *(k)* one of the laft places, that were taken by the Romans after the fiege of Jerufalem was over.

Obj. 3. According to our Evangelifts, the daughter of Herodias obtained the promife of John the Baptift's head at the time of a public entertainment. And it was delivered to her prefently. But how could that be done, if John was imprifoned at Machaerus, at a great diftance from Herod's court?

To which I anfwer, *firft,* that Herod the Tetrarch may have kept his birth-day, and made that entertainment at *Machaerus.* For his father, Herod the Great, had built a palace there, with large and beautifull *(l)* apartments. Says Tillemont: "We *(m)* learn from Jofephus, that he was beheaded, at Machaerus, where it is eafily fuppofed, that Herod made his feaft. [*Mald. in Matt. p.* 304. *a.*] For it was a palace, as well as a citadel." *Secondly,* fuppofing the entertainment to have been made at the capital city of Galilee, the promife

---

(k) Vid. De B. J. l. 7. *cap. vi.*
(l) Μέσον δὲ τᾶ περιβόλε βασίλειον ᾠκοδό-μήσατο, μεγέθει τε ᾗ κάλλει τῶν οἰκήσεων ϖο-

λυτελές. κ. λ. *De B. J. l.* 7. *c. vi.* §. 2.
(m) S. Jean Battifte, art. viii. p. 102. *Mem. Ec. T. i.*

Ch. IV.   *Of John the Baptist.*

promise might be made at the time of the entertainment: but the execution might be deferred till the next day, or till several days after.

Obj. 4. Still it may be said, that this paragraph contradicts our Evangelists. For, according to them, it was at the solicitation of Herodias, and her daughter, that John was beheaded. But here it is said, that Herod put John to death, because he feared, he might be the cause of a sedition.

But there is no inconsistence in these things. For Herod might, as is said in this paragraph, have apprehensions from John's popularity, and be disposed, upon that account, to take him off. Lesser differences there may be in several historians, who write of the same matter with different views. And some circumstances may be mentioned by one writer, which are omitted by others.

I shall give an instance from the writings of the New Testament. Acts ix. 22 .. 25. *But Saul encreased the more in strength, and confounded the Jews which dwelt at Damascus, proving, that this is very Christ. And after that many days were fulfilled, the Jews took counsel to kill him. But their lying in wait was known to Saul. And they watched the gates day and night to kill him. Then the disciples took him by night, and let him down by the wall in a basket.* So says St. Luke. Let us now observe St. Paul himself. 2 Cor. xi. 31 . . . 33. *The God and Father of our Lord Jesus Christ, who is blessed for evermore, knoweth that I lye not. In Damascus the Governour under Aretas the King, guarded the city of the Damascenes, desirous to apprehend me. And through a window in a basket was I let down by the wall, and escaped him.* St. Luke and St. Paul write of the same thing, as is apparent, and is allowed by all Commentators and Ecclesiastical Historians. Nevertheless here is a very considerable difference of circumstances. St. Paul says nothing of *the Jews*, and St. Luke says nothing of *the Governour of Damascus*. But we can conclude from St. Paul, that the Jews had engaged the Governour in their interest, who with his sol-

U 2   diers

diers kept strict guard at all the gates of the city. But there was a window, or opening, in some part of the wall, to which his friends had accesse: and through that they let him down by the side of the wall, in a basket, held by a rope, and he escaped. The danger was very pressing. And the Apostle was much affected with it.

So far from contradicting the Evangelists, this account in the paragraph greatly confirms them. In the preceding paragraph Josephus assures us of the unlawfull contract made by Herod, that Herodias should leave her first husband, and come and live with him. In this paragraph he gives an account of John's doctrine very agreeable to that in the Gospels: That he earnestly recommended the practise of righteousnesse toward men, and piety toward God: that he taught men, not to relye on baptism, or any other external rites, for the forgivenesse of their sins, unless their minds were also purified by righteousnesse. And he assures us, that John was in great esteem with the Jewish people. The same is also said by our Evangelists, who tell us, that *all men held John for a Prophet*. He likewise says, that John, called the Baptist, was imprisoned by Herod, and afterwards put to death by his order.

We may be the more induced to admit the genuinnesse of this paragraph, because there is nothing in it out of character. Josephus did not receive our Jesus as the Christ. Nor is there here any mention made of that part of John's character: that he was the forerunner of the Christ, or referred men to him.

There may have been many Jews, who had a great regard for John, and yet did not believe in Jesus as the Christ. St. Paul met with twelve Jews of that sort at Ephesus, about the year of our Lord 53. as appears from a historie at the begining of Acts xix. *He said unto them: Have ye received the Holy Ghost, since ye believed? They said unto him: We have not so much as heard, whether there be any Holy Ghost. And he said unto them: Unto what then were ye baptised? And they said: unto John's baptism. Then said Paul: John verily baptised with the baptism of repentance, saying unto the people, that*

Ch. IV.   *Of John the Baptist.*   149
that they should believe on him, which should come after him, that is, on *Christ Jesus*. These men had received John's baptism, as the baptism of repentance, but they had not attended to that other part of his preaching, that *they should believe on him who came after him*, till they were reminded of it by St. Paul. And then they were presently satisfied. *When they heard this, they were baptised in the name of the Lord Jesus.* And what follows.

A. D. 76.

Possibly those men, or most of them, had seen and heard John, and been baptised by him. And left Judea, before Jesus had begun his public ministrie. And being at a distance from the land of Judea, had never had any distinct account of the transactions there. But now, being informed of them, and being open to conviction, they became disciples of Jesus, and believed in him, as the Christ.

But many other Jews, not so well disposed, might stand out. They might retain a great respect for John, as we suppose Josephus to have done, as an holy man, of an austere character, who had recommended the practise of virtue, and had been put to death by the Tetrarch of Galilee, without believing in Jesus as the Christ.

Origen was well acquainted with the Jewish sentiments, having often conversed with their learned men. And in his answer to Celsus he puts him in mind, " that (*n*) the Jews always make a difference between John and Jesus, and between the death of each of them."

Indeed both were for a while in great repute with the Jewish people. But Jesus had greatly disappointed them, in not assuming the character of a temporal prince, as they expected the Messiah should do. And John was put to death by a prince, not much beloved. But Jesus was crucified at the importunate demand of the Jewish rulers and people in general.

Jo-

(*n*) . . . ἀναγκαῖον αὐτῷ παραστῆσαι, ὅτι ᾗ τοῦτο οὐκ εἰκέως τῷ Ἰουδαϊκῷ πρεσβεύω περιέθηκεν. 'Οὐδὲ γὰρ συνάπτουσι τὸν Ἰωάννην οἱ Ἰουδαῖοι τῷ Ἰησοῦ, ᾗ τὴν Ἰωάννου τῇ τοῦ Ἰησοῦ κολάσει. *Contr. Celf. l. i. cap.* 48. *p.* 38.

Josippon, in the ninth or tenth centurie, though he says nothing of *Jesus Christ*, or *James, the Lord's Brother*, mentions the death of *John the Baptist*, and more agreeably to the Evangelists, than this passage of Josephus, which we are considering. He represents the Tetrarch Herod as a very wicked prince. He says, " that (*o*) he " took to himself to be his own wife, the wife of his brother Phi- " lip, though his brother was still living, and she had children by " him. He killed many wise men in Israel. And he killed that " great priest John, the Baptizer, because he had said to him, It is " unlawfull for thee to have thy brother's wife." Many Jews, as it seems, have respected John the Baptist, as an eminently good man, without allowing him to have any connexions with Jesus Christ.

Concerning Jesus Christ.

II. In the same eighteenth book of Josephus's Jewish Antiquities, but in a chapter, preceding that, in which is the account of John the Baptist, just considered, is this paragraph.

" At (*p*) that time lived Jesus, a wise man, if he may be called " a man. For he performed many wonderfull works. He was a " teacher of such men as received the truth with pleasure. He drew " over to him many Jews, and Gentiles. This was the Christ. And " when Pilate, at the instigation of the chief men among us, had con- " demned

---

(*o*) Ipse accepit uxorem Philippi fratris sui adhuc viventis in uxorem, licet illa haberet filios ex fratre ejus: eam, inquam, accepit sibi in uxorem. Occidit autem multos sapientes Israel. Occidit etiam Jochanan Sacerdotem magnum ob id quod dixerat ei: Non licet tibi accipere uxorem fratris tui Philippi in uxorem. Occidit ergo Jochananem Baptistam. *Josipp. l.* 6. *cap.* 63. *p.* 274.

(*p*) Γίνεται δὲ κατὰ τῦτον τὸν χρόνον Ἰησῦς, σοφὸς ἀνὴρ, εἴγε ἄνδρα αὐτὸν λέγειν χρή. Ἦν γὰρ παραδόξων ἔργων ποιητὴς, διδάσκαλος ἀνθρώπων τῶν ἡδονῇ τ'ἀληθῆ δεχομένων. Καὶ πολλὰς μὲν Ἰυδαίες, πολλὰς δὲ κ̀ τῶ Ἑλληνικῶ ἐπηγάγετο. Ὁ Χριστὸς ἕτος ἦν. Καὶ αὐτὸν ἐνδείξει τῶν πρώτων ἀνδρῶν παρ' ἡμῖν, σαυρῷ ἐπιτετιμηκότος Πιλάτε, ἐκ ἐπαύσαιτο ὅγε πρῶτον αὐτὸν ἀγαπήσαντες. Ἐφάνη γὰρ αὐτοῖς τρίτην ἔχων ἡμέραν πάλιν ζῶν, τῶν θείων προφητῶν ταῦτά τε κ̀ ἄλλα μυρία θαυμάσια περὶ αὐτῦ εἰρηκότων. Εἰς ἔτι νῦν τῶν Χριστιανῶν ἀπὸ τῦδ'ε ὠνομασμένων οὐκ ἐπέλιπε τὸ φῦλον. *Antiq. Jud. l.* 18. *cap. iii.* §. 3.

Ch. IV. *Of Jesus Christ.*

"demned him to the crosse; they who before had conceived an affection for him, did not cease to adhere to him. For on the third day he appeared to them alive again, the divine prophets having foretold these and many other wonderfull things concerning him. And the sect of the Christians, so called from him, subsists to this time."

This passage is received by *(r)* many learned men, as genuine. By others *(s)* it is rejected, as an interpolation. It is allowed on all hands, that it is in all the copies of Josephus's Works, now exstant, both printed and manuscript. Nevertheless it may be for several reasons called in question. They are such as these.

1. This paragraph is not quoted, nor referred to by any Christian writers, before Eusebius, who flourished at the begining of the fourth centurie and afterwards.

If it had been originally in the works of Josephus, it would have been highly proper to produce it in their disputes with Jews and Gentils. But it is never quoted by *Justin Martyr*, or *Clement of Alexandria*, nor by *Tertullian*, or *Origen*, men of great learning, and well acquainted with the works of Josephus. It was certainly very proper to urge it against the Jews. It might also have been fitly alleged against Gentils. A testimonie so favorable to Jesus in the works of Josephus, who lived so soon after the time of our Saviour, who was so well acquainted with the transactions of his own countrey, who had received so many favours from Vespasian and Titus, could not be overlooked, or neglected by any Christian Apologist.

If

(r) Cav. H. L. in Josepho. Huet. Dem. Ev. Prop. iii. p. 32. &c. Fab. Bib. Gr. l. 4. cap. vi. Tom. 3. Whiston in his first dissertation. Spanhem. Opp. T. i. p. 531. Tillem. Ruine des Juifs, art. 81. and note al. H. E. Tom. i.

(s) J. Ittigii Prolegom. ap. Havercamp: p. 89. Blondel des Sibylles. p. 18. Tan. Faber. ap. Havercamp. p. 267. &c. Cleric. H. E. An. 25. n. iv. et Ars Crit. P. 3. cap. xiv.

If this passage had related only to some one of the first followers of Jesus, the omission had not been so remarkable. But it relates to Jesus himself. It declares his proper character, his miracles, his crucifixion, and resurrection, and that all this was agreeable to the predictions of the Prophets.

This passage is not only not quoted by *Origen*: but we can perceive, that he had it not. For in the words next following the notice taken of John the Baptist, as mentioned by Josephus, and before quoted by us, he adds: "The (*t*) same writer, though he did not
"believe Jesus to be the Christ, inquiring into the cause of the over-
"throw of Jerusalem, and the demolition of the temple, when he
"ought to have said, that their attempt upon Jesus was the cause of
"the ruin of that people, forasmuch as they had put to death the
"Christ before prophesied of: he, as it were unwillingly, and not
"erring far from the truth says: These things befell the Jews in
"vindication of James called the Just, who was the brother of Jesus
"called the Christ: forasmuch as they killed him who was a most
"righteous man. That James is the same, whom Paul, that genuine
"disciple of Jesus, says, he had seen, and calls the Lord's brother,
"[Gal. i. 19.] not so much for the sake of consanguinity, as their
"common education, and agreement in manners and doctrine. If
"(*u*) therefore he says, the destruction of Jerusalem had befallen the
"Jews for the sake of James; with how much more reason might
"he have said, that this had happened for the sake of Jesus, who
"was the Christ, to whose divinity so many churches bear witnesse:
"who being now recovered from the pollutions of vice, have given
"up themselves to the Creator, and endeavour to please him in all
"things."

Afterwards,

---

(1). Ὁ δ' αὐτὸς, καίτοιγε ἀπιςῶν τῷ Ἰησῦ ὡς Χριςῷ, ζητῶν τὴν αἰτίαν τῆς τῶν Ἱεροσολύμων πτώσεως, ᾗ τῆς τῦ ναῦ καθαιρέσεως δέον αὐτὸν εἰπεῖν, ὅτι ἡ τῦ Ἰησῦ ἐπιβυλὴ τέτων αἰτία γέγονε τῷ λαῷ, ἐπεὶ ἀπέκτειναν τὸν προφητευ- όμενον Χριςόν. κ. λ. *Contr. Cels. l.* 1. *c.* 47. p. 35.

(u) Εἴπερ ἔν διὰ Ἰάκωβον συμβεβηκέναι λέγει τοῖς Ἰεδαίοις τὰ κατὰ τὴν ἐρήμωσιν τῆς Ἱερυσαλήμ, κ. λ. *ib.*

Afterwards, in his second book against Celsus, he argues our Saviour's knowledge of futurities from his predictions concerning the destruction of Jerusalem, which had not been effected till the times of Vespasian and Titus. " Which (x) as Josephus writes, happen-
" ed upon account of James the Just, the brother of Jesus called
" the Christ: but in truth upon account of Jesus the Christ, the
" Son of God."

Origen speaks again to the like purpose in his commentarie upon St. Matthew, and says, " that *(y)* this James, the same that is men-
" tioned by Paul in his epistle to the Galatians [i. 19.] was so re-
" spected by the people for his righteousnesse, that Flavius Josephus,
" who wrote the Jewish Antiquities in twenty books, being desirous
" to assign the cause, why that people suffered such things, so that
" even their temple was demolished to the foundations, says, that
" those things had happened, because of the anger of God against
" them for what they had done to James the brother of Jesus cal-
" led the Christ. And it is wonderfull, that he who did not receive
" our Jesus as the Christ, should ascribe such righteousnesse to
" James. He says, that the people also were of opinion, that they
" suffered these things upon account of James."

After Origen, the same saying of Josephus concerning James is also alleged by (z) Eusebius, and (a) Jerome: but without saying, any more than Origen, what work of Josephus, or what book of his works, it was in.

There is not now any thing of that kind in any of his works. Nor is it easily conceivable, that *(b)* there ever was. But what I now

---

(x) ... ὡς μὲν Ἰώσηπος γράφει, διὰ Ἰάκωβον τὸν δίκαιον, τὸν ἀδελφὸν Ἰησοῦ τοῦ λεγομένου Χριστοῦ· ὡς δὲ ἡ ἀλήθεια παρίστησι, διὰ Ἰησοῦν τὸν Χριστὸν τὸν υἱὸν τοῦ Θεοῦ. *Contr. Cels.* l. 2. §. 13 p. 69.

(y) *Comm. in Matt. Tom. x.* §. 17. p. 463. T. 3. *Bened. T. i. p.* 223. *Huet.*

(z) *H. E. l.* 2. *cap.* xxiii. *p.* 65.

(a) Tradit idem Josephus, tantae eum sanctitatis fuisse, et celebritatis in populo, ut propter ejus necem creditum sit, subversam esse Hierosolymam. *De V. I. cap.* 2. *vid. et cap.* 13.

(b) Quod vero attinet ad ista, ταῦτα συμ-

A. D. 76.

now allege these passages of Origen for, is to shew, that it may be hence evidently and certainly concluded, that Origen never read in Josephus that testimonie to Jesus, which we now have in his works.

I have above mentioned no other Latin author, but *Tertullian*, to *(c)* whom Josephus was well known. But I might have also insisted upon the silence of the other Latin Apologists for Christianity, of the first three centuries, as *Minucius Felix, Cyprian, Arnobius*, and *Lactantius*. To whom so extraordinarie a testimonie to our Saviour, in so celebrated a Jewish writer, would not have been unknown, if it had been in him.

Eusebius, then, who flourished about the year of Christ 315. and afterwards, is the first Christian writer, in whom this paragraph is found. And by him *(d)* it is twice quoted at large. After him, as is well known, it is quoted by *(e) Jerome, (f) Sozomen*, and many other following writers.

But it is observable, that this paragraph is never quoted by *Chrysostom:* Whom I suspect to have had but little regard for Eusebius of Cesarea. He several times refers to Josephus, as a proper writer, from whom men might learn what miseries the Jewish people had undergone in their war with the Romans, *be (g) not being a believer, but a Jew, and zealous for the Jewish rites even after the rise of Christianity.*

συμβιζνειν Ιεδαιοις κατα εκδικησιν Ισκαζα τε διχεις. κ. λ. quae tanquam a Josepho probata in Antiquitatum libris, affert Origines, .. et ex eo, ut puto, Eusebius, aliique, verisimile est, ea referri debere μνημονιω αμαρτηματι Origenis . . . Certe nullibi, quod sciam, haberi potuerunt in Antiquitatibus, ut quae non agant de Hierosolymorum excidio. *Hudson. annot. ad Jos. Antiq. l. 20. cap. ix.* §. 1. *p.* 976. *ed. Hav. Vid. et Cleric. Ars Crit. P.* 3. *cap.* xiv. §. 8. 9. 10.

(c) .. et qui istos aut probat aut revin-

cit Judaeus Josephus, antiquitatum Judaicarum vernaculus vindex. *Tert. Ap. c.* 19. *p.* 19.

(d) H. E. l. 1. *cap. xi. Dem. Ev. l.* 3. *p.* 124.

(e) De V. I. cap. 13.

(f) Soz. l. 1. *cap. i. p.* 399.

(g) .. κ γαρ Ιεδαιος ην, κ σφοδρα Ιεδαιος, κ ζηλωτης, κ των μετα την Χριστ παρεσιαν. *In Matt. hom.* 76. *al.* 77. *T.* 7. *p.* 732. *Vid. et in Matt. hom.* 75. *al.* 76. *p.* 727. *et in Jo. hom.* 64. *al.* 65. *T.* 8. *p.* 390.

Ch. IV.   *Of Jesus Christ.*   155

stianity. He refers likewise *(h)* to what Josephus says of John the Baptist: though inaccuratly, as must be acknowledged. But he never takes any notice of this testimonie to JESUS. Which, surely, he would not have omitted, in his many arguments with the Jews, if he had been acquainted with it, and had supposed it to be genuine.

Some have supposed, that this testimonie of Josephus was alleged by *Macarius* in the time of Diocletian. But Fabricius *(i)* has honestly, and judiciously observed, that there is no reason to take that passage of *Macarius* for genuine.

2. This paragraph was wanting in the copies of Josephus, which were seen by *Photius* in the ninth centurie.

I make a distinct article of this writer, because he read, and revised the works of Josephus, as a critic. He has in his Bibliothèque *(k)* no less than three articles concerning Josephus, but takes no notice of this passage. Whence it may be concluded, that it was wanting in his copies, or that he did not think it genuine. But the former is the more likely. He refers to the passage concerning John the Baptist in this manner. " This *(l)* Herod, Tetrarch of Galilee and " Peroea, son of Herod the Great, is he who put to death the great " John, the fore-runner, because, as Josephus says, he was afraid, he

X 2   " would

(*h*) *In Jo. hom.* 12. *al.* 13. *T.* 8. *p.* 73. *A.*

(*i*) Hoc Josephi loco non utuntur Justinus, Tertullianus, Chrysostomus, alique complures, quando contra Judaos disputant. Non produxit Origenes, alia Josephi laudans in libris contra Celsum. Nec Photius quidem tanto junior meminit, in cujus Bibl. Antiquitates Josephi bis recensentur. cod. 76. et 238. Ante Eusebium tamen ... allegaverit illum Macarius quidam cubiculi imperatorii praefectus, siquidem genuinus sit hujus ad Diocletianum sermo, qui refertur in Actis Sanctorum Macarii a Cl. viro W. E. Tenselio, primum in Dialogis menstruis Germanice editis, A. 1697. p. 556. Sed merito existimandum, haec Acta martyriis Macariani, si non longe post Diocletianum plane conficta, saltem interpolata, atque locum Josephi insertum a recentiore manu esse. *Fabr. Bib. Gr. T.* 3. *p.* 237.

(*k*) *Cod.* 48. 76. *et* 238.

(*l*) *Cod.* 238. *p.* 973.

"would ſtirr up the people to rebellion. For all men paid great "regard to John upon account of his tranſcendent virtue. In his "time alſo our Saviour ſuffered." How fair an occaſion had Photius here to refer alſo to the teſtimonie given to Jeſus, which we now have, if he had ſeen it? Upon this article of Photius the very learned *Ittigius* in his Prolegomena to Joſephus (*m*) has juſt remarks, invincibly aſſerting the abſolute ſilence of this great critic concerning this paragraph of Joſephus.

And very obſervable is what Photius ſays in his article of Juſtus of Tiberias. "This (*n*) writer, laboring under the common preju- "dice of the Jews, and being himſelf a Jew, makes not any the "leſt mention of the coming of Chriſt, or the things concerning "him, or the miracles done by him." This is very remarkable. This ſilence of *Juſtus* concerning our Saviour was not peculiar to him, but was common to other Jewiſh writers with him, very probably intending Joſephus. If Joſephus had been an exception, he would not have been omitted, but would have been expreſsly mentioned.

3. This paragraph concerning Jeſus interrupts the courſe of the narration. And therefore is not genuine, but is an interpolation.

In the preceding paragraph Joſephus gives an account of an attempt of Pilate to bring water from a diſtant place to Jeruſalem with the ſacred money: Which occaſioned a diſturbance, in which many Jews were killed, and many others were wounded.

The paragraph next following this, about which we are now ſpeaking, begins thus. "And (*o*) about the ſame time another ſad calamity gave the Jews great uneaſineſſe." That calamity was no

leſs

(*m*) *Ap. Havercamp. p.* 89.

(*n*) ὡς δὲ τὰ Ιυδαίων νοσῶν, Ιυδαῖος τε κ̄ ἀυτὸς ὑπάρχων τὸ γένος, τῆς Χριςῦ παρουσίας, κ̄ τῶν περὶ αὐτὸν τελεσθέντων, κ̄ τῶν ὑπ' ἀυ- τῦ τερετυργηθέντων, ὐδενὸς ὅλως μνήμην ἐποιήσατο. *Cod.* 33. *p.* 20.

(*o*) Καὶ ὑπὸ τὸς ἀυτὸς χρόνος ἕτερόν τι δ εινον ἐθορύβει τὸς Ιυδαίυς. *L.* 18. *cap.* 3. §. 4.

Ch. IV.   Of Jesus Christ.

less than banishing the Jews from Rome by order of the Emperour Tiberius: "occasioned *(p)* as he says, by the misconduct of some Jews in that city."

This paragraph therefore was not originally in Josephus. It does not come from him. But it is an interpolation inserted by some body afterwards. This argument must be of great weight with all, who are well acquainted with the writings of Josephus, who is a cool and sedate writer, very exact in connecting his narrations, and never failing to make transitions, where they are proper, or needfull.

I believe, it is not easie to instance in another writer, who is so exact in all his pauses and transitions, or so punctual in the notice he gives, when he has done with one thing, and goes on to another. That must make this argument the stronger.

Tillemont was very sensible of this difficulty, though he thinks, that the writers, who maintain the genuinnesse of this passage, have made good their point. "It *(q)* must be owned, however, says he,
" that there is one thing embarrassing in this passage, which is, that
" it interrups the course of the narration in Josephus. For that
" which immediatly follows begins in these terms. *About the same*
" *time there happened another misfortune, which disturbed the Jews.*
" For those words, *another misfortune*, have no connexion with what
" was just said of Jesus Christ: which is not mentioned as an un-
" happinesse. And on the contrarie, it has a very natural reference
" to what precedes in that place: which is a sedition, in which ma-
" ny Jews were killed, or wounded. Certainly it is not so easie to
" answer to this difficulty, as to the others. I wish, that Mr. *Huet*,
" and Mr. *Roie* had stated this objection, and given satisfaction upon
" it. As for my-self, I know not what to say to it: but that Josephus
" himself might insert this passage after his work was finished. And
" he

A. D. 76.

(*p*) Καὶ εἰ μὲν διὰ κακίαν τεσσάρων ἀνδρῶν ἐλαύνοντο τῆς πόλεως. §. 5. fin.

(*q*) *Ruine des Juifs.* note xl. *Hist. des Emp. Tom.* i.

A. D. 76.

"he did not then think of a more proper place for it, than this, "where he passed from what happened in Judea under Pilate to "somewhat that was done at the same time at Rome. And he for-"got to alter the transition, which he had made at first."

Undoubtedly, the difficulty presses very hard, which will allow of no better solution.

4. Let us now observe the paragraph itself, and consider, whether it be suitable, or unsuitable, to the general character of Josephus.

At the same time lived Jesus, a wise man, if he may be called a man. For he performed many wonderfull works.

But, why (r) should Josephus scruple to call Jesus *a man?* Were not Moses, Elijah, Elisha, and other prophets, men? The wonderfull works, done by them, were not done by their own power, but by the power of God, bearing testimonie to their commission, or supporting them in the execution of it. Moreover Moses himself, who (s) is so highly extolled and magnified by Josephus, is (t) often called by him a man. Why then should he scruple to say the same of Jesus? However, it should be owned, that he has this expression concerning Moses: "So (u) that his legislation, which was from "God, made this man to be thought superior to his own nature."

He

(r) Sed quo judicio scriptum est quod sequitur: ἤγε ἄνδρα αὐτὸν λέγειν χρή. Quaenam, quaeso, ratio est? Quia, inquit, παραδόξων ἔργων ποιητής ᾖν. Itaque adeo, quando ita vult, dubitabitur in posterum a nobis, dii an homines appellandi sint Moses, Elias, Elisaeus? Nam et illi fuerunt παραδόξων ἔργων ποιηταί. Deinde, cum ait ἤγε ἄνδρα αὐτὸν λέγειν χρή, quid, quaeso, aliud innuere vult, nisi Jesum Dominum esse Deum? In quo graviter errat hic pius impostor. Judaei enim ne suspicabantur quidem, Messiam seu Christum fore Deum, sed praestantissimum aliquem principem ex semine Davidis. Tan. Fab. ap. Havercamp. Joseph. p. 269.

(s) *Antiq. l. 3. cap. xv. l. 4. cap. viii. et alibi.*

(t) Θαυμαστὸς δὲ τῆς ἀρετῆς ὁ ἀνὴρ. κ. λ. *Ant. l. 3. c. xv. §. 3.*

(u) "Οὕτως ἡ νομοθεσία τῦ Θεῦ δοκῦσα τὸν ἄνδρα πεποίηκε τῆς αὐτῦ φύσεως κρείττονα νομίζεσθαι. *Ibid.*

Ch. IV. *Of Jesus Christ.*

He was a teacher of such men, as received the truth with pleasure. Very honorable to Jesus, and his followers! But would Josephus say this of them? And would he call the Christian Religion *the truth?*

He drew over to him many Jews and Gentils. That is not true of the Lord Jesus, if intended of his own personal preaching, before his crucifixion. It was done indeed afterwards. But this manner of speaking is more suitable to a writer of the second, or third centurie, than to Josephus.

This was the Christ. Jerome in his article of Josephus, in his book of Illustrious Men, quoting this passage, puts it thus: *And (x) he was believed to be the Christ.* Which is a qualifying expression, for which there is no ground. Nor (y) did Sophronius, Jerome's Greek interpreter, follow that translation, but puts it, as it is in Eusebius, and other Greek (z) writers. *This was the Christ.* But it cannot be supposed, that Josephus either thought, or said, that Jesus was the Christ.

It follows: *And when Pilate at the instigation of the chief men among us had condemned him to the crosse: they who before had conceived an affection for him, did not cease to adhere to him. For on the third day he appeared to them alive again, the divine prophets having foretold these and many other wonderfull things concerning him.*

All must be sensible, that this could not be said by any man, but a professed Christian. Which Josephus was not. Therefore he could not write this.

And the sect of the Christians, so called from him, subsists to this day.

Which Mr. *Whiston* translates in this manner. *And the tribe of Christians, so named from him, are not extinct at this day.* But Mr. W... who thinks this passage to be Josephus's, should not have rendred

---

(*x*) et credebatur esse Christus. (*z*) See particularly Sozomen, *l.* 1. *cap.*
(*y*) Ὁ Χριϛὸς ὅτος ἦν. i. *p.* 399.

A. D. 76.

dred φυλον *tribe:* becaufe φυλη is the word always ufed by Jofephus for *tribe.* And φυλον, which we have here, always fignifies *nation* (a) in Jofephus. Nor were the Chriftians a *nation,* or political fociety in the firft three centuries.

Here it is put for *feɛt.* It cannot fignify any thing elfe in this place. Jefus is called a *wife man,* and is faid to have been *a teacher of fuch as received the truth with pleafure.* And though he had been crucified, *they who had before conceived an affection for him, did not ceafe to adhere to him, becaufe he appeared to them alive again.*

Here the word denotes *feɛt.* But αἱρεσις, *herefie,* is the word generally ufed by Jofephus, in fpeaking (b) of the Pharifees, Sadducees, and Effens, the three prevailing fects, or different ways of philofophizing among the Jews.

The phrafe (c) χριϛιανῶν φῦλον, here ufed, refembles the phrafe χριϛιανῶν ἔθνος, which was in ufe, in the time of Eufebius, at the begining of the fourth centurie, and denotes *the feɛt of the Chriftians.*

Moreover, the expreffion, *fubfifts to this time,* or, *is not extinɛt at this day,* imports a confiderable fpace of time, fince the crucifixion of Jefus. And does very reafonably lead us to think, that the compofer of this paragraph lived later than Jofephus.

Thefe confiderations, as feems to me, are fufficient to determine the point in queftion, and to fatisfy all men, that Jofephus was not the author of this paragraph. However, I fhall add one confideration more.

5. If Jofephus were the author of this paragraph, it would be reafonable

---

(a) ... ἔσω κ᾽ Πέρθοι, τὸ πολεμικώτατον φῦλον. De B. J. l. 2. c. 16. §. 4. p. 189. Hav. Πᾶν ὑμῶν τὸ φῦλον. Ib. p. 191. *et paffim.*

(b) *Vid. De. B. J. l.* 2. *cap. viii. Ant. Jud. l.* 13. *cap. v.* §. 9. *cap. x.* §. 5. *l.* 14. *cap. i. Et paffim.*

(c) ... τῷ ἔθνει τῶν χριϛιανῶν ἑαυτὲς συμμεμιχότας. *Maximin. ap. Eufeb. H. E. l.* 9. *cap. ix. p.* 360. C. ... ad Chriftianorum fectam fe applicuiffe cernerent, *Valef.*

Ch. IV.   Of Jesus Christ.   161

reasonable to expect in him frequent mention of Christ's miracles. Whereas, he is every where silent about them.

A. D. 76.

Josephus was a Pharisee. He believed the miracles of Moses, and the Jewish Prophets. He believed a Divine Providence, superintending human affairs, the immortality of the soul, and the rewards of a future state. And he is willing enough to relate extraordinarie things, or such things as had an appearance of being so.

Therefore (c) he tells a storie of *Eleazar*'s dispossessing a demon by virtue of some incantations, and the use of a certain root called *Baanas*.

Therefore (d) he relates a dream of *Archelaus*, and then another of *Glaphyra*, as very extraordinarie, as (e) confirming the doctrine of the immortality of souls, and the belief of a Divine Providence, concerning itself about human affairs. Those dreams are related by him both in the historie of the Jewish War, and in his Antiquities. And yet that dream of *Glaphyra* is now considered (f) by divers learned men, as a mere fiction.

I might refer to another silly storie of the fulfilment of a prediction of *Judas*, an *Essen*: which (g) is related by him also in both those works, the War and the Antiquities.

Would any man please himself with such poor things as these, and relate them to the world, as matters of importance, if he had any respect for the doctrine and miracles of Jesus Christ? No. He was either unacquainted with them, or resolutly silent about them.

(c) *Vid. de B. J. l. 7. cap. vi. Ant. l.* 8. *cap.* ii. §. 5.

(d) *Antiq. l.* 17. *cap.* xiii. §. 3. 4. 5. *De B. Jud. l.* 2. *cap.* vii.

(e) ... τότε ἀμφὶ τὰς ψυχὰς ἀθανασίας ἐμφερὴς, κὴ τῇ θεῖα προμηθείᾳ τὰ ἀνθρώπινα παρειληρότος τῇ αὐτῶ, καλῶς ἔχειν εὔμισα εἰπεῖν. *Ant. l.* 17. xiii. 5.

(f) *Vid. Noris. Censtaph. Pis. Diss.* 2. *cap. xii. p.* 238. *et le Clerc, Bib. Ch. T.* iv. *p.* 60.

(g) *De B. J. l.* 1. *cap.* iii. §. 4. 5. *Ant. l.* 13. *cap.* xi. §. 2.

Y   And

A. D. 76. And never can be supposed author of the honorable testimonie here bore to Jesus as the Christ.

Supposing these arguments to be of great weight, some may ask, how this paragraph came to be in the works of Josephus? In that case I should answer, that probably some learned christian, who had read the works of Josephus, thinking it strange, that this Jewish historian should say nothing of Jesus Christ, wrote this paragraph in the margin of his copie, and thence it came to be afterwards inserted into many copies of the works of Josephus. But for a good while it was not in all. And therefore *Photius* did not see it in that copie, which he made use of.

Who was the first author of this interpolation, cannot be said. *Tanaquil Faber (h)* suspected Eusebius. I do not charge it upon him. But I think it was first made about his time. For, if I am not mistaken, we have seen sufficient reason to believe, that this paragraph was not quoted by Origen, nor by any ancient Christian writer before Eusebius, that we have any knowledge of.

Though many learned men have maintained the genuinnesse of this paragraph, others have rejected it. And for avoiding the charge of singularity, and for giving satisfaction to some scrupulous persons, I shall, beside the authors *(i)* before referred to, transcribe at the bottom of the page *(k)* the observations of *Vitringa*. And I add the judgement

(h) Itaque constet necesse est, id intra illud tempus admissum fuisse, quod ab Origene ad Eusebium fluxit. Mihi autem inprimis credibile fit, auctorem hujus τεχνάσματος esse Eusebium. *Faber ap. Havercamp. p.* 272.

(i) See *p.* 151. *note* (1).

(k) Sed vehementer dubito, post doctissimas etiam Huetii curas, an non hic foetus Josepho sit suppositus, et ab aliena manu in textum intrusus. Utique pro certo et indubio habeo, totum locum, ut nunc apud Josephum habetur, e calamo Josephi non effluxisse: sed si omnino Josephus Christi Jesu hoc in contextu meminerit, locum a manu Christiana esse interpolatum mutatumque. Quod jam si dicamus, ne sic quidem omnis sublata erit diffi-

Ch. IV.   *Of James, the Lord's Brother.*

judgement of Dr. *Warburton*, now Bishop of Gloucester, who has expressed himself upon the subject in very clear and strong terms. "If a Jew, says (*l*) his Lordship, owned the truth of Christianity, he must needs embrace it. We, therefore, certainly conclude, that the passage, where Josephus, who was as much a Jew as the religion of Moses could make him, is made to acknowledge, that *Jesus is the Christ*, in as strong terms as words could do it, is a rank forgerie, and a very stupid one too."

III. There is yet one passage more in the works of Josephus, which ought to be here taken notice of. It is in the twentieth book of his Antiquities, and to this purpose. *Concerning James, the Lord's Brother.*

"The (*m*) Emperour having been informed of the death of Festus, sent Albinus to be prefect in Judea. And the King [*meaning Agrippa the younger,*] took away the high-priesthood from Joseph, and bestowed that dignity upon the son of Ananus, who also was named Ananus... This younger Ananus, who, as we said just now, was made High-Priest, was (*n*) haughty in his behaviour, and very enterprising. And moreover, he was of the sect of the Sadducees, who, as we have also observed before, are above all other Jews severe in their judicial sentences. This then being the temper of Ananus, and he thinking he had a fit opportunity, because Festus was dead, and Albinus was yet upon the road, calls

"a

---

difficultas : sed restat longe maxima de cohaeretia horum verborum Josephi, quibus Christo testimonium perhibet cum sequentibus: *Circa eadem tempora aliud etiam Judaeos turbavit incommodum,* &c. Quae tamen verba, si testimonium de Christo e contextu Josephi sustuleris, egregie cum praecedentibus conspirabunt. Ad quam difficultatem removendam nuper nihil aliud a doctissimo Tillemontio

produci potuit, quam verba Josephi, quae de Christo agunt, contextui παρεντιθέως inferta esse. In quo tamen dubito, an docti acquieturi sint. *Vitring. Observ. Sacr. l.* 4. *cap.* 7. §. *xi. p.* 971.

(*l*) See *Divine Legation of Moses*, B. 2. *Sect.* 6. *p.* 295. *vol. i.*
(*m*) *L.* 20. *cap. ix.* §. 1.
(*n*) θρασὺς ἦν τὸν τρόπον, καὶ τολμητὴς διαφερόντως.

A. D. 76.

"(o) a council of judges. And bringing before them James the bro-
"ther of him who is called Chrift, and fome others, he accufed them
"as tranfgreffors of the laws, and had them ftoned to death. But
"the moft moderate men of the city, who alfo were reckoned moft
"fkilfull in the laws, were offended at this proceeding. They there-
"fore fent privately to the King, [*Agrippa before mentioned*,] entreat-
"ing him to fend orders to Ananus, no more to attempt fuch things.
"And fome went away to meet Albinus, who was coming from
"Alexandria, and put him in mind, that Ananus had no right to
"call a Council without his leave. Albinus approving of what they
"faid, wrote to Ananus in much anger, threatening to punifh him
"for what he had done. And King Agrippa took away from him
"the high-priefthood, after he had enjoyed it three months, and
"put in Jefus, the fon of Damnaeus."

This paffage is cited from Jofephus by *(p) Eufebius*, and from the 20. book of his Antiquities. It is alfo quoted by *(q) Jerome*, but very inaccuratly. We perceive likewife, that *(r)* it was in the copies of Jofephus, in the time of *Photius*.

Neverthelefs there are learned men of good judgement, who (*s*) think, that the words, which we now have in Jofephus, concern-ing James, are an interpolation.

They were in Jofephus in the time of Eufebius, and afterwards. But it does not follow, they were always there. Indeed, there is a good deal of reafon to believe, that they were not originally in Jo-phus.

I have

(o) ... καθίζει συνέδριον κριτῶν· ϰ παραγαγὼν ἐκ αὐτὸ τὸν ἀδελφὸν Ἰησοῦ τοῦ λεγομένου
Χριστοῦ, Ἰάκωβος ὄνομα αὐτῷ, ϰ τινας ἑτέρους,
ὡς παρανομησάντων κατηγορίαν ποιησάμενος,
παρέδωκε λευσθησομένους.

(p) H. E. l. 2. cap. 23. p. 65. 66.

(q) De V. I. cap. ii. De Jacobo fratre Domini.

(r) ... αὐθεντίσας καθίζει συνέδριον, ϰ Ἰάκωβον τὸν ἀδελφὸν τοῦ κυρίου, σὺν ἑτέροις, παρανομίαν αἰτιασόμενος, λίθοις ἀναιρεθῆναι παρασκευάζει. κ. λ. Phot. cod. 238. p. 977.

(s) Facile quidem crediderim, Jerofoly-mitanos proceres graviter tuliffe, quod fy-nedrium fuâ auctoritate inftituiffet, cum dudum 'us gladii a Romanis effet Judaeis ademtum :

Ch. IV. Of James, the Lord's Brother.

I have elsewhere (t) carefully examined the most ancient accounts of the death of James, called the Just, and the brother of Jesus. Those disquisitions will be of use here. The persons, of whom Josephus speaks, who were tried and condemned by the Jewish council, at the instigation of *Ananus*, were put to death by *stoning*, and probably without the city. But according to the historie of the death of James, given by *Hegesippus*, a learned Jewish believer, and writer in the second centurie, the death of James was effected in a tumultuous manner. The disturbance began at the temple, and he died there, or near it. Some flung him down, and threw stones at him: but his death was compleated by a blow on the head with a long pole, such as fullers make use of in beating wet cloths. This is said by Clement of Alexandria, in his Institutions, as cited by *(u)* Eusebius and by *(x)* Hegesippus, as cited also by him. That therefore is the true and ancient account of the death of James, the Lord's brother. And the Christians of the second centurie knew nothing of

---

ademtum: quod iterum inconsulto Caesare ab Anano usurpatum timebant, ne genti suae gravi sortasse poenâ luendum esset. Sed quae de *Jacobo, Jesu, qui Christus dicebatur, fratre*, habentur, merum adsumentum, male seriati Christiani, esse videntur. *Cleric. H. E. ann. 62. n. ii. p. 415.*

Sunt quoque rationes sat graves, quae persuadeant haec suisse interpolata, et scripsisse duntaxat Josephum: ϗ παραγαγὼν εἰς αὐτὸ τινας, ϗ ὡς παραιομησάντων κατηγορίαν ποιησάμενος. κ. λ. Statutosque coram eo nonnullos, et accusatos perfractae legis, tradidit lapidibus obruendos. *Id. Ars Crit. P. 3. cap. 14. §. 12. Vol. 2. p. 289.*

Illa de Jacobo, *Jesu, qui Christus dicebatur, fratre.* (licet agnita ab Eusebio, aliisque eum sequutis, disertimque a Photio.) pro meio adsumento male seriati Christiani habentur a nonnullis: quam recte, κριτικωτέρων ἔστω judicium. *Hudson. annot. ad Antiq. l. 20. c. ix. §. 1.*

(t) *See the third volume of the Supplement, &c. p. 25. 26. 27. and p. 36. . . . 57.*

(u) Διὸ δὲ γεγόνασιν Ἰάκωβοι ἕις ὁ δίκαιος, ὁ κατὰ τὸ πτερὺγιν βληθεὶς, ϗ ὑπὸ κναφέως ξύλῳ πληγεὶς εἰς θάνατον. *Clem. A. ap. Euseb. H. E. l. 2. c. i. p. 38. D. Conf. ib. cap. 23. p. 63. C. et 65. C. And see the third vol. of the Supplement to the Credibility, &c. p. 27.*

(x) Καὶ λαβὼν τις ἀπ᾽ αὐτῶν ἕν τῶν γναφέων τὸ ξύλον ἐν ᾧ ἀπεπίεζε τὰ ἱμάτια, ἤνεγκε κατὰ τῆς κεφαλῆς τοῦ δικαίου. Καὶ οὕτως ἐμαρτύρησιν. *Hegesipp. ap. Euseb. H. E. l. 2. cap. 23. p. 65. B.*

of that account of his death, which we now have in Josephus. Therefore, probably, there was then nothing in him about it. For if there had, they would not have been ignorant of it.

Moreover, it is very observable, that according to the long and particular historie of the death and martyrdom of *James*, which we have in *Hegesippus*, that Apostle suffered alone. There was no attempt made upon any others, as the passage, now in *Josephus*, intimates. And it is inconsistent with the whole narrative, that any others should be joyned with him.

And that James suffered martyrdom, not by order of Council, as now in Josephus, but in a tumultuous manner at the Temple, or near it, and by a blow on the head with a fuller's pole, appears to have been the general and prevailing opinion of Christians in the fourth centurie, as well as before. For it is mentioned by *(y)* Jerome, and *(z)* Epiphanius, very agreeably to Hegesippus.

In this place therefore Josephus gave an account of some, who were accused by *Ananus*, and condemned by his Council, as transgressors of the Jewish laws. And what Ananus did was upon several accounts disliked by many discreet and moderate men. But there is not sufficient reason to believe, that *James* was particularly mentioned by him, as one of them.

It is certain, we ought to be very cautious in admitting quotations from Josephus, by later Christian writers. For they had a great regard for him, and were fond of having his testimonie, whether there was ground for it, or not. Theophylact upon John xiii. 33. and
referring

(y) Qui cum praecipitatus de pinna templi, confractis cruribus, adhuc semivivus . . . fullonis fuste quo uda vestimenta extorqueri solent, in cerebro percussus interiit . . et juxta templum, ubi et praecipitatus fuerat, sepultus est. *Hier. de V. I. cap. 2.*

Qui et ipse postea de Templo a Judaeis praecipitatus successorem habuit Simonem, quem et ipsum tradunt pro Domino crucifixum. *Id. Comm. in ep. ad Gal. cap. i, T. 4. p. 237.*

(z) *Haer.* 78. *num. xiv. p.* 1046.

Ch. IV.   *Of James, the Lord's Brother.*   167

referring also to John vii. 34. says, " The (*a*) Jews sought him, A. D.
" when their city was taken, and the wrath of God fell upon them, 76.
" on all sides: as also Josephus testifies, that those things happened
" to them upon account of the death of Jesus."

So says Theophylact. But from Origen, as before seen, we have good Reason to believe, that there was no such account in the works of Josephus, and that he never said any such thing.

In Suidas is a long article at the word JESUS, where it is said, " that *(b)* Josephus, who is often quoted by Eusebius Pamphili in " his Ecclesiastical Historie, expressly says, in his historie of the " Jewish War, that Jesus sacrificed with the priests at the temple."

There is no such thing there now. And probably never was in any good copies of the works of Josephus. But as he was an author in great repute with Christians, and he was often appealed to, and too often quoted inaccuratly, (of which Jerome, in his *(c)* article of St. James, is a remarkable instance,) his works were as likely to suffer some interpolations, as any writer's whatever.

Blondel supposed, that to this desire of *making an advantage from Josephus*, we owe the insertion of the remarkable testimonie to Jesus, which we have above so largely considered. What Blondel says, appears to me so judicious, and so apposite to the purpose, that I shall transcribe him below in his own *(d)* words. And let his judgement

---

(*a*) ... ὡς καὶ Ἰώσηπος μαρτυρεῖ, διὰ τὸν θανάτον τοῦ Ἰησοῦ ταῦτα αὐτοῖς γενέσθαι. *In Ev.* p. 762. *A.*

(*b*) Εὕρομεν ἐν Ἰωσήπῳ, τὸν συγγραφέα τῆς ἁλώσεως Ἱεροσολύμων, (ὃ μνήμην πολλὴν Εὐσέβιος ὁ Παμφίλου ἐν τῇ ἐκκλησιαστικῇ αὐτοῦ ἱστορίᾳ ποιεῖται) φαιερῶς λέγοντα ἐν τοῖς τῆς Αἰχμαλωσίας αὐτοῦ ὑπομνήμασιν, ὅτι Ἰησοῦς ἐν τῷ ἱερῷ μετὰ τῶν ἱερέων ἡγίαζε. *Suid. V.* Ἰησοῦς.

(*e*) *De V. I. cap. ii.* To *Jerome* 'might' have been added Eusebius, and divers o-

ther Christian Writers. Concerning Eusebius's inaccurate quotations of Josephus somewhat was said formerly. *Credib. P.* 2. *Vol. viii. p.* 59. 60. And they have been observed and censured by Scaliger, and other learned moderns.

(*d*) A mesme dessein, de tirer avantage de Josephe, quelque main hardie a' inseré dans ses Antiquitez. lib. 18. c. 4. des paroles qui luy sont d'autant moins convenables, qu'elles contiennent un tesmoignage

A. D. 76.

ment be added to thofe of *Vitringa*, and the Bifhop of *Glouceſter* above quoted.

Concluding Obſervations upon the Writings and Teſtimonies of Joſephus.

IV. Suppoſing Joſephus not to have ſaid any thing of Jeſus Chriſt, ſome may aſk: What could be the reaſon of it? And how can it be accounted for?

To which I might anſwer, that ſuch a queſtion is rather more curious, than judicious and important. And it may be difficult to propoſe a ſolution, that ſhall be generally approved of. However, I ſhall hazard a few obſervations upon the point.

It is eaſie to believe, that all Jews, who were contemporarie with Chriſt, or his Apoſtles, and did not receive Jeſus as the Chriſt, muſt have been filled with much enmity againſt him and his followers. We are aſſured by early Chriſtian writers, of good credit, ſuch as *(e)* Juſtin Martyr, *(f)* Tertullian, and others, that the ruling part of the Jewiſh nation induſtriouſly ſpread abroad falſe and injurious reports among the nations concerning the followers of Jeſus. But the polite and learned writers, ſuch as *Juſtus of Tiberias*, and *Joſephus*, might think it expedient to be ſilent. They had nothing to ſay againſt Jeſus, or the Chriſtians, with any appearance of truth and credibility. They therefore thought it better to be ſilent, and thereby, if poſſible, bury them in utter oblivion.

It is not eaſie to account for the ſilence of Joſephus any other *(g)* way.

moignage honorable, tant de la perſonne de noſtre Seigneur, que de la ſainteté et verité du Chriſtianiſme, de la profeſſion duquel cét Autheur a toujours eſté tres eloigné: et d'ailleurs qu'elles ſont notorement une piece d'attache ſans liaiſon avec le reſte de ſon diſcours, tant precedant que ſuivant, et placée à l'endroit qu'elle occupe par affection de parti pluſtoſt que par raiſon. *Blondel Des Sibylles.* p. 28.

(e) Dial. cum Tryph. p. 234 D. Par. §. 18. p. 102. Bened.

(f) Ad Nat. l. i. cap. 13. p. 59. D. et adv. Marcion. l. 3. cap. 23. p. 498.

(g) Le Cardinal Noris ſe fâche avec raiſon contre Joſeph, de ce qu'il expedie en dix lines les neuf années du regne d'Archelaus ... pour raconter au long les deux ſonges, dont on a parlé cideſſus. Mais on a encore plus de ſujet de ſe plaindre

Ch. IV. *Concluding Observations upon his Testimonie.*

way. Many things are omitted by him, of which he could not be ignorant. He must have known of the massacre of the infants at Bethlehem soon after the birth of Jesus. The arrival of the Wise Men from the East, who were conducted by a star, gave concern not only to Herod, but to all Jerusalem. Matt. ii. 8. Josephus was a Priest. He could not but have heard of the vision of *Zacharias* the father of John the Baptist at the temple. Luke i. And it was a thing very proper to have had a place in his historie. The prophecies of *Simeon* and *Anna* at the temple, and other things that happened there about that time, as we may think, must have been well known to him. Then the preaching and miracles of our Saviour and his Apostles at Jerusalem, and in Galilee, and all over Judea: the crucifixion of Jesus at Jerusalem, at the time of a Passover, the darknesse for three hours at Jerusalem, and all over Judea, the death of James the brother of John, at Jerusalem, by Herod Agrippa. All these things must have been well known to him.

Moreover, before Josephus had finished his work of the Jewish Antiquities, or even the historie of the Jewish War, christianity had spread very much in Asia, and in other parts, and at Rome itself, where also many had suffered, and that several years before the final ruin of Jerusalem, and the Jewish nation. The progresse of the Christian Religion was a very considerable event. And it had it's rise in Judea.

The sect of the Christians, which had it's rise in Judea, and consisted partly of Jews, partly of men of other nations, was as numerous, or more numerous, in the time of Josephus, than any of the

---

indre de la negligence, ou plutôt du silence affecté de cet Historien, touchant le denombrement, dont S. Luc parle, et touchant le meurtre des enfans de Bethlehem, du tems de la naissance de notre Seigneur : pour ne pas parler de sa vie, et de sa mort, dont il ne dit rien non plus : car on ne peut guere douter, que le passage, où il en est parlé, ne soit fourré, par un Chrétien mal-habile, dans Joseph. S'il eut dit seulement un mot du denombrement, et du massacre de Bethlehem, on n'auroit point la peine de chercher le tems de la naissance de Notre Seigneur. Mais ce Juif malicieux a voulu, autant qu'il étoit en lui, ensevelir cette histoire dans un éternel oubli, en haine des Chrétiens. *Le Clerc. Bib. Ch. T. 4. Art. i. p. 74 75.*

three Jewish sects, the Sadducees, Pharisees, and Essens, whose principles are particularly described by him in the (*) War, and in (**) the Antiquities. And therefore, as we may think, were deserving of notice. But they were not Jewish enough. They were not entirely Jewish. And they were followers of a leader, whom our Author did not, and could not esteem, consistently with his prevailing views and sentiments.

Josephus was well acquainted with affairs at Rome, and in all the settlements of the Jewish people in Asia, and parts adjacent. He is as exact in the account of the several successions in the Roman Empire, as any Roman Historian whatever. What *(b)* a long and particular account has he given of the conspiracie against Caligula, and his death, and the succession of Claudius?

I do not say, that Josephus had read the books of the New Testament. He might have come to the knowledge of most of the things just mentioned another way. They are great and remarkable events, about which a contemporarie, and a man of good intelligence, engaged in public life, could not be ignorant. His silence therefore about Christian affairs is willfull, and affected. It cannot be owing to ignorance. And must therefore be ascribed to some other cause, whatever it may be.

His profound silence, however, concerning the affairs of the Christians in his time, is no objection to their truth and reality. The historie of the new Testament has in it all the marks of credibility, that any historie can have. Heathen historians (*i*) of the best credit, have born witnesse to the time of the rise of the Christian Religion,

(*) *De B. J. l. 2. cap. viii.*
(**) *Antiq. l. 13. cap. v. et l. 18. cap. i.*
(*b*) *Antiq. l. 19. cap. i. ii. iii.*
(*i*) ... quos vulgus Christianos appellabat. Auctor hujus nominis Christus, qui Tiberio imperante, per procuratorem Pontium Pilatum supplicio affectus erat. Repressaque in praesens extiabilis superstitio rursus erumpebat, non modo per Judaeam originem ejus mali, sed per Urbem etiam, &c. *Tacit. Ann. l. 15. cap. 44.*

Ch. IV. *Concluding Observations upon his Testimonie.* 171

ligion, the countrey, in which it had it's origin, and who was the Author of it, and it's swift and early progresse in the world.

A. D. 76.

Of all those things, which are recorded in the Gospels, and of the progresse of Christianity afterwards, we have uncontested evidence, from the evangelical writers themselves, and from ancient Christian authors, still exstant, and from Heathen writers, concurring with them in many particulars.

And Josephus, the Jewish Historian, who believed not in Jesus, has recorded the historie of the Jewish people in Judea, and elsewhere: and particularly the state of things in Judea, with the names of the Jewish Princes, and Roman Governours, during the ministrie of our Saviour, and his Apostles. Whereby as *(k)* formerly shewn at large, he has wonderfully confirmed, though without intending it, the veracity, and the ability, of the evangelical writers, and the truth of their historie. He has also, as we have now seen in this volume, bore testimonie to the fulfilment of our Lord's predictions concerning the coming troubles and afflictions of that people: which is more credible, and more valuable, than if given by a believer in Jesus, and a friend and favourer of him. So that though all the passages in his works, which have been doubted of, should be rejected; he would be still a very usefull writer, and his *(l)* works very valuable.

Josephus knew how to be silent, when he thought fit, and has omitted some things very true, and certain, and well known in the world.

(k) In the first Part of the Credibility of the Gospel Historie.

(l) Evangelicam quoque et apostolicam historiam Josephus confirmat in multis, etiamsi vel maxime ponamns dubitandum esse de γνησιοτητι locorum de Christo Servatore lib. xviii. Antiq. cap. 4. de Johanne Baptista lib. xviii. cap. 7. de Jacobo, l. xx. c. 8. et quae de dirutis propter Jaco-

bi necem injustam Hierosolymis .. ex iisdem Josephi libris laudant Origenes, 1. contr. Cels. et l. 2. et in Matthaei cap. xiii. Eusebius. l. 2, c. 23. H. E. Hieronymus Catalogo Script. Ec. cap. 2. et 13. Suidas Ἰώσηπος, et Ἰησῖς, hodie vero in Josephi libris non reperiuntur. *Fabric. Bib. Gr. l. 4. cap. vi. T. 3. p. 237. 238.*

JOSEPHUS. Ch. IV.

A. D. 76.

world. In the preface to his Jewish Antiquities, he *(m)* engages to write of things, as he found them mentioned in the sacred books, without adding any thing to them, or omitting any thing in them. And *(n)* yet he has said nothing of the golden calf, made by the Jewish people in the wilderness: thus dropping an important narrative, with a variety of incidents, recorded in one of the books of Moses himself, the Jewish Lawgiver, the most sacred of all their scriptures.

The sin of the *Molten calf* is also mentioned in other books of the Old Testament in the confessions of pious Israelites: as Neh. ix. 18. and Ps. cvi. 19. Nevertheless Josephus chose to observe total silence about it.

A learned critic observed some while ago, as somewhat very remarkable, that *(o)* Josephus has never once mentioned the word *Sion*, or *Zion*, neither in his Antiquities, nor in his Jewish War: though there were so many occasions for it: and though it is so often mentioned in the Old, as well as the New Testament. And he suspects that omission to be owing to design and ill-will to the Christian cause.

And

(m) Τίνα δὴ διὰ ταύτης ποιήσειν τῆς πραγματείας, ἀπήγγειλάμην, οὐδὲν προσθεὶς ἰδ᾿ εὖ παραλιπών. *Antiq. Pr.* §. 3. *p.* 4.

(n) Eruditionem, diligentiam, prudentiam, fidem, omnes collaudant, praeterquam ubi nimio est in suam gentem affectu. v. gr. in rebus Mosis et Salomonis .. silentium nonnunquam affectatum, ut in iis quae probro cederent suae genti. Qualis ex. gr. fuit Vituli Aurei fabrica, et adjuratio, tacita Josepho: ita et in iis quae faverent Christianae rei, eruditi passim notarunt, et nos subinde in locis suis. F. Spanhem. *H. E. T.* i. *p.* 258. Conf. *J.* Otton. *Animadversiones* in *Joseph.* §. ii. *p.* 305. *Havercamp.*

And by all means see Tillemont's Remarks upon this Author's Antiquities. Ruine des Juifs, art. 81.

(o) Sion, Tzion nomen, montem, munimentum semel iterumque apud Josephum quaerens, nullibi inveni, neque iis etiam in locis, ubi expugnationem arcis Tzion expresse tractat: quum tamen centies et millies ipsi occasio data fuerit, ita ut plane sentiam ipsum studio et data opera hoc tam gloriosum pro Novo Testamento nomen pressisse silentio &c. *J. B. Ottii Animadversiones in Joseph. ap. Havercamp. T.* 2. *p.* 305.

Ch. IV. *Concluding Observations upon his Testimonie.*

And if I was not afraid of offending by too great prolixity, I should now remind my readers of a *(p)* long argument of old date, relating to the assessment made in Judea, by order of Augustus, at the time of our Saviour's nativity, near the end of Herod's reign, recorded by St. Luke ch. ii. I *(q)* then quoted a passage from the Antiquities of Josephus, whence it appears, that there were then great disturbances in Herod's familie. And there were some *Pharisees, who foretold,* or gave out, *that God had decreed to put an end to the government of Herod, and his race, and transfer the kingdom to another.* Josephus here takes great liberties. And though he was himself a Pharisee, and at other times speaks honorably of that sect, he now ridicules them. He says *(r) they were men, who valued themselves highly for their exact knowledge of the laws. And talking much of their interest with God, were greatly in favour with the women. Who had it in their power to controll Kings: extremely subtle, and ready to attempt any thing against those whom they did not like.* But it appears, that the King, who was then talked of, and who was to be appointed, *according to the predictions of the Pharisees,* was a person of an extraordinarie character. For he says, that *Bagoas,* an eunuch in Herod's palace, *was elevated by them, with the prospect of being a father and benefactor to his countrey, by receiving from him a capacity of marriage, and having children of his own* ***.

All these particulars, though not expressed with such gravity, as is becoming an historian, and is usual in Josephus, cannot but lead us to think, that he was not unacquainted with the things related in the second chapter of St. Matthew's Gospel. Says the Evangelist: *Now when Jesus was born in Bethleëm of Judea, in the days of Herod the King, behold there came wise-men from the East to Jerusalem, saying:*

Were

(p) Credibility. P. i. B. 2. ch. i. Vol. 2. p. 628. . . 645. the third edition.

(q) The quotation is, as above, p. 628. . . . 630. taken from the Antiquities. l. 17. cap. 2 § 4 p. 831. Havercamp.

(r) P. 629.

*** Whiston translates: *And for Bagoas, he had been puffed up by them for that this King would have all things in his power, and would enable Bagoas to marry, and to have children of his own body begotten.*

A. D. 76.

Where is he that is born King of the Jews? For we have seen his star in the East, and are come to worship him. When Herod the King had heard all these things, he was troubled, and all Jerusalem with him. The word rendred *troubled*, is of a midle meaning. How Herod was *moved*, may be easily guessed, and is well known. The inhabitants of Jerusalem were differently *moved* and agitated: partly with joyfull hopes of seeing their Messiah, *King of the Jews:* partly filled with apprehensions from Herod's jealousie, and the consequences of it.

It seems to me, that Josephus had then before him good evidences, that the Messiah was at that time born into the world. But he puts all off with a jest. Perhaps, there is not any other place in his works, where he is so ludicrous. We are not therefore to expect, that ever after he should take any notice of the Lord Jesus, or things concerning him, if he can avoid it.

And why should we be much concerned about any defects in this writer's regard for Jesus Christ, and his followers: who out of complaisance, or from self-interested views, or from a mistaken judgement, or some other cause, so deviated from the truth, as to ascribe the fulfilment of the Jewish ancient prophecies concerning the Messiah, to *Vespasian*, an idolatrous prince, who was not a Jew by descent, nor by religion: who was neither of the church, nor of the seed of Israel?

Josephus was a man of great eminence and distinction among his people. But we do not observe in him a seriousnesse of spirit, becoming a Christian: nor that sublimity of virtue, which is suited to the principles of the Christian Religion. Nor do we discern in him such qualities, as should induce us to think, he was one of those, who were well disposed, and were *not far from the kingdom of God.* He was a Priest by descent, and early in the magistracie, then a General, and a Courtier, and in all shewing a worldly mind, suited to such stations and employments. Insomuch that he appears to be one of those, of whom, and to whom, the best judge of men and things said: *How can ye believe, who receive honour one of another, and seek not the honour that cometh from God only!*

Mark xii. 34.

John v. 44.

CHAP.

CHAP. V.

The Mishnical, and Talmudical writers.

I. *The Age, and the Authors of the Mishna, and the Talmuds.* II. *Extracts from the Mishna, with Remarks.* III. *Extracts from the Talmuds,* 1. *of our Saviour's Nativity.* 2. *His journey into Egypt.* 3. *His Disciples.* 4. *James, in particular.* 5. *His last Sufferings.* 6. *The power of Miracles in Jesus, and his Disciples.* 7. *A Testimonie to the Destruction of the Temple by Vespasian and Titus, with Remarks.*

I. THE word *Talmud* is used in different senses. Sometimes it denotes the *Mishna*, which is the text. At other times it is used for the commentaries upon the *Mishna*. At other times it includes both. I shall generally use it, as distinct from the Mishna, denoting the commentaries upon it, of which there are two, the Jerusalem and the Babylonian. Of all which good accounts may be seen in Wagenseil's preface to his *Tela Ignea Satanae*, and in Dr. Wotton's *Discourses upon the Traditions of the Scribes and Pharisees*, and in many other writings. The most authentic account is that of M. Maimonides, in his preface to the Order of Seeds, which is the first of the six Orders, into which the whole work is divided. And may be seen in *Pocock's Porta Mosis*. As it is also prefixed to the first volume of Surenhusius's edition of the Mishna.

A. D. 180.

The Time and Authors of the Mishna, and the Talmuds.

The

A. D.
180.

The compiler of the Mishna is *Rabbi Jehudah Hakkadosch*, or the holy, upon whom the highest commendations are bestowed by Maimonides (a) as eminent for humility, temperance, and every branch of piety, as also for learning, and eloquence, and likewise for his riches: which are magnified by him, and other Jewish writers, beyond all reasonable bounds of probability.

But it may not be amiss for me to give my readers some farther infight into this work, by reciting an article of Dr. Prideaux in his Connexion of the History of the Old and New Testament. He observes, how the number of Jewish traditions had encreased. "And " (b) thus, says he, it went on to the midle of the second centurie " after Christ, when Antoninus Pius governed the Roman Empire, " by which time they found it necessarie to put all these traditions " into writing. For they were then grown to so great a number, " and enlarged to so huge a heap, as to exceed the possibility of be- " ing any longer preserved by the memorie of men. And there- " fore there being danger, that under their disadvantages they might " be all forgotten and lost, for the preventing hereof, it was re- " solved, that they should be all collected, and put into a book. And " *Rabbi Judah, the son of Simeon,* who from the reputed sanctity of " his life, was called *Hakkadosh,* that is, the Holy, and was then " Rector of the school, which they had at Tiberias in Galilee... " undertook the work, and compiled it in six books, each consist- " ing of several tracts, which all together make up the number of " sixty three... This is the book, called the *Mishnah.* Which book " was forthwith received by the Jews with great veneration through- " out all their dispersions, and hath been ever since held in high " esteem among them... And therefore, as soon as it was publish- " ed, it became the object of the studies of all learned men. And " the chiefest of them employed themselves to make comments up-
" on

(a) *Ap. Pocock. Port. Mosis. p. 35. 36. &c. Vol. i.* (b) *The Year before Christ. 446. p. 326.*

Ch. V.   Of the Mishna, and the Talmuds.

" on it, and these with the Mishna make up both the Talmuds, "that is, the *Jerusalem Talmud*, and the *Babylonish Talmud*. These "comments they call the *Gemara*, that is, the complement, because "by them the *Mishna* is fully explained, and the whole traditiona- "rie doctrine of their law and their religion compleated. For the "*Mishna* is the text, and the *Gemara* the comment, and both to- "gether is what they call *the Talmud*. That made by the Jews of "Judea is called *the Jerusalem Talmud*, and that made by the Jews "of Babylonia, the *Babylonish Talmud*. The former was compleated "about the year of our Lord three hundred, and is published in one "large folio. The later was published about two hundred years "after, in the begining of the sixth centurie, and has had several e- "ditions since the invention of printing: the last published at Am- "sterdam, is in twelve folios. And in these two Talmuds is con- "tained the whole of the Jewish religion, that is now professed a- "mong them. But *(c)* the *Babylonish Talmud*, is that which they "chiefly follow."

The same learned author again, afterwards computes, that the *Mishna* was composed about the one hundred and fiftieth year of our Lord, the *Jerusalem Talmud*, about the three hundredth year, and the other *Talmud* about the five hundredth year of our Lord.

And *Wagenseil* observes, that *(d)* Rabbi Jehuda was contempora- rie with Antonin the Pious. Mr. *Lampe (e)* speaking of several of

A. D. 180.

(c) Dr. *Wotton*, as above, p. 22. 23. says: "The Jerusalem Talmud wants "the impertinences, and, consequently, "the authority of the Babylonish Gema- "ra... It has little of that hyperbolical "and fabulous stuff, for which the other "is so highly valued by the modern Tal- "mudists."

(d) Rabbi Jehudam, qui Sancti cogno- men inter suos meruit, et Antonini Pii

Imperatoris aequalis fuit, metus invaserat, ne ob tantas gentis suae miserias, et in re- motissimis terris deportationes, Oralis Lex plane in hominum animis obliteraretur. *Wagens. Pr. p.* 55.

(e) Sed praecipue eminuit R. Jehuda, quem Sanctum nominant, Mishnae auc- tor, qui circa annum 194. aut secundum alios 230 obiisse creditur. *Lampe Synops. H. E. P.* 111.

A. D. 180.

the Jewish Rabbins celebrated about this time, fays, that *R. Jehuda*, author of the Mifhna, died about the year of Chrift 194. or according to others in the year 230.

Dr. Lightfoot, [*Fall of Jerufalem* §. vii. *Vol. i. p.* 369.] fays, "that "R. Judah outlived both the Antonins, and Commodus alfo." And afterwards, in the fame page. " He compiled the Mifhnah " about the year of Chrift 190. in the later end of the reign of Com- " modus: or, as fome compute, in the year of Chrift 220. an hun- " dred and fifty years after the deftruction of Jerufalem."

I do not take upon me to conteft at all what *Prideaux* fays of the times of the two Talmuds. But I muft fay a few things about the time of the *Mifhna*. I allow, that Rabbi Jehudah, the compofer of it, was contemporarie with Antonin the Pious: though the ftories told by the Jewifh writers of the favours fhewn him by that Emperour, muft be reckoned partly fabulous. But allowing him to be contemporarie with *Antonin*, who died in the year 161. it does not follow, that the Mifhna was compofed fo foon, as the year of Chrift 150. R. Jehuda is fuppofed to have had a long life. And the compiling the Mifhna, which muft have been the work of many years, and much leifure, and deliberate thought and confideration, may not have been finifhed before the year 190. or *(f)* later. If therefore I place this work at the year 180. I think, I place it foon enough. Befides, it is faid, that R. Jehudah had feveral ficknefles, fome of long continuance, which are particularly mentioned, both in the Jerufalem and the Babylonian Talmud, though with fome variations. Thefe muft have been obftructions to him in his ftudies, and muft have prolonged the labours of his work. The nature of the work alfo required time. It is not a fpeculation, which might be

---

(f) Talmudici Operis fundamenta hoc feculo jacta, circa A. C. cxc. Magiftri citius, imperante Antonino Pio. *Fred.* Spanh. *Opp. T. i. p.* 687. *Vid. et p.* 793.

Ch. V.   *Of the Mishna, and the Talmuds.*   179

be spun out of a man's head at once. But it is a collection *(g)* of traditions from all quarters, and from the contributions of other learned men of the nation, who had treasured up these hitherto unwritten traditions in their memories.

One thing more I may premize here, that *(h)* it is the opinion of divers learned men, well skilled in this part of learning, that in the *Mishna*, which is a collection of Jewish traditions, there is little or nothing concerning our Saviour, or his followers. I allow also, that here are none of those open blasphemies, which may be found in some other Jewish writings.

II. I shall now make some extracts out of the *Mishna*.

1. In the tract concerning *Fasts* are these words: " Five *(i)* heavie " af-

---

(g) Quamobrem, adhibitis in consilium auxiliumque sapientissimis quibusque, sedulo ab iis, quibus licebat, Judaeis, voce ac per epistolas sciscitatus est, quaenam a parentibus oralis legis scita didicissent, quin et schedas undique conquisivit, quibus hactenus memoriae caussa traditiones inscriptae fuerant. Ea omnia, secundum certa doctrinae capita disposuit, et in unum volumen redegit, cui nomen hoc *Mishna*, hoc est, δευτέρωσις imposuit. *Wagenseil Pr. p.* 55.

(h) Scilicet, si per Talmud solam Mishnam intelligam, vere affirmavero, nullam in toto Talmude reperiri blasphemiam, nihil Christianis adversum, nullam fabulam quoque, immo nec quicquam quod valde a ratione sit alienum. Continet enim meras tantum πατροπαραδόσεις, et est, ceu diximus, corpus juris Judaici olim non scripti. Rem ita se habere, testem idoneum ac locupletem sistere possumus, virum harum rerum scientissimum, omnique dignum praeconio Josephum de Voisin. ... *Wagenseil. Praef. p.* 57.

Quippe, quod in praefatione hujus voluminis satis dixi, id tamen nunc iterum dico, in universa Mishna, de Jesu servatore, nec vola nec vestigium ullum apparet, immo ne de Christianis quidem, ejus nomen profitentibus. *Id. in Confut. Toldos Jeschu. p.* 10. §. 4.

(i) Quinque res luctuosae patribus nostris acciderunt die septimo decimo mensis Tammuz [sc. *Junii.*] totidemque die nono mensis Abh [sc. *Julii.*] Nam xvii. Tammuz fractae sunt tabulae Legis: cessavit juge sacrificium : Urbis moenia perrupta : Lex ab Apostemo combusta, idolumque in templo statutum. Nono autem die mensis Abh, decrevit Deus de patribus nostris, non ingressuros eos in terram promissam: desolatum est templum primum et secundum : capta est urbs Bither: diruta urbs sancta. Unde ex quo

"afflictions have befallen our anceſtors on the ſeventeenth day of
"the month Tammus [June] and as many on the ninth day of the
"month Ab. [*July*.] For on the ſeventeenth day of Tammus, the
"tables of the law were broken: the perpetual ſacrifice ceaſed: the
"walls of the city were broke open: the Law was burnt by *Apoſ-*
"*temus*, and an idol was ſet up in the temple. On the ninth day of
"the month Ab, God determined concerning our fathers, that they
"ſhould not enter into the promiſed land: the firſt and ſecond tem-
"ple was deſolated: the city *Bither* was taken: the holy city was
"deſtroyed. For which reaſon, as ſoon as the month Ab begins, re-
"joycings are abated." *⁎*

quo menſis Abh incipit. laetitiam immi-
nuunt. Tract. de *Jejuniis* cap. 4. §. 7.
Pars. 2. p. 382. edit. Surenh.

(*⁎*) I think it cannot be diſagreea-
ble to my readers, if I here tranſcribe
ſome obſervations of Dr. Lightfoot, from
what he calls a *Parergon*. *Concerning the
Fall of Jeruſalem*. Of his Works, Vol.
i. p. 362. though they are long, "The
temple was burnt down, as Joſephus a
ſpectator ſetteth the time, *on the tenth day
of the month Lous*. Which he ſaith was a
fatal day to the temple. For it had been
burnt down by the Babylonians before, on
that day. *De Bell. l.* 6. *cap. vii.* And
yet his countreymen, who write in the
Hebrew tongue, fix both theſe fatalities to
the ninth day of that month, which they
call the month Ab. And they account
that day fatal for three other ſad occurrences beſides. *On the ninth day of the
month Ab*, ſay they, *the decree came out a-
gainſt Iſrael in the wilderneſs, that they
ſhould not enter into the land*. On it was
*the deſtruction of the firſt Temple, and on it
was the deſtruction of the ſecond*. On it the
*great city Bither was taken, where there were
thouſands and ten thouſands of Iſrael, who
had a great King over them*, [Ben Cozba.]
*whom all Iſrael, even their greateſt wiſe
men, thought to have been Meſſias*. *But he
fell into the hands of the Heathen, and there
was great affliction, as there was at the deſtruction of the Sanctuarie. And on that
day, a day allotted for vengeance, the wicked
Turnus Rufus ploughed up the place of the
Temple, and the places about it, to accompliſh
what is ſaid, Sion ſhall become a ploughed
field*. Talm. in Taanith. per. 4. halac. 6.
Maimon. in Taanith. per. 5."

"It is ſtrange, that men of the ſame
nation, and in a thing ſo ſignal, and of
which both parties were ſpectators, ſhould
be at ſuch a difference: and yet not a difference neither, if we take Joſephus's report of the whole ſtory, and the other Jews
conſtruction of the time. He records, that
the Cloiſter walks, commonly called *the
Porticoes of the Temple*, were fired on the
eighth day, and were burning on the ninth:
but that day Titus called a council of war,
and carried it by three voices, that the
temple ſhould be ſpared. But a new buſt-
ling of the Jews cauſed it to be fired,
though

Ch. V. Extracts out of the Mishna.

Who is meant by *Apostemus*, or *Appostomus*, is not very material. And therefore, I do not inquire. I allege this passage, as an early Jewish testimonie to the destruction of the holy city, or *Jerusalem*, and the *second temple*, as it is here called.

2. In the tract concerning *the Woman suspected of Adulterie*, are these words: " When *(k)* the war of *Vespasian* began, the coronets " and bells of bridegrooms were forbidden by a public decree.

" When though against his will, on the next day. *Joseph. ubi supr.* cap. 22. 23. 24. Now their Kalendar reckons, from the midle day of the three that fire was at it, as from a centre. And they state the time thus : *It was the time of the evening, when fire was put to the temple. And it burnt till the going down of the sun of the next day. And behold what Rabban Jochanan benzaccai saith : If I had not been in that generation, I should not have pitched it upon any other day, but the tenth, because the most of the temple was burnt that day. And in the Jerusalem Talmud it is related, that Rabbi, and Joshua ben Levi, fasted for it the ninth and tenth days both.* Gloss. in Maim. in Taanith. per. 8."

" Such another discrepancy about the time of the firing of the first temple by Nebuchadnezzar, may be observed in 2 Kings xxv. 8. 9. where it is said, that *in the fifth month, on the seventh day of the month, came Nebuzaradan, Captain of the guard, and burnt the House of the Lord.* And yet in Jer. lii. 12. it is said to have been *in the fifth month, on the tenth day of the month.* Which the Gemarists in the Babylon Talmud reconcile thus: *It cannot be said, on*

the seventh day, because it is said, On the tenth. Nor can it be said On the tenth, because it is said, On the seventh. How is it then? On the seventh day the aliens came into the Temple, and eat there, and defiled it, the seventh, eighth, and ninth days. And that day toward night, they set it on fire, and it burnt all the tenth day, as was the case also with the second Temple. Taanith. fol. 29."

" The ninth and tenth days of the month Ab, on which the Temple was burnt down, was about the two and three and twentieth of our July. And the city was taken, and sacked, the eighth day of September following. Joseph. supr. cap. 47." So *Lightfoot*.

(*k*) Orto bello Vespasiani, decreto publico abrogatae sunt coronae sponsorum, et tympana. Orto bello Titi cautum est de coronis sponsarum, et ne quis filium in Graecanicis erudiret. Propter postremum belli impetum, prohibebatur sponsa in publicum prodire sub uranisco. Sed magistris nostris visum est, facultatem ejus rei indulgere. *Tractat. de Uxore Adulterii suspectae, num.* 14. P. 3. p. 304. *Edit, Surenh.*

A. D. 180.

"When the war of *Titus* began, the coronets of brides were forbidden, and that no man should educate his son in Greek learning. Becaufe of the final iffue of that war, every bride was forbid to come abroad under an umbrella. Neverthelefs, our Mafters have [fince] thought fit to allow of it."

This alfo is an early teftimonie to the war, in which the Jewifh people were fubdued by thofe two great Generals, *Vefpafian* and *Titus*.

3. I fhall now tranfcribe below another long paffage from the fame tract. A part of which fhall be tranflated.

"When *(l)* Rabbi *Meïr* died, there were none left to inftruct men in wife parables."...

"... When

(l) Mortuo R. Meir defecere, qui homines erudicbant [*doctii*] parabolis.... Mortuo R. Simeone Filio Gamalielis, venerunt locuftae, et auctae funt calamitates. .. R. Ahiba mortuo decus legis evanuit. .. Mortuo R. Gamaliele Sene, evanuit honor legis, fimulque mundities et fanctimonia, intermortuae. R. Ifmaele filio Babi defuncto, occubuit fplendor facerdotii. Mortuo Rabbi [*Juda Sancto*] ceffavit modeftia, et timor peccati. R. Pinchas F. J. ait diruto templo pudore fuffufi funt Sapientes pariter et Nobiles : obnubuntque capita. Liberales ad pauperiem funt redacti, contra invaluerunt violenti, et calumniatores: nec fupereft explicans, nec quaerens, nec interrogans. Cui ergo in nitendum eft nobis ? Patri noftro coelefti. R. Eliezer, cognomento Magnus, ait : Ex quo templum devaftatum eft, coepere Sapientes fimiles effe Scribis, Scribae Aedituis, Aeditui vulgo hominum. Vulgus autem hominum, in pejus in dies ruit : nec quis rogans, aut quaerens, fupereft. Cui ergo innitendum ? Patri noftro coelefti. Paullo ante adventum Meffiae impudentia augebitur, et magna erit annonae caritas. Vitis proferet fructum, fed vinum nihilominus care vendetur. Summum in orbe Imperium obruetur opinionibus pravis, et nulli locum habebit correptio. Synagogae convertentur in lupanaria, limites Judaeae defolabuntur, et regio quanta quanta eft devaftabitur. Viri infignes oppidatim circuibunt, nec ulla humanitatis officia experientur. Faetebit fapientia Magiftrorum, a delictis fibi caventes fpernentur, et Veritatis magnus erit defectus. Juvenes confundent ora Senum. Senes coram junioribus furgent. Filius irritabit patrem. Nata infurgat adverfus matrem, nurufque contra focrum. Denique, fuos quifque domefticos inimicos habebit. Scilicet feculo illo canina facies

Ch. V.   *Extracts out of the Mishna.*   183

"...When *Simeon*, fon of Gamaliel died, there came locufts, and   A. D.
"calamities were encreafed... When R. *Akiba* died, the glorie of   180.
"the law vanifhed away. Upon the death of *Gamaliel*, the *aged*,
"the honour of the law vanifhed, and there was an end to purity
"and fanctimonie. When Rabbi *Ishmael*, fon of Babi, died, the
"fplendour of the prieſthood was tarnifhed. When *Rabbi* [Judah]
"died, there was no more any modeſtie, or fear of tranfgreffion.
"Rabbi *Pinchas*, fon of Ifhmael, faid, when the temple was de-
"ftroyed, all men were covered with fhame, both Wife men and
"Nobles. And all now cover their heads. The bountifull are re-
"duced to poverty, and the violent and flanderers prevail. Nor is
"there any to explain the law, nor are there any who afk and in-
"quire. What then fhall we do? Let us truft in our heavenly Fa-
"ther. R. *Eliezer*, furnamed the great, fays: from the time that
"the temple was deftroyed, the Wife Men began to be like Scribes,
"the Scribes like Sextons, and Sextons like the Vulgar. And the
"Vulgar are continually degenerating from bad to worfe. Nor are
"there any who afk and inquire. What then fhall we do? Let us
"truft in our heavenly Father. A fhort time before the coming of
"the Meffiah, Impudence will be encreafed: and great will be the
"price of provifions. The vine will bear fruit. Neverthelefs wine
"will be fold at a high price. The fupreme Empire of the world
"will be overwhelmed with bad opinions. Nor will there be room
"for any to correct them. Synagogues will be turned into brothel-
"houfes, and the whole land of Judea will be laid wafte. Excel-
                                                                    "lent

facies erit, nec verebitur filius parentem. Cui. ergo confidendum? Patri coelefti. .. R. Pinchas F. J. ait: Providentia cauf-fa alacritatis... Timor fceleris ducit ad pietatem. Pietas cauffa eft [*gratiae*] S. Spiritus. Spiritus S. [*fideles*] facit participes refurrectionis mortuorum. Refurrectio mortuorum obtinget interventu Eliae, cujus memoria facra efto, et fancta... Deus aeternus benigne concedat ut adventu illius cito falvi fanique fruamur. Amen. *Tr. de uxore adulterii fufpecta. num.* 15. P, 3. *p.* 308. 309. *Surenh.*

A. D.
180.

"lent men will wander from town to town, and experience no offices of humanity. The Wisdom of the Masters will be slighted, and all who strive to avoid transgression will be contemned, and great will be the dearth of truth. Young men will cover the faces of the aged with shame. And the aged will rise before the Young. The son will dishonour the father. And the daughter will rise up against her mother: and the daughter-in-law against her mother-in-law. And a man's enemies will be they of his own houshold. In a word, that age will have a canine appearance. Nor will the son reverence the father. What then shall we do? Let us trust in our heavenly Father.... *May the coming of Elias be hastened. And may the eternal God graciously vouchsafe, that we may be preserved to that time.*"

This passage may deserve an attentive regard, and will require divers observations. But I shall take no particular notice of what is here said about *the coming of Elias*, that not being reckoned certainly genuine.

1. In the first place, this passage ought to be compared with *Jerome's* commentarie upon If. ch. viii. 14. where (*l*) he mentions divers of the Jewish Masters, who flourished, and were very eminent about the time of our Saviour, and some while after: *Sammai, Hillel, Meir, Akibas, Johanan*, the son of *Zachai*, and some others. In (*m*) ano-

---

(*l*) Duas domus Nazaraei .. duas familias interpretantur, Sammai et Hillel: ex quibus orti sunt Scribae et Pharisaei, quorum suscepit scholam Akibas, quem magistrum Aquilae proselyti autumant: et post eum Meir, cui successit Johanan filius Zachai: et post eum Eliezer, et per ordinem Delphon: et rursum Joseph Galilaeus: et usque ad captivitatem Jerusalem Josue. Sammai igitur et Hillel non multo prius quam Dominus nasceretur, orti sunt in Judaea, quorum prior *dissipator* interpretatur, sequens *prophanus:* eo quod per traditiones et δευτερώσεις suas legis praecepta dissipaverit, atque maculaverit. &c. *In If. cap. viii.* T. 3. p. 79.

Ch. V. *Extracts out of the Mishna.*

A. D. 180.

(m) another place he censures the numerous traditions, or secondarie laws of the Pharisees. Undoubtedly *Jerome* was not unacquainted with Jewish traditions. But I cannot say, that these passages amount to a proof, that he had seen the volume of the *Mishna*.

2. Here is another testimonie to the destruction of the Temple at Jerusalem.

3. I suppose likewise, that here is a reference to the disasters of the Jews, occasioned by the rebellion of *Barchochebas* in the time of Adrian. This I suppose to be intended in these words: *And the whole land of Judea will be laid waste, and excellent men will wander from place to place, and experience no offices of humanity.* Moreover in the passage first cited, *the taking of the city Bither* is mentioned, as one of the most remarkable calamities that had befallen the Jewish people. It was the concluding event of the Jewish war with Adrian, about the year 136. Which shews, that the Mishna was not composed, till some while afterwards.

4. *Meïr*, the first Rabbi here mentioned, is said to have been *(n)* one of the principal of the Jewish doctors after the destruction of Jerusalem.

5. Rabbi *Akibas (o)* is a man, upon whose praises the Jewish writers enlarge mightily. And his sayings are often mentioned in the

---

(m) Quantae traditiones Pharisaeorum sint, quas hodie vocant δευτερώσεις, et quam aniles fabulae, evolvere nequeo. Neque libri patitur magnitudo: et pleraque tam turpia sunt, ut erubescam dicere. *Ad Algas. Qu. x. T.* 4. *P. i. p.* 207.

(n) See *Basnag. Hist. des Juifs. l.* 6. *ch.* x. §. *iv, &c.*

(o) Of *Akibas* may be seen *Basnage Hist. des Juifs. liv. vi. ch. ix.* §. 14. . . . 25. *Vid. et Basnag. ann.* 134. *num. iii.* Raymund. *Martini Pug. Fidei. p.* 256. 257. . . . 264. *Edzardi Avodazara. Vol. i. p.* 162. 338. *Lightfoot, in the Fall of Jerusalem.* §. *iv. vol. i. p.* 366. 367. *Dr. Sharpe's Argument for Christianity. p.* 55.

Mishna,

Mishna, and the Talmud. He was a zealous follower of the impostor *Barchochebas*, who took upon him the character of the Messiah, in the time of *Adrian*, about the year of Christ 132. And he perished with him. This shews the temper of *Akibas*. And we can hence conclude, how he stood affected to the Lord Jesus. The honorable mention here made of him shews also the temper of the compiler of this work, the *Mishna*.

6. *Gamaliel the aged* is supposed to be Gamaliel, St. Paul's master, mentioned by him Acts xxii. 3. and in ch. v. 34. to be *one of the Council, a Pharisee, and doctor of the law, had in reputation with all the people*. From what is here said of him, in the passage now before us, he appears to have been in great esteem with the Jewish people. And he is often mentioned in the Mishna. What is here said of him, therefore confirms the truth of what is said of him in the book of the Acts. Moreover, we are hereby assured, that *Gamaliel* never was converted to Christianity, as some Christians, especially of the Church of Rome, have fondly and weakly imagined. And indeed from what St. Paul says, in the text before quoted, it may be argued, that Gamaliel was still a firm Jew. Otherwise, it had not been to the purpose, to take notice of his education under him, in the critical circumstance, which he was then in.

7. Of *Rabbi*, [Jehudah,] the compiler of the Mishna, here, and elsewhere called *Rabbi*, or the *Master*, without any other distinction, so much has been said already, that little more needs to be added now. It is here said, *that when he died, there remained no longer any modestie, or fear of transgression*. Maimonides in his character of *Jehudah the Holy*, did not omit *(p)* this particular. But here is somewhat,

---

(p) In summo etiam pietatis, et humilitatis, et abstinentiae a voluptatibus gradu: uti etiam dixerunt: Ex quo mortuus est Rabbi, cessavit humilitas, et timor peccati. *Maim. Porta Mosis. p.* 35.

Ch. V.   *Extracts out of the Mishna.*   187

somewhat, which could not be said by himself. It must have been inserted after his death. *Wagenseil* therefore acknowledgeth, that *(q)* there were some additions made to the Mishna. But he says, they are not many, and they were soon made, and chiefly regard R. *Jehuda* himself, which I see no reason to contest. For I am willing to allow this volume to be a work of the second centurie. Nevertheless this manner of speaking, may perhaps induce us to think, that more hands than one were employed in compiling it.

A. D. 180.

8. Once more, in the eighth place. *This whole passage appears to me to be a disguised, and invidious representation of the state of things, under the gospel-dispensation, since the appearance of Jesus, whom his disciples and followers have received as the Messiah: and especially, after the destruction of Jerusalem, when Christianity prevailed, and Judaism declined.*

For 1.) The destruction of the Jewish temple is acknowledged. Nevertheless here are no tokens of repentance and humiliation, but complaints and reflexions upon others. The times were bad. But the blame is all laid upon others.

2.) The *supreme Empire of the world*, he says, *will be*, or *is overwhelmed with bad opinions*: meaning, as I think, the Christian Religion, and the several sects and heresies, which arose in the second centurie, and some of them, not far from the begining of it.

3.) *Synagogues will be turned into brothel-houses.* He refers to the common reports among the vulgar, that the Christians practised promiscuous lewdnesse in their religious assemblies. And he adopts the calumnie.

4.) In what follows, the Author adopts the words of our Lord, recorded Matt. x. 35, 36. and Luke xii. 51...53. Which words are also

Bb 2   in

(q) Accessisse post obitum R. Judaei, quasdam interpolationes, non negaverim: sed eae paucae sunt, ac mature fuerunt — adjectae, ipsumque R. Judam potissimum respiciunt. *Wag. ib. p. 55.*

in Micah vii. 6. concerning the diffenfions that would be in families, fome chearfully embracing his doctrine, whilft others obftinatly rejected it, and were bitter toward thofe who received it. Which the compiler of this work reprefents, as the utmoft diftreffe and miferie, and as hitherto unknown and unparalleled wickedneffe.

5.) And what do all the clamours of this paragraph mean concerning the *failure* or dearth *of truth, the multiplicity of bad opinions, whilft there was no room left for reproof or correction?* What is intended by the complaints, that *the wifdom of the mafters was flighted, that there was an end to purity and fanctimonie, to modeftie and the fear of tranfgreffion, and that the Young covered the faces of the aged with fhame, and the aged rofe up to the Young,* and the reft.

All thefe complaints, as feems to me, refer to the refolution and fteadineffe of the converts to Chriftianity, from Judaifm, and Gentilifm, who judged for themfelves, and admitted the evidences of the truth of the new religion, which overpowered their minds. Of which therefore they made an open profeffion, notwithftanding the fophiftrie, the entreaties, and the menaces of the world about them: many of whom were their fuperiors in age, learning, and outward circumftance and condition. Of all this we have in this paffage, as feems to me a graphical defcription.

I cannot but underftand this paffage after this manner. And I refer thefe thoughts to the confideration of my readers. This paragraph, if my interpretation be right, is very curious.

I am unwilling to enter into a controverfie about the Mifhnical tract *Avoda zara, de cultu peregrino,* of ftrange, or idolatrous worfhip. I pay a great regard to the judgement of thofe learned men, who fay, there is in it no reference to the Chriftians. Neverthelefs there feems to me a defect in their reafonings upon that point. I think, that when the *Mifhna* was compiled, the Chriftians were more numerous, more confiderable, and of more confequence, than thofe learned men fuppofe in their argument concerning that tract.

III.

Ch. V. *Of our Lord's Nativity.*

The Nativity of Jesus.

III. I have done with the *Mishna*. I proceed to the *Talmud*.

1. The first passage to be taken thence will relate to our Lord's nativity.

" Upon *(r)* a certain day, when several Masters were sitting at
" the gate of the city, two boys passed by before them: one of
" whom covered his head, the other had his head uncovered.
" Concerning him, who contrarie to all the rules of modestie, had
" boldly passed by with his head uncovered, *Eliefer* said, he believ-
" ed he was spurious. R. *Joshua* said he believed he was the son
" of a woman set apart. But R. *Akiba* said, he was both. The
" others said to *Akiba*, Why do you differ from the rest of your bre-
" thren?

(r) Juramentis vero illorum nihil prorsus est tribuendum, quia in ipso Talmude docentur, posse juramenta, dum praestantur, confestim in mente aboleri, ut non obligent. Exemplo est R. Akisa, de quo *Cod. Kalla fol.* 18. *col.* 2. *med.* sequens refertur historia. Cum aliquando Seniores sederent in porta [urbis] praeterierunt ante ipsos duo pueri, quorum alter caput texerat, alter retexerat. Et de eo quidem, qui caput [proterve, et contra bonos mores] retexerat, pronunciavit R. Eliefer, quod esset spurius. R. Josua autem dixit, eum esse a muliere menstruata conceptum. At R. Akisa subjecit, esse illum et spurium, et filium menstruatae. Unde ceteri interrogarunt R. Akisam, quomodo tam audacter collegis suis contradiceret. Sed ille regessit, se dicta sua esse confirmaturum. Abiit ergo ad matrem pueri istius, quam cum videret sedentem in foro, et vendentem legumina, dixit ad illam. Filia mea, si tu mihi ingenue indicaveris id quod sum interrogaturus, efficiam ut potiaris vita seculi futuri. Ipsa autem postulante, ut jurejurando assertum suum roboraret, juravit R. Akisa labiis suis, sed corde suo jusjurandum hoc statim reddidit irritum. Tum R. Akisa: Dic, inquit, mihi qualis sit hic filius tuus? Ad quae illa: Quando ego nuptias celebrarem, laborabam a menstruis. Ideoque secessit a me maritus, paranymphus autem meus [occasione arrepta] congressus mecum est. Atque ex eo concubitu exstitit mihi filius hic. Unde apparuit, puerum istum esse non modo spurium, sed et menstruatae filium. Cumque id percepissent ceteri assessores, dixerunt: Magnus est Akisa, quando correxit doctores suos. *Edzard. Aveda Sara. Tom. i. p.* 279. *Conf. Wagenseil. Confut. Tol. Jeschu. p.* 14. 15. *et Buxtorf. Syn. Jud. cap. vii. p.* 132, 133.

The Nativity of Jesus. Ch. V.

A. D. 500.

" thren? He anſwered, that he would prove the truth of what he
" had ſaid. Accordingly he went to the mother of the boy, whom
" he found fitting in the market, and ſelling of herbs. He then ſays
" to her, *My daughter, anſwer me a queſtion, which I am going to
" put to you, and I aſſure you of a portion of happineſſe in the world
" to come.* She anſwered : *Confirm what you ſay with an oath.* A-
" *kiba* then ſwore with his lips, but at the ſame time abſolved him-
" ſelf in his mind. Then he ſaid to her : *Tell me the origin of this
" your ſon?* Which ſhe did, and confeſſed, that it was as he had
" ſaid. When he returned to his collegues, and told them the diſ-
" coverie he had made, they ſaid : Great is Akiba, who had cor-
" rected the reſt of the maſters."

An abſolute fiction, the fruit of deep-rooted malice! Though (s) no perſon is here named, there can be no doubt, who is intended. And it is adopted by (t) the author of Toldoth Jeſchu.

Our Lord's Journey into Egypt

2. Upon Matt. ii. 14. *Lightfoot* obſerves as follows *(u)* " There
" are ſome footſteps in the Talmudiſts of this journey of our Savi-
" our into Egypt, but ſo corrupted with venomous blaſphemie, (as
" all their writings are,) that they ſeem only to have confeſſed the
" truth, that they might have matter more liberally to reproach him.
" For ſo they ſpeak [Bab. Sanhedr. fol. 107. a.] *When Jannay the
" King ſlew the Rabbins, R. Joſhua Ben Perachiah and Jeſus went a-
" way unto Alexandria in Egypt. Simeon Ben Shelah ſent thither, ſpeak-
" ing thus. From me Jeruſalem the holy city, to thee, o Alexandria in
" Egypt, my ſiſter, health. My huſband dwells with thee, while I in the
" mean time ſit alone. Therefore he roſe up, and went. And a little after.*
" He

(s) Haec hiſtoria tecte videtur loqui de Chriſto. *Buxtorf. ubi ſupr.* p. 133.

Ac de infantia quidem et natalibus Jeſchu, credo ego, creduntque Judaei hoc mecum, ſermonem eſſe, quamquam nomine penitus ſuppreſſo, in Maſſechet Calla,

quam et ipſam allegare convenit. *Wagenf. ut ſupr.* p. 14.

(t) *Apud Wagenf.* p. 5.

(u) *Hebrew and Talmudical Exercitationi.* p. 111. 112.

Ch. V.   Our Lord's Journey into Egypt.

" He brought forth four hundred trumpets and anathematifed [Jefus.]   A. D.
" And a little before that. Elizaeus turned away Gehazi with both his   500.
" hands, and R. Jofhua Ben Perachiah thruft away Jefus with both
" his hands."
" And [Schabb. fol. 104. 2.] Did not Ben Satda bring enchantments
" out of Egypt in the cutting which was in his flefh? Under Ben
" Satda they wound our Jefus with their reproaches."

The ftorie of our Lord's journey to Alexandria with *Jofhua Ben Perachia*, when King Jannay killed the Rabbins, may be feen more at large in fome other authors (x) to whom I refer. And I fhall tranfcribe it (y) below, though I do not tranflate it entire. It is obfcure. Neverthelefs, the folly, the malice, and the falfhood of it are apparent.

It

(x) *Vide B. Scheidii. Loca Talmudica, in quibus Jefu et difcipulorum ejus fit mentio. p.* 6. *et Wagenfeil. Confutatio, libr. Toldos Jefchu. p.* 15. 16.

(y) *In Tr. Sanhedrin f.* 107. 2. *et Sota f.* 47. 1. Quum Jannai Rex interficiebat Rabbinos, fugiebat R. Jofua filius Parachiae et Jefus Alexandriam Aegypti. Pace reddita, in hacc verba Simeon Sel etachides R. Jofuae Perachiae filio fcribit. Hierofolymae civitas fancta, tibi Alexandriae Aegypti. O foror mea, maritus meus in medio tui degit, at ego fedeo defolata. Surgens ergo ille veniebat eo, et pervenit ad quandam hofpitam, quae omnibus honoris officiis cum profequebatur. Tum dicebat [Jofua] Quam pulchrum eft hoc hofpitium Sed difcipulus de hofpita fermonem excipiens, dicebat ei : Mi magifter, oculi ejus funt teretes. Cui ille refpondebat : Impie, taliane tu curas? atque feminas fpectas intentius? Nec mora. Producls ergo 400 tubis, proclamari curabat cum [Jefum] effe excommunicatum. Saepenumero adibat [difci-

pulus] magiftrum, obfecrans, ut fefe denuo reciperet. Verum ipfe ejus nullam habuit rationem. Die quodam, cum recitaffet [Jofua Perachides] lectionem, Audi Ifrael, Deut. vi. 4 accedit [Jefus] Perachidem. Nam putabat fe receptum iri. Indicabat ei R. Jofua filius Perachiae manu fua, quod vellet recipere eum. Ipfe [Jefus] putabat, quod repellendo repelleret fe. Abibat ergo, et fufpendens laterem, eam adorabat. Dicebat [Perachides] illi : Refipifce. Cui ille refpondebat : Sic a te ipfo didici : Quod nulli, qui peccavit, et ad peccandum multis fuit auctor, facultas agendi poenitentiam fuppeditetur? Nam dixerat Mar *doctor Talmudicus*] Jefus ad magiam feduxit, et crimen, Deut. xiii. 5. 6. impulfionis, vetitum commifit, et Ifraelitis ad peccandum auctor fuit. Ergo, *ceu Gemarici volunt, deferto Perachide praeceptore, Jefchu totum fe deinde magicis artibus in Aegypto addixit : cunique has intus et in cute teneret, in Judaeam fe contulit.* Apud Scheid. et Wagenf. ubi fupra.

It should be observed, that this storie of our Lord's journey into Egypt, with *Joshua Ben Perachiah*, has little agreement with the true historie in Matt. ii. 13...23. For according to the Evangelist, Jesus was carried thither, when an infant, and was soon brought back again into Judea. But according to the *Talmudists*, Jesus was a young man, when he went thither with *Joshua Perachides*, who is supposed to have been his master or tutor. And according to them, when *Perachides* and *Jesus* had been some while in Egypt, they were informed, that peace was restored in Judea. As they were returning back, they were well received at an inn. Here Perachides and Jesus disagreed, and parted asunder. Nor could they ever be reconciled again, though some attempts on both sides were made toward a reconciliation. After that Jesus, as is said, wholly gave up himself to magical practises, and was excommunicated.

If by *King Jannai* be intended *Alexander Jannaeus*, here is a great anachronism. For he died fourscore years (z) before the Christian epoch. But I do not insist upon that. For, perhaps, it is owing to design, and not to ignorance.

If in the discourse between *Perachides* and *Jesus*, at the inn, where they first disagreed, there be an aspersion of our Lord's moral character, as if he too attentively observed the faces of women: it is of a piece with another charge of theirs, that Jesus endeavored to seduce men to idolatrie. Which we shall see presently.

I do acknowledge, however, that when I first observed this paragraph, I was not a little surprized. For *Origen* says, " that *(a)*
" though innumerable lies and calumnies had been forged against
" the venerable Jesus, none had dared to charge him with any in-
" tem-

(z) *Prideaux's Connexion, year before Christ* 79. p. 396. 397.

(a) ... πρὸς τὸν σεμνὸν ἡμῶν Ἰησῦν, ἵν μηδὲ ἐν μίμα κατηγορήσαντες, κỳ ψευδῆ ὅσα περὶ αὐτῶ λέγοντες, δεδύνηνται κατειπεῖν, ὡς κ'ἂν τὸ τυχὸν ἀκολασίας κ'ἂν ἐπ' ὀλίγον γευσαμένε. *Contr. Cels.* l. 3. num. 36. *Bened.* p. 32. *Spenc.*

Ch. V.   Our Lord's Journey into Egypt.

" temperance whatever." So says *Origen* about the midle of the third centurie. He speaks confidently, with full assurance. If he had ever met with such a calumnie, he would not have denied it. For he was perfectly honest and sincere. And if such a calumnie had appeared, he was as likely to know it, as any man. For he was acquainted with all sorts of people. And he had often conversed with the learned men of the Jewish nation, as well as others. This storie therefore was not in being in his time, not till after it. But reflexions upon a man's character unknown, till long after his departure out of the world, are destitute of authority, and deserve no regard. They only shew the bad temper of those who receive, or who invent and forge them.

Let me add one thought more here. We may reasonably conclude, and reckon it certain from Origen's work, that *Celsus* knew nothing of this storie. Consequently, it was not yet invented. For he had conversed with Jews, and made use of them to assist him in his argument against the Christians: and had picked up all the scandal he could get.

I must be allowed to observe yet farther. Celsus had made use of some disparaging expressions concerning our Saviour. Whereupon Origen says: " If (**) Celsus had alleged any kind of infa-
" mous actions in the life of Jesus, we would have done our best
" to answer to every thing that might appear so to him. As to the
" miserable death of Jesus, the same may be objected to *Socrates* and
" *Anaxarchus*, just mentioned." Celsus therefore knew not of any such thing.

Finally, I do not recollect in the remains of Celsus, who wrote in the second, nor in Origen, who wrote in the third centurie, any

---

(**) Ἐι γὰρ τὰ εἴδη τῦ ἐπιρρητοτάτυ βίυ ἐν ταῖς πράξεσιν αὐτῦ φαινόμενα αὐτῷ ἐκτιθέμενος ἦν, κἂν ἠγωνισάμεθα πρὸς ἕκαςον τῶν δοκύντων ἔιναι αὐτῷ ἐπιρρητοτάτων. *Contr. Cels.* l. 7. §. 56. *Ben.* p. 369. f. *Sperc.*

traces of this *journey of our Lord into Egypt with a tutor*. This story therefore is a late, as well as a malicious fiction without ground.

The second quotation in *Lightfoot* shall now be more distinctly transcribed. "In (b) the Mishnical tract, called *Schabbath*, it is said:
"If any one, especially on the Sabbath, draws a line, or makes a
"cut in his flesh, he is obliged to bring a sin-offering. But the
"wise men absolve him. Upon which words it is remarked in the
"*Gemara*. A tradition. R. *Eliefer* said to the wise men. But did
"not the Son of Stada bring magical arts out of Egypt, in a cutting
"in his flesh? The *Gloss* says: The reason of that was, that he
"could not bring them away in writing, because the Priests dili-
"gently searched all at their going away, that they might not carry
"out magical arts, to teach them to men dwelling in other coun-
"treys."

This is said, I suppose, to insinuate, that all the great works, ascribed to our Saviour, were performed by virtue of magical arts, which he had learned in Egypt. This insinuation has been considered, and well confuted by Grotius (c) to whom I now refer. Hereafter I shall transcribe his words at length, in the chapter of *Celsus*, where this charge will come over again.

3. Let us now observe, whether Jesus gained any disciples.

Lightfoot

(b) In tractatu *Schabbath* fol. 104. 2. in *Mishna* dicitur. Si quis [die Sabbathi] lineam ducat, feu incisuram faciat super carnem suam, R. Eliefer eum reum censet sacrificii peccati. Sapientes autem absolvunt. Postea in *Gemara*, ad haec verba notatur: Traditio. Dixit R. Eliefer ad Sapientes: At annon Filius Stadae extulit magicas artes ex Aegypto, in incisura, quae erat super carne ejus? *Glossa*. Quia non poterat eas efferre, vel educere, scriptas: quia Magi diligenter inquirebant in omnes qui exibant, ne efferrent artes magicas, ad docendum eas alios homines alibi terrarum habitantes. *Scheid.* ib. p. 1. et *Wagenseil. Confut. Told. Jescbu.* p. 17.

(c) *De V. R. Chr. l. 5. cap. iii.*

Ch. V.   *Of the Disciples of Jesus.*   195

A. D. 500.

Lightfoot upon Mat. ix. 9. speaks to this purpose. " Five disci- Of
" ples of Christ are mentioned by the Talmudists. [Bab. Sanhe- *Christ's*
" drim. fol. 431.] Among whom Matthew seems to be named. *The Disciples.*
Rabbins deliver, there were five disciples of Jesus, Matthai, Nahai,
" *Nezer, Boni, and Thodah.* These they relate, were led out, and
" killed. Perhaps five are only mentioned by them, because five
" of the disciples were chiefly employed among the Jews: namely
" Matthew, who wrote his Gospel in Judea, Peter, James, John,
" and Judas."

I shall now transcribe at length the passage of the Babylonian Talmud, to which Lightfoot refers: though it is so silly, that, when produced, some may think, it might have been omitted.

" The *(d)* Rabbins have taught, that there were five disciples
                                  C c 2   " of

(d) Sanhedr. cap. vi. fol. 43. fin. Quinque tantum discipuli dicuntur fuisse Jesu Nazareno, quorum nomina, Matthai, sc. Matthaeus, Nakai, Nezer, Boni, et Toda, sc. Thaddaeus, qui alio nomine Lebbaeus fuit appellatus. Matt. x. 3. Verba integre ita habent... Rabbini docuerunt, quinque discipulos fuisse Jesu, Matthai, Nakai, Nezer, Boni, et Toda. Cum adduxissent Matthai, [ut capitis ipsum damnarent,] dixit ille ad Judices: Num Matthai occidetur? Atqui scriptum est: Quando [Matai] veniam, ut compaream coram facie Dei? Ps. xlii. 2. Sed illi regesserunt: Omnino, Matthai occidetur, quia scriptum est, Quando [Matai] morietur, ut pereat nomen ejus? Ps. xli. 5. Cum adduxissent Nakai, dixit ille : Num Nakai occidetur? Atqui scriptum est. Ex. xxiii. 7. Insontem [naki] et justum non occides. Sed illi responderunt: Omnino, Nakai occidetur, sicut scriptum est. Ps. x. 8. In latibulis occidit insontem. [Naki]. Cum adduxissent Nezer, dixit ad illos : Num Nezer occidetur? Atqui scriptum est, Es. xi. 1. Nezer e radicibus ejus fructum feret. Sed illi reposuerunt. Omnino Nezer occidetur, quia scriptum est. Es. xiv. 9. Tu autem ejectus es e sepulchro tuo, ut surculus [nezer] abominabilis. Cum adduxerunt Boni, dixit ille : Num Boni occidetur? Atqui scriptum est Ex. iv. 22. Filius meus [Beni] primogenitus est Israel. Sed illi regesserunt : Omnino Boni occidetur, sicut scriptum est Ex. iv. 23. Ecce ego occidam filium tuam [bincka.] primogenitum. Cum adduxissent Todam, dixit ad illos : Num Toda occidetur ? Atqui scriptum exstat. Ps. c. 1. *Psalmus* [Lethoda] *eucharisticus*. Sed illi responderunt : Omnino Toda occidetur, quemadmodum
                                                                                      scrip-

A. D. 500.

"of Jesus, Matthai, Nakai, Nezer, Boni, and Toda. When
"Matthai was brought forth [*to be condemned to death*] he said to
"the Judges: Shall Matthai be flain? But it is written: *When shall*
"*I come* [Matai] *and appear before God!* Pſ. xlii. 2. But they an-
"ſwered: Yes, Matthai ſhall be ſlain. For it is written: *When*
"[Matai] *ſhall be die, and his name periſh!* Pſ. xli. 5. When Na-
"kai was brought out, he ſaid: Shall Nakai be ſlain? But it is
"written: *Thou ſhalt not kill the innocent,* [Nakai] *and the juſt.* Ex.
"xxiii. 7. But they ſaid: Yes, Nakai ſhall be ſlain. For it is
"written: *In the ſecret places does he murder the innocent.* [Naki.]
"Pſ. x. 8. When they brought forth Nezer, he ſaid to them. And
"ſhall Nezer be ſlain? But it is written, *A branch* [Nezer] *ſhall*
"*grow out of his roots.* Iſ. xi. 1. But they anſwered: Yes, Nezer
"ſhall be ſlain. For it is written: *Thou art caſt out of thy grave, as*
"*an abominable branch.* Iſ. xiv. 19. When they brought out Boni,
"he ſaid: And ſhall Boni be ſlain? But it is written: Iſrael is *my*
"*ſon* [Beni] *even my firſt-born.* Ex. iv. 22. But they ſaid: Yes,
"Boni ſhall be ſlain. For it is written: *Behold, I will ſlay thy ſon,*
"[bineka.] *thy firſt-born.* Ex. iv. 23. When they brought out
"Toda, he ſaid to them: *And ſhall Toda be ſlain?* It is written:
"*A pſalm to praiſe.* [Lethoda.] Pſ. c. But they anſwered: Yes,
"Toda ſhall be ſlain. For it is written: *Whoſo offereth praiſe,* [To-
"da] *gloriſieth me."*

Here it may be aſked: Why do the Talmudiſts ſpeak only of five diſciples of Jeſus? *Lightfoot*, as before ſeen, ſuppoſeth it to be, that theſe five men were chiefly employed among the Jews. *Edzardus* ſays: "We *(e)* hence ſee, how falſe and fabulous every thing is,

---

ſcriptum eſt. Pſ. l. 23. Qui ſacrificat laudem [Toda] is honorabit me. *Ap.* Edzard *Avoda Sara.* T. i. p. 298. 299. *Conf.* B. *Scheidii Loca Talmudica de Jeſu et Diſ-*cipulis ejus et *Wagenſel. Conſut.* T. I. p. 17.

(*e*) Quod ſi autem quinque tantum diſcipuli hi Jeſu Nazareno fuerunt, unde ergo

is, which the Talmudists say of Christ, and his disciples." Which, surely is not amiss. However, to me it seems, that the Jewish Rabbins affected silence and reserve about Jesus, and his historie, and said little about it, the better to keep their own people in ignorance, and bondage. *Wagenseil*'s reflexions upon this passage, are somewhat different. I place them *(f)* below: though nothing material can be said upon what is so exceeding trifling.

A. D. 500.

4. It may be questioned, whether *James* be one of the five disciples there named. I shall therefore allege a passage of the Talmud, where he is mentioned.

R. *Akiba* and Rabbi *Eliefer* are talking together. " Eliefer *(g)* " says, O Akiba, you have brought something to my mind. As I " was walking in the high street of Zipporis, I met one of the dis- " ciples of Jesus of Nazareth, whose name is James, a man of the " town of Shecaniah. He said to me: In your law it is written. " *Thou shalt not bring the hire of a harlot.* Deut. xxiii. 18. I did
" not

go sextus, Jacobus Sechanienfis, cujus nomen inter quinque numeratos non apparet? Constat hinc, quam fabulosa sit Talmudistarum narratio de iis quae contra Christum atque discipulos ejus deblaterent. Ut alia confutatione non sit opus, cum seipsos suis contradictionibus jugulent. *Edz. ibid. p.* 299.

(f) Apparet, ista huc tendere, quasi in viros illos, quorum nomina exprimuntur, ultimis poenis fuerit animadversum : etsi magis est ut credamus, ab otioso aliquo, et scripturae dicta, in lusum et jocum sic detorquente, delirantis ingenioli ostentandi caussa, ineptias has esse confictas. *Wagenf. ibid. p.* 18.

(g) In Tr. Avoda Sara. f. 16. 2. Tradiderunt Rabbini. . . . Tum P. Eliazar.

In memoriam mihi, o Akiba revocasti, aiebat: me aliquando spatiatum in foro superiori urbis Zipporis, obvium habuisse aliquem ex discipulis Jesu Nazareni, cui nomen erat Jacobus, civis Caphar, vel viri Saccanienfis, qui dicebat mihi. In Lege vestra scribitur ; *Non afferes mercedem meretricis.* . . . Quo audito, nihil prorsus ei respondebam. Illo autem pergente mihi dicere. Sic docuit me Jesus Nazarenus. *Si ex mercede meretricia, meretrix quid colligat, usque ad mercedem meretricis revertetur.* Ex loco impuro si qua venerint, in locum impurum redibunt. Et profuit mihi verbum hoc opera hujus. . . . *ap. Scheid. Loca Talmud. p.* 5. 6. *Et Conf. Edzardi Avoda Sara. Vol.* i. *p.* 130.

A. D. 500.	"not make him any anfwer. But he added, and faid to me. Jefus of Nazareth taught me the meaning. *She gathered it of the hire of a harlot. And they shall return to the hire of a harlot.* Mic. i. 7. *From an impure place they came. And to an impure place they shall return.* Which interpretation, (fays Eliezer,) did not difpleafe me."

5. We will now obferve fome paffages concerning our Saviour's laft fufferings.

Of the Death of Jefus. Says *Lightfoot* upon Matt. xxvii. 31. "Thefe things (*h*) are delivered in Sanhedrim [cap. vi. Hal. 4.] of one that is guilty of ftoning: *If there be no defenfe found for him, they lead him out to be ftoned, and a Cryer went out before him, faying aloud thus. N. N. comes out to be ftoned, becaufe he has done fo and fo. The witneffes againft him are N. N. Whofoever can bring any thing in his defenfe, let him come forth and produce it.* On which thus the Gemara of Babylon. *The tradition is, that on the evening of the Paffover Jefus was hanged, and that a cryer went before him for forty days, making this proclamation: This man comes forth to be ftoned, becaufe he dealt in forceries, and perfuaded, and feduced Ifrael. Whofoever*

(*h*) I fhall put here an exact Latin verfion of the fame. Tr. Sanhedrim. fol. 43. Mifhna. Inventa reoc paitis innocentia, reus ille liber dimittitur. Sin minus, exit, ut lapidetur. Praeco autem exit ante eum, his verbis proclamans: Vir ifte N. N. Filius alicujus N. N. exit, ut lapidetur, quia tranfgreffus eft talem tranfgreffionem. Cujus rei teftes funt hi, N. N. et N. N. Quicunque noverit aliquid de ejus innocentia, veniat, et doceat de eo. Poftea in Gemara ad verba Mifhnae: *praeco autem exit ante eum, &c.* notatur. Atqui traditio eft: Die Parafceves Sabbathi fufpenderunt Jefum, et praeco exibat ante eum 40. diebus, his verbis prolatis proclamans: Exit ut lapidetur, quia magicas artes exercuit, feduxit, et impulit Ifraelitas. Quicunque ergo noverit aliquid de ejus innocentia, veniat, et doceat de eo. Cum autem nihil de ejus innocentia comprobanda inveniri potuifiet, fufpenderunt cum die Parafceves Pafchatis. Dixit Ula: Et putetur, quod filius verforum feu contrariorum innocentiae ipfe feductor eft. Dixit autem Deus, Deut. xiii. 8. Non parces, neque teges fuper eo." Deut. xiii. 8. et Conf. 5. et 6. *Scheid. Loca Talmud.* p. 7. 8. *Conf. Wag. Confut. T. I. p.* 19.

Ch. V.   *Our Lord's last Sufferings.*   199

"*soever knows of any defense for him, let him come forth, and produce*   A. D.
"*it. But no defense could be found. Therefore they hanged him upon*   500.
"*the evening of the Passover. Ulla saith, his case seemed not to ad-*
"*mit of any defense, since he was a seducer, and of such God has said:*
"*Thou shalt not spare him, nor conceal him.*" Deut. xiii.

There is another place relating to the same event, the death of our Saviour, to be taken from the Babylonian Talmud. "The (*i*) "*Mishna* explaining Deut. xiii. and shewing, who is the seducer there "spoken of, says, Of all that are adjudged to die, to none of them "are snares to be laid, excepting a seducer. For, if he has at- "tempted two, and they bear testimonie against him, he is to be "stoned. Upon this it is said in the *Gemara*. Against none are "snares to be laid, except against a seducer of the people. [Mean- "ing one who seduces to idolatrie.] And that is done after this "manner. They light a candle in a closet or inner room, and "place witnesses in another room, so that they may see him, and
                                                                     "hear

---

(*i*) *Sanhedrim* f. 67. 1. *Mishna, de quo Deut. xiii.* 6. Ex omnibus qui morti adjudicantur in Lege, nulli insidiae collocantur, hoc excepto. . . . Postea, in Gemara notatur: Ex omnibus, qui morti adjudicantur in Lege, nulli insidiae collocantur, hoc excepto [*seductori, qui aliud ad idololatriam, et cultum alienum cupit seducere.*] Quomodo faciunt id ei? Accendunt illi candelam in conclavi interiori, et testes collocant in cubiculo exteriori, ut hi ipsum videre, et vocem ejus audire possint. Sed ipse non videt illos. Tum ille, quem antea conatus erat seducere, dicit ei, Repete, quaeso, id quod ante hac dixisti hic privatim. Tum, si id dicat, hic regerit ei: Quomodo relinquemus Deum nostrum in Coelis, et serviemus idolis ⊦

Ad hoc si convertatur, poenitentia acta, bene est. Si vero dicat: Hoc est officium nostrum, atque ita omnino decet nos facere, testes exterius audientes, eum ad domum judicii abducunt, et lapidant. [Conf. Schabbath. f. 104. 2.] sic fecerunt filio Stadae, [vel Stadtae] in Lud, et suspenderunt eum in vespera Paschatis, seu pridie d.ei Paschatis. Filius Stadae filius Pandirae c°. Dixit R. Chasda: Maritus seu procus matris ejus fuit Stada, iniens Pandiram. . . . Maritus Paphus filius Judae ipse est. mater ejus Stada, mater ejus Maria, plicatrix capillorum mulierum erat: sicut dicimus in Pompedita. Declinavit haec a marito suo. Glossa: Ideo quia scortata haec erat, vocabatur ita. *Schedii Loca Talmud.* p. 1. *et* 2.

"hear his voice, but he does not see them. There he, whom some
"time before he had endeavored to seduce, (*being with him,*) says to
"him. Repeat to me now in private, what you before said to me. If
"he then repeats it, the other says to him: How can we leave our
"God who is in the heavens, and serve idols? If he then owns his
"fault, and repents, all is well. But if he says: This is our duty, and so
"we ought to do: the witnesses, who are in the outer room, carry him
"to the house of judgement, and stone him. So they did to the son
"of Stada in Lud, and hanged him on the evening of the Passover.
"Rabbi Chasda said: the son of Stada is the son of Pandera....
"His mother was Stada. She was Mary the plaiter of womens
"hair: as we say in Pompedita, she departed from her husband. In
"the Gloss it is said: she was so called, because she transgressed
"the laws of chastity."

This is translated by Lightfoot upon Matt. xxvii. 56. p. 270. after this manner. *They stoned the son of Satda in Lydda, and hanged him up on the evening of the Passover. Now this son of Satda was son of Pandira. Indeed Rabbi Chasda said, the husband [of his mother] was Satda, her husband was Pandira, her husband was Papus, the son of Juda. But yet I say his mother was Satda, namely Mary the plaiter of womens hair: as they say in Pombeditha, she departed from her husband.*

In several other places of these Talmudical writers Mary is called a *plaiter of womens hair*, as may be seen in Lightfoot, p. 270. (k) And from some things alleged just now, it seems, that thereby they denote a transgressor of the laws of purity. And we are led to think, that by this description they intended to represent not her outward condition, but her moral character.

Upon the two foregoing passages relating to the event of our Saviour's death, we may now make some remarks.

First,

(k) *Vid. et Scheid. Loca Talmud.* p. 3.

Ch. V.   *Our Lord's laſt Sufferings.*

Firſt, it is here acknowledged, that Jeſus ſuffered death as a malefactor. And that he was put to death at the time of a Jewiſh Paſſover, or on the *evening* of it, as the expreſſion is.

Secondly, But here are many great and notorious falſhoods. It is here ſaid, that Jeſus was put to death at *Lud :* whereas it is certain, that he ſuffered at *Jeruſalem*. It is inſinuated, that he endeavoured to perſuade men to forſake the true God, and worſhip falſe gods, and idols. Another abominable falſhood. It is alſo inſinuated, that he carried on this evil deſign of ſeducing men from the worſhip of the true God in a *clandeſtine* manner : whereas nothing is more certain, than that Jeſus lived, and acted, and taught publicly before all the world. Farther, it is intimated, that for many days before his death, proclamation was made, that any who could ſay any thing in his defenſe might appear and plead for him. But no defenſe was made. It is alſo ſaid, that he was put to death by *ſtoning*, and then *hanged* up. Which indeed was the uſual method among the Jews, firſt to put criminals to death, and then hang them up. But Jeſus was *crucified*. And though the Jews were his proſecutors, he was condemned, and put to death by a Roman magiſtrate.

It is truly ſurprizing to ſee ſuch falſities, contrarie to well known facts. For the ſufferings of Jeſus, and the circumſtances of them, are recorded in the Goſpels, well known hiſtories, writ in a language, which was then almoſt univerſal in Europe, Aſia, and Africa. That Jeſus was crucified at Jeruſalem, when *Pontius Pilate* was Governour of Judea, under the Emperour *Tiberius*, was in all Chriſtian Creeds, and atteſted by Roman Authors of good credit, and indeed was well known to all Greeks and Romans in general. How then was it poſſible for the Jewiſh Rabbins, whoſe teſtimonies are collected in their Talmuds, to ſpeak in the manner, which we have now ſeen ? Perhaps it is not eaſie to be accounted for. But I apprehend the Caſe to be this. The Rabbins taught and wrote in a language little known to any in the fourth and fifth centuries, but themselves, and the men of their own nation. Their people were ignorant, and they endeavored to keep them so. Their people had a great respect for them, and so they presumed to say whatever they pleased.

The power of Miracles in Jesus, and his Disciples.

6. There seems to be in these writings an acknowledgement of the power of miracles in Jesus, and his disciples. "In *(l)* the Gemara, " upon Avoda Sara, in Bareitha, it is said : No man may converse " with heretics, nor receive medicines from them, though the dis- " ease be mortal and desperate. Of this there is an example in the " son of Dama, nephew to R. Ismael by his sister. When he had " been bit by a serpent, James of Shechania [*a disciple of Jesus*] " came to heal him. But R. Ismael did not allow it to be done. " The son of Dama said to R. Ismael: O Rabbi Ismael, my uncle, " let me be healed by him. I will allege a text out of the Law, " which allows of it. But before he had finished all he would say, " he expired. Then Ishmael pronounced this speech over him: " Thou art happy, o son of Dama. For thy body has remained pure, " and thy soul also has gone pure out of it. And thou hast not " transgressed the words of thy brethren."

This

(l) Similis locus habetur infra in *Gemara fol.* 27. *col.* 2. *med.* Sed insto ego. In Bareitha docemur. Non conversabitur quisquam cum haereticis, neque licet medicinam ab illis admittere, etsi morbus videatur ita desperatus, ut aegrotus non sit ultra unius horae spatium superfuturus. Estat quoque hujus rei exemplum in filio Damae, nepote R. Ismaelis ex sorore, quem cum inomordisset serpens, venit Jacobus Secaniensis ad sanandum ipsum. Sed non permisit ei R. Ismael. Dicebat quidem filius Damae ad R. Ismaelum: O Rabbi Ismael frater, [*i. e. cognate, avuncule*,] mi! Sine ipsum, ut saner ab ipso. Afferam enim textum e Lege, qui id concedat. Sed nondum absolverat omnia, quae constituerat dicere, cum jam efflaret animam, atque moreretur. Tum R. Ismael sequentem super ipsum concionculam habuit. Beatus es, o fili Damae! quod corpus tuum manserit mundum, etiamque anima tuo corpore exierit munda, neque fueris transgressus verba Sociorum tuorum. &c. *Edzard. Avoda Sara. Vol.* i. *p.* 312. *Conf. Martini Pug. Fidei. P.* 2. *cap.* 8. *p.* 289.

Ch. V.   *Miracles wrought by Christ's Disciples.*   203

This (*m*) is supposed to be an acknowledgement of the power of working miracles in the name of Jesus, at the same time that it shews the virulent temper of the Jewish Doctors against him and his disciples.

A. D. 500.

There is another like instance alleged from the Jerusalem Talmud. "A (*n*) child of a son of Rabbi Joses, son of Levi, swallow-
"ed somewhat poysonous. There came a man, who pronounced
"some words to him in the name of Jesus, son of Pandira, and he
"was healed. When he was going away, R. Joses said to him:
"What word did you use? He answered, such a word. R. Joses
"said to him: Better had it been for him to die, than to hear such
"a word. And so it happened, that is, he instantly died."

Another (*o*) proof this of the power of miracles inherent in the disciples of Jesus, and at the same time, a mark of the malignity of the Jewish Rabbins.

That passage I have transcribed, as it is in the *Pugio Fidei*. I shall now (*p*) put it down below, as it stands in *Edzardi Avoda Sara*.

D d 2   7. It

(*m*) Memorabile hujus rei exemplum occurrit Cod. Abhoda zara f. 27. 2. de R. Ismaele vetante aliquem sanari in nomine Jesu . . . *Exemplo est B. Dama* . . . Insignis sane historia, et praeclarum veritatis Evangelicae testimonium, ab ipsis Judaeis dictum. *J. Rhenferd. Diss. de Redemtione Marcosiorum et Heracleonit.* §. L. p. 215.

(*n*) Item in lib. *Sabbat Jerosolymitana*, distinctione Shemona Scheratzin. . . . Filius filii R. Jose filii Levi glutiverat toxicum scilicet, vel aliud morbiferum. Venit itaque vir quidam et conjuravit ei in nomine Jesu Panderini, et sanatus est, five quievit. Cumque exivisset, ait ei, quomodo conjurasti eum? Ait ei, tali verbo.

Ait ei, tali verbo. Ait ei: Remissius fuisset ei, si mortuus fuisset, ut non audivisset verbum tale. Et factum est sic ei: id est, statim mortuus est. *Pug. Fid. ib. p. 290.*

(*o*) Si quis diligenter advertat has duas traditiones, in nomine Domini nostri Jesu Christi fuisse facta miracula Judaicarum scripturarum testimonio comprobabit. *Roym. Martin. ib.*

(*p*) Similis textus est in Talmude Hierosolymitano Avoda S. Fol 40. 4. et Schabb. fol. 14. 4. med. . . . Nepos R. Josuae filii Levi laborabat ab absorpto. [id est, diglutiverat aliquid, quod ipsi in gutture haerebat, et suffocationem minabatur.] Venitque quidam, qui illi clam insusurravit, [id est, jussit ipsum convalescere.]

A. D. 500.

Of the Destruction of Jerusalem.

7. It will certainly be worth the while, to take a testimonie from these writers to the destruction of Jerusalem, and the temple there. I shall therefore transcribe and translate almost word for word a long passage out of the Babylonian Talmud, in the title *Gittin*, chapter *Hannisab*.

" This *(q)* is the tradition. Rabbi Eliaser said: Go, and see how
" the

lescere.] in nomine Jesu filii Pandirae. Unde confestim respiravit. Quando autem egressus est inde, dixit ad eum R. Josua filius Levi. Quid insusurrasti ei ? Respondit ille, vocem hanc [i. e. nomen Jesu.] Tum R. Josua: Praestitisset ipsum fuisse mortuum, et non audivisse nomen illud. Atque hoc ipsum etiam ei [haud longe post] contigit. *Edzard, Avoda zara. Vol.* 2. *p.* 311. 312.

(q) Traditio est. Dixit R. Eleaser: Exi, et vide quanta est virtus pudoris, quia ecce Deus Sanctus et Benedictus juvit Bar-kamtza, et destruxit domum suam, et exussit templum suum, et desolavit Jerusalem. ... Ivit Romam, et dixit Neroni Caesari: Judaei rebellarunt contra te. Dixit ei : Quis dicit ? Dixit ei mitte illis sacrificium. Videbis, si illi offerent. Ivit filius Kamtza, et misit per manus ejus vitulum trimam. Ipse autem rediens impressit in ea maculam in ora labii ejus. Alii dicunt, quod in pupilla oculi ejus maculam impressit : secundum aliquorum opinionem est macula. et secundum opinionem aliorum non est macula. Rabbini censebant itaque illam 'acrificandam propter pacem regni. Dixit eis R. Zacharias filius Onkelos: dicetur, Maculata offeruntur super altare. Voluerunt occidere eum ne iret, et diceret. Dixit eis R.

Zacharias, dicent : Mittens maculam in Sanctuarium occidetur? Dixit R. Jochanan : Superstitio R. Zachariae destruxit domum nostram, et combussit templum nostrum, et urbem nostram evertit, et fecit ut nos e terra nostra captivi duceremur. Misit itaque Bar-Kamtza super his ad Neronem Caesarem. Quando venit, jecit sagittam ad orientem. Cecidit ad Jerusalem ad occidentem... Dixit puero. Lege mihi versum tuum. Dixit ei Ezech. xxv. 14. ... Dixit Nero: Deus sanctus, benedictus, vult per me destruere domum suam. Misitque contra illos Vespasianum, qui venit, et obsedit Jerusalem tres annos, et dimidium. Interim venit nuncius ad eum, dicens illi : Surge, quia mortuus est Nero Caesar, et consenserunt tibi optimates Romanorum, ut te constituant principem.... Ivit, et misit Titum impium filium suum.... Hic est Titus impius, qui blasphemavit, et maledixit contra Justum, i. e. Deum. Quid fecit ? Cepit meretricem in manu sua, et ingressus in Sancta Sanctorum stravit librum legis et transgressus est super illum transgressionem. Et accepit gladium, et dirupit vela, et factum est miraculum. Et fuit sanguis erumpens et exiens. Et putavit occidisse ipsam substantiam Dei sancti benedicti, i. e. ipsum Deum.... Quid fecit? Accepit vela, et fecit

Ch. V.   Of the Destruction of Jerusalem.

"the blessed and holy God helped Bar-kamtza, and he destroyed his house, and burnt up his temple, and made Jerusalem desolate." [*Here is inserted an account of a trifling discourse and difference between some Rabbins.*] "Whereupon he [Bar-kamtza] went to Rome, and said to the Emperour Nero, the Jews have rebelled against thee. Who says this, said the Emperour? Kamtza answered: Send to them a sacrifice. See if they will offer it. Bar-kamtza returned. Nero sent by him a heifer three years old. As he was going, he made a blemish in the mouth of it. Others say, in the pupil of it's eye. According to the opinion of others, it was no blemish. The Rabbins therefore thought it ought to be offered for preserving the peace of the nation. But Rabbi Zacharias, son of Onkelos, said: shall blemished sacrifices be offered upon the altar? He that brings blemished sacrifices into the sanctuarie, ought to be put to death. R. Jochanan said. The superstition of R. Zacharias has destroyed our house, and burnt up our temple, and overthrown our city, and caused us to be led captive out of our land. Bar-kamtza therefore sent an account of these things to Nero.... Nero said: the great and blessed God has determined, by me to destroy his house. And he sent against them Vespasian, who came, and besieged Jerusalem three years and a half. In the mean time there came a messenger to him, who said: Arise, for the Emperour Nero is dead, and the Nobles of
"the

---

fecit illa sicut saccum, et adduxit omnia vasa quae erant in Sanctuario, et posuit illa in illo. Et collocavit illa in navi, ut iret, et gloriaretur in urbe sua. . . . Stetit contra Draco, vel tempestas, in mari, ut demergeret illum in mari. Dixit: Puto ego, quod Deus horum nullam habet potentiam non in mari: Venit Pharao, et submersit cum in mari. Stat etiam contra me, ut me submergat. Si fortis est, ascendat in siccam, et faciat bellum mecum. Exivit filia vocis, et dixit ei, Impie fili impii, fili filii impii Esau: Creatura vilis est mihi in mundo meo, et culex est nomen ejus. Ascende in siccam, et bellum contra illam geres. Statim innuit Deus mari, et quievit. Ascendit in siccam, et venit culex, et ingressus est in nasum ejus, et perforavit illi cerebrum septem annis, et occidit illum. *Ex libro Gittin. capite Hannisakin. ap. R. Martin. Pug. Fid. P.* 3. *cap. xxi. p.* 703. 704.

A. D. 500.

"the Romans have agreed to make thee Emperour. He went, and
"sent the impious Titus, his son.... This is the impious Titus,
"who blasphemed the Most High, even God himself. What did
"he do? He took a harlot into the holy of holies, and there lay
"with her. And he took a sword, and cut the veils. At the same
"time there was a miracle. For bloud burst out. He thought he
"had killed God himself... Well, what did he? He took the veils,
"and made a sack of them, and put into it all the vessels of the
"Sanctuarie. And then put them in a ship, that he might go and
"triumph in his city... There stood against him a dragon, that he
"might drown him in the sea. He said, I think the God of these
"men has no power but in the sea. Pharaoh arose, and he drowned
"him in the sea. He has a mind to destroy me in the like man-
"ner. If he has power, let him come upon the dry land, and
"make war with me. There went forth a voice, and said to him:
"O Impious son of the wicked man, o son of the impious son of
"Esau, there is a contemptible creature in my world, called a gnat.
"Go upon the dry land, and you shall make war against it. God
"presently rebuked the sea, and it was calm. He went out upon
"the dry land, and the gnat came, and entered into his nose, and
"gnawed his brain seven years, and killed him."

J. De Voisin, in his notes upon this passage, particularly the last words of it, quotes some Jewish authors, who say, "the (r) storie of the fly is not to be understood literally, but mystically, and allegorically, intending to insinuate in men's minds a persuasion of the power of God, and that he is able to abase those who rise up against him, and to punish the proudest of men by very contemptible creatures."

(r) Alii asserunt illud de culice, sive musca ejusmodi, non juxta literalem sensum intelligendum esse, sed sensum habere mysticum.... Itaque poteris de historia Titi libere pronuntiare, quod narratio ejus nihil aliud sit, quam inventio, sive fabula, atque modus doctrinae usitatus apud eruditos ad stabiliendum in corde plebis, quod magnus est Dominus noster, et potentissimus, ad retribuendum illis qui contra ipsum insurgunt: sed in primis ad puniendum superbos etiam per minimam creaturam. *Ap. Pugion. Fid. p.* 714.

Ch. V.   *Of the Destruction of Jerusalem.*

tures." Nor is it any wonder, that some should be ashamed of this silly storie of the fly, getting up a man's nose, and dwelling there seven years. But men of true wisdom can find out more cleanly allegories than this, when they are disposed to make use of that kind of instruction.

A. D. 500.

Nor has *Voisin* alleged any Jewish authors, who condemn the horrible storie of Titus defiling the sanctuarie of the temple with lewdnesse: though *Martini* has alleged another Jewish writing in great repute, where (s) the same storie is told, with all the same horrible, or yet more horrible circumstances of filthinesse, if such there can be. Nor is the concluding part of that narrative of the Talmud there omitted. But I presume, the Divine Being never arms his feeble creatures to destroy, or annoy men for no fault at all: for none, but such as are only imputed to them by those who give a loose to their tongues, to lye and calumniate, as they please. For Titus, when he went into the temple at Jerusalem all in flames, neither committed lewdnesse there, nor did he blaspheme the Deity.

Behold then the temper, the incorrigible temper of the Jewish people, and their Rabbins, the Talmudical writers. Their temple had been burnt up, their city destroyed, their land laid wast, and they carried into captivity. But instead of repenting, they revile him, who under God had been the instrument of their chastisement: a Prince, who, as good authority says, was as remarkable for the humanity,

(s) Hucusque Talmud. Legitur quoque in *Midrash Kohelet* super illud Eccles. cap. v. 8. ... Dixit Deus sanctus benedictus Prophetis: *Quid vos putatis, quod si vos non eatis in missionem meam, non sit mihi alius nuncius? In omni ego do missionem vel legationem meam, etiam per serpentem, vel scorpium, vel culicem, vel ranam. Titus impius ingressus est in Sancta Sanctorum, quando destruxit domum Sanctuarii, et gladius ejus districtus in manu sua, et diruspit duo vela, et accepit duas meretrices in manu illarum, et coivit cum illis, cum una super altare, cum altera super librum legis, et exivit, et gladius ejus plenus sanguine. Et incepit blasphemare, et execrari. Quid fecit? Collegit omnia vasa Sanctuarii, et posuit illa in saccho, et descendit ad navem. Et reliqua, sicut modo ex Talmude citata junx. Ibid. p. 704. 705.*

manity, the compassion, and equity, in his manner of subduing them, as for his militarie skill and courage. Who then, are the men, who exalt themselves against God?

But I may no longer indulge myself in such reflexions as these. Let us attend for our own benefit. Here is a testimonie to the destruction of Jerusalem from Talmudical writers. They agree very much with *Josephus*, in their account of the origin of the war. He says " that (*t*) Eleazar, then captain at the temple persuaded those " who officiated in sacred things, not to accept the gift or sacrifice " of a stranger. Which was the occasion of the war." The Talmudists say the same thing, in different words, after their manner. According to this account also, the war broke out near the end of the reign of *Nero*, who sent *Vespasian* General into Judea. Whilst Vespasian was there, carrying on the war, Nero died, and he was chosen to succeed him. When he was chosen Emperour at Rome, he sent *Titus* to carry on the war in Judea: The issue of which was, that the temple was burnt up, their city destroyed, and their whole government overthrown, and they carried into captivity. Moreover, as they here own, Titus was in possession of the veils, and sacred vessels of the temple, which he took with him to adorn his triumph at Rome. All this, (though they relate not particularly the distresses of the siege of Jerusalem) is said, not very differently from *Josephus*, and more agreeably to him, in some respects, than by *Josippon*, who afterwards wrote at length the historie of the war: as we shall see by and by.

(*t*) *De B. J. l. 2. cap. 17. §. 2. p. 192.*

CHAP. VI.
JOSEPH BEN GORION, or JOSIPPON.

I. *His Age, Work, and Character.* II. *Extracts from his Work, shewing his Historie of the Jewish War with the Romans, and the Destruction of Jerusalem.* III. *Concluding Remarks.*

1. WE are now coming to an Author of a very extraordinarie, or even a singular character, writer of *(a) the Jewish Historie* in six Books, who stiles himself JOSIPPON, or JOSEPH BEN GORION.

A. D. 930.

His Time, and Work.

He had a very high opinion of himself, and has now been for some while in great reputation with the learned men of the Jewish nation.

At the begining of the thirty sixth chapter, which is the first chapter of the fifth book, he writes: " So *(b)* says *Joseph Ben Go-* " *rion* the Priest, who has writ the things which have happened to

---

(*a*) Josippon, sive Josephi Ben-Gorionis Historiae Judaicae libri sex. Ex Hebraeo vertit, Praefatione et Notis illustravit Joannes Gagnier. A. M. Oxon. 1706. 4to.

(*b*) Sic ait Joseph Ben Gorion Sacerdos, qui rerum historiam texuit, quae contigerunt Israeli, et calamitatem ejus, ut sit memoria earum in documentum, et eruditionem posteris ejus. . . .
Hic autem liber ab hac die, et deinceps futurus est in testimonium ceteris scriptoribus, qui post me venturi sunt, et aggredientur scribere, et testimonia allegare. Dicent enim: " Sic et sic memoriae prodidit Joseph Sacerdos, qui est princeps scriptorum omnium, qui libros ediderunt quotquot reperti sunt in Israel, exceptis quidem scriptoribus quatuor et viginti librorum Sanctorum. *lib.* 5. *cap.* 36. *p.* 170.

" Israel,

"Israel, and his calamities, to be a memorial and instruction to his "posterity... From this day, and henceforward, this book is to be "a testimonie to other writers, who shall come after me, and at- "tempt to write of the same things, and shall allege proofs of what "they write. For they will say: So and so has recorded *Joseph* the "Priest, who is the prince of all writers, who have published books "among the people of Israel, excepting only the writers of the four "and twenty sacred books."

And indeed so it has happened. For Rabbi *Tham*, who published this work in the Hebrew original at Constantinople in the year 1510. and made another edition of it at Venice in 1544. says of it in his preface. "Although (*c*) this book resembles other books in some "respects, it is very different from them in others. The great dif- "ference between books consists in their truth, or their falshood. "The words of this book are all justice and truth, nor is there any "thing perverse in it. The evidence of it is this, that it approach- "eth nearer to prophecie, than any book writ since the sacred Scrip- "tures. For it was writ before the Mishna, and the Talmud. Up- "on that man was the hand of the Lord, when he wrote this book. "And it may be said, that his words are well-nigh equal to the "words of a man of God."

This work is not so ancient as the author and his admirers pretend, as will be shewn presently. But from the time that he has begun to be taken notice of, as Mr. *Gagnier* observes in the preface to his edition

(*c*) Quamvis autem hic liber cum ceteris libris in genere conveniat, tamen ratione argumenti plurimum ab eis differt. Differentia autem illa praecipue consistit in veritate aut in falsitate. Porro hujus libri verba omnia sunt justitia et veritas: neque perversitas ulla invenitur in eo. Cujus quidem rei signum est, quod propius accedat ad Prophetiam, quam ceteri omnes libri, qui post Scripturas sacras editi sunt. Siquidem ante Misnam et Talmud scriptus fuit. Adde quod super virum illum fuit manus Jehovae, dum hunc librum componeret; et parum abest, quin ejus verba sint verba viri Dei. *Praef. R. Tham. De Scopo Libri.*

Ch. VI.   *His Time, Work, and Character.*

A. D. 930.

edition of this work, " all *(d)* Jewish writers, whether Commenta-
" tors, or Historians, or Philologers, continually allege it, and quote
" authorities and testimonies from it, as an authentic and funda-
" mental book... As for the Greek *Josephus*, they have little re-
" gard for him, or rather none at all: but declaim against him as
" a lying historian, full of falshoods and flatteries. But their *Josip-*
" *pon* they extol and magnify as true, and almost divine."

But Christian Critics, of the best credit, have argued, that the work is the production of a late age. They shew this from the work itself: in which, as *(e) Joseph Scaliger* has observed, people and countreys are called by modern names, not in use till more than six hundred years after our Saviour's nativity. And he supposeth him to be a Jew, that lived in France. He therefore considers him as an Impostor.

Fabricius (f) has argued in the like manner. He supposeth him to

---

(d) Deinde omnes qui secuti sunt Judaei Scriptores, sive Commentatores, sive Historici, sive Philologi, ubique eum allegant, et tanquam ex libro fundamentali atque authentico testimonia et auctoritates depromunt. ... Nam quod ad Josephum, Graecum adtinet, illum non in magno solent habere pretio, imo ei nullam habent fidem, et tanquam in Historicum mendacem et adulatorem adversus illum acriter invehuntur. Suum vero Josippon quasi hominem veracem et pene divinum summis laudibus ad sidera evehunt, extollunt, et praedicant. &c. *Gagnier in Praef. p. xxix.*

(e) De Josepho Gorionide satis est, si ostendero cujas fuit, quando vixit, cujusmodi scriptor est. Gallum Judaeum fuisse ex agro Turonensi non difficile est colligere, ut qui plus de illis quam de aliis Galliae tractibus agat. Recentem admodum fuisse arguunt verba locorum recentia, quibus utitur, Tours, Amboise, Chinon. Quae loca post DC annos a natali Christi adhuc Turones, Ambasia, Kainon Vocabantur. Quare cum Munsterus videret eum Francorum et Gothorum mentionem facere, et Francos interfuisse exequiis Herodis, quos Γαλάτας Josephus vocarit, ex eo solo potuit edorari hunc scriptorem recentissimum esse, ac proinde planum, qui nomen Josephi Historici sibi vindicarit. *Jo. Scalig. in Elencho Trihaer. Vid. Gagnier. Praef. p. xlviii.*

(f) Ceterum eruditis hodie plerisque dubium non est, Josephum huncce Hebraicum ex Graeco, vel potius ex Latina Josephi versione esse expressum, vel exerptum

A. D. 930.

to have been a Jew, who lived in Bretagne, in France, in the ninth or tenth centurie. The many modern names of people and countreys made use of by him, plainly declare his late age. His Hebrew historie is translated, or more properly extracted from the g eek of Josephus, or rather from a Latin translation of him: taking from him what he likes, omitting some things, and adding others.

To the like purpose *Gagnier*, in his preface, already cited more than once. Who also says, " that *(g)* Rabbi *Saadias Gaon*, who " wrote his commentarie upon the book of Daniel in the year of " Christ 936. is the first author who has mentioned *Josippon Ben* " *Gorion*. He does not expressly name his work, though probably " he refers to it." *Gagnier* adds: " The *(h)* first writer, who has " expressly mentioned this work, with the name of *Josippon Ben* " *Gorion*, and quoted authorities from it, is Rabbi *Solomon Jarchi*, " who flourished about the year of Christ 1140."

I refer likewise to (*i*) *Ittigius*, and *Basnage*, who in (*k*) his Historie of the Jews, has a long article concerning this writer and his work. He says, *Josippon* lived in the tenth or eleventh centurie. Which he argues after this manner. " *Solomon Jarchi* (*l*) who wrote
" in

tum potius : nec Josephum ipsum auctorem, sed longe recentiorem aliquem, qui in Britannia Galliae Armorica non ante nonum vel decimum seculum vixit, et pro lubitu digessit, addidit, interpolavit, omisit quaecunque ipsi videbantur addenda esse vel omittenda. . . . Ita recentiora longe Josepho tempora arguit, quod memorat Francos, et Burgundiae populum, et Daniscos, ac Danemanam, et Anglicam gentem, et quae in Irlandia sive Hibernia. *Fab. Bib. Gr. lib.* 4. *cap.* 6. *T.* 3. *p.* 249. *et apud Havercamp. Joseph. T.* 2. *p.* 68.

(*g*) R. Saadias Gaon, qui scribebat circa annum 696. min. suppul. Christ. 936. in suo commentario in Danielem primus omnium Josephi Ben Gorionis meminit. . . . *Gagn Pr. p. xxvii.*

(*h*) R. Salomo Jarchi, qui florebat circa annum Christi 1140. primus est, qui diserte citat hunc librum sub nomine Josippon, vel Josephi Ben Gorionis, et auctoritates ex eo adducit, quarum loca habes infra in Testimoniis. *Gagn. ib. p. xxviii.*

(*i*) *Ittigii Prolegom. ap. Joseph. Havercamp. Tom.* 2. *p.* 87.

(*k*) *Basnag. Hist. des Juifs. liv.* 7. *ch.* vi. *p.* 1539. . . . 1570.

(*l*) *Ib.* §. *xxv. p.* 1564.

Ch. VI.   His Time, Work, and Character.

"in the year 1140. is the first, who has quoted this Hebrew Joseph. *Abraham Ezra*, and *Abraham Ben Dion*, who by their quotations gave the work credit, lived in the same age. It would be very strange, that a work should be unknown for three or four hundred years, to the nation for whose sake it was composed. But, if it was writ near the end of the tenth, or the begining of the eleventh centurie, it is not at all strange, that it did not begin to be taken notice of till some while after."

A. D. 930.

I say nothing more in the way of introduction. I shall now make such extracts out of this work, as may be sufficient to shew the writer's character, and his testimonie to the destruction of the temple, and Jerusalem by Vespasian and Titus. I have placed him in the tenth centurie, not very far from the begining of it, in the year of Christ 930.

II. The work is divided into six books, and 97 chapters. The sixth and last of which books consists of five and fifty chapters.

Extracts from this Work.

The 43. chapter, which is the first of the sixth book, begins in this manner. "Thus (*m*) says Joseph Ben Gorion, the Priest, the same who is also called Josippon... This is the book, which I have entitled THE WARS OF JEHOVAH, because it contains the historie of the calamities of the house of our sanctuarie, and of our land, and our glorie."

My readers cannot but remember, that our Greek (*n*) *Josephus*, when

---

(*m*) Sic dicit Joseph Ben Gorion sacerdos. Ipse est Josippon, nomine quidem diminutivo Josippon... Hic est liber ille, quem appellavi titulo, BELLA JEHOVAE, eo quod continet historiam calamitatum desolationis Domus Sanctuarii nostri, et terrae nostrae, et gloriae nostrae. *Lib.* 6. *cap.* 43. *p.* 189.

(*n*) *De B. J. l.* 2. *cap.* 20.

when he gives an account of the determination of the Jewish people to go to war with the Romans, informs us, that they appointed *Joseph Ben Gorion*, and *Ananus* the High-Priest to preside at Jerusalem. Others were sent as Generals into several parts of the countrey: and himself, *Joseph son of Matthias*, was appointed Governour of the two Galilees, together with the prefecture of Gamala annexed to them.

Our author's account of the same determination is to this purpose: "The (*o*) Jews out of their Generals which were at Jerusalem chose "three princes valiant for war, Me *Joseph* the Priest, valiant for "war with the help of Jehovah, and *Ananus* the Priest, and *Elea-* "*zar* his son, Priests also, and by lot they divided to them the several "parts of the countrey, in which they should carry on the war. "The third part, which was the first lot, containing the land "of Galilee and Naphtali, came out to *Joseph Ben Gorion the* "*Priest*. And they called him *Josippon*, by way of praise and ho- "nour: forasmuch as he was then anointed with the militarie oint- "ment for the war. The second lot came out to *Ananus* the High- "Priest, to govern at Jerusalem and the adjoyning countrey. The "third lot came out to *Eleazar*, son of Ananus, and what follows." This should be compared with what is writ by (*p*) *Josephus*.

Thus he adopts the appellation of *Joseph son of Gorion* *₊*. But per-

---

(*o*) Quae omnia cum audissent Judaei, elegerunt e ducibus, qui erant in Juda et Jerusalem, tres principes fortissimos bello, Me scilicet, Joseph Sacerdotem fortissimum bello cum auxilio Jehovae, et Anani Sacerdotem, et Eleazar Sacerdotem filium ejus, et praefecerunt illos super terram, et partiti sunt terram Judae inter illos per sortem, dederuntque illis praesidio manum Judaeorum ad bellum gerendum. Et obtigit tertia pars terrae per primam sortem scilicet, omnis terra Galileae a terra Nephtali, et deinceps, Josepho filio Go- rionis Sacerdoti, in honorem et gloriam. Et appellaverunt illum Josippon in titulum dignitatis et laudis: quia tunc unctus fuit unctione militari. Deinde sors secunda exiit pro Anano Sacerdote magno, Jerusalem scilicet, et omnia circum vicina loca, ... Sors denique tertia egressa est Eleazaro filio Anani. &c. *Josipp*. *cap.* 67. *p.* 293.

(*p*) *De B. Jud. lib.* 2. *cap.* 20. §. 1. 2. 3.

(*₊*) Gagnier in his notes upon this place, p. 293. assigns some reasons, why this

Ch. VI.   His Historie of the Jewish War.

A. D. 930.

personates *Joseph son of Matthias*. And like him, he is appointed Governour of Galilee. And all along he will be Josephus in the main, and another person, when he pleaseth. He will also transcribe the Greek Josephus, and copy a large part of his historie of the Jewish war, without taking any notice of him. If he differs from him, and adds to him, it is not taken out of any other writers better informed, but from his own invention only.

Being come into *Galilee*, he there orders things very agreeably to what we have formerly seen in our Greek Josephus. At length he (*q*) flyes from Vespasian and Titus, and the Roman armie, and shuts himself up in *Jotapata*. Vespasian (*r*) with his armie comes before Jotapata. The (*s*) city is taken after a siege of eight and forty days. *Joseph* (*t*) himself, and with him forty more, go out of the city, and hide themselves in a cave. Vespasian sends Nicanor to Joseph with offers of peace and safety, if he would surrender. But (*u*) the forty men, who were with him, choose rather to dye by their own hands. After long arguing Joseph proposeth, that they should cast lots, till they were all killed. Which being done, there were none left alive, but Joseph, and one more, who at length consented to

---

this writer chose to be thought *the son of Gorion*, rather than *the son of Matthias*. Cur autem hic noster Gorionis filius quam Matthiae esse voluerit, ratio videtur fuisse, quod cum nomen *Gorionis* cujusdam insignis viri mentio aliquando in Talmude occurrat, atque etiam *Nicodemi* filii Gorionis, in eam familiam ipsi se adoptare visum est, ut prodiret in lucem gratior contribulibus suis, eisque facilius imponeret. *Vid. reliqua ibid. Et Conf. not.* (*p*) *ap. J. s. Havercamp. p.* 207.

(*q*) At vero ut audivit Josephus, quod venit Vespasianus, et cum eo filius ejus Titus, omnisque exercitus ejus, ut praelium committeret, fugit Josephus a facie eorum in Jotapatam urbem magnam, quae est in Galilaea: et inclusit se Josephus et omnis exercitus intra illam. *cap.* 68. *p.* 299.

(*r*) *Cap.* 69. *p.* 300. *et cap.* 70. *p.* 301. *&c.*

(*s*) *Cap.* 71. *p.* 307.

(*t*) Tunc surrexit Josephus ipse, et quadraginta viri ex militibus, qui residui erant cum illo, et egressi sunt ex urbe, fugeruntque in sylvam, ubi inventa caverna illuc intraverunt, delitueruntque omnes in illa caverna. &c. *Cap.* 71. *p.* 307.

(*u*) *Cap.* 72. *p.* 315. . . . 319.

A. D. 930. to surrender. Joseph *(x)* then calls to Nicanor, and they yield up themselves to him. Vespasian, when Joseph was brought before him, treated him kindly, and carried him about with him from place to place, together with *(y) Agrippa*.

So far there is a great agreement between our *Josephus*, and *Joseph Ben Gorion*. But now they differ. For Josippon entirely omits the compliments, which our Josephus paid to Vespasian.

Upon *(z)* the death of Nero, and after the short reigns of Galba and Vitellius, Vespasian is declared Emperour by the soldiers in Judea, and after some hesitation he is persuaded to accept of the diadem from them.

Some while *(a)* after that Vespasian takes part of the armie, and goes to Rome: but leaves the other part with Titus to carry on the siege of Jerusalem. However, he orders Titus to stay at Alexandria, till he shall send to him from Rome.

" When *(b)* Vespasian left Judea to go to Rome, he took with him Agrippa, and his son Monbaz, least they should rebel against him. With himself, and them, he also took me Joseph the priest, bound with iron chains." And when Vespasian was come to Rome, he ordered, that *(c)* Joseph should be sent to prison, and kept bound there.

Ves-

(*x*) *Cap.* 73. *p.* 319. &c.

(*y*) Cum ergo audivisset Vespasianus Titum filium suum, recta visa sunt verba illius in oculis ejus, et clementia usus est erga Josephum sacerdotem, et prohibuit, quo minus moreretur gladio, et constituit cum principem, et magnum inter principes suos, et secum ducebat de urbe in urbem cum Agrippa rege. *Cap.* 73. *p.* 321.

(z) *Cap.* 75. *p.* 333. 334.

(*a*) *Cap.* 77. *p.* 340.

(*b*) Abiit itaque Vespasianus Romam. Cumque pergeret, ut iterum acciperet illic coronam regni, duxit secum Agrippam regem, et Monbaz filium ejus. Dixerat enim, ne forte rebellent contra me. Duxit praeterea cum eis, et secum, meipsum Josephum sacerdotem vinctum catenis ferreis. *Cap.* 77. *p.* 340.

(*c*) Tunc jussit, et vinxerunt me in domo carceris. Agrippam vero et filium ejus ipsorum arbitrio reliquit. *Ib. p.* 341.

Ch. VI.   *His Historie of the Jewish War.*

Vespasian upon his arrival at Rome was received joyfully by the Senators and all the people in general. And *(d)* in a short time he is inaugurated with great solemnity. Agrippa and his son are allowed to be with the Senators. And Joseph himself, though a prisoner, is allowed by the keeper of the prison, to have a place, where he may see all.

The *(e)* coronation is then described by him, in a pompous manner, seven Electors of the Empire attending, agreeably to the coronations of the Emperours in late ages, a good while after the time of Charles the Great, as *(f) Gagnier* observes in a note, which I shall place below. *Basnage* thinks, that *(g)* this Hebrew Joseph intends the coronation of Otho the first, or his son Otho the second. And he considers this article, as a proof, that Josippon lived in the tenth, or rather in the eleventh centurie.

" Soon after his coronation, as this author says, Vespasian *(h)* was

A. D. 930.

(d) Postridie illius diei congregati sunt omnes Senatores Romani, ut Vespasianum Caesarem crearent, secundum jus Caesareae dignitatis pro consuetudine Romana. Porro Agrippa et filius ejus erant cum illis. At ego supplex rogavi principem domus carceris. . . . Et inveni gratiam in oculis ejus, et introduxit me in confessum regni, ubi fieri debebat Inauguratio Caesaris : attamen vinctum catenis ferreis, et collocavit juxta se in loco, unde vidi omnia quae facta sunt. *Ib. p.* 341.

(e) Cum itaque perventum est ad illum locum, accedunt ad eum septem Reges coronis suis insignes, quas acceperunt de manu Caesaris, Electi vero jussu Senatus Romani. &c. *Ibid.*

(f) Fingit hic fabulator Josephum, id est, seipsum a Vespasiano Romam perduc-

tum fuisse, ut ibi spectator adesset ejus coronationis, quam describit cum omni illa ceremonia inaugurationis Caesarum, qualis longe post tempora Caroli Magni, sub Romanis Pontificibus instituta fuit, praesentibus nempe et ministrantibus Septem Imperii Electoribus, cum toto illo apparatu, quem fuse et lepide narrat.   *Gagn. p.* 341.

(g) Tous ces caractères nous font croire, que le Josephe Hebreu n'a vécu qu' à la fin de dixiéme, ou plutôt dans l'onzième siécle, et que le couronnement, dont il a laissé la description, est celui d' Othon I. ou de son fils Othon II. *Basnag. ut supr.* §. *xxiv. p.* 1563.

(h) Post aliquot autem dies, ex quo Vespasianus Caesar factus fuit, indignatus est adversus Agrippam, quia calumniati sunt eum

F f

was offended with Agrippa upon account of some calumnies cast upon him, which he had received from wicked men of the Jewish nation. Whereupon he slew Agrippa, and his son Monbaz with the sword. Which was done three years and a half before the desolation of the house."

So writes this author. Supposing Agrippa to have been put to death at this time, I do not conceive, how it could be done, *three years and a half* before the destruction of the temple. Besides, Agrippa survived the Jewish war and the destruction of Jerusalem many years: as is attested not only by Josephus, but also by ancient medals (*i*) still extant.

Rabbi Isaac, in his *Munimen Fidei*, writ in the *(k)* sixteenth centurie, has quoted this passage of our author. And I have put down his words in the margin: though, perhaps, they may be taken notice of again, hereafter.

In *(l)* the same year and month that Agrippa and his son were put to death, Vespasian sent for Joseph, and spake comfortably to him, and released him from his bonds. Joseph complained of the death of Agrippa. But Vespasian assured him, he had good reason for so doing. And now Vespasian sent Joseph to Titus at Alexandria, with a letter of recommendation. Joseph goes to Alexandria. Titus

---

cum impii Israel, dicentes eum cogitasse perfide agere in illum, et idcirco misisse litteras in Jerusalem ea de re. Interfecit itaque illum et filium ejus Monbaz gladio. Quod quidem contigit tribus annis cum dimidio ante desolationem domus. &c. *Cap.* 77. *p.* 344.

(*i*) *Vid. Gagnier in loc.*

(*k*) Verba, *Vae pastori meo nihili, derelinquenti gregem.* [Zach. xi. 17.] Agrippam respiciunt, qui Romam se contulit, atque inde evocavit Vespasianum, hujus-

que privignum Titum, adversus Hierosolymas, tandem autem irasci illi coepit Vespasianus, eumque una cum Monbaso filio securi percussit tribus et dimidio annis ante templi desolationem. Ceterum ob illam, quae inter regem Agrippam et improbos duces factiosorum exorta fuerat contentionem, denique desolatum fuit templum, uti ex Josepho constat. *Munimen Fidei*. p. 417.

(*l*) *Cap.* 78. *p.* 344.

Ch. VI. Of the Siege of Jerusalem.

Titus *(m)* and all his counsellors rejoyced at the arrival of Joseph. "For he was full of the spirit of wisdom and understanding, the spirit of counsel and valour, the spirit of knowledge, and of the fear of the Lord." After *(n)* some consultation, it was determined to go up to Jerusalem, and besiege it. "For Joseph knew that it was of the Lord, and that it was not possible, that the word of the Lord should be turned back." Titus therefore went from Alexandria to Judea.

A. D. 930. Isa. xi. 1. 2.

In *(o)* the first year of the reign of Vespasian, in the tenth month, and the seventh day of the month, came Titus with Joseph, and all his forces, and his armie, to the delightfull city of Cesarea. Where he was employed in collecting his forces from all parts, till he had compleated his armie for besieging Jerusalem. There *(p)* he stayed all the winter, till the month of Abib, or March. During this whole year,

---

(m) Postea profectus Josephus Romā venit Alexandriam. Cumque audisset Titus de adventu Josephi, laetatus est plurimum ipse, et omnes seniores et sapientes, qui cum illo erant. Josephus enim plenus erat spiritu sapientiae et intelligentiae, spiritu consilii et fortitudinis, spiritu scientiae, et timoris Jehovae. *Cap.* 78. *p.* 346.

(n) Postea consilium inierunt inter se, ut ascenderent in Jerusalem, et obsiderent eam. Sciebat enim Josephus a Jehova hoc esse, neque possibile esse, ut verbum Jehovae convertatur retrorsum. *Ib. p.* 347.

(o) Anno primo regni Vespasiani, mense decimo, die septimo mensis venit Titus cum Josepho, et cum omnibus copiis suis, et exercitu suo in urbem Cesareae gratissimam et desideratissimam omnibus, qui illam viderunt. *Cap.* 79. *p.* 347.

(p) Mansitque illic, donec complerentur dies brumae, et dies hiemis, et donec venirent dies Abib. Toto autem hoc anno primo regni Vespasiani, quo erectus est super regnum Romanorum, ... ingruerunt praelia durissima in medio Jerusalem inter habitatores ejus per crudelitatem irae et furoris, et percutiebant unusquisque proximum suum, nulla interposita quiete aut mora. Quinetiam nulla cessatio belli fuit inter illos tota hieme, ut post est universae terrae, sed et aestate et hieme duraverunt praelia Simonem inter et Jehochananem. Porro tertius fuit Eleazarus. Atque hoc ab ipso die, quo proficiscens Vespasianus de terra Juda abiit Romam, ut illic de novo susciperet regnum Caesareae dignitatis, secundum jus consuetudinis Romanae. *Ibid.*

JOSIPPON. Ch. VI.

A. D. 930.

year, the firſt year of the reign of Veſpaſian, were grievous wars and fightings in the midſt of Jeruſalem. From the time that Veſpaſian left Judea to go to Rome, there to receive the confirmation of the Empire, in ſummer and winter, were perpetual quarrels and contentions between the three parties, into which the people of Jeruſalem were divided, and headed by three leaders, *Simon, John,* and *Eleazar*. "For *(q)* at that time God poured out a ſpirit of inſenſibility in the midſt of Jeruſalem. And they deſtroyed, as *(r)* this writer ſays, a thouſand and four hundred garners, filled with things that might have been uſefull in a ſiege. For there were in them proviſions, ſufficient to maintain two hundred thouſand people for twenty years. But by the madneſſe of theſe robbers all was conſumed by fire. Which brought on the famine in Jeruſalem.

Iſ. xxix. 10.

And now this writer makes a long and grievous lamentation over *(s)* Jeruſalem. Which in the Hebrew original, as *(t) Gagnier* obſerves, is a ſort of metrical compoſition, not in uſe among the Jews, till long after the ſuppoſed time of the author.

Titus *(u)* draws out his numerous forces, and reviews them in a plain near Ceſarea, and then moves toward Jeruſalem.

It is not my intention to relate particularly from this writer, as I have

(q) Eo anno effudit Jehova ſpiritum vertiginis in medium Jeruſalem. . . . *p.* 348.

(r) Porro numerus horreorum illorum in Jeruſalem erat mille et quadringentorum : et omnia plene commeatibus victus pro tempore obſidionis. Tempore autem, quo Veſpaſianus venit in urbes Galileae, Seniores et viri fide digni, qui aeſtimaverunt quantitatem proventus horreorum illorum, invenerunt in illis eſſe commeatus et victus pro ducentis mille animabus per viginti annos. Et tunc in bello latronum,

haec omnia cremata ſunt. Caepitque fames in Jeruſalem. *p.* 350.

(s) Lamentatus eſt itaque Joſephus lamentationem hanc ſuper Jeruſalem, et dixit. . . . *cap.* 80. *p.* 350. . . . 355.

(t) Lamentatio Joſephi. In Hebraeo eſt carmen rithmicum. Quod genus poëſeos multis poſt ſeculis a recentioribus Judaeis, Arabum exemplo, uſurpatum eſt. *Gagn. not. p.* 350.

(u) Poſtea Titus venit in planitiem Caeſareae cum exercitu, et recenſuit exercitum ſuum, &c. *cap.* 81. *p.* 355.

Ch. VI. Of the Siege of Jerusalem.

have done from Josephus, the attacks of Titus, and the defenses of the people in the city. I shall pass over a great deal.

A. D. 930.

" Whilst *(x)* they hard pressed by the Romans, the three
" parties within agreed, and joyned together in opposing the common
" enemie. But as soon as the Romans gave them any respite, the three
" rulers of the robbers within exercised a cruel war with one ano-
" ther: insomuch that the bloud of the citizens ran like a torrent out
" of the gates of Jerusalem, in the sight of the Romans, who could
" not forbear to pity them." Those expressions are extravagant. But what is here said may be compared with Josephus de B. J. l. 5. cap. vi. §. 1. Upon this occasion our author made another lamentation.

After *(y)* having carried on the siege for some while, Titus draws off from the city, and for several days ceaseth to make any attacks. And by Joseph, who addresseth them in a very long speech, in their own language, he makes them offers of peace, that he might preserve their temple and city. But they hardened their necks, and would not hear. In *(z)* this speech he tells them, not disagreeably to

---

(x) Quando instabat praelium Romanorum, omnes ad invicem coalescebant, tanquam unus vir ad pugnam, et pugnabant contra Romanos, fugabantque illos a se. Et postquam fugaverant a se Romanos, revertebantur ad se et incipiebant pugnare unusquisque in fratrem suum. Tuncque fiebat praelium magnum et durum inter tres principes latronum crudelium, donec egrederetur sanguis extra portas Jerusalem, tanquam torrens scaturiens de scaturigine aquarum. Videbantque Romani sanguinem egredientem de portis Jerusalem. Et conterebatur cor eorum in medio ipsorum, et flebant, et dolebant ea de re. Josephus autem Sacerdos stabat cum eis. Tunc lamentatus est Josephus lamentationem hanc iterum super Jerusalem. Et prolocutus est Josephus alte proferens vocem lamentationis, et dixit. &c. *cap.* 82. *p.* 362. *&c.*

(y) Tunc temporis jussit populum suum discedere a muro extra urbem, et cessare a bello per aliquot dies, ut clamaret pacem in auribus Judaeorum. *cap.* 84. *p.* 369... 377. *et cap.* 85. *p.* 378... 385.

(z) Nunc autem videte malum vestrum esse maximum, et quod Jehova non sit in medio vestri, quia propter bella, quae geritis unusquisque cum fratre suo mox brevi siccatae sunt apud vos aquae Siloe. At vero in castris Gentium, quando congregatae sunt contra vos, ecce aquae Siloe redundant, et fluunt instar torrentis, et fluvii magni pleni super omnes margines suos. *Cap.* 85. *p.* 383. *m.*

to what the Greek Josephus says [de B. J. l. 5. cap. ix. p. 350.] that for their sins, the waters of Siloam had before failed on a sudden: but now they flowed plentifully in the camp of the Gentils, fighting against them. In this speech he goes on, and says: "though *(a)* " I am in the camp of the Romans, I am still considered as one of " you. For with you is my dear wife, the wife of my youth, whom " I still embrace, though I have had no children by her. With " you also are my Father and Mother. He is now an hundred and " three years old, and my mother eighty five. I am sixty four years " of age, and have not yet attained to the term of human life."

Many *(b)* he says, wept at hearing him, and many people of meaner rank would willingly have gone out of the city, to surrender themselves to Titus. But the three leaders of the factions, Simon and Eleazar, and John, prevented them by their severe threatenings, and the strict guard they kept over them.

In *(c)* the mean time the famine encreased, and was very grievous.

The

(a) Porro, quamvis ego sim in castris Romanorum, tamen reputor idem, ac si essem vobiscum : quia ecce nunc uxor mea dilectissima, carissima, vobiscum est, uxor nempe juventutis meae. Neque respuo illam, et licet filii ex ea non sint mihi, nihilominus illam diligo plurimum, cum sit ex familiis nobilissimis et optimis populi Dei, et populi virorum. Quin et pater meus et mater mea, infelices, pauperes, sancti, senes, provecti in diebus apud vos sunt. Nam et pater meus est centum et trium annorum hodie. Mater vero mea octoginta et quinque annorum est hodie. Ego vero paucos et malos, et per varias tribulationes et aerumnas sexaginta et quatuor annos exegi, ac nondum attigi terminum, qui postulet mortem juxta viam naturae. &c. *Cap.* 85. *p.* 383. *fin.*

(b) Cum ergo audivisset populus verba Josephi sacerdotis, fleverunt plurimum... Et quidem summopere optabat plebs infima exire ad Titum, et pacem inire cum illo juxta consilium Josephi. Sed astabant Simon, Eleazarus, et Jochanan, principes latronum, et praeposuerunt viros fortissimos ad portas. . . . &c. *cap.* 86. *p.* 385.

(c) Interea fames ingravescebat in Jerusalem. . . . Crescebat autem malum eo usque, ut populus comederet omne genus reptilium terrae a mure usque ad araneam, et ad serpentem, et mustellam, et bufonem. . . . Si forte inveniretur in Jerusalem cadaver equi, aut cadaver cujuslibet bestiae, multi ex Israel inter se pugnabant, et mortui corruebant, dum pugnarent super cadaver bestiae, aut super cadaver ferae. . . . *cap.* 86. *p.* 385. 386.

Ch. VI.   *Of the Siege of Jerusalem.*   223

A. D. 930.

The people ate mice, spiders, weasels, serpents, toads. And if the carcase of a horse, or other beast was found in any of the streets of Jerusalem, multitudes contended for it.

Titus *(d)* continues his attacks, but the Jews gain great advantages over him. They killed a great number of his men, and destroyed his platforms, which *(e)* gave him great concern.

Soon after that *(f)* Titus, as this author says, received numerous recruits from all nations and countreys, subject to the Roman Empire. At their arrival, Titus represents to their Generals and chief men the state of things, and how the Jews had prevailed, and still had great strength remaining. These recruits however, are very willing to engage with the Jews. And *(g)* out of the vast numbers of fresh men, supposed to be capable of doing more than the Romans, who were fatigued, and worn out, and discouraged with the fatigues of a long siege, were selected eighty thousand men, Macedonians, Britans, Syrians, Africans, Burgundians, Persians, Chaldeans. All these, without any Romans joyned with them, marched in order toward

---

(d) Cap. 87. *p.* 388. ... 391.
(e) Cap. 88. *p.* 391. 392.
(f) Eo tempore congregatae sunt innumerae turbae ex omnibus gentibus, et venerunt contra Jerusalem in auxilium Romanorum ex omnibus dominiis Caesareae dignitatis ad Romam pertinentibus. ... Narravit autem Titus senioribus gentium, quae sibi venerant in auxilium, ea omnia, quae sibi contigerant dum oppugnavit Jerusalem. ... Narravit etiam, quomodo perdiderant milites suos, et principes suos, ... omnesque machinas suas dirutrices, et omnia instrumenta belli, quae secum habebat, corruperant. *Cap.* 88. *p.* 393. 394.

(g) Electi sunt itaque ex turmis nationum illarum octoginta millia virorum, scilicet decem millia Macedonum, viginta millia virorum Britanniae, quinque millia Syrorum, decem millia virorum Africae, decem millia fortissimorum ex viris Borgoniae, quinque millia de filiis Cedar, decem millia militum ex fortissimis Persarum et Chaldaeorum. Et progressi sunt eo ordine, quo venerunt: neque unus Romanus ex illis. Abierunt autem in planitiem, quae erat e regione Sepulchri Jchochanan Sacerdotis magni. Et ceperunt miscere praelia cum Judaeis, qui erant super murum, et admovere scalas cum instrumentis ligneis quibus tegebantur, ut ascenderent ad eos supra murum. *Ib. p.* 394. 395.

A. D 930.

toward Jerufalem, and encamped near it. And then they began to attack the wall, and to fight with the Jews that were upon it.

" Now (b) the three leaders within the city, John, and Simon, and Eleazar, confult together between themfelves, and with their friends, what was beft to be done. It was agreed, that two fhould go out of the city, and the other abide within. John then, and Eleazar went out, having with them fifteen hundred of the moft valiant of their men. They prevailed, and flew their enemies with the edge of the fword from morning to evening. The day on which this battle was fought, he fays, was the ninth day of the month Thebet, which was the tenth month from the arrival of Titus before Jerufalem. And they flew of the hofts of the Gentiles, feven and fifty thoufand and five hundred. They took captive three thoufand of their chiefs, putting the reft to flight. Of the Jews there fell on that day feven men. And they brought off their dead and their wounded to Jerufalem : where they buried their dead, that the uncircumcifed might not infult them."

" Whereupon (i) John and Eleazar returned to Jerufalem with " their brethren, finging a hymn of triumph, and offering praifes

" to

(b) Egreffi funt ergo Jehochanan et Eleazarus cum mille et quingentis fortiffimis Latronum et percufferunt turmas gentium plaga gladii, . . a mane diei pugnae ufque ad vefperam. Quod quidem contigit nona die menfis Thebet, qui fuit decimus ab adventu Titi in Jerufalem, et proftraverunt ex turmis gentium illarum quinquaginta feptem millia cum quingentis. Et ceperunt ex eis vivos ter mille principes, ceteris in fugam conjectis. Ex judaeis autem ceciderunt illa die feptem viri, et vulneratos fuos fecum extulerunt latronés, ut illos fepelirent, ne infultarent eis incircumcifi. *Ib. p.* 395.

(i) Venerunt itaque Jehochanan et Eleazarus in Jerufalem cum fratribus fuis cantantes hymnum, et gratiarum actiones Jehovae. Reliquiae autem fugientium ex turmis nationum illarum reverfae funt ad caftra Titi cum ignominia. . . . Poftridie Latrones acceperunt tria millia principem, quos comprehenderant vivos, effoderunt unicuique eorum oculum, manumque amputaverunt, atque ita remiferunt eos ad caftra Titi, ut ipfi effent dedecori et opprobrio. *Ib. p.* 395.

Ch. VI. *Of the Siege of Jerusalem.*

" to Jehovah. The rest of those nations returned to the camp of
" Titus, in shame and confusion... The day after the Robbers took
" the three thousand chiefs, whom they had brought captives, and
" put out an eye of every one of them, and also cut off one of their
" hands, and so sent them back to the camp of Titus."

A. D. 930.

All fiction, surely, without any ground or authority from Josephus, or any other ancient writer, that we know of! We here plainly see, that the author was an artfull man. He knew how to flatter and please his own nation. And he has obtained his end. He is in admiration with them.

At that *(k)* time Titus consulted with his Generals, and his soldiers, and his whole armie, that it might be determined what was best to be done, especially considering the strength and fortitude of the Jewish people. After a long consultation, the opinion of Titus, which he was resolved to adhere to, was, that the siege of the city should be continued, without making any attacks upon it. For says he, their provisions fail already, and will be all speedily consumed. Moreover, they will quarrell among themselves, and thus hasten their ruin. And we shall overcome.

" And indeed, says *(l)* this writer, the famine prevailed greatly.

(k) Eo tempore Titus consilium inivit cum principibus, et militibus suis, et cum filiis populi sui Romanis, et cum populo omnium nationum, quae cum eis convenerant, dicens: Quid faciemus contra Israelem, et contra fortitudinem ejus?... At consilia eorum omnium contemtui fuerunt coram Tito.... Dixit ergo eis Titus. Hoc est consilium meum, quod a me ipso juxta rectam rationem profertur, neque ab eo recedam. Cedo, teneamus urbem hanc obsessam, neve oppugnemus illam amplius. Victus enim et commea-

tus eorum omnino defecerunt, neque cibus est apud illos. Haud dubium, quin fames illos consumptura est: neque etiam dubium est, quin, quando viderint nos non amplius miscere praelia cum illis, ipsi praelia misceant inter se, unusquisque adversus fratrem suum.... *Ib. p.* 395. 396.

(l) Porro, nisi grassata fuisset fames in Jerusalem, nunquam perrupta fuisset urbs, neque capta in aeternum. Fortes enim Israel erant velociores aquilis, et fortiores leonibus. *Ib. p.* 396.

G g

" And

"And, if it had not, the city could not have been broken up, nor "taken for ever. For the valiant of Israel were *swifter than eagles,* "*and stronger than lions.* 2 Sam. i. 23. But the famine consumed "them. The streets were filled with dead bodies, nor were there "any to bury them. And when Titus saw the dead cast out from "the city, like dung upon the earth, he was much affected at the "sight, and lifting up his hands to heaven, he fell down upon his "knees, and said: This is not my work. He had desired peace. "But the people would not accept of it."

In *(m)* the following, the 89 chapter, is an account of several acts of cruelty, committed by Simon in putting to death *Amittai*, or *Mattbias*, and others.

In (*n*) the mean while, as he says, in the 90 chapter, *Gorion*, the Priest, father of Joseph, who wrote this book for Israel, to be a memorial and testimonie to them, was a prisoner in one of the towers upon the wall, bound in iron fetters. Joseph came near to the place, hoping to see his aged father. But the Jews cast stones at him, and wounded him. And now likewise he at length gets a sight of his mother. She was not bound with chains, though she was kept prisoner in the house of Simon. But she got upon the wall to see her son, and make her lamentations to him. His father was about 103 years of age, and his mother 85.

It is observable, that about this time, after the slaughter of *Amittai* or *Mattbias* and his sons by order of *Simon*, *Josephus* (*o*) also makes mention of his father and mother, as being in Jerusalem. And about

---

(*m*) *Cap.* 89 *p.* 397... 406.

(*n*) Interea Gorion sacerdos, pater Josephi sacerdotis, qui scripsit hunc librum Israeli, ut esset illis in testimonium, et in memoriale, tunc erat victus catenis ferreis, et in vinculis aereis in una e turribus Jerusalem. Ipse autem senex processerat in diebus, natus scilicet centum et trium annorum. ... Eo tempore venit Josephus, filius ejus versus murum e regione turris, in qua erat pater ejus Gorion sacerdos tunc illic vinctus. .. *Cap.* 90. *p.* 406. *&c.*

(*o*) *De B. J. l.* 5. *cap. xiii. num.* 1, 2. 3.

Ch. VI.   *Of the Siege of Jerusalem.*   227

about this time also Josephus was wounded: not for attempting to see his father, or mother, but as he was going round the city, near the walls of it, proposing arguments to the people within to surrender to Titus for their benefit.

A. D.
930.

The *(p)* famine being very severe in the city, many Jews in good circumstances went out in order to go over to the Romans. But it being found, that some of them had gold and jewels hid in their bowels, they were ript up by the Arabian and Syrian soldiers, which were in the armie of Titus. Some of the Roman soldiers did the like. In this practise the Arabians and Syrians killed a thousand Jews. When Titus heard of it, he was exceedingly grieved and provoked. And he gave orders, that all who had done this thing should be put to death, and that their goods should be given to living Jews, heirs of the dead. Upon this occasion six thousand Arabians and Syrians suffered death.

A most unlikely thing, and mere romance! No General would shew such favour to a resolute people, whom he was besieging with an armie. Josephus says, that *(q)* two thousand of the Jews were thus cruelly destroyed by the Syrian and other soldiers for the sake of the gold hid in their bodies. He also says, Titus was much displeased,

G g 2

(p) Porro Judaei, qui egressi fuerant de Jerusalem ad castra Romanorum . . . deglutierunt aurum et argentum, et gemmas et lapides pretiosos. . . . Cumque animadvertissent nonnulli ex Syris et Arabibus illos ita facere, indicavit rem unusquisque socio suo. . . . Tum apprehenderunt illos, et scissis eorum visceribus, invenerunt intra viscera aurum, et lapides pretiosos. . . . Factusque numerus scissorum per manus Syrorum et Arabum mille animarum. Cumque audivisset Titus rem illam pessimam, . . . indignatus est, et accensus est furor ejus admodum. Tunc jussit comprehendi omnes, qui patraverunt hujusmodi facinus pessimum, et jugulari, ac deinde dari omnes facultates eorum Judaeis vivis haeredibus mortuorum. Et mortui sunt propter hoc facinus, jussu Titi, tum ex Syris, tum ex Arabibus sex millia virorum. *Cap.* 91. *p.* 411. 412.

(q) De B. J. l. 5. *cap. xiii.* §. 4. 5. *p.* 361. 362.

pleafed, and would have ordered his horfe to furround the criminals, and kill them with darts. But he confidered, that the number of the guilty exceeded that of the flain. He therefore was obliged to content himfelf with forbidding that cruelty for the future, upon the pain of heavie punifhment.

This author moreover fays, "that *(r)* ftrict inquiry was made by Titus after the Romans, who had been guilty of the like action. And they were found to be three hundred and twenty men, whom Titus ordered to be burnt to death, in one pit or ciftern. After which all Jews, who came over to Titus were treated by the foldiers very civilly, and they lived very quiet and unmolefted in his camp." All fiction from this author's fruitfull invention! And the ftorie is made out, as it feems, to do honour to his nation, at the fame time, that their city was falling into ruin, and they going into captivity!

He likewife tells the ftorie which Jofephus has done of the crucifixion of the Jews before the walls of the city, five (*s*) hundred in a day, and fometimes more, as Jofephus fays. But this author tells it very differently in this manner. Some (*t*) went out of the city with

---

(*r*) Fuitque numerus eorum, qui reperti funt, tum eorum qui fecerunt, tum eorum qui noverant, trecentorum et viginti virorum. At juffit Titus fervis fuis, et combufferunt omnes in medio cifternae unius. Et deinceps Judaei cum fiducia in caftris Titi degebant, neque ultra fuit adverfarius, aut incurfus malus. Sed quotiefcunque Romanus inveniebat Judaeum aliquem perplexum aut errantem extra caftra procul, clam illum deducens comitabatur ufque dum ad caftra incolumem, et tranquille, et cum fecuritate bona reduxiffet. *Cap.* 91. *p.* 413.

(*s*) *De B. J. l.* 5. *cap. xi. n* 1.

(*t*) Quando aliqui ab urbe exibant cum uxoribus, et filiis, et filiabus, et parvulis fuis, ut invenirent herbas, .. Romani qui illos inveniebant, jugulabant natos eorum, et dicebant: Jugulemus hos parvulos, ne adolefcant, et fucceffu dierum pugnent nobifcum, ficut patres illorum. Idcirco Romani trucidabant infimam plebem, quotquot exibant ab urbe, et fufpendebant illos

Ch. VI. Of the Siege of Jerusalem.

with their wives, and sons and daughters, and little ones, to gather herbs for food. And the Romans slew all the young people, saying: *Let us kill these, least they grow up and fight against us, as their fathers have done.* So the Romans acted from day to day, till the number of slain, and hanged up, amounted to five hundred. The like to this was done within the city by Simon and John and Eleazar. They killed and hung up upon the walls all the Romans, which they could catch, and all their own people who endeavored to go out of the city, till they amounted also to the number of five hundred. Which when Titus saw, he gave strict orders to all the men of his armie, not to kill any Jews that came out of Jerusalem. If any did so, they should be put to death. For his bowels yearned over Israel.

So says this fantastical writer.

He computes the taking of *Antonia* to have been on the fifth day of Sivan, the third month, on the eve of the feast of Weeks, or Pentecost, the fourteenth month from the coming of Titus to besiege Jerusalem. So (*u*) at the end of ch. 91.

He

---

illos ad arbores ex adverso portae Jerusalem. Sicque faciebant Romani quotidie. Pervenitque numerus occisorum, et suspensorum ad quingentas animas. Idem etiam faciebant Simon, Jehochanan, et Eleazarus, iis omnibus, quos capiebant ex cohortibus Romanorum, postquam illos per insidias circumvenerant. Eodem modo animadvertebant in eos, qui quaerebant exire, ut perfugerent ad illos. Jugulabant enim eos, et cadavera suspendebant super murum ex adverso Romanorum.... Fuitque numerus suspensorum per manus Latronum quingentorum virorum, tot scilicet numero, quot suspendebant Romani ex Judaeis. Itaque Titus praecepit omnibus viris exercitus sui dicens: Quicunque interfecerit aliquem ex iis, qui egrediuntur de Jerusalem, morietur. Et quidem ita fecit Titus, quia flagrabant viscera ejus super Israel. *cap.* 86. *p.* 386.

(*u*) Ut autem vidit Titus Turrim Antoniam esse in Laqueum Romanis, jussit Titus ut diruerent illam. Quod quidem contigit in quinta in Sivan, mense tertio, in vespera festi Hebdomadarum. Ipse est mensis quartus decimus ab adventu Titi ad obsidendam Jerusalem. *cap.* 91. *in fin. p.* 420.

He proceeds (x) in the 92 ch. to relate contentions and fightings of the Jews and Romans at the Temple or near it, which I need not rehearse particularly: especially, since it is not all exact truth, or matter of fact, but exaggeration agreeable to this author's fansie.

At the begining of the (y) 93 chapter, he tells the story of Mary, who in the extremity of the famine killed her only child, and dressed it, and ate a part of it. The same storie, that is told by (z) Josephus: but their harangues upon the event are different.

In the next chapter (a) the temple is on fire, and the doors of the house of the sanctuarie were opened on the ninth day of the fifth month, the same day of the month, in the which it had been opened in the time of the Chaldeans. The soldiers rejoiced greatly. But

(x) P. 420...431.
(y) P. 431.
(z) De B. J. l. 6. cap iii. §. 4.
(a) Postridie congregati Romani miserunt ignem in Sanctum Sanctorum in circuitu.... Mox incaluit aurum, et combusta sunt ligna valvarum, et ceciderunt in terram, et aperta fuit Domus Sancti sanctorum in oculis omnium mense quinto nona die mensis, eo ipso die, quo aperta fuerat Domus Sancti sanctorum in diebus Chaldaeorum. Et statim ut aperuerunt Romani portam Sancti Sanctorum, et ceperunt illud, tunc vero vociferati sunt clamore magno, mirum in modum prae laetitia.... Cucurrit autem Titus totis viribus suis, ut extingueret ignem.... Ac tandem defessus defatigatusque corruit ad terram viribus exhaustus.... Postquam itaque incensa fuit Domus Sancti sanctorum, surrexit Titus, et ingressus in Sanctum sanctorum vidit gloriam Domus, et decorem ejus, et splendorem illius.... Nondum enim tota Domus incendio consumpta erat, ut pulchritudinem illius, et majestatem ejus contemplaretur. Tunc dixit Titus: Nunc cognovi, quia non est hic aliud, nisi Domus Dei. Hoc est habitaculum Dei coelorum, et tabernaculum ejus.... Quia magna est majestas Domus hujus, et magnus splendor majestatis Templi ejus longe supra Templum Romanorum, et omnia Templa nationum, quae vidi.... Deinde surrexerunt Romani, et exstincto incendio, idola, et imagines suas in Templo statuerunt. Et obtulerunt eis holocausta, et probro affecerunt Judaeos, et Legem eorum coram idolis suis plasphemarunt. Cap. 94. p. 436....438.

Ch. VI.   *Of the Siege of Jerusalem.*   231.

But Titus was much concerned, and ran toward the temple, and did all in his power to have the fire extinguished, calling aloud to his men, till he was hoarse, and persisting in his exclamations; as this author says, till he fell to the ground almost dead. And the Priests at the temple fought, as long as they were able. And when they saw the fire prevail, they threw themselves into it. As there remained no hopes of preserving the temple, Titus, before it was entirely consumed, went in, and greatly admired it... Soon after that the Romans sat up their idols, and images in the temple, and, offered sacrifices to them, and reviled the Jews, and blasphemed their law, before their idols.

A. D.
930.

He now comes to the signs and prodigies, foresignifying the calamities that were coming upon the Jewish people, which also are mentioned by Josephus *(b)* in this same place, after the burning the temple. "Nor *(c)* did the Jews attend to the words of the signs, "which happened in Jerusalem, though they were very awful. For "a year before Vespasian came, there appeared over the temple a "blazing starr in the shape of a man, in whose hand were drawn "swords. The day in which this sign was seen, was the first of the "feast of the Passover: and during the whole night the temple was "illuminated, as if it had been day. And so it continued through- "out the seven days of the Passover." Thus confounding, as it seems, the first two signs in Josephus, and making them one only, and likewise representing the blazing star somewhat differently from

Jo-

(b) De B. J. l. 6. cap. v. num. 3.
(c) Neque Judaei animum adverterant ad verba signorum, quae contigerunt in Jerusalem. . . . Nam anno uno antequam veniret Vespasianus, apparuit super Templum stella quaedam scintillans instar formae hominis, in cujus manu gladii districti. Dies autem, quo visum est signum illud, fuit primus ex diebus festi Paschatis: et tota nocte illius diei Templum fulsit, et resplenduit tanquam lux diei, et ita factum est per totos septem dies Paschatis . . . *Cap.* 94. *p.* 438.

JOSIPPON. Ch. VI.

A. D. 930.

Jofephus. Then follow in him the other figns taken from Jofephus. But I fhall not rehearfe them. He has, particularly, that of the man of low rank, who, for feveral years travelled through the ftreets of Jerufalem, with his mournfull denunciation of *Woe to the city.* Whom (⁎) he calls *Joſhua, fon of Hananiah.*

When *(d)* the Romans had got poſſeſſion of the temple, the Jews, fled to mount Sion. Here our author uſeth a different ſtile from Jofephus, who has never uſed the word *Sion* in his writings, but always deſcribes that part of the city by other Names.

Now *(e)* fome Prieſts came to Titus, entreating mercie. But he would not grant it, and ordered them to be put to death.

Now *(f)* alfo John and Simon fent meſſengers to Titus, propoſing to furrender to him, if he would grant them their lives. But Titus rejected their propoſal, and reproached them feverely.

Whereupon *(g)* Titus ordered the war to be renewed, and carried on by his armie with vigour.

At *(h)* this time *Zarach* [or *Izates,*] of royal defcent, and his brothers,

---

(⁎) Porro quatuor annis ante haec figna fuit vir quidam in Jerufalem, de populo terrae, feu plebeius, nomine Jehoſhua, filius Chananiae, et coepit clamare voce magna die ipfo fefti Tabernaculorum. ... Oderunt autem illum omnes cives urbis. &c. *Ibid. p.* 439.

(d) Poftquam itaque ingreſſus fuit omnis exercitus Romanorum in Templum, diffugerunt Judaei ad montem Sion. *Cap.* 95. *in p.* 440.

(e) Poftquam autem libaverunt Romani, coram Domino fuo Tito, ecce pars Sacerdotum, qui capti fuerant juxta Templum, deprecati funt Titum, ut feipfos vivos fervaret, neve interficeret. . . . Tunc Romani irruerunt in illos, et mortui funt omnes. *Cap.* 95. *p.* 440.

(f) Simon autem et Jehochanan miferunt ad Titum fermones pacis, et deprecationis, orantes pro feipfis, ut vivos fervaret. . . . *Ibid. p.* 440.

(g) Tunc juſſit Titus Romanis inftaurari bellum cum principibus Latronum Jehochanane et Simone, quandoquidem fe tam pertinaciter gerebant. . . . . *Ib. p.* 441.

(h) Eo tempore furrexit Zarach, qui quidem

Ch. VI. Of the Siege of Jerusalem.

thers, came down from mount Sion, and surrendered to Titus, and were well received by him. Whereupon Simon and his adherents set fire to their goods and treasures, which they had left behind them, that they might not come into the hands of the Romans.

Simon *(i)* and John escape, and hide themselves in a cavern. Many Jews of good condition surrender to Titus, and he receives them favourably.

Joshua (k) a Priest, son *of Shebuthi* High Priest, comes to Titus, bringing with him two golden candlesticks, which were in the sanctuarie, and golden tables, and divers other rich utensils of the temple, and vestments of the Priests, and precious stones. All which he made a present of to Titus, who received him graciously.

At *(l)* this time also came out *Gorion*, the Priest, father of the writer

A. D. 930.

quidem erat de filiis Regum, de monte Sion cum fratribus suis, et cum omnibus filiis feminis regii, ... et venerunt ad Titum, qui excepit illos cum honore, ... et benigne tractavit.... Cum ergo vidissent Jochanan et Simon principes Latronum abiisse Izatam cum ceteris filiis Regis, ... abierunt ipsi, et combusserunt omnia, quae pertinebant ad filios Regis, et incenderunt Domum, et omnes thesauros ejus combusserunt, ne acciperent eos Romani. ... *p.* 441.

(i) Tunc temporis fugientes Simon et Jehochanan, in quadam latebra absconderunt se, quocunque se contulerint. Ceteri vero eorum, qui erant cum eis, et principes Jerusalem, et nobiles Juda, ... statim atque viderunt fugisse Simonem et Jehochananem, ... tunc descenderunt ... et venientes ad Titum, procubuerunt ante faciem ejus in terram ... Et Titus benigne excepit illos... *ib. p.* 442.

(k) Sub id tempus venit ad Titum Jehoshua, sacerdos, filius Shebuthi, Sacerdotis Magni, et attulit secum duo ex candelabris aureis, quae fuerant in Sanctuario. Avexit autem secum omnes mensas aureas, et omnia vasa aurea, ... et crateres, et a- cerras, ... et scutellas, ac etiam vestes Ministerii, et vestes sanctitatis coopertas auro, et circumcinctas lapidibus petiosis, cum magna copia gemmarum. ... Quae omnia donavit Tito, a quo benigne acceptus est, ... *Ib. p.* 442.

(l) Tunc temporis egressus est Gorion, sacerdos, pater Josephi Sacerdotis, Authoris Historiarum libri hujus, de carcere suo, de turri videlicet domus Simonis Latronis, cum uxore sua, et cum filio Honian. Is erat frater Josephi Sacerdotis natu minor. Ille quoque Honian fuit sapiens, magnus, et sacerdos sanctus. ... Nam reliquit eum Titus in Jerusalem, neque abductus fuit ab eo, quemadmodum Josephus.

H h

A. D. 930.

writer of this Historic, and his mother, with their son *Bonian*. They came out of the house of Simon, in which they had been kept prisoners. *Gorion* *** lived twenty months after taking the city of Jerusalem. *Bonian* was a wife, and good man. Titus did not take him to Rome with himself, as he did Joseph: but left him to preside over the Priests in that countrey. Now also *Phineas*, a Priest, brought more of the holy things out of the temple to Titus. But our author blames both these Priests, for delivering such things into the hands of an enemic of the people of God. However, I do not perceive him to make any mention here of the book of the Law.

At (*m*) that time therefore was taken Jerusalem, with all it's desirable

phus. Vixit autem pater Josephi postquam capta est Jerusalem, viditque Josephum filium suum, per viginti menses, et mortuus est. Tunc etiam temporis captus est Phinehas Sacerdos, custos cellarum sacrarii, in quas contulerat omnes thesauros sacerdotum, et vestes sacerdotum sanctas, et dedit Tito Thesaurum unguenti optimi, et aromata, et vestes purpureas, quibus sanctificaverant Sanctuarium Reges Domus secundae, et omnia vasa aurea, quae apud se habebat de vasis Domus Jehovae. *Ib. p.* 443.

(***) *According to Josephus, Gorion was put to death by the zealots, before the siege of the city began. See above, p.* 170. *and De B. J. l.* 4. *cap.* vi. §. 1. *What therefore this Author says of his father and mother must be all fiction and falshood.*

(*m*) Tunc itaque temporis capta fuit Jerusalem, cum omnibus rebus desirabilibus ejus. Deinde ascendit Titus in montem Sion, et cepit illum. Jussit autem destrui murum civitatis Sion. Jam vero elapso triduo deficiebat anima Jehochana-

nis principis Latronum, prae fame. Surrexit itaque de loco ubi latebat, et egressus inde abiit ad Titum, et corruens ante faciem ejus, et deosculatus pedis ejus dixit ei: Serva, quaeso, Domine mi Rex. Tunc jussit illum Titus constringi vinculis ferreis gravissimis, et abduci illum, et circumvehi per totum exercitum suum, atque ignominiose tractari . . . tandem post septem dies mortuus est strangulatus. . . . Postea egressus est etiam Simon Latro, homicida impius, de loco latebrae suae, quia fames graviter premebat illum. . . . Tunc dixit eis: Venite, et vocate mihi ducem, et tradam me illi. . . . Et vocaverunt Rupha, . . qui tunc erat Rector seu praefectus militiae Romanorum. . . . Et sic fecit ille, deduxitque eum ad Titum. Statim autem ut vidit Titus Simonem, jussit illum vinculis constringi, . . . et abduci, et circumvehi per totum exercitum suum, et ignominiose tractari, et subsannari, quemadmodum fecerant Jehochanani. Erat autem vinctus catenis aereis. Tum denique jussit Titus interfici illum in vinculis. Itaque

Ch. VI. *Of the Siege of Jerusalem.* 235

sirable things. And then Titus went up to mount Sion, and took it, and ordered, that the wall of the city of Sion should be demolished. And three days after that *John* one of the princes of the Robbers, being pinched with hunger, came out of his hiding place, and surrendered to Titus, begging mercie of him. But Titus commanded him to be bound with heavie iron chains, and gave orders that he should be led about before his soldiers to be derided and insulted by them, and after seven days he was hanged. And now also immediatly in the same connexion, he relates the appearance of *Simon*, though it could not be, till some while afterwards. He was first brought before the Roman General *Rupha*, or Rufus, and then before Titus. Who commanded him to be bound, and to be led round the whole armie, to be exposed and insulted by them, as *John* had been. After which he was beheaded, and his body was cut to pieces, and thrown to the dogs."

Moreover (*n*) as he goes on, the number of the people that were slain,

que amputaverunt illi caput antequam moreretur. Tum dissecuerunt eum in partes, et projecerunt membra cadaveris ejus canibus. *Ib. p.* 443. 444.

(*n*) Porro numerus totius populi eorum, qui occisi sunt, quatenus potuerunt cognosci tunc gladio cecidisse sive per Romanos, sive per Latrones, ex populo Judaeorum, sive qui de proximo, sive qui de longinquo venerant ad festum, festum scilicet Johovae in Jerusalem, et restiterant illic propter obsidionem, corruerunt que gladio: numerus, inquam, fuit millia millium, et centum millia: praeter illos, qui quidem occisi sunt, sed cognosci non potuerunt, ut numerarentur. Illi enim tantummodo numerati sunt, qui sepulti et cogniti fuerunt. Qui autem cognosci non potuerunt, non recensiti sunt in numerum. Praeter eos quoque, qui postea mortui sunt cum Eleazaro, filio Anani sacerdotis, post mortem Jehochananis, et Simonis, Latronum et Tyrannorum crudelium.

Numerus autem populi ex Judaeis, qui abierunt cum Tito in captivitatem, et quos abduxit secum Romam, sexdecim millia. Et abduxit quidem Romam Josephum Sacerdotem: Bonian vero ejus fratrem reliquit in Antistitem super Sacerdotes, qui remanserunt in Jerusalem. Ita enim deprecatus fuerat Josephus frater ejus, et suscepit faciem ejus, et ita fecit. .. Nam

slain, so far as could be found, who were killed by the Romans, or the robbers, of all the people of the Jews, who from the neighboring countrey, or from far off, had come up to Jerusalem, to the feast, the feast of the Lord, and were shut up in the city by the siege, was eleven hundred thousand, beside many others, whose number was not found, and beside those who died with *Eleazar*, after the death of *John* and *Simon*.

The number of the people of the Jews, who were taken captive by Titus, and carried with him to Rome, he says, were sixteen thousand. He also took with him to Rome *Joseph* the Priest. But *Bonian*, his brother, he left to preside over the Priests in that countrey. But as for those, whom he took captives, he says, that Titus put to death at Jerusalem all, and every one of them in an ignominious manner, excepting only such, as he reserved to take with him. And them he caused to die in a very ignominious manner. For in all the cities, where he made any stay, in his return to Rome, he ordered some of them to be thrown to lions, and other wild-beasts, untill all, whom he had taken with him, were destroyed.

So says our author. The number of the captives, according to Josephus [De B. J. l. 6. ix. 3.] were ninety and seven thousand. Many of whom, according to him, were sold for slaves. But this, so far

as

...Nam quoad ceteros ex eis, quos Titus cepit vivos, ne unum ex eis vivere passus fuit: sed omnes Latrones residuos, quotquot vivos comprehendit, interfecit Titus morte probrosa, et ignominiosa in Jerusalem. Quosdam tamen ex eis secum superstites asservavit, ut contumelia eos afficeret per singulas urbes transitus sui cum contenderet Romam. Cum itaque profectus est Titus de Jerusa'em, accepit eos secum, et abduxit etiam secum reliquum populum captivitatis, quem captivum fecerat ex Judaeis: cumque morabatur in singulis urbibus transitus sui, dum iter faceret Romam, in quacunque urbe, ubi castra metabatur, educebat quosdam ex latronibus illis, et jubebat illos objici leonibus, et feris pessimis, ut devorarent illos, donec consumpti sunt omnes latrones, quos secum habebat. *Cap.* 95. *p.* 444. 445.

Ch. VI. *Of the Siege of Jerusalem.*

as I see, is quite omitted by our Author, as also the triumph of Vespasian and Titus for their conquest of Judea.

But why does he omit these things? To me it seems, to be owing to the pride of his heart. The Temple had been burnt, Jerusalem was destroyed. The whole countrey of Judea had been subdued by the Romans, uncircumcised and idolatrous people. Facts which he could not deny, or disown, however dishonorable and reproachfull to his nation. And he has himself related these events, in his way and manner. But yet he was, as it seems, desirous to save his nation from some circumstances of reproach, and dishonour. He therefore forbore to say any thing of the triumph of Vespasian and Titus: though performed in the metropolis of the vast Empire of the Romans, and published and recorded in public and durable monuments, as well as in writings of the best credit. From the same principle of pride and vanity, he forbore to say, that at this time many Jews, the people of Israel, had been sold for slaves, to live in slaverie to uncircumcised Gentiles. So it seems to me. And I think it may deserve to be taken notice of by us, that in the fictitious historie, which he has given of his journey to Rome, and the inauguration of Vespasian there, he has mentioned a particular, somewhat resembling this. "For after the coronation of Vespasian, and "the death of Agrippa, and his son Monbaz, before-mentioned, "when Vespasian began to shew favour to Joseph, and ordered his "chains to be struck off, Joseph (o) presented a petition to Vespasi-
"an,

(o) Dixit vero Josephus: Nonne opprobrium mihi est referari a me catenas ferreas, et interim vincula filiorum Israel, qui mecum sunt Romae, non etiam referari tuo jussu? Si ergo nunc audieris me, quandoquidem inveni gratiam in oculis tuis, solves quaeso, vincula omnium Israelitarum, qui mecum sunt Romae, et ero tibi consiliarius fidelis omnibus diebus, et inimicus ero inimicus tuis, et adversabor adversariis tuis. Fecit itaque Vespasianus secundum sermonem Josephi, et solvit omnia vincula omnium vinctorum filiorum Israel, qui erant cum Josepho Romae. *Lib.* 6. *cap.* 78. *p.* 346.

A. D. 930

"an, in behalf of all sons of Israel, who were then in prison at
" Rome, entreating that they might be set at liberty: and upon that
" condition promising, that he would for the future be a faithfull
" counsellor to the Emperour, and serve him according to the ut-
" most of his ability. Which petition was granted by the Empe-
" rour, and all Israelites, who had been bound at Rome, were set
" at liberty." Which must be allowed to be one of the fictitious
events of that voyage to Rome, which is throughout the fiction of
this writer's fertil invention, who says what he pleaseth.

After this our Author (*p*) tells the storie of *Eleazar*, and his men at *Massada*, but somewhat differently from (*q*) Josephus. He does not say, that they determined to kill themselves and one another. His account is, that (*r*) after the speech of *Eleazar*, they killed their wives and daughters, that they might not fall a prey into the hands of the enemie. And (*s*) then the men went out of the city, and fought with the Romans. Of whom they slew very many, till they were themselves all killed. And, says he, " Here end the wars of the second House."

After which follows (*t*) this Author's final lamentation, and in a rithmical

(*p*) Cap. 96. p. 447. 448. *et cap.* 97. p. 452.

(*q*) Vid. De B. J. l. 7. cap. viii. ix.

(*r*) Tunc surgentes viri uxores suas, et filias suas accesserunt, quas osculati, et complexi ita alloquuntur. Melius est in oculis nostris, ut moriamini in terra vestra cum sanctitate et honore, quam ut eatis in captivitatem, et cum opprobrio in terram inimicorum vestrorum, et cum idolis gentium, ... et contumelia moriamini. ... *Cap.* 97. *p.* 452.

(*s*) Postea egressus est Eleazarus Sacerdos cum omnibus viris bellatoribus qui secum erant ex urbe, et miscuerunt ingentem pugnam cum multitudine exercitus Romanorum, et occiderunt multos ex eis absque numero. Ac tandem pugnantes Judaei contra proprias ipsorum animas, donec omnes absumerentur in praelio illo mortui pro Jehova, et pro sanctuario ejus. Huc usque desinunt Bella Domus secundae. *Cap.* 97 *p.* 452.

(*t*) Tunc lamentatus fuit Josephus Sacerdos Dei, lamentationem hanc. ... *p.* 452.

Ch. VI. *The Conclusion of the War.*

rithmical fort of poesie, as *Gagnier* (*u*) observes, very different from that among the Hebrews at the time when their temple was destroyed.

A. D. 930.

" Woe (*x*) is now unto us!
For the City of our glorie is laid waste,
                                                                And

(*u*) Lamentatio Ben Gorionis ultima, eaque Rithmica, quam ut Leoninae cujusdam inter Judaeos specimen poeseos non injucundum hic Hebraice subjunximus. Et credat Lector, si potest, sine risu, hanc ab ipso Flavio Josepho compositam fuisse tempore Templi excidii. *Gagnier Not. p.* 472.

(*x*) Vae nunc nobis.
Quia desolata est civitas gloriae nostrae.
Et eversa est Domus Sanctuarii nostri.
In quo posita fuit spes nostra.
Et omnia desideria cordium nostrorum.
Et incensum est Templum nostrum.
Et migravimus de terra nostra.
Et ex haereditate Patrum nostrorum.
Neque ad Deum [extendimus] manus nostras.
Ut liberaremur de exiliis nostris
Quae aggravaverunt super nos.
In illum [commissae] iniquitates nostrae.
Et redegerunt nos in captivitatem peccata nostra.
Et humiliaverunt in terram capita nostra praevaricationes nostrae.
Sed adhuc veniet dies, et terminus
Redemtionis, et adjiciet Deus noster,
Ut recordetur juramenti sui ad Patres nostros.
Et aedificabit civitatem nostram,
Et restaurabit Templum nostrum,
Et colliget dispersos nostros,
Et reducet captivitatem nostram,
Et accelerare faciet Messiam nostrum,
Et festinabit ad redimendum nos.
Et prosternet inimicos nostros.
Et humiliabit osores nostros.
Et perdet, et delebit hostes nostros.
Et nos restituet, sicut in principio.
Cap. 97. *p.* 452. 553.

And the House of our Sanctuarie is thrown down.
In which our hope was placed,
And all the defires of our hearts.
And our **Temple** is confumed with fire.
And we have been carried out of our countrey,
And from the heritage of our Fathers.
Nor have we ftretched out our hands to God,
That we might be delivered from our exiles.
And our fins and iniquities
Have been aggravated upon us.
Our tranfgreffions have carried us into captivity,
And our apoftafies have brought us down to the earth.
But the day will come, and the time of our Redemption.
And our God will deliver us.
He will remember the oath made with our Fathers.
And will build up our city,
And reftore our Temple,
And gather our difperfions.
And will bring back our captivity.
And haften the coming of our Meffiah,
And will fpeedily deliver us.
And will caft down our enemies,
And will humble thofe who hate us.
And will deftroy, and root out all our adverfaries.
And will reftore us, as at the begining.

 Here, befide other things, which an attentive reader will obferve, he expreffeth his expectation of the rebuilding the temple at Jerufalem. So likewife, when he gave an account of Herod's building, or repairing the temple, he defcribes the rejoicings made upon that occafion: " For *(y)* the building, fays he, of the houfe of the Lord, which

(*y*) Et laudaverant Jehovam cum gaudio ... propter aedificium Domus Jehovae, quam vidimus, et aedificatam, devaftatam. Sed adhuc reaedificabitur tertio cum

Ch. VI. *The Conclusion of the War.*

which we have seen, both built, and destroyed. But it shall be raised a third time in honour and glory, and shall be established for ever." And in like manner in another (*z*) place. He is therefore a good witnesse to the destruction of the temple at Jerusalem, which had been raised after the return from the Babylonish captivity. In which, as we say, the Prophets had foretold, the Messiah would make his appearance. See Hag. ii. 6... 9 and Mal. iii. 1.

After his lamentation this author adds, "But (*a*) Titus left a remnant of Israel in the land of Israel, in the city Jabne, and it's towns, and in the city Bether, and in it's towns, and in Osha, and it's towns." Of all which cities, as Gagnier (*b*) in his notes observes, there is no notice taken by Flavius Josephus: though there is in the Talmudical writings, and he refers to Lightfoot's works such as are inquisitive.

This author proceeds. "Moreover (*c*) Titus reigned two years

---

cum laude, et celebritate, et gloria, et firmabit eam Jehova in aeternum. *l.* 6. *cap.* 55. *p.* 243.

(*z*) *Cap.* 65. *p.* 288. *sub fin. et p.* 289.

(*a*) Reliquit autem Titus Israeli reliquias in terra Israel, in urbe Jabne, et in oppidis ejus, in urbe Bether, et in oppidis ejus, et in Osha, et oppidis ejus. *Cap.* 97. *p.* 454.

(*b*) Tres illas urbes, vid. Jabneh, Bether, et Oshah, hoc loco commemorat Ben-Gorion noster, non ex Josepho auctore suo, qui nihil hic habet de hac Belli Judaici Coronide, sed ex Pandectis Talmudicis, ubi frequentissima illarum mentio occurrit. De quarum urbium situ et celebritate maxime post eversa Hierosolyma, consulenda est doctissimi Lightfooti

Chronographia Terrae Israelis. *Cap. xv. lii. et lxxxiv. Gagn. Not p.* 474.

(*c*) Regnavit autem Titus duobus annis postquam cepit Jerusalem, et mortuus est. Porro Titus Rex fuit sapiens, magnus in scientia eloquentiae, tum in lingua Graeca, tum in lingua Romana, et composuit libros multos cum sapientia Graece et Romane. Fuitque Titus vir justus et rectus, et omnia judicia ejus erant cum justitia. Verum necessitate coactus desolavit et delevit Jerusalem. Et quidem desolavit et delevit eam, quia omne malum illud, quod venit super Jerusalem, non venit nisi per Latrones, qui erant in Israel, et propter impietatem illorum, uti memoravimus. *Cap.* 97. *p.* 456.

"after

"after he had taken Jerufalem, and then died. Titus was a wife
" King, and compofed many valuable books both in the Greek, and
" in the Roman language. Titus was a juft and upright man, and
" all his judgements were in righteoufneffe. But being compelled
" by neceffity he deftroyed and laid wafte Jerufalem. All which
" evil came upon Jerufalem, becaufe of the robbers, which were
" in Ifrael, and becaufe of their wickedneffe, as we have fhewn in
" this hiftorie."

He here fays, that *Titus reigned two years, after he had taken Jerufalem*. Which is very inaccurate. Vefpafian did not die before
the year of our Lord 79. After him Titus reigned more than two
years and died in the year, of Chrift 81. Nor does our author fay
any thing here of Vefpafian, as he ought to have done. But we
muft not ftay to remark upon the defects or inaccuracies of this writer. If we had fo done, we fhould never have got through his
work. And every reader is able to obferve many fuch things, without my mentioning them.

This author gives a good character of Titus. And he could do
no lefs, after having before related fo many favours and civilities
conferred by him upon the Jews. Titus alfo, as all know, is much
commended in the Hiftorie of the Jewifh War, writ by Flavius Jofephus: from which this writer had all his materials, that are of
any value. But *(d)* herein he differs from the Talmudical writers,

---

(d) Hic magna eft difcordia Ben-Gorionem inter et Talmudicos Doctores, quam
non diffitentur ipfi Rabbini. Nec deeffe
tamen afferunt Sapientes, qui illam con-
tradictionem concilient, quemadmodum
affirmat R. David Ganz. Sed quo judicio id tentaverint, judicium fit penes lec-
torem.
Quoad noftrum Ben-Gorionem, illum
hoc loco fibi conftare fatendum eft. Cum
enim in verfione Rufini ubique magnas
Titi Imp. virtutes fummis laudibus prae-
dicari legerit, ipfeque Flavium Jofephum
fecutus illum faepius multis elogiis orna-
viffet, non aufus fuit fuos Doctores Talmudicos cum famae fuae difpendio fequi,
ne videlicet fibi contrarius videretur.
Gagn. p. 456.

as Gagnier obferves in his notes upon this work. For they reprefent Titus as exceeding impious and profane, as we alfo have feen. How the learned Jews can reconcile thefe contradictions is not eafie to comprehend. But they continue to pay refpect to this author, as well as to the Talmudical Doctors.

Reland (e) likewife, in his notes upon the Triumphal Arch of Titus, takes notice of the grievous reproaches and fcandalous reflexions upon him in the Jewifh writers. Whereby they have fhewn that they are fkilfull in the art of flandering, and fpare not, when they attempt it. Moreover in this their enmity to Titus they bear witneffe to that great event, the overthrow of their city and temple, of which he was, under God, the inftrument.

III. I may now make fome general remarks. But they need not to be many, nor long.

Concluding Remarks.

1. This writer is evidently an impoftor, a deteftable character, which cannot be too much difliked, nor too much cenfured. He did not live in the time of Vefpafian and Titus, as he pretends. Nor is he *Jofeph the fon of Gorion*, the Prieft, who was appointed to prefide in Jerufalem, or to govern in Galilee.

2. Neverthelefs he is a witneffe to the burning of the temple, and the taking of Jerufalem, and the conqueft of Judea, by the forementioned

---

(e) Hebraei narrant, fed ex odio Titi, quem *illum impium* vocant, ac fi hominem longe poft homines natos fceleratiffimum diceres, non modo velis facris eum vafa templi impofuiffe, fed et contaminaffe adytum impio facinore, in Gemara Gittin. fol. 56. 2. *Cepit meretricem, eaque inducta in fanctum fanctorum, ftratoque Legis volumine, facinus patravit fuper illud.* Dein ftricto gladio velum perrupit, unde fanguis, facto miraculo, miffus eft, fic ut exiens Titus putaret fe Deum ipfum peremiffe.... *Reland. de Spoliis Templi in Arcu Titian). cap.* 13. *p.* 130, 131.

mentioned Emperours. To thofe events he has bore his teftimonie, and his teftimonie is received by the people of his own nation, efpecially by the learned among them.

3. He fays, that *Titus was compelled by neceſſity to deſtroy Jeruſalem, and that all this evil had come upon Jeruſalem, becauſe of the robbers, and their wickedneſſe.*

He therefore does not afcribe the calamities, which befell the Jews in the time of Vefpafian and Titus, to their fin in rejecting Jefus, and not receiving him, as the Meſſiah. Their calamities he owns, and thereby bears witneſſe to the fulfilment of our Saviour's prophecies concerning the deftruction of Jerufalem. But he does not acknowledge any guilt contracted by his people in crucifying the Lord Jefus, and perfecuting his followers. Nor does Jofephus. Nor (A) indeed do I well fee how any unbelieving Jews can make fuch acknowledgements. Rabbi Ifaac in his *Munimen Fidei* above quoted, which is writ againſt the Chriſtians, quotes John xix. 15. The chief-prieſts anfwered : *We have no King, but Cefar.* Upon which he remarks in this manner. "This (f) fhews, that before
" Jefus

(A) It is faid by fome learned men, that *Maimonides aſcribes the deſtruction of Jeruſalem to our Lord.* So Dr. Sharpe in his *Argument. &c. p.* 38. 39. And De Voifin in Pr. Rugion. Fidei. p. 127. Certe R. Mofes in tract. De Regibus, et De Bell. cap. 11. propter Jefum Chriftum excidium Jerofolymitanum contigiffe fatetur. ... Id eſt, " Ille, qui vifus eſt effe Meffias, et occifus eſt fententia judiciali, &c. ille fuit cauffa, cur Ifrael gladio perierit, et reliquiae Ifrael difperfae fint, et depreffae, et cur lex mutata fit." But how this is to be underſtood, I cannot well fay. I have not the tract of Maimonides, here referred to.

(f) Haec ibi. Ecce hoc dicto oftenditur, ante Jefu cruci affixionem jam dum Caefares Romanos Judaeis imperitaffe. Atque is Caefar [*de quo ibi fermo,*] Tiberius fuit, qui Pilatum Hierofolymis praefecerat, ceu conſtat ex capitis III. Lucae initio. Valebit hoc pro refponfo adverfus objectionem Nazaraeorum, qua clamitant, Judaeos propter peccatum fufpenfionis Jefu perdidiffe regnum fuum. &c. R. *Iſacci Munimen Fid.* p. 446. *Conf. p.* 55. 56. *ibid.*

"Jesus was crucified, the Jews were subject to the Roman Empe-
"rours. The Emperour here intended was Tiberius, who sent Pi-
"late to preside at Jerusalem, as appears from the third chapter of
"Luke at the begining. This may suffice for an answer to an ob-
"jection of the Nazareans, who say, the Jews lost their kingdom,
"for their sin in hanging Jesus." This, though it be no better than
an evasion, shews the Jewish temper and principles. I say, it is no
better than an evasion. The Jewish people, as we know very
well, were subject to the Romans in our Saviour's time. But the
case was much altered with them afterwards. They were then very
happy, and were so for some good while after that, enjoying, under the mild government of the Romans, the free exercise of their
religion, and the temple-worship, and many other privileges. The
distresse, and other circumstances of the siege of Jerusalem, were
very uncommon, sufficient to raise the attention of all serious men.
And the long duration, and other circumstances of their captivity
and dispersion ever since, are also very uncommon and extraordinarie. But this is not a time or place for me to enlarge upon them
any farther. But it is reasonable to think, that unbelieving Jews
must endeavor, some how or other, to evade the argument in favour
of Christianity, taken from the destruction of Jerusalem, and their
long continued captivity and dispersion. And beside the passage just
now alleged, the same Rabbi *Isaac*, in the place before referred to,
relating to the death of Agrippa, says, " that *(g)* the differences be-
"tween King Agrippa and the wicked leaders of the factions, at
"length brought on the desolation of the Temple."

4. This work of *Josippon* confirms the historie of the Jewish war
writ by *Flavius Josephus*, son of Matthias. And it must induce us
to set a real value upon Josephus, and raise our esteem for him.
They

(g) Ceterum, ob illam, quae inter Re- que desolatum fuit Templum, uti ex Jo-
gem Agrippam et improbos Duces factio- sepho constat. *Munim. Fid.* p. 417. And
sorum exorta fuerat contentionem, deni- see before p. 218. note (*k*).

They are both fond of their own people. But Jofephus was indeed contemporarie with the events, which he records, and with the principal actors in them: and therefore he muſt have the preference. This author is a plagiarie, and knows nothing of the war, of which he writes, but what he has ſtolen from another, without naming him. And with all his Greek politeneſſe, Jofephus has more the air of ſincerity and ſimplicity than this Hebrew writer. Indeed, it would have been a bad exchange, if inſtead of *the Hiſtorie of the Jewiſh War*, writ by *Flavius Joſephus*, we had palmed upon us *the Hiſtorie of the Wars of Jehova*, writ by *Joſippon*, who neither was *the ſon of Gorion*, who preſided at Jeruſalem, nor *the ſon of Matthias*, who governed in Galilee.

CHAP. VII.

A Recollection of the foregoing Articles, and Reflexions upon them.

I. *The preceding Articles recollected.* II. *Reflexions upon them.* III. *Concluding Observations.*

I. **I** QUOTE no more Jewish (*a*) Writers. I therefore now pro- *The pre-* ceed to recollect what we have seen, and to make remarks. But *ceding Ar-* I need not recollect the first two chapters. I hope they have not been *collected,* im-

(*a*) Some learned men have of late appealed to a book, entitled *Toldoth Jeschu*. I am of opinion, that Christianity does not need such a testimonie, nor such witnesses. I have looked it over several times, with an intention to give some account of it. But, after all, I could not persuade myself to attempt it. For it is a modern work, writ in the 14. or 15. centurie, and is throughout, from the begining to the end, burlesque and falshood. Nor does the shameless writer acknowledge any thing that has so much as a resemblance of the truth, except in the way of ridicule. I shall however put down here the short censure of *Grotius* upon this work, though he does not mention the title of it: not thinking it, as I suppose, worthy to be named. " Some of the Jews ascribe the " miracles of Jesus to a certain secret " name, which was put in the temple by " Solomon, and kept by two lions for " above a thousand years, but was conveyed thence by Jesus. Which is not " only false, but an impudent fiction : " [non mendaciter modo, sed et impu- " denter confictum est.] For as to the " lions, so remarkable and wonderful a " thing, neither the Books of the Kings, " nor the Chronicles, nor Josephus, men— " tion

improperly premised to this work. But they need not to be brought in here, in the way of recapitulation, and recollection. I shall recollect only what we have seen in Jewish writers, begining with Josephus.

Two things are to be regarded by us, their testimonie to the Lord Jesus Christ, and to the Destruction of Jerusalem.

In Josephus there is a paragraph, where JESUS is mentioned very honorably, and agreeably to his true character. But it is not universally received by learned men as genuine. Many are rather of opinion, that it has been inserted in his works, since his time.

There is in him another paragraph, concerning *John the Baptist*, which is generally received as genuine. And it is a valuable testimonie to his preaching, and therein calling men to the practise of virtue. He likewise says, that he was put to death by Herod the Tetrarch. But he says nothing of that part of his character, that he appeared as the fore-runner of the Messiah.

He likewise acknowledgeth, that there was then in Judea a general expectation of a great person to arise from among them, who should obtain the empire of the world: and that this expectation was one great occasion of the war with the Romans: and that it was built upon an oracle found in their sacred writings: and that many of their wise men embraced it, and acted upon it in their engaging in the war. He has also spoken of many false-prophets, who appeared at that time, promising great advantages to the people, if they would follow them, and that many were deceived by them. If they

---

" tion any thing of them. Nor did the
" Romans, who before the times of Jesus
" entered the temple with Pompey, find
" any such thing." *Grotius, of the Truth*
*of the Christian Religion. B. 5. §. iv. in the
version of Dr. John Clarke. And I refer
to Wagenseil's Confutation of the Toldeth
Jeschu.*

Ch. VII. *A Recollection of the preceding Articles.*

they did not call themselves Chrifts, as well as Prophets, they did in effect take upon them the character of the Meffiah.

In the *Mifhna* it is allowed, that there is no exprefs mention of Jefus Chrift, the defign of that work being to make a collection of the numerous traditions, which hitherto were unwritten. But I have alleged a paragraph (✣) which I think, contains an invidious reprefentation of the ftate of things under the gofpel-difpenfation, in the fecond centurie.

In the *Talmudical* writings Jefus is mentioned. But as Lightfoot, who was well acquainted with them, fays, it is chiefly with a view to wound and reproach him. They call his mother by the name *Mary*. But they have afperfed her character, and have affigned to Jefus a fpurious nativity. They have mentioned feveral of our Saviour's difciples, who, as they fay, were put to death. They fay, our Saviour fuffered as a malefactor, at one of the Jewifh Paffovers, or, in the *eve* of it, as the expreffion is. They feem in fome places, to acknowledge the power of miracles in Jefus, and his difciples. And if they had not known, that many miraculous works were afcribed to him, they would not have infinuated, that he learned magical arts in Egypt, and brought them thence in a private manner, and then fet up himfelf among his countrey-men, as an extraordinarie perfon.

That is the fum of their teftimonie upon this article. It would be in vain to expect a great deal from Jews upon this head, who are our enemies. Such are their prejudices, that they are, and always have been, the moft inveterate enemies of Jefus, and his followers.

(✣) *See above, p.* 182 .... 188.

K k

Concerning the other point, the *deſtruction of Jeruſalem*, their teſtimonie is more material, indeed very valuable. *Joſephus*, without intending it, has bore teſtimonie to the fulfilment of all our Saviour's predictions concerning the miſeries of the ſiege of Jeruſalem, the deſolation of the land of Judea, and the diſperſion of his nation. We have above tranſcribed his account at large. His teſtimonie has been repeated, with ſome variations, in *Joſippon*'s Hiſtorie of the Jewiſh war. And the *Miſhna*, and the *Talmuds* likewiſe acknowledge the conqueſt of Judea by Veſpaſian and Titus, the burning of the temple, or the *ſecond houſe*, and the overthrow of Jeruſalem, which was dug up to the foundation.

Reflexions upon the preceding Articles.

II. But how ſhould this be? How could this come to paſs? What ſhould be the reaſon of it? Does not this deſerve ſerious conſideration? Amos iii. 6. *Shall there be evil in a city, and the Lord has not done it?* Such things are not the effect of chance, but are owing to the direction of Providence. Iſa. xlv. 7. *I form the light, and create darkneſſe: I make peace, and create evil: I the Lord do all theſe things.* But if God inflict calamities upon any people, it is not without reaſon. For all his works are done in truth. So again, in the forecited chapter of Amos ver. 1. and 2. *Hear this word, that the Lord hath ſpoken againſt you, o children of Iſrael, againſt the whole familie, which I brought up from the land of Egypt, ſaying: You only have I known of all the families of the earth. Therefore I will puniſh* [or viſit] *you for all your iniquities.*

It is a reaſonable maxim: *Unto whom much is given, of him ſhall be much required. And to whom men have committed much, of him they will aſk the more.* Luke xii. 48. The people of the Jews had been favoured by God with many privileges. A ſuitable emprovement might be expected. If they tranſgreſs the laws of God, their puniſhment will be exemplarie. Nor could any thing elſe, but ſin,

alienate

Ch. VII. *Reflexions upon the preceding Articles.*

alienate the mind of God from them. If. lix. 1. 2. *Behold the Lord's hand is not shortened, that it cannot save: neither is his ear heavie, that it cannot hear. But your iniquities have separated between you and your God.* And Lam. i. 8. *Jerusalem has grievously sinned. Therefore she is removed.* According to the declarations of Moses and all the Prophets, the prosperity and adversity of this people would be proportionate to their regard or disregard of the laws of God. For this I refer to Leviticus ch. xxvi. and Isaiah ch. i. And I shall make quotations from the book of Deuteronomie ch. xxviii. 1. 2. *And it shall come to pass, if thou shalt hearken diligently unto the voice of the Lord thy God, to observe and do all his commandments, which I command thee this day, that the Lord thy God will set thee on high above all the nations of the earth. And all these blessings shall come on thee, and overtake thee, if thou shalt hearken unto the voice of the Lord thy God...* ver. 15. *But it shall come to pass, if thou wilt not hearken unto the voice of the Lord thy God to observe to do all his commandments, and his statutes, which I command thee this day, that all these curses shall come upon thee, and overtake thee:* 25. *The Lord shall cause thee to be smitten before thy enemies. Thou shalt go out one way against them, and flee seven ways before them, and shalt be removed into all the kingdoms of the earth...* ver. 37. *And thou shalt become an astonishment, and a proverb, and a bye-word among all the nations, whither the Lord shall lead thee...* ver. 49. 50. *The Lord shall bring a nation against thee from far, from the end of the earth,* [as swift] *as the eagle flieth, a nation, whose tongue thou shalt not understand: a nation of fierce countenance, which shall not regard the person of the old, nor shew favour to the young:* .. ver. 52... 59. *And he shall besiege thee in all thy gates, untill thy high and fensed walls come down, wherein thou trustedst throughout all thy land. And he shall besiege thee in all thy gates, throughout all thy land, which the Lord thy God hath given thee. And thou shalt eat the fruit of thy own body, the flesh of thy sons and thy daughters, which the Lord thy God hath given thee, in the siege, and in the straightnesse, wherewith thy enemies shall distress thee. So that the man, who is very tender among you, and very delicate, his eye shall be evil toward his brother, and toward the wife of his bosom, and toward the remnant of his children, which he shall leave: so that he will not give to any of them of the flesh of his children, which he shall eat: because he has nothing left him in the siege, and in the straightnesse, wherewith thy enemies shall distress thee in all thy gates. The tender and delicate woman among you, which would not adventure to set the sole of her foot upon the ground, for delicatenesse and tendernesse, her eye shall be evil toward the husband of her bosom, and toward her son, and toward her daughter, and toward her young one that cometh from between her feet, and toward her children which she shall bear. For she shall eat them for the want of all things secretly in the siege and straightnesse, wherewith thy enemie shall distress thee in thy gates. If thou wilt not observe to do all the words of this law, which I have written in this book, that thou mayest fear this glorious and fearfull name, the Lord thy God: then the Lord will make thy plagues wonderfull, and the plagues of thy seed, even great plagues, and of long continuance, and sore sicknesses, and of long continuance.*

We may be hence apt to think, that Moses foresaw the distresses of the siege of Jerusalem, in the year of our Lord 70. and all the calamities endured by the Jewish people about that time, throughout their whole land, and their dispersion afterwards. If he did not foresee them, the words spoken by him, were then fulfilled. And all the calamities, which then befell the Jewish people, or have since befallen them, are exactly according to the original plan of Divine Providence concerning them.

When the law of the ten Commandments was delivered at mount Sinai, the people were greatly terrified. And they earnestly requested, that God might speak to them no more in that way. If he would be pleased to speak to them by Moses, they engaged to hear and obey him. God accepted of this request, and assured them,

that

Ch. VII.   *Reflexions upon the preceding Articles.*

that for the future, he would reveal his mind to them in a more familiar manner. He would speak unto them by Moses, and afterwards by Prophets, like unto him. And that there might be no room for mistake, deceit, or delusion, he would furnish those, whom he should send unto them, with sufficient credentials of their mission. If any should come to them in his name, without such credentials, they might be slighted, and despised. But if they came with proper credentials, they ought to be heard, and obeyed. And if not, it would be resented. This is related several times in the books of Moses, and deserves to be attended to by us.

Ex. xx. 18. 19. *And all the people saw the thundrings, and the lightenings, and the noise of the trumpet, and the mountain smoaking. ... And they said unto Moses: Speak thou with us, and we will hear. But let not God speak with us, least we dye.*

Deut. v. 22...29. *These words the Lord spake unto all your assemblie in the mount, out of the midst of the fire, of the cloud, and of the thick darknesse, with a great voice... And it came to pass, when ye heard the voice out of the midst of the darknesse, (for the mountain did burn with fire,) that ye came near unto me, even all the heads of your tribes, and your Elders. And ye said: Behold, the Lord our God has shewn us his glorie, and his greatnesse, and we have heard his voice out of the midst of the fire... Now therefore why should we die? For this great fire will consume us. If we hear the voice of the Lord our God any more, we shall die... Go thou near, and hear all that the Lord our God shall say: and speak thou unto us all that the Lord our God shall speak unto thee: and we will hear and do it. And the Lord heard the voice of your words, when ye spake unto me. And the Lord said unto me: I have heard the voice of the words of this people, which they have spoken unto thee. They have well said all that they have spoken. Oh that there were such an heart in them, that they would fear me, and keep all my commandments always, that it might be well with them,*

and

Reflexions upon the preceding Articles. Ch. VII.

and with their children for ever! Which words are supposed to be wonderfully emphatical, expressive of a most ardent wish and desire.

Once more Deut. xviii. 15...18. *The Lord thy God will raise up to thee a Prophet, from the midst of thee, of thy brethren, like unto me. Unto him shall ye hearken. According to all that thou desiredst of the Lord thy God in Horeb, in the day of the assemblie, saying: Let me not hear again the voice of the Lord thy God: neither let me see this great fire, any more, that I die not. And the Lord said unto me, they have well spoken that which they have spoken... I will raise them up a Prophet from among their brethren,* and what follows.

Here is the origin of the prophetical character, *men sent from God with a special commission to declare to mankind his mind and will.* And from the occasion of this institution, (the great terrours of mount Sinai, and the request thereupon made,) it might be argued, that if ever a Prophet should arise among the people of Israel, like unto Moses, and meeker than he: and if his miracles, the signs and proofs of his mission, should be more universally saving and beneficent, than those of Moses, it should not be any disadvantage to him, nor lessen the respect fit to be shewn unto him.

We proceed in considering the texts lying before us.

Deut. xviii 18...22. Says God to Moses: *I will raise them up a prophet from among their brethren, like unto thee, and will put my words in his mouth, and he shall speak unto them all that I shall command him. And it shall come to pass, that whosoever will not hearken to my words, which he shall speak in my name, I* WILL REQUIRE IT OF HIM. *But the prophet, which shall presume to speak a word in my name, which I have not commanded him to speak, or that shall speak in the name of other gods, even that prophet shall dye. And, if thou say in thy heart, How shall we know the word, which the Lord has not spoken?*

Ch. VII. *Reflexions upon the preceding Articles.*

ken? *When a prophet speaketh in the name of the Lord, if the thing, follow not, nor come to pass, that is the thing, which the Lord has not spoken, but the prophet has spoken presumptuously. Thou shalt not be afraid of him.*

Here is a general rule for difcerning the miffion of prophets, or fuch as fhould come in that character, as from God. It is a rule, that would be of ufe in all ages. And is here delivered for that purpofe.

If the thing follow not, nor come to pass. Thofe words do not intend any prediction of fome diftant good or evil, to come fome while hereafter. But they intend a *prodigie*, or fome work above the ordinarie courfe of nature. Which he who takes upon him the character of a prophet, propofeth, as a fign, or token, or proof of his miffion. If the fign propofed by any man, as a token and proof of his miffion be performed, he ought to be hearkened to. If it is not performed, there is no reafon to apprehend any harm from defpifing and rejecting him. He has no meffage from God. *He has spoken presumptuously. Thou shalt not be afraid of him.*

This may appear farther from what is faid ch. xiii. 1. 2. 3. *If there arise among you a prophet, or a dreamer of dreams, and he giveth a sign, or a wonder:* that is, propofeth fome great work, as a proof of his miffion: *and the sign, or the wonder come to pass, whereof he spake unto thee, saying, Let us go after other gods (which thou hast not known) and serve them: thou shalt not hearken to the words of that prophet, or dreamer of dreams. For the Lord Your God proveth you, to know whether you love the Lord Your God with all your hearts, and with all your soul...* ver. 5. *And that prophet, or that dreamer of dreams shall be put to death....So shalt thou put the evil away from the midst of thee.*

Here is a cafe put, which never would happen. Never would any man be able to perform a miracle, in order to induce the people

ple of Ifrael to worfhip other gods. But fuppofing it, he was neverthelefs to be difregarded.

In all other cafes the rule here laid down for judging of prophets would hold, and was to be obferved by all. If a man propofed fome extraordinarie work, as a proof of his miffion, which was not performed, he was not to be regarded. So all the falfe-prophets, fpoken of by Jofephus, who appeared in the times of *Felix*, *Feftus*, and other Governours of Judea, fome while before the deftruction of Jerufalem, in order to induce people to follow them, in hopes of deliverance from fubjection to the Romans, engaged that they fhould *fee the walls of Jerufalem fall down before them*, to give them eafie entrance into the city: or that they *fhould fee the waters of Jordan divided*, that they might go over upon dry ground, or *that God would fhew them figns in the wildernefse*, and the like. But nothing of that kind came to pafs.

But if a prophet *gave*, or propofed a *fign* or *wonder*, in proof of his miffion, and it came to pafs, or was performed, it would be decifive in his favour. So, when there were murmurings and difputings among the people of Ifrael in the wildernefse, which tribe fhould have the priefthood: it was propofed, that *twelve rods, each having the name of the prince of the tribe upon it, and another rod, with Aaron's name upon it, for Levi, fhould be laid up in the tabernacle, before the teftimonie:* and his rod which bloffomed, fhould be known to be the man, whom God had chofen. *Mofes then laid up the rods before the Lord, in the tabernacle of witnefse. And it came to pafs, that on the morrow Mofes went into the tabernacle of witnefse: and behold, the rod of Aaron, for the houfe of Levi, budded, and brought forth bloffoms, and yielded almonds. And Mofes brought out all the rods from before the Lord unto all the children of Ifrael. And they looked, and took every man his rod.* Numb. xvii. So that point was determined, and the *murmurings of the children of Ifrael ceafed.* And

fa

Ch. VII.   *Reflexions upon the preceding Articles.*

so it must be in all other like cases. If a *sign* or *wonder* has been *given*, or proposed, and it is performed, or *comes to pass*, it is decisive.

Here then is the rule. If a man come, and speak in the name of God, and prove his commission by signs and wonders, he is to be regarded, and received as a Prophet. And God declares, *whosoever will not hearken unto my words, which he shall speak in my name, I* WILL REQUIRE IT OF HIM. Deut. xviii. 19. It cannot be otherwise. The consequence of disobedience to the word of the Lord, so manifested, and confirmed, must be dreadfull.

Let us now apply this. Jesus spoke in the name of God, faithfully delivered the words, which he had received from God, and performed many miracles, in proof of his commission. John xii. 49. 50. *For I have not spoken of my-self. But the Father, which hath sent me, he gave me commandment, what I should say, and what I should speak. And I know that his commandment is life everlasting. Whatsoever I speak therefore, as the Father said unto me, so I speak.* Ch. viii. 42. *I have proceeded forth, and came from God. Neither came I of my-self, but he sent me.*

And in proof of his mission, he appealed to his works, which were great, and numerous, and openly performed in the view of all men. John v. 31. 32. 33. *If I bear witnesse of my-self, my witnesse is not true. There is another that beareth witnesse of me. And I know, that the witness, which he witnesseth of me, is true. Ye sent unto John, and he bare witnesse unto the truth.* 36. *But I have greater witnesse than that of John. For the works, which the Father hath given me to finish, they bear witnesse of me, that the Father hath sent me.* And ch. xv. 24. *If I had not done among them the works, which no other man did, they had not had sin: but now they have both seen and hated both me and my Father.*

L l

If Moses and the ancient Prophets wrought miracles, there (b) is as good reason to believe, that Jesus likewise did so, and more than any of them, or than all of them together. For the testimonie of the writers of the New Testament is as credible, as that of the writers of the Old Testament. And if it be said, that Elijah was taken up to heaven, it (c) is as credible, that Jesus was raised from the dead, and afterwards ascended up to heaven.

Our Lord asserted his prophetical character, and his peculiar character of the Messiah: and often reminded the Jews of the terrible consequences of rejecting him, who spake in the name of God: or in the words of Moses, that it *would* BE REQUIRED OF THEM. John viii. 24. *If ye believe not that I am He, ye shall die in your sins.* ver. 25. *They said unto him, Who art thou? Jesus said unto them, even the same that I said unto you from the beginning,* John the Baptist often said the same: that *he was not the Christ, but was sent before him.* John iii. 28. And see ch. i. 19...37.

But not to multiply texts, I shall quote Matt. xxi. 33...44. *Hear another parable. There was a certain housholder, who planted a vineyard, and hedged it round about, and digged a wine-presse in it, and built*

(b) Si quis Paganus ab ipsis Judaeis quaerat, cur credant miracula a Mose facta, nihil dicant aliud, quam inter suos adeo perpetuam constantemque ejus rei fuisse famam, ut non potuerit, nisi ex testimonio eorum qui vidissent proficisci. Sic ab Elisaeo [2. Reg. cap. iv.] auctum apud viduam oleum purgatum [cap. v.] subito a mala scabie Syrum, hospitae [ib. iv.] filium ad vivum revocatum, et similia alia credunt Judaei, non aliam ob caussam, quam quod testes bonae fidei id proditum ad posteros transmiserunt. *Grot. de V. R. C. l. v. §. ii.*

(c) De Eliae vero in coelum raptu unius Elisaei, tanquam viri omni exceptione majoris, testimonio fidem habent. At nos de Christi adscensu in coelum duodecim proferimus testes vitae inculpatae: de Christo post mortem in terris viso multo plures. Quae si vera sunt, verum sit necesse est Christi dogma: planeque nihil a Judaeis pro se adferri potest, quod non et nobis pari, aut potiori jure possit aptari. *Grot. ib.*

Ch. VII.   Reflexions upon the preceding Articles.

built a tower, and let it out to husbandmen, and went into a far countrey. And when the time of the fruit drew near, he sent his servants to the husbandmen, that they might receive the fruits of it. And the husbandmen took his servants, and beat one, and killed another, and stoned another. Again, he sent other servants unto them, more than the first. And they did unto them likewise. Last of all, he sent unto them his Son, [the Messiah] *saying: They will reverence my Son. But when the husbandmen saw the Son, they said among themselves: This is the heir. Come, let us kill him, and let us seize on his inheritance. And they caught him, and cast him out of the vineyard, and slew him. When therefore the Lord of the vineyard cometh, what will he do unto those husbandmen? They say unto him: he will miserably destroy those wicked men, and will let out his vineyard unto other husbandmen, which shall render him the fruits in their season. Jesus saith unto them: Did you never read in the scriptures, The stone, which the builders rejected, the same is become the head of the corner? This is the Lord's doing, and it is marvellous in our eyes. Therefore I say unto you: The kingdom of God shall be taken from you, and shall be given to a nation bringing forth the fruits thereof. And whosoever shall fall on this stone, shall be broken: but on whomsoever it shall fall, it will grind him to powder. And when the Chief-priests and Pharisees had heard his parables, they perceived that he spake of them.* This should be compared with Luke xx. 9...18.

Psal. cxviii. 22, 23.

Here our Lord speaks of the ancient Prophets, and then of himself, and shews the dreadfull consequences of rejecting Him, and his message. There is another thing, that should be observed, which is what our Lord added concerning the treatment to be given to his Apostles and Evangelists, the Prophets of the New Testament, also sent to the Jewish people. Matt. xxiii. 29...39. *Woe unto you, Scribes and Pharisees, hypocrites, because ye build the tombs of the Prophets, and garnish the sepulchres of the righteous. And say, If we had been in the days of our fathers, we would not have been partakers with them*

them in the bloud of the Prophets. Wherefore ye are witnesses to yourselves, that ye are the children of them who flew the Prophets. Fill ye up then the measure of your fathers. Ye serpents, ye generation of vipers, how can ye escape the damnation of hell? Wherefore, behold I send unto you, prophets and wise men, and scribes. And some of them ye will kill and crucify, and some of them ye will scourge in your synagogues, and persecute them from city to city, that upon you may come all the righteous bloud shed upon the earth, from the bloud of righteous Abel, to the bloud of Zacharias son of Barachias, [rather, son of Jehoiada. 2 Chron. xxiv. 17... 22. *(d)*] *whom ye flew between the temple and the altar. Verily I say unto you, all these things shall come upon this generation. O Jerusalem, Jerusalem, thou that killest the Prophets, and stonest them that are sent unto thee! How often would I have gathered thy children together, even as a hen gathereth her chickens under her wings, but ye would not. Behold, your house is left unto you desolate. For I say unto you: ye shall not see me henceforth, till ye shall say, Blessed is he that cometh in the name of the Lord.*

All this is properly said by our Lord in his prophetic denunciations. Not only the rejection of Jesus himself, would be *required of them*, but likewise their refusal to hearken to his Apostles. For they likewise were Prophets, and spake by divine inspiration. They spake in the name of God, and delivered his mind and word, and proved their mission by miraculous works. If therefore, after having crucified the Lord Jesus, the Jewish people should proceed to treat in like manner, his Disciples, who were sent to them: if they should *scourge them in their synagogues*, and put some of them to death, *and persecute them from city to city*, (as he foresaw they would) they would then bring upon themselves in the end, a terrible condemnation: and such miseries would befall them, that it would seem as if all the righteous bloud shed from the foundation of the world, had been required of them.

And

(d) *See Credib. Part* i. *p.* 915. *&c.*

Ch. VII.   *Reflexions upon the preceding Articles.*

And that they did so treat the Apostles and other disciples of Jesus, appears from the books of the New Testament. These things may have been already taken notice of by us. Nevertheless they must be here briefly recollected. How the Apostles of Jesus were apprehended, imprisoned, beaten, and farther threatened, may be seen in the book of the Acts ch. iv. and v. Some while afterwards, ch. vi. and vii. Stephen was stoned, *and there was a great persecution against the church, which was at Jerusalem, and they were all scattered abroad, throughout the regions of Judea and Samaria, except the Apostles.* Some time after this, when Herod Agrippa had been advanced to the kingdom of Judea by the Romans, we are informed, ch. xii. 1...4. *that he stretched forth his hands to vex certain of the church. And he killed James, the brother of John with the sword. And because he saw it pleased the Jews, he proceeded farther to take Peter also.* But after he had been imprisoned, he was miraculously delivered out of the hands of Herod, and from the expectation of all the people of the Jews. St. Paul writing to the Hebrews, ch. x. 33. 34. bids them *call to remembrance the former days, in which, after they had been illuminated, they had endured a great fight of afflictions:* partly, says he, *whilst ye were made a gazing-stock, both by reproaches and afflictions, and partly, whilst ye were companions of those who were so used. For ye had compassion upon those who were in bonds, and bore joyfully the spoiling of your goods: knowing that ye have in heaven a better, and a more enduring substance.* And we have good reason to believe, that *James,* called *the Lord's brother,* the Apostle, who generally resided at Jerusalem, was put to death by the Jews there in a tumultuous manner, about the year of Christ 62.

How Paul acted in the early days of the gospel, and whilst he was under the direction of the Chief-priests and Pharisees, we know partly from the Acts of the Apostles, and partly from his own Epistles. It is said Acts viii. 1. that he *was consenting to the death of of Stephen.* And ch. vii. 58. *When he was stoned, the witnesses laid down their cloths at a young man's feet, whose name was Saul.* And afterwards ch. ix. 1. 2. *But Saul yet breathing out threatenings and slaughter against the disciples of the Lord, went unto the High-Priest and desired of him letters to Damascus, to the synagogues, that if he found any of this way, whether they were men or women, he might bring them bound to Jerusalem.* And in his speech before King Agrippa, and the Governour Festus, Acts xxvi. 9 ... 12. he says himself. *I verily thought with my-self, that I ought to do many things contrarie to the name of Jesus of Nazareth. Which thing I also did in Jerusalem. And many of the saints did I shut up in prison, having received authority from the Chief-Priests. And when they were put to death, I gave my voice against them. And I punished them oft in every synagogue, and compelled them to blaspheme. And being exceedingly mad against them, I persecuted them even into strange cities. Whereupon, he set out for Damascus, with authority and commission from the Chief-Priests.* But in his way thither, he met with a check, received new light, to which he submitted, and became a true penitent, and sincere convert, and then preached the faith which for some while he had endeavoured to destroy. Compare Gal. i. 13 ... 24. 1 Cor. xv. 8. 9. Eph. iii. 8. 1 Tim. i. 12 ... 14.

How he was treated by the Jews, after his conversion, we know from the historie in the Acts, and from his own Epistles. For when he began to preach the gospel at Damascus, *the Jews laid wait for him, and they watched the gates day and night to kill him. But the disciples took him by night, and let him down by the wall in a basket.* Acts ix. 23. 24. Of which great danger, and his wonderfull escape, he speaks himself in an affecting manner. 2 Cor. xi. 31. ... 33. When he came to Jerusalem, from Damascus, *and disputed with the Grecians,* or Jewish proselytes. Acts ix. 29. *They went about to slay him.* Acts ix. 29. For which cause the disciples found

it

Ch. VII.   *Reflexions upon the preceding Articles.*   263

it prudent to bring him down to Cefarea, that he might go to Tarfus.

The Jews out of Judea acted in the like manner. At *Antioch in Pifidia*, Paul having preached there with fome fuccefs, both among Jews and Gentils, *the Jews moved with envie ſtirred up the devout and honorable women, and the chief men of the city, and raiſed perfecution againſt Paul and Barnabas, and expelled them out of their coaſts.* Acts xiii. 50. And fee ver. 45. They therefore went to *Iconium*, where alfo they had fome converts among Jews and Gentils. *But the unbelieving Jews ſtirred up the Gentils, and made their minds evil affected toward the brethren... But the multitude of the city was divided... And when there was an aſſault made both of the Gentils and of the Jews, with their rulers, to uſe them deſpitefully, and to ſtone them; they were aware of it, and fled to Lyſtra, and Derbe, cities of Lycaonia, and unto the region that lyeth round about. And there they preached the goſpel.* ch. xiv. 1...7. At Lyſtra, a great miracle was wrought by Paul, upon a *lame man, who had been a creeple from his mother's womb, and never had walked.* And the people of the place were difpofed to give divine honours to Paul and Barnabas, which they refuſed to accept. *But there came thither certain Jews from Antioch and Iconium, who perſuaded the people. And having ſtoned Paul, they drew him out of the city, ſuppoſing he had been dead. Howbeit, as the diſciples ſtood round about him, he roſe up, and came into the city. And the next day he departed with Barnabas to Derbe.* ch. xiv. 1...20. And having paffed through feveral places, they returned to *Antioch in Syria*, from which place they had been fent out with fpecial recommendations to the grace of God. ver. 21...28. All which things therefore happened in what is fometimes called the firſt peregrination of Paul and Barnabas.

How the Jews acted at *Theſſalonica*, may be feen Acts xvii. 1...9. at *Berea*, may be feen ver. 10....15. How they behaved at *Corinth*, may be feen ch. xviii. ver 5...20. And when Paul came

to

to Jerusalem afterwards, in the year of Christ 58. as we compute, he was very hard pressed by the Jews there, where was their great Council, and where the whole nation was gathered together at the feast of Pentecost, as is related Acts xxi. and xxii. Nor was there any visible means of his escaping out of their hands with his life, but by appealing to the Emperour himself, notwithstanding the favourable dispositions of the Roman Governours, *Felix* and *Festus*, to shew him equity: by which appeal he obtained leave to go to Rome, where he lived *two whole years* in a kind of free custodie, *receiving all that came in unto him, and preaching the kingdom of God, and those things which concern the Lord Jesus, with all confidence, no man forbidding him.* ch. xxviii. 30. 31. And then he was set at liberty, and went abroad again.

Thus the Jews resisted the counsel of God, and went on accumulating guilt, and laying up a store of vengeance to fall upon them, when God saw fit, and when the measure of their iniquity was full. As St. Paul says to the Thessalonians, 1. ep. ii. 14. *For ye, brethren, became followers of the churches of God, which in Judea are in Christ Jesus. For ye also have suffered the like things of your countrymen, even as they have of the Jews: who have killed the* LORD JESUS, *and their own* PROPHETS, *and have persecuted* US, *and are contrarie to all men: forbidding us to speak to the Gentils, that they may be saved, to fill up their sins always. For the wrath is come upon them to the uttermost.*

For certain such things cannot be overlooked by the Sovereign Lord and Governour of all nations, and of the Jewish nation, especially. For he has said, and it is agreeable to reason, and to all the rules of right government, that *if he raiseth up a Prophet, and put his words in his mouth, and he speaks all that he has commanded him: It shall come to pass, that whosoever will not hearken unto my words which he shall speak in my name,* I WILL REQUIRE IT OF HIM. Deut.

Ch. VII.   *Reflexions upon the preceding Articles.*   265

Deut. xviii. 18. 19. This rule was laid down and promulgated by Moses himself, the great Lawgiver of the Jews. And, as before observed, it was to be a standing rule. If faithful messengers, who deliver truly the message they have received from God, are rejected, and not only not hearkened to, but abused, the God of the Prophets will resent it, and shew his displeasure. Accordingly, soon after the events before related, wrath did come upon the Jewish people, to a very remarkable degree. And the numbers of those who perished at Jerusalem, and in Judea, by the famine, and by the sword, and by intestin feuds and divisions, or otherwise, was very extraordinarie, and even unparalleled, as we know from *Josephus*, a contemporarie writer of their own nation, and from *Josippon*, a Jew likewise, and from others.

Josephus, who was a witnesse of that awful scene, often acknowledgeth the hand of God in it. *Cestius Gallus*, President of Syria, made a successful attempt upon Jerusalem, and then withdrew. Whereupon, he says, (*e*) *If Cestius had continued the siege a little longer, he would have taken the city. But God, as I think, for the wickednesse of the people, abhorring his own solemnities, suffered not the war to come to an end at that time.* When *John* of Gischala escaped from out of the hands of Vespasian, and got to Jerusalem, he says, (*f*) *It was the work of God, who saved John for the destruction of Jerusalem*. In another place (*g*) he says, *that God had blinded their minds for the transgressions, which they had been guilty of.* And (*h*) *Never did any city endure so great calamities. Nor was there ever from the begining of the world any time more fruitfull of wickednesse.* Again, (*i*) *Indeed, it was God, who had condemned the whole nation, and defeated every method taken for their preservation.* When the

(*e*) See before in this volume. p. 73.   (*h*) p. 95.
(*f*) p. 82. 83.   (*i*) p. 98.
(*g*) p. 93.

M m   Temple

Temple was burning, he says, *(k) Certainly the divine sentence had long ago condemned it to the fire.* He also observes, that *(l) they did not attend to the prodigies, which evidently foretold their desolation. But like men infatuated, who have neither eyes to see, nor minds to consider, they disregarded the divine denunciations.* He also observes, *(m) that the whole nation was then shut up, as in a prison. And the Romans encompassed the city, when it was crowded with inhabitants. Accordingly, the multitude of them who perished therein, exceeded all the destructions that ever man or God brought upon the world. And (n) the whole circumference of the city was so thoroughly laid even with the ground by them who dug it up to the foundation, that there was nothing left to make those who came thither believe, it had ever been inhabited.* So writes *Josephus*, in the Greek language, in the face of the whole world, not many years after the Jewish war was ended. And says *Eleazar*, in his speech at *Massada*, recorded by the same Historian, *(o) the Metropolis of the whole nation, the City, which we believed to have God inhabiting it, has been rooted up to the foundation, and the holy temple has been profanely dug up to the foundation.*

Such was the end of the siege of Jerusalem in the second year of Vespasian, and the year of Christ 70. And thus were accomplished the predictions of Jesus concerning the city of Jerusalem, and the Temple, and the Jewish People, if they did not repent.

Here I might conclude. But if any should be desirous to see this argument in all it's force, and in it's full light, it will be requisite to look farther back, and ascend up to the origin of this people: and then trace their historie, through the several periods of it. For they

are

(*k*) p. 103.
(*l*) p. 104.
(*m*) p. 119.

(*n*) p. 121.
(*o*) p. 122.

Ch. VII.   *Reflexions upon the preceding Articles.*

are a people separated from all other nations, chosen of God for very great ends and purposes, to uphold the belief of the Divine Unity, the doctrine of a Divine Providence, concerning itself in the affairs of mankind, upon the belief of which all religious worship depends, and to preserve the expectation of the coming of a great person to redeem the human race from errour and vice, and the bad consequences of their deviations from truth and virtue.   Gen. iii. 15.

For these ends God chose Abraham, and brought him out of *(p) Ur of the Chaldees. When he called him, out of his countrey, and from his kindred, and from his father's house, he said: I will make thee a great nation, and I will bless thee, and make thy name great, and thou shalt be a blessing. . . . And in thee shall all the families of the earth be blessed.* Gen. xii. 1. . . 3. The fulfilment of which magnificent promise was limited to *Isaac*, or his seed by Sarah. Gen. xvii. and afterwards to *Jacob*, Gen. *xxvii. xxviii.*   And when his posterity was greatly encreased, after their sojourning a while in Egypt, where they had been treated in a servile manner, God brought them out of that countrey, with a *mighty hand, and an out-stretched arm*, working many great and conspicuous miracles for their safety. Whilst they were in the wildernesse he gave to them a system of laws, the ten principal of which were delivered from mount Sinai with great solemnity, and then engraved on tables of stone by the finger of God.   God then brought them into the land of Canaan, where they became a flourishing and powerfull nation, according to the promise made to Abraham concerning *Sarah*, when she was yet barren, that *She should be a mother of nations, and Kings of people should be of her.* Gen. xvii. 16.

David intended to build a House for the name of the Lord. But that honour was reserved for his son Solomon.   The divine approbation of David's design is manifest.   And God, by inspiration, gave him

(p) Gen. xv. 7. Neh. ix. 7.

him the form and dimensions of the house, and the order of the worship to be performed there. 1 Chr. xxviii. 11...13. *Then (q) David gave to Solomon his son the patterns of the porch, and of the houses thereof* [or of the House, and the apartments thereof] *and of the treasures thereof, and of the upper chambers thereof, and of the place of the mercy-seat: and the pattern of all that he had by the spirit of the courts of the house of the Lord, and of all the chambers round about, of the treasuries of the House of God, and of the treasuries of the delicate things. Also for the courses of the Priests and the Levites, and for all the work of the service of the house of the Lord...* ver. 19. *All this,* said David, *the Lord made me to understand in writing* [as if it were inscribed on his mind] *by his hand upon me, even all the words of this pattern.*

When the house was finished, and dedicated by a prayer suitable to the great occasion. 2 Chr. v. vi. we are informed, ch. vii. 12. *that the Lord appeared to Solomon by night, and said unto him: I have heard thy prayer, and have chosen this place to my-self for an house of sacrifice.* 15. 16. *Now my eyes shall be open, and my eyes attent unto the prayers that are made in this place. For now have I chosen and sanctified this house, that my name may be there for ever, and my eyes and my heart shall be there perpetually...* 19...22. *But if ye turn away, and forsake my statutes and my commandments, which I have set before you, and serve other gods, and worship them: then will I pluck them up by the roots out of my land which I have given them. And this house, which I have sanctified for my name will I cast out of my sight, and make it to be a proverb, and a by word among all nations. And this house, which is high, shall be an astonishment to every one that passeth by it, so that he shall say: Why has the Lord done thus unto this land, and to this house? And it shall be answered, Because they forsook the God of their fathers, which brought them out of the land*

(q) *Dedit autem David Salomoni filio suo descriptionem.... id est,* dedit ei formam conspicuam, qualem Deus animo inscripserat, ut dicitur infra ver. 19. *Grot.*

Ch. VII. *Reflexions upon the preceding Articles.*

land of Egypt, and laid hold on other gods, and worshiped them, and served them: therefore has he brought all this evil upon them.

And though God is ever mercifull, and full of compassion, *and forgave their iniquity, and many a time turned away his anger, and did not stirr up all his wrath.* [Pf. lxxviii. 38. and what follows, and Neh. ix.] yet at length the provocation of their repeated idolatries, and grofs immoralities, after the renewed admonitions of his Prophets, was fuch, that God gave them up into the hands of their enemies. So this is related 2 Chron. xxxvi. 15...20. *And the Lord God of their fathers sent unto them by his messengers, rising up early, and sending them, because he had compassion upon his people, and his dwelling place. But they mocked the messengers of God, and despised his words, and misused his Prophets, untill the wrath of the Lord rose against his people, till there was no remedy. Therefore he brought upon them the King of the Chaldees, who flew their young men with the sword, in the house of their sanctuarie, and had no compassion upon young man or maiden, old man, or him that stooped for age. He gave them all into his hand. And all the vessels of the house of God, great and small, and the treasures of the house of the Lord, and the treasures of the King, and of his Princes. All these things brought he to Babylon. And they burnt the house of God, and brake down the walls of Jerusalem, and burnt all the palaces thereof with fire, and destroyed all the goodly vessels thereof. And them that escaped from the sword carried he to Babylon: where they were servants to him, and his sons, untill the reign of the kingdom of Persia.*

That was the overthrow of the Temple and city of Jerufalem, and the kingdom of Judah at that time. All which is related at large, and rather more particularly, in the lii. and laft chapter of the book of Jeremiah. And may be feen alfo in 2 Kings ch. xxiv. xxv.

And it may be worth the while to obferve here Jerem. xxv. 1...11. *The word that came unto Jeremiah concerning all the people of Judah, in the fourth year of Jehoiakim the son of Josiah, King of Judah,*

Reflexions upon the preceding Articles. Ch. VII.
dah, which was the first year of Nebuchadnezzar King of Babylon. Which Jeremiah the Prophet spake unto all the people of Judah, and to all the inhabitants of Jerusalem, saying: From the thirteenth year of Josiah the son of Amon, King of Judah even unto this day, (that is, the three and twentieth year) the word of the Lord has come unto me. And I have spoken unto you, rising early, and speaking. But ye have not hearkened. And the Lord has sent unto you (r) all his servants the Prophets, rising early, and sending them. But ye have not hearkened, nor inclined your ear to hear. THEY SAID, *Turn ye again now every man from his evil way, and from the evil of your doings, and dwell in the land, that the Lord has given to you, and to your fathers for ever. And go not after other gods to serve and to worship them, and provoke me not to anger with the works of your hands, and I will do you no hurt. Yet ye have not hearkened unto me, faith the Lord, that ye might provoke me to anger, with the works of your hands to your hurt. Therefore thus faith the Lord of hosts, because ye have not heard my words, behold, I will send and take all the families of the north, faith the Lord, and Nebuchadnezzar the King of Babylon my servant, and bring them against this land, and against the inhabitants thereof... And this whole land shall be a desolation, and an astonishment. And these nations shall serve the King of Babylon (s) seventy years.*

It ought to be here particularly observed by us, that this calamity is said to have been brought at length upon this people, *because they had refused to hearken to the words of God, spoken to them by the Prophets.*

The

(r) Jeremiah seems there to intend, as Prophets of former times, so also some, who were contemporarie with him, two of which are mentioned in scripture, *Zephaniah*, whose prophecies we have, and *Urijah*, mentioned here ch. xxvi. 20 *See Louth upon the place.* And says Grotius upon ver. 1. *A tertio anno regni Josiae.*

... Nam 31 annis regnavit Josias. Ab his deme 12 et adde annos 4 Joakimi, fiunt ipsi anni 23. Per quos nullo labore et se et socios suos abstinuisse ait Jeremias, ut ad meliorem frugem populum reduceret.

(s) Praedictio insignis, ob ita exactam temporis designationem. *Grot.*

Ch. VII. *Reflexions upon the preceding Articles.*

The veffels of the temple were carried to Babylon, and lodged in the temple there dedicated to Belus. 2 Chr. xxxvi. 7. *Nebuchadnezzar alfo carried of the veffels of the houfe of the Lord to Babylon, and put them in his temple at Babylon.* They are more particularly enumerated, Jer. lii. 17...23. This, undoubtedly, was intended, by way of fcorn and infult to the conquered people of Ifrael, and as a triumph over the God, whom they worfhiped. Neverthelefs they were thereby preferved, and many of them were afterwards returned. That they were there near the end of the captivity, we learn from the profane and unfeafonable feaft made by Belfhazzar, as related Dan. v. 1...4. *Who then commanded to bring the golden and filver veffels, which his father Nebuchadnezzar had taken out of the temple, which is at Jerufalem, that the King and his princes, and his wives and concubines might drink therein.* At the end of the captivity, when Cyrus permitted the people to return to their own countrey, he alfo gave orders for the reftoring of thefe veffels, as related at the begining of the book of Ezra ch. i. 1...11. *Now in the firft year of Cyrus King of Perfia, (that the word of the Lord by the mouth of Jeremiah might be fulfilled) the Lord ftirred up the fpirit of Cyrus King of Perfia, that he made proclamation, throughout all his kingdom, and put it alfo in writing, faying: Thus faith Cyrus King of Perfia, The Lord God of heaven hath given me all the kingdoms of the earth, and he has charged me to build him an houfe at Jerufalem, which is in Judah. Who is there among you of all his people? His God be with him, and let him go to Jerufalem, which is in Judah, and build the houfe of the Lord God which is at Jerufalem. ... Alfo Cyrus the King brought forth the veffels of the houfe of the Lord, which Nebuchadnezzar had brought forth out of Jerufalem, and had put them in the houfe of his god. Even thefe did Cyrus King of Perfia bring forth by the hand of Mithredath, the treafurer, and numbered them unto Shefhbazzar the Prince of Judah. And this is the number of them: thirty chargers of gold, a thou and chargers of filver, nine and twenty knives: thirty bafins of gold: filver bafins of a fecond fort four hundred and ten,*

and

and other veſſels a thouſand. All the veſſels of gold and ſilver, were five thouſand and four hundred. All theſe did Sheſhbazzar bring up with them of the captivity, that were brought up from Babylon unto Jeruſalem.

The firſt thing that was done by them, after their return to Jeruſalem, was reſtoring the altar for burnt-offerings. Ezra. iii. 2. *Then ſtood up Joſhua the ſon of Jozedech and his brethren the prieſts, and Zerubbabel, the ſon of Shealtiel, and his brethren, and builded the altar of the God of Iſrael to offer burnt-offerings thereon... From the firſt day of the ſeventh month began they to offer burnt-offerings unto the Lord. But the foundation of the temple of the Lord was not yet laid.* The building of the temple met with oppoſition, and therefore it was ſeveral years, before it was finiſhed. Which is mentioned Ezra vi. 14...16. *And the Elders of the Jews builded, and they propheſied through the propheſying of Haggai the Prophet, and Zachariah the ſon of Iddo, and they builded, and finiſhed it, according to the commandment of Cyrus, and Darius, and Artaxerxes King of Perſia. And this houſe was finiſhed on the third day of the month Adar, which was in the ſixth year of the reign of Darius the King. And the children of Iſrael, the Prieſts and the Levites, and the reſt of the children of the captivity, kept the dedication of this houſe with joy.*

At firſt they were diſcouraged by the little proſpect they had of raiſing the temple ſuitably to their wiſhes. Ezra iii. 12. *Many of the Prieſts and Levites, and chief of the fathers, who were ancient men, who had ſeen the firſt houſe, when the foundation of this houſe was laid before their eyes, wept with a loud voice, and many ſhouted aloud for joy.* But God himſelf encouraged them to proceed with the moſt gracious aſſurances. Haggai ii. 1...7. *In the ſeventh month, in the one and twentieth day of the month, came the word of the Lord by the Prophet Haggai, ſaying: Speak now to Zerubbabel, the ſon of Shealtiel, Governour of Judah, and to Joſhua the ſon of Joſedech the High-Prieſt, and to the reſidue of the people. Who is left among you that*

ſaw

Ch. VII.   *Reflexions upon the preceding Articles.*

saw this house in its first glorie? And how do ye see it now? Is it not in your eyes in comparison of it, as nothing? Yet now be strong, o Zerubbabel, saith the Lord: and be strong, o Joshuah, son of Josedech, the Priest, and be strong all ye People of the land saith the Lord of hosts, and work. I am with you saith the Lord of hosts. According to the word that I covenanted with you, when ye came out of Egypt, so my Spirit remaineth among you. Fear ye not. For thus saith the Lord of hosts. Yet once a little while... And I will shake all nations, and the desire of all nations shall come. And I will fill this house with glorie, saith the Lord of hosts. See likewise ch. i. and Zach. i. ii. iii. and viii.

And now they restored the worship of God at the temple, according to the prescriptions of the law of Moses for offering sacrifices. They kept the feast of the Passover, and other great feasts according to the law of Moses, and the Priests and Levites were set to officiate in their courses. So, after the setting up the altar of burnt-offering, and their begining to lay the foundation of the temple, it is said. Ezra. iii. 18. *And when the builders laid,* or were laying, *the foundation of the temple of the Lord, they set the Priests in their apparel with trumpets, and the Levites the sons of Asaph, with cymbals, to praise the Lord after the ordinarie of David King of Israel.* And afterwards, when the temple was raised, it is said, Ezra vi. 18. *And they set the Priests in their divisions, and the Levites in their courses, for the service of God, which is at Jerusalem, as it is written in the book of Moses.* Then it follows ver. 19. *And the children of the captivity,* that is, who were returned from their captivity, *kept the Passover, upon the fourteenth day of the first month.*

Thus the worship of God was again restored, and set up, at his temple in Jerusalem. And though, undoubtedly, in the intermediate space, the Jews met with various difficulties from surrounding enemies, and were now in subjection to the Romans; yet in the time of our Saviour and his Apostles, the Jewish people had free accesse to the Temple, performed their sacrifices there, kept the Passover,

Passover, and Pentecost, and other great solemnities according to the appointments of the law of Moses. And the genealogies of their tribes were in being. Jesus, our Lord, was of the tribe of Judah, and of the familie of David, though then in low circumstances. Matt. i. and ii. Luke i. and ii. *Zacharias*, father of John the Baptist, was of the course of Abia, and his wife *Elisabeth* was of the daughters of Aaron. And he executed the priests office before God at the temple, in the order of his course. Luke i. 5 ... 12. *Anna*, *a prophetesse*, is said to have been *the daughter of Phanuel, of the tribe of Asher, a widow of fourscore years of age, who departed not from the temple, and served God with fastings and prayers, night and day.*

But it is not needful to add any thing more, it being apparent from the books of the New Testament, and from Josephus, as well as from other writings, that the worship at the Temple in Jerusalem subsisted, till the second year of Vespasian, and the year of Christ 70. in which year, they had come up in great numbers to keep the Passover, and were suddenly shut up in the city by the Roman armie.

The times of the first and second Temple are computed by Dr. Lightfoot in this manner. "The (*t*) time of the standing of the " first Temple, from it's finishing in the eleventh year of Solomon, " to it's firing by Nebuzaradan, was four hundred and twenty " years." "From the (*u*) first year of Cyrus, (in which he proclaim- " ed redemption to the captives, and gave commandment to restore " and build Jerusalem) to the death of Christ, were four hundred " and ninety years, as they are summed up by an angel, Dan. ix. " and from the death of Christ to the fatal and final destruction of
" Jeru-

(*t*) *The Temple, as it stood in the time of our Saviour Ch.* 40. *p.* 2063.

(*u*) *Ib. p.* 2064.

Ch. VII. Reflexions upon the preceding Articles.

" Jerusalem, were forty years more, five hundred and thirty years
" in all." Which two sums make no more than nine hundred and
fifty years. In another place (*x*) he computes the times of the two
temples to be exactly one thousand years. Others may make different computations. But now we need not concern ourselves about
a nice exactness. However, I refer to (*y*) Prideaux, who may be
consulted.

III. I shall now shut up these reflexions with some concluding observations.

Obs. 1. The Temple at Jerusalem was designed by David, and
erected by Solomon with divine approbation: and the worship there
performed, was of divine appointment. And as the building itself,
and the worship there, had a divine sanction; it was fit, that a suitable respect should be shewn to the place itself, and to the ordinances there enjoyed, by all the worshipers of the true God.

Solomon (*a*) and all understanding Israelites, were persuaded of
the divine omnipresence. Nevertheless, as God had determined to
make peculiar manifestations of himself at the Temple, it was fit,
that respect should be shewn to it. 1 Kings viii. 27... 30. *But will
God dwell on this earth? Behold, the heaven of heavens cannot contain
thee. How much less this house that I have built? Yet have thou respect*

(*x*) " If Jerusalem was destroyed ex-
" actly forty years after our Saviour's
" death, as it is apparent, ... then that
" destruction of it befell just in the four
" thousandth year of the world. And
" so, as the Temple of Solomon had
" been finished anno mundi, exactly 3000.
" so in anno mundi exactly 4000. both
" the City and the Temple that then
" was, were destroyed never to be re-
" paired, or rebuilt again. And from

" that time most properly began the *king-
" dom of heaven, and the new Jerusalem*,
" when that earthly kingdom, and that
" old city, were utterly ruined." *Harmony of the four Evangelists. Vol. i. p.*
487.

(*y*) *See his Connexion &c. year before
Christ* 458. *Vol.* i. *p.* 262. &c.

(*a*) *See his Letter to Hiram, King of
Tyre.* 2 *Chr.* ii. 1. ... 7.

spect unto the prayer of thy servant... That thy eyes may be open toward this house, night and day, even toward the place, of which thou hast said: my name shall be there: [Deut. xii. 11.] *and hearken thou to the supplication of thy servant, and of thy people Israel, when they shall pray toward this place. And hear thou in heaven thy dwelling place, and when thou hearest, forgive.* See likewise ver. 46... 48.

And when Solomon had made an end of praying, fire came down from heaven, and consumed the burnt-offering, and the sacrifice. And the glorie of the Lord filled the house. 2 Chr. vii. 1. *And the Lord appeared to Solomon by night, and said unto him: I have heard thy prayer, and have chosen this place to myself, for an house of sacrifice. If I shut up heaven, that there be no rain... or, if I send pestilence among my people: if my people, which are called by my name, shall humble themselves, and pray, and seek my face, and turn from their wicked ways: then will I hear from heaven, and will forgive their sin, and will heal their land... For now have I chosen, and sanctified this house, that my name may be there forever: and my eyes, and my heart shall be there perpetually.* ver. 12... 16.

Accordingly, Daniel, who was renowned for secular wisdom, as well as for divine illuminations, and eminent piety, when his fidelity to God met with a severe trial, as we are told, ch. vi. 10. *he went into his house, and his window being open in his chamber, toward Jerusalem, and kneeled down upon his knees three times a day, and gave thanks before his God, as he did afore-time.* Comp. 1 Kings viii. 48. Ps. v. 4. Jonah ii. 4. And the Lord Jesus was often at Jerusalem, especially at the great festivals. And twice in the course of his ministrie cleared the Temple of some abuses and incumbrance, and severely rebuked those who practised those indecences, or connived at them.

Obs. 2. The Temple and the City of Jerusalem were twice destroyed, once by the Chaldeans, a second time by the Romans.

The city of Jerusalem was besieged, and taken several times besides: by *Antiochus Epiphanes, Pompey,* and *Herod the great,* and others.

others. But now we confine ourselves to those seasons, when the city was ruined, and the Temple also was destroyed.

Obs. 3. The taking of Jerusalem by the Chaldeans was a very grievous calamity.

The particulars are related Jer. lii. 2 Kings xxiv. xxv. 2 Chron. xxxvi. Daniel, in his confessions, ch. ix. 12. says: *For under the whole heaven has not been done, as has been done upon Jerusalem.* It was a calamity, not easie to be paralleled, in all it's circumstances. Which was agreeable to the maxim before observed, *that where much is given, there also much will be required,* and to the words of God, by the Prophet Amos. *You only have I known of all the families of the earth. Therefore I will punish you for all your iniquities.*

Obs. 4. The final captivity of the Jewish People by the Romans has been a much greater calamity, than that by the Chaldeans. It exceeds in many respects.

1.) The distresses of the siege of Jerusalem, and the numbers that perished there by famine, or sword, by the hand of the Romans, or by their own intestin divisions, and the numbers carried captive, exceeded all the desolations, that ever were. It happened, when the city was crowded with people, they being assembled together at one of their festivals. And the city itself, it's buildings, it's walls, and the Temple were demolished, and thrown down to the foundation, so as they had never been before. So our Lord foretold Matt. xxiv. 21. *For then shall be great tribulation, such as was not from the begining of the world, to this time: no, nor ever shall be.* So Jesus said, it would be. And Josephus says, it was so, and that *it exceeded all the destructions, ever brought upon the world by God or man.*

2.) The captivity by the Romans has exceeded the former in duration.

This

This second captivity has now already lasted almost seventeen hundred years, without any the left prospect of a period to it. That was limited to *seventy* years only according to the word of God by Jeremiah. ch. xxv. 12. .. 18. xxix. 10. .. 14. and Dan. ix. 1. 2.

3.) During the captivity by the Chaldeans, the Jewish People had Prophets among them: but now they have none.

In this second captivity, as they are without altar, and sacrifice, and Temple, and City of their own; so are they, all this while, without visions, and prophecies, and divine illuminations of every kind.

In the former captivity they had several Prophets, of great eminence. *Jeremiah* continued to prophesy to the remains of the people in Judea several years after the begining of the captivity. *Ezekiel* and *Daniel* prophesied in Babylon. These, and other good men may, have been of great service for bringing men to repentance, and fitting them for the expected deliverance. And during that period of seventy years, there were miraculous deliverances vouchsafed to some: the preservation, particularly, of the three young men in the fiery furnace: Dan. iii. Then Daniel's satisfactorie interpretations of Nebuchadnezzar's dreams, ch. ii. and iv. and Daniel's great advancement, and some other extraordinarie occurrences, were much in their favour. They must have tended to influence the minds of the great princes, to whom they were subject. And must have been means of facilitating their deliverance, and accomplishing their safe return into their own countrey, and to their happy settlement in it. But we hear not of any such like favorable appearances in the present captivity and dispersion.

Obs. 5. All these calamities, those of the former, and of the later captivity, have happened to the Jewish People, agreeably to the original plan of divine dispensations concerning them.

This observation was mentioned formerly. But it is repeated here, as a thing of great importance. And we have an acknowledgement

of

Ch. VII.   Concluding Observations.

of it, in Daniel's confessions, with regard to the Babylonish captivity. ch. ix. 11. *Yea, all Israel have transgressed thy law, even by departing, that they might not obey thy voice. Therefore the curse is poured upon us, and the oath that is written in the law of Moses the servant of God, because we have sinned against him.* . . . 13. *As it is written in the law of Moses, all this evil is come upon us.* See Lev. xxvi. 14. . . . 46. Deut. xxviii. 15. &c. What is here said of the captivity by the Chaldeans, is as true of the captivity by the Romans, and ought to be in like manner acknowledged.

Obs. 6. Our blessed Lord's predictions therefore of evil coming upon Jerusalem and the people of Judea, did not proceed from private resentment, enmity, malice, ill-will, or any other unsociable affection, from which the mind of the blessed Jesus was always free: but they were declarations of the counsel of God, prophetical denunciations of evil to come, if men did not repent, faithfull warnings to men to take heed to themselves, and earnest and affectionate calls to repentance and reformation, that the impending and threatened calamities might be averted and avoided.

A Prophet, who is entrusted with the mind of God, must faithfully deliver both promises to obedience and threatening to disobedience, as he is required. Says Moses to the people under his care, for whose welfare and prosperity he was greatly concerned. Deut. iv. 5. *Behold, I have taught you statutes and judgements, even as the Lord my God commanded me.* . . . ver. 25. 26. . . . *But if thou do evil in the sight of the Lord thy God, to provoke him to anger: I call heaven and earth to witnesse, that ye shall soon utterly perish from off the land, whereunto you go over Jordan to possess it: ye shall not prolong your days upon it. But shall utterly be destroyed.* Nor was Jeremiah to be charged with ill will to the Jewish people, when he foretold the desolations of the Chaldean captivity.

Obs.

Obſ. 7. The great aggravation of the tranſgreſſions of the Jewiſh people, lay in their not hearkening to the meſſages of the Prophets, which God ſent among them.

This was obſerved before from 2 Chron. xxvi. 15. 16. and from Jerem. xxv. 1...11. to which I now add, that it is particularly mentioned by Daniel in his devout and humble confeſſion of the ſins of that people, which brought upon them the Babyloniſh captivity. ch. ix. 5. 6. *We have ſinned, and have committed iniquity, and have done wickedly, and have rebelled even by departing from thy precepts and thy judgements. Neither have we hearkened unto thy ſervants the prophets, who ſpoke in thy name to our Kings, our Princes, and our fathers, and to all the people of Iſrael.* By which, certainly, theſe Prophets manifeſted their fidelity. And the reaſon of this is, that refuſing to hearken to meſſages of God, faithfully delivered by his Prophets, demonſtrates obſtinacie and irreclaimableneſſe. This is repreſented by our Lord in the parable of the *fig-tree.* Luke xiii. 6...10. and of the *huſbandmen.* Matt. xxi. 33. &c. and in other parables and diſcourſes. The parable of the fig-tree juſt mentioned, is thus. *A certain man had a fig-tree, planted in his vineyard. And he came, and ſought fruit thereon, and found none. Then ſaid he to the dreſſer of the vineyard: Behold theſe three years I come ſeeking fruit on this fig-tree, and find none. Cut it down. Why cumbreth it the ground? And he anſwering ſaid: Lord, let it alone this year alſo, till I ſhall dig about it, and dung it. If it bear fruit, well. If not, thou ſhalt cut it down.* So God ſaid of old to the people of Iſrael by Iſaiah, after having in a like manner repreſented his care and cultivation of his vineyard. Iſ. v. 3. 4. 5. *And now, o inhabitants of Jeruſalem, and men of Judah, judge, I pray you, betwixt me and my vineyard. What could have been done more to my vineyard, than I have done in it? Wherefore when I looked, that it ſhould bring forth grapes, brought it forth wild grapes? I will tell you, what I will do to my vineyard? I will*

Ch. VII. Concluding Observations.

will take away the hedge thereof, and it shall be eaten up: and break down the wall thereof, and it shall be trodden down.

This was the case in the time of our Saviour. After all other Prophets, came Jesus, who taught the people in the name of God, and faithfully delivered his mind to them, and called them to repentance, and wrought many wonderfull works. There was then a great profusion of spiritual gifts in Himself, and his Apostles. If their message was not hearkened to, but rejected, and they abused: it would be an aggravated provocation, and would be required of the people, to whom they had spoken in the name of God.

Obs. 8. Finally, in the eighth and last place, let us now inquire and consider, what was the sin, what the sins, or offenses, that occasioned the great calamity, which befell the Jewish people, about forty years after the times of the Lord Jesus, under the conduct of those two Generals, *Vespasian*, and *Titus*.

We have seen accounts in Josephus, and other Jewish writers, of the distresses then suffered by the Jewish people at Jerusalem, and in other parts of Judea, and of the destruction and demolition of their city, and temple, and their captivity and dispersion, which still continue. And we have seen evident proofs, that the hand of God was therein, and that all came to pass by the over-ruling providence of God. It is an affecting subject. And if we make inquiries into the reasons and causes of these great calamities, we should do it seriously, and impartially, and may be disposed also to compassion and candour.

When God appeared to Solomon after he had finished and dedicated the Temple, he graciously assured him, that he accepted the prayer, which he had made, and that he would hearken to the prayers, which his people should make to him toward that place in their distresses. Nevertheless he declares, 2 Chron. vii. 19...22. *But if ye turn away, and forsake my statutes, and my commandments, which I have set before you, and serve other gods, and worship them: then will I pluck them up by the roots out of my land which I have given them.*

them. *And the house, which I have sanctified for my name will I cast out of my sight, and will make it to be a proverb, and a by-word among all nations. And this house, which is high, shall be an astonishment to every one that passeth by it: so that he shall say: Why has the Lord done thus unto this land, and unto this house. And it shall be answered, Because they forsook the Lord God of their fathers, who brought them out of the land of Egypt, and laid hold on other gods, and worshiped them, and served them. Therefore has he brought all this evil upon them.*

This was fulfilled in the *Babylonish* captivity, when Jerusalem was taken, and the Temple, built by Solomon, was burnt down. That was an event, which occasioned inquiries into the reasons and causes of it. And shall not we consider, and make like inquiries, concerning the captivity by the *Romans*, which has been attended with so many awfull circumstances? Shall we not say: *Why has the Lord done thus, unto this land, and to this house,* meaning the second house, built after the return from the Babylonish captivity. For that *house* also was *high*. And had been erected with divine approbation and encouragement. And the worship had been restored there according to the appointment of Moses: and was so continued there, till it's final desolation.

If now we ask, *Why has the Lord done thus to this land and people, and to this house:* It cannot be said, *because they laid hold on other gods, and worshiped them, and served them.* For after the return from the Babylonish captivity, they were for the most part free from the sin of idolatrie, into which they had so often relapsed before. Nor are they now guilty of that sin, for which their dispersion should be continued. For some while before the last destruction of Jerusalem, they appear, from all accounts, to have been generally very zealous for the law of Moses, and the rites of it, and very diligent in their attendance on the temple at Jerusalem, to which they resorted

Ch. VII. Concluding Observations.

sorted in great numbers from all parts of the world, where they inhabited, at the solemn festivals: and where a large part of the nation was assembled to keep the Passover, when the final overthrow befell them.

We are therefore led to think, that these calamities befell the Jewish people, because they rejected, and crucified the Lord Jesus, who was a Prophet, mighty *in deed and word, before God and all* *the people,* who spake as never man spake before, and performed many wonderfull works, which none had done before. And God has *required it of them,* as he said by Moses, he would do. Deut. xviii. 19. And I must again recite here those affecting, and awfull, but true sayings of our Lord, recorded John xv. 22. 24. *If I had not come, and spoken unto them, they had not had sin : but now have they no cloak* [or excuse *for their sin. If I had not done among them the works, which no other man did, they had not had sin : but now they have both seen and hated, both me and my Father.*

Lu xxiv. 19.

The expectation of the Messiah is no new thing. It had not it's rise from Jesus, or his Disciples. It was in being, long before the nativity of Jesus. We are assured *(b)* by *Suetonius,* and *Tacitus,* and *Celsus,* Heathen writers of great learning, as well as from *Josephus : That there had been for a long time, all over the East, a notion firmly believed, that at that very time, some coming from Judea should obtain the Empire of the world.* Heathen writers say, this was *contained in the book of the fates :* Josephus, who at the time of his writing the historie of the war, was disposed to think, as the Heathen writers above mentioned do, that Vespasian was thereby intended, says, that this expectation was founded upon an *ambiguous oracle.* Nevertheless he owns, that the expectation was general among the Jewish people,

O o 2

(*b*) See *the passages of those Heathen Authors, and of Josephus, all alleged, Credib.* P. i. Vol. i. p. 284. ... 290.

people, and that it was embraced by *many of the Wife men among them*, as well as by others, and that it was the thing, which *principally encouraged them to undertake the war with the Romans*. But upon this head there is now no difference between the Jews and us. All allowing that the expectation of a Meffiah is founded on the writing of Mofes and the Prophets.

That this was the time of his appearance, they may have argued and collected from divers texts of fcripture, as Dan. ii. 34... 45. vii. 14. ix. 24. and from Hag. ii. 4... 9. Mal. iii. 1. iv. 5. 6.

How general and prevailing the expectation of the appearance of the Meffiah then was, among all forts of men, the rulers, as well as the common people, we farther know from the books of the New Teftament. Luke iii. 15. 16. *And as the people were in expectation, and all men mufed in their hearts of John, whether he were the Chrift, or not: John anfwered, faying unto them all: I indeed baptize you with water. But one mightier than I cometh, the latchet of whofe fhoes, I am not worthy to unloofe. He will baptife you with the Holy Ghoft, and with fire.* And from John i. 19... 34. we know, that the Jews fent *Priefts and Levites*, who were of the fect of the *Pharifees*, to John, where he was baptizing, to afk him, who he was. He declared, *he was not the Chrift, but was fent before him. And faid: There ftandeth one among you, whom ye know not. He it is who coming after me, is preferred before me. Whofe fhoes latchet I am not worthy to unloofe.* I need not cite any other texts.

At that very time Jefus appeared, and wrought many wonderfull works, irrefragable atteftations to his divine miffion and authority, and the truth of his doctrine: of which we are as well affured from the concurring and unanimous teftimonie of all the writers of the New Teftament, as we can be of any thing that ever was done in the world: or as the Jews are of the miracles wrought by Mofes and the Prophets.

Here

Ch. VII. Concluding Observations.

Here therefore we may adopt the words of our Lord spoken to his disciples, Matt. xvii. 12. *But I say unto you, that Elias is come already. And they knew him not, but have done unto him whatsoever they listed. Likewise shall also the Son of Man suffer of them.* As he did soon afterwards. For which God has reckoned, and is still reckoning with them.

However, though the treatment given to Jesus and his Apostles, was a very great offense: there may have been other provocations, which occasioned the displeasure of God against his people, and concurred to bring down the vengeance of heaven upon them. One sin is never alone. There is generally a complication of guilt in all great and aggravated transgressions. Though the Jewish people often fell into the practise of Heathen idolatrie, and that was one great occasion of the Babylonish captivity, that was not the only sin, with which they were chargeable. All sorts of immoralities abounded among them. And Daniel, in the confession which he makes of the sins of his people, says: ch. ix. 5. *We have sinned, and have committed iniquity, and have done wickedly, and have rebelled, even by departing from thy precepts and thy judgements.* So now the greatnesse of their guilt lay in rejecting and crucifying Jesus the Messiah. But that would not have been done, if wickednesse had not greatly prevailed among them. Josephus owns, that *never was there a time more fruitfull of wickednesse, than that.* In the Gospels the men of that time are spoken of, as an *untoward generation, and a wicked and adulterous generation.* They were chargeable with all kinds of evil, and were openly reproved for them, by the faithfull teacher, and Prophet, whom God sent among them, and whom they so ungratefully used. They were covetous and worldly minded. Luke xvi. 14 15. They were exceeding proud and ambitious of respect and honour. *They did all their works to be seen of men. They made broad their phylacteries, and enlarged the borders of their garments. They loved the uppermost rooms at feasts, and the chief seats in the synagogues,*

and

Reflexions upon the preceding Articles. Ch. VII.

and to be called of men Rabbi, Rabbi. Matt. xxiii. 5. 6. And fee Mark xii. 38. 39. and Luke xx. 46. and Luke xiv. 7. They were extremely uneafie, and impatient under the Roman government, to which, by the difpofal of Divine Providence, they were fubject. *They were very deceitfull* and hypocritical, who *devoured widows houfes, and for a pretenfe made long prayers.* Mark xii. 40. And fee Matt. xxiii. 23...28. At the fame time they depended upon their defcent from Abraham, and other external privileges. Which rendred all exhortations to repentance fruitlefs and ineffectual. See Matth. iii. 9. John viii. 33. and 39. Accordingly they are reprefented to have *hardened their hearts, and fhut their eyes.* For which reafon, they did not underftand, nor attend to the figns of the times, and the evidences of truth fet before them. Matt. xiii. 14. 15. John xii. 37...41. And moreover they were at this time, very fond of traditions, which made void the moral law of God.

All thefe charges, now collected from the Gofpels, might be verified by examples, and obfervations in Jofephus. Thefe evil difpofitions prevailing among them, efpecially in their great men, who had the chief influence on the people, they did not, and could not believe, but rejected, and ill treated the Lord Jefus Chrift. Let me recite here John v. 39...44. *Search the Scriptures, impartially. For in them ye think ye have eternal life. And they are they which teftify of me. And ye will not come unto me, that ye might have life. I receive not honour from men. But I know you, that ye have not the love of God in you... How can ye believe, which receive honour one of another, and feek not the honour that cometh from God only?*

One thing more I muft add here. That the time in which our Lord appeared, was not a time of grofs ignorance. The Jews now had fynagogues every where, in all parts of Judea, and in many places out of it: where the Law of Mofes and the Prophets were read, and explained. The common people in general were well acquainted with thofe Scriptures, and with the explications given of them by their Rabbins.

Ch. VII. *Concluding Observations.*

Rabbins. Among the Scribes and Pharisees were many men of very good abilities. Their acuteness and subtlety are manifest in their cavils with our Saviour. Nor were the Jewish people now altogether unacquainted with the Greek literature. Their three sects of the *Pharisees*, *Sadducees*, and *Essens*, had occasioned disputes and controversies, and spread the knowledge of the things of religion among them.

It is amazing, that a prophet, who teaches men a reasonable doctrine, and works many miracles, all usefull and beneficent, should be rejected. And it would be still more amazing, were it not, that we are in some measure able to account for it, by the bad dispositions, before taken notice of. Jesus gave no sign from heaven to induce them to expect from him (what suited their carnal and ambitious views) a deliverance from the Roman government. And all other works of mighty power, and of great goodnesse, were slighted, and despised. Thus prejudice and passion prevailed against evidence. And it is a great aggravation of the guilt of any men, who are knowing and discerning, if they reject the truth, of which good evidences are set before them. Our Lord having made some remarks after the cure of the man born blind, and after his being excommunicated by the Pharisees, John ix. 39...41. Some of them, who heard him, *said unto him: Are we blind also? Jesus said unto them: If ye were blind, ye should have no sin. But now ye say, We see: therefore your sin remaineth.*

Thus they were incurable. And these evil dispositions, prevailing in them, brought on that great sin of rejecting and crucifying the Lord Jesus, which God has required of them.

The destruction therefore of the City of Jerusalem, and the Temple, and the continued dispersion of the Jews, are a cogent argument for the truth of the Christian Religion. They confirm the historic of the New Testament, and every part of it. If they had not sinned, as they are there said to have done, these calamities had not befallen them. Their sufferings bear witnesse to the spotless life, and

and excellent doctrine, and wonderfull works of the Lord Jesus. They testify, that there had been one among them greater than *Jonah*, and wiser than *Solomon*. But they slighted all his wisdom, and repented not, as the people of Nineveh did, at the preaching of Jonah.

They confirm particularly the historie, recorded in Luke xxiii. 1...25. *And the whole multitude of them,* [that is, many of the Jewish Council] *arose, and led him unto Pilate, saying: We found this man perverting the nation, and forbidding to give tribute to Caesar, saying, that he himself is Christ, a King. Pilate then asked him, saying: Art thou the King of the Jews? And he answered him, and said, Thou sayest it.* [It is as you say.] *Then said Pilate to the* CHIEF-PRIESTS, AND TO THE PEOPLE: *I find no fault in this man. And they were the more fierce, saying: He stirreth up the people, teaching throughout all Judea, begining from Galilee to this place.* He then sent Jesus to Herod, who sent him back again to Pilate. *After which, when Pilate had called together* THE CHIEF-PRIESTS AND THE RULERS, AND THE PEOPLE, *he said unto them: ye have brought this man unto me, as one that perverteth the people. And behold, I having examined him before you, have found no fault in this man, touching these things, whereof ye accuse him. No, nor yet Herod. For I sent you to him. And lo, nothing worthy of death is done unto him. I will therefore chastise him, and release him. For of necessity he must release one unto them at the feast. And they cried out, all at once, saying: Away with this man, and release unto us Barabbas. Who for a certain sedition made in the city, and for murder, was cast into prison. Pilate therefore willing to release Jesus, spake again to them. But they cried, saying: Crucify him, crucify him. And he said unto them the third time: Why, what evil has he done? I have found no cause of death in him. I will therefore chastize him, and let him go. And they were instant with loud voices, requiring, that he might be crucified. And the voices of them and the Chief-Priests prevailed. And Pilate gave*

Ch. VII. Concluding Observations.

gave sentence, that it should be as they required. And he released unto them him that for sedition and murder was cast into prison, whom they desired: but he delivered Jesus to their will. Or as in Matt. xxvii. 24. 25. 26. *When Pilate saw, that he could prevail nothing, but that rather a tumult was made, he took water, and washed his hands before the multitude, saying: I am innocent of the bloud of this just person. See ye to it. Then answered all the people, and said: His bloud be upon us, and our children. Then released he Barabbas unto them. And when he had scourged Jesus, he delivered him to be crucified.*

To these things the destruction of Jerusalem, and the present circumstances of the Jews, bear witnesse: as also to the resurrection of Jesus, and his ascension to heaven, and to the plentifull effusion of spiritual gifts, afterwards upon his Apostles, and others: whereby they were enabled to preach the heavenly doctrine, in which their Lord and Master had instructed them. He commanded them to *preach repentance and remission of sins in his name, beginning at Jerusalem.* Luke xxiv. 47. And that they did so, *preaching repentance toward God, and faith toward our Lord Jesus Christ*: or, that they did earnestly call upon the Jewish people in Judea, and elsewhere, to repent of their sins, and believe in the Lord Jesus; and that they did not receive their instructions and warnings, but *killed some of them, scourged others, and persecuted them from city to city:* To all these things, the destruction of Jerusalem and the Temple, and other calamities brought upon the Jewish people, bear witnesse. And thus they filled up the measure of their iniquity.

The argument, upon which I have now insisted, is not new. It is old. And has been well managed by divers ancient Christian writers. I shall place below the observations made upon the long captivity of the Jews by Jerome (d) and by Prudentius (e) in their own language.

(d) Multa, Judace, scelera commisisti, cunctis circa te servisti nationibus. Ob quod factum? Utique, propter idololatriam. Quumque servisses, crebro misertus tui

Reflexions upon the preceding Articles. Ch. VII.

guage. I believe, they will be perufed with pleafure by fome of my readers. And I refer to a *(f)* place of Chryfoſtom, which was *(g)* formerly quoted more at large. I likewife refer to *(h)* Origen.

Nor

tui eſt Deus: et miſit judices et ſalvatores, qui te de famulatu Moabitarum et Ammonitarum, Philiſtiim quoque et diverſarum gentium liberarunt. Noviſſime fub regibus offendiſti Deum, et omnis tua provincia, gente Babylonica vaſtante, deleta eſt. Per ſeptuaginta annos templi ſolitudo permanſit. A Cyro rege Perſarum eſt laxata captivitas. Eſdras hoc et Nehemias pleniſſime referunt. Exſtructum eſt templum ſub Dario rege Perſarum a Zorobabel filio Salathiel, et Jeſu filio Joſedec, ſacerdote magno. Quae paſſi ſitis a Medis, Aegyptis, Macedonibuſque non enumero. Nec tibi adducam in memoriam, Antiochum Epiphanem, crudeliſſimum omnium tyrannorum: nec Cn. Pompeium, Gabinium, Scaurum, Varum, Caſſium, Soſiumque replicabo, qui tuis uibibus et praecipue Jeroſolymae inſultavere. Ad extremum ſub Veſpaſiano et Tito urbs capta, templumque ſubverſum eſt. Deinde civitatis uſque ad Hadrianum principem per quinquaginta annos manſe-

re reliquiae. Poſt everſionem templi paullo minus per quadringentos annos et urbis et templi ruinae permanent. Ob quod tantum facinus? Certe non çolis idola, ſed etiam ſerviens Perſis atque Romanis, et captivitatis preſſus jugo, ignoras alienos deos. Quomodo Clementiſſimus quondam Deus, qui nunquam tui oblitus eſt: nunc per tanta ſpatia temporum miſeriis tuis non adducitur, ut ſolvat captivitatem, et, ut verius dicam, exſpectatum tibi mittat Antichriſtum? Ob quod, inquam, facinus, et tam execrabile ſcelus, avertit a te oculos ſuos? Ignoras? Memento vocis parentum tuorum. *Sanguis ejus ſuper nos, et ſuper filios noſtros. Et: Venite, occidamus eum, et noſtra erit haereditas. Et: Non habemus regem, niſi Caeſarem.* Habes quod elegiſti, uſque ad finem mundi ſerviturus es Caeſari, donec gentium introeat plenitudo, et ſic omnis Iſrael ſalvus fiet: ut qui quondam erat in capite, vertatur in caudam. *Hieron. ad Dardan. T.* 2. *p.* 610. 611.

(e) Quid mereare, Titus docuit: docuere rapinis
Pompeianae acies: quibus extirpata per omnes
Terrarum pelagique plagas tua membra feruntur.
Exiliis vagus, huc illuc fluitantibus errat
Judaeus, poſtquam Patriâ de ſede revulſus,
Supplicium pro caede luit, Chriſtique negati
Sanguine reſperſus commiſta piacula ſolvit.

Prud. Apoth. ver. 38. *&c.*

(f) Adverſus Judaeos Or. vi. T. i. p. 652. 653.

(g) See the Circumſtances of the Jewiſh People an Argument for the Truth of the Chriſtian Religion. p. 47.

(h) Contr. Celſ. l. 2. §. 13. *Bened. p.*

69.

Ch. VII. Concluding Observations.

Nor can it be said, that God has been unrighteous in his dealings with them. All these judgements befell them, according to the original plan of Providence concerning them, and according to the prophetic denunciations of their Lawgiver Moses. Nor can it be said, that their continued dispersion is unrighteous, since they persist in the sin, which first occasioned it, and reject Him, whom God has sent unto them: and not only reject him, but reproach and revile him, so as no other people do. And, finally, whenever they repent, they may obtain forgivenesse, and be received into the Church of Christ, and partake in all the privileges of it, and in the end obtain everlasting life, which God through Jesus Christ has promised to all those who love him. *For God has not cast away his people, whom he foreknew. And if they abide not still in unbelief,* they will be graciously received. Rom. xi. 2. and 23.

The circumstances of the Jewish People deserve the attentive regard, and serious consideration of all mankind, Jews and Christians, and the men of all nations and religions, where their historie is known: as it now generally is, from the books of the Old and New Testament, and from Josephus, and other writings.

The writings of the Apostles and Evangelists, contained in the New Testament, are faithfull records of the life of Jesus, and the promises of the gospel. And the continued subsistence of the Jewish people in a dispersed condition, all over the earth, bears testimonie to the truth of every thing related by them. Thus God, the Sovereign Lord of all, in his great wisdom, has provided a perpetual, and universal, living monument to the memorie of the transactions and sufferings of Jesus in Judea: and of his own veracity in *performing the mercie promised to their fathers, and the oath which he sware to Abraham.* Luke i. 72. 73. Gen. xxii. 15... 18. and, that *when the fullnesse*

---

69. *Spenc. l.* 4. §. 22. *Bened. p.* 174. *Sp.*   *Ben. p.* 405. *Spenc. seu Cantab. et* §. 73. *Ben. p.* 212. *Sp. l.* 8. §. 42.

fullneſſe of the time was come, he ſent forth his Son, made of a woman, made under the law, to redeem mankind from idolatrie, and all vice, and from all burdenſome rites, whether of Jewiſh, or Heathen original. Gal. iv. 4. 5.

The circumſtances of the Jewiſh People confirm the faith of Chriſtians, and are a loud call to themſelves, to think, and conſider, and repent, and believe. And it ſhould in a like manner affect, and awaken all other people. It is a voice, which may be heard by thoſe, who have not yet ſeen the Goſpels, and perhaps are averſe to them. And it ſhould induce them to look into them, and carefully examine them.

That Jeſus is the Chriſt, is manifeſt from his agreeing to all the prophetic deſcriptions concerning that great perſon, which are recorded in the Jewiſh Scriptures, that he might be known, when he came. He is the ſeed of Abraham, and the ſon of David: *the rod out of the ſtem of Jeſſe.* . . . *And the Spirit of the Lord reſted on him; the ſpirit of wiſdom and underſtanding, the ſpirit of counſel and of might, the ſpirit of knowledge and of the fear of the Lord. And to him the Gentils have ſought.* Iſ. xi. 1. 2. 3. 10. He was born of a *virgin.* Iſ. vii. 14. *at Bethlehem in Judea.* Mic. v. 2. *In him all the families of the earth have been bleſſed,* according to the promiſe made to Abraham. Gen. xii. 3. xviii. 18. xxii. 18. He is *the ſervant of God, whom he upheld, his elect, in whom his ſoul delighteth,* [or God's well beloved ſon.] *and he has brought forth judgement to the Gentils.* Iſ. xlii. 1. *He has been a light to lighten the Gentils, and ſalvation to the ends of the earth.* Iſ. xlix. 6. *The iſles waited for his law, and have received it.* Iſ. xlii. 4. *And the earth is now full of the knowledge of God, as the waters cover the ſea.* Iſ. xi. 9. We have *a new heaven, and a new earth,* Iſ. lxv. 17. *All the gods of the earth have been famiſhed.* Zeph. ii. 11. Heathen idolatrie, once ſo general, and ſo much delighted in by princes and people, is now no more in this part of the world.

Ch. VII.   *Concluding Observations.*   293

world. Their temples are demolished, or put to other uses. Their oracles are silent. Nor do they receive human, or other sacrifices. And God himself, the Lord of heaven and earth, is no longer served with sacrifices of animals, or oblations of fruits of the earth: but with prayers and praises, and good works of righteousnesse and mercie. Nor is his worship now confined to any one particular place. The time is come, *when men should neither at mount Garizim, nor at Jerusalem, worship the Father: and when the true worshipers of God should worship him in spirit and in truth,* John iv. 21. . . . 23. And *in every nation, he that feareth God, and worketh righteousnesse, is accepted of him.* Acts x. 35. Jesus had *the words of eternal life.* John vi. 68. And *God has poured out of his spirit upon all flesh.* Joel ii. 28. Is. xliv. 3. Acts ii. 17. And *all men now know God from the least to the greatest of them.* Jerem. xxxi. 3. All have just sentiments, and are able to discourse rationally, concerning God, the Creator of all things, and his overruling Providence, and future rewards and punishments. We now worship God on earth, through Jesus Christ, in a reasonable, spiritual, liberal manner, in hopes of obtaining, hereafter, perfection of holinesse and happinesse in the kingdom of our heavenly Father.

Jesus, then, is the promised Messiah, who was to come. Not is there any reason, why we should look for another.

I have formerly treated *(k)* this subject. But the large and copious testimonie of *Josephus* to the fulfilment of our Saviour's predictions concerning the destruction of Jerusalem, and the miseries coming upon the Jewish people, and the repeated acknowledgments of the destruction of the Temple in the *Mishnical* and *Talmudical* writers, have compelled me to enlarge here, as I have now done.

Finally,

(k) The Circumstances of the Jewish People an argument for the Truth of the Christian Religion.

Finally, to put an end to this long argument: If we have obtained the invaluable *treasure* of the gospel, that *pearl of great price*; let us be thankful to God, who has so enriched us by Jesus Christ. And let us be careful to keep it entire, and in all it's purity, unalloyed with base mixtures, and undisguised by false colourings. Our own glorie and the credit of our Religion depend upon this.

Matt.
xiii. 44.
. . 46.

As for the Jewish People, I believe, all good Christians will readily joyn with the Apostle Paul, and say: *our hearts desire, and prayer to God for Israel, is, that they might be saved.* Rom. x. 1. Nevertheless I acknowledge, that I see no immediate prospect of their general conversion: and must assent to what the same Apostle says, in another place, who had great dealings with them, after his conversion to the christian faith, as well as before, and had full experience of their untractable temper: which is still too much the same, that it was in his time. *But their minds were blinded. For untill this day remaineth the same vail, untaken away, in the reading of the Old Testament. Which vail is done away in Christ. But even unto this day, when Moses is read, the vail is upon their heart. Nevertheless, when it shall turn to the Lord, the vail shall be taken away.* 2 Cor. iii. 14. . . 16.

God grant, that we may all know, and mind the things, which are conducive to our true interests, both here and hereafter!

The End of Jewish Testimonies.

TESTIMONIES
OF ANCIENT
HEATHEN AUTHORS.

CHAP. I.

The Epistle of Abgarus King of Edessa to Jesus, and the Rescript of Jesus to Abgarus.

S the authority of these Epistles depends entirely upon Eusebius, I shall here transcribe his account at length, which is in the 13. or last chapter of the first book of his Ecclesiastical Historie.

A. D. 33.

" *A (a) Historie concerning the Prince of the Edessens.*"

" The Divinity of our Lord and Saviour Jesus Christ, says Euse-
" bius, being every where talked of by reason of his wonderfull
" power in working miracles, it drew after him many people from
" other countreys, and some very remote from Judea, who were
" filled with hopes of relief under all sorts of pains and sicknesses.

(a) Ισορία περὶ τȣ τῶν Ἐδεσσηνῶν δυναςȣ. *H. E. l. i. cap.* 13. *p.* 31.

" For

"For which reason King Abgarus, who *(b)* with honour governed the nations beyond the Euphrates, laboring under a grievous distemper, incurable by human skill, when he heard of the fame of Jesus, which was much celebrated, and his wonderfull works attested by the unanimous testimonie of all men, sent a letter to him by a messenger, entreating him to cure his distemper. But he did not then comply with his request. Yet he vouchsafed to write to him a letter, wherein he promised to send to him one of his disciples, who should cure his distemper, and also bring salvation to him, and to all with him. Which promise was not long after fulfilled. For after the resurrection of Christ, and his ascension to heaven, Thomas, one of the twelve Apostles, moved by a divine impulse, sent Thaddeus, one of Christ's seventy disciples to Edessa, to be a preacher and an Evangelist of Christ's doctrine. By whom all things promised by our Saviour were fulfilled. The evidence of this we have from the records of the city of Edessa. For among the public records, wherein are entred the antiquities of the city, and the actions of Abgarus, these things are still found preserved to this day. It *(c)* will therefore be worth the while to attend to the letters, as taken by us, [or for us] from the archives, and translated word for word from the Syriac language."

"*The Copie of the Letter, which was writ by Abgarus the Toparch, to Jesus, and sent to him at Jerusalem, by the courier Ananias.*"

"Abgarus, Toparch [or Prince] of Edessa to Jesus the good Saviour, who has appeared at Jerusalem, sendeth greeting. I have heard of thee, and of thy cures, performed without herbs, or other medicines. For it is reported, that thou makest the blind to see, and the lame to walk, that thou cleansest lepers, and castest out

---

(b) Who governed the nations beyond the Euphrates. That is the lofty stile of the eastern people. Abgarus was governour of only a small territorie.

(c) ... ἀπὸ τῶν ἀρχείων ἡμῖν ἀναληφθεισῶν, ᾗ τόνδε αὐτοῖς ῥήμασιν ἐκ τῆς συρῶν φωνῆς μεταβληθεισῶν τὸν τρόπον. p. 32. B.

Ch. I.   *with our Saviour's Refcript.*   299

"out unclean fpirits and demons, and healeft thofe who are tor-
"mented with difeafes of a long ftanding, and raifeft the dead.
"Having heard of all thefe things concerning thee, I concluded in
"my mind one of thefe two things, either that thou art God come
"down from heaven to do thefe things, or elfe that thou art the
"Son of God, and fo performeft them. Wherefore I now write
"unto thee, entreating thee to come to me, and to heal my diftem-
"per. Moreover I hear, that the Jews murmur againft thee, and
"plot to do thee mifchief. I have a city, fmall indeed, but neat,
"which may fuffice for us both." " Now let us attend, *fays Eu-*
"*febius*, to the letter, which Jefus returned by the fame courier,
"fhort indeed, but very powerfull. It is in thefe words."

A. D.
33.

"*The Refcript of Jefus to the Toparch Abgarus fent by the Courier*
"*Ananias.*"

"Abgarus, thou art happy, forafmuch as thou haft believed in
"me, though thou haft not feen me. For it is written concerning
"me, that they who have feen me fhould not believe in me, that
"they who have not feen me might believe, and live. As for what
"thou haft written to me, defiring me to come to thee: it is necef-
"farie that all thofe things, for which I am fent, fhould be fulfilled
"by me here: and that after fulfilling them, I fhould be received
"up to him that fent me. When therefore I fhall be received up,
"I will fend to thee fome one of my difciples, that he may heal thy
"diftemper, and give life to thee, and to thofe who are with thee."

John xx.
29.

"To thefe epiftles, as Eufebius goes on to fay, are fubjoyned the
"following things, and in the Syriac language: That after Jefus had
"been taken up, [or after his afcenfion,] Judas, called alfo Thomas,
"fent the Apoftle Thaddeus, one of the feventy: who, when he
"came to Edeffa, took up his abode with Tobias, fon of Tobias.
"When his arrival was rumoured about, and he had begun to be

"known

The Epistle of Abgarus to our Saviour, Ch. I.

"known by the miracles which he wrought, it was told to Abgarus, that an Apostle was sent to him by Jesus, according to his promise. Thaddeus therefore by the power of God healed all sorts of maladies, so that all wondred. But when Abgarus heard of the great and wonderfull works which he did, and how he healed men in the name and by the power of Jesus Christ, he was induced to suspect, [ἐν ὑπονοίᾳ γέγονεν,] that he was the person, about whom Jesus had writ to him, saying, *When I am taken up, I will send to thee some one of my disciples, who shall heal thy distemper.* Sending therefore for Tobias, at whose house he was, he said to him: I hear that a man, endowed with great power, and come from Jerusalem, is at thy house, and that he works many cures in the name of Jesus. To which Tobias answered: Yes, Sir, there is a stranger with me, who performs many miracles. Abgarus then said: Bring him hither to me. Tobias coming to Thaddeus, said to him: The *(d)* prince Abgarus, has bid me bring thee to him, that thou mayest heal his distemper. Whereupon Thaddeus said: I go. For it is upon his account, chiefly, that I am sent hither. The next day early in the morning Tobias taking Thaddeus came to Abgarus. As he came in, the Nobles being present, there appeared to Abgarus somewhat very extraordinarie in the countenance of Thaddeus. Which *(e)* when Abgarus saw, he worshiped Thaddeus. Which appeared strange to all present. For they did not see that brightnesse, which was discerned by Abgarus only. He then asked Thaddeus, if he were indeed the disciple of Jesus the son of God, who had said to him: *I will send to thee some one of my disciples, who shall heal thy distemper, and give life to all with thee.* Thaddeus answered: Forasmuch as thou hast great faith in the Lord Jesus, therefore am I sent unto thee. And if thou shalt encrease in faith in him, all the desires of thy heart will be fulfilled according to thy faith.

"Then

(d) ὁ τοπάρχης.
(e) ὅπερ ἰδὼν Ἀβγαρος προσεκύνησε τῷ Θαδδαίῳ. p. 33. D.

"Then Abgarus said to him: I have so believed in him, that I
" would go with an armie, to extirpate the Jews, who crucified him,
" if I were not apprehensive of the Roman power. Then Thadde-
" us said: Our Lord and God Jesus Christ has fulfilled the will of
" his Father. And having fulfilled it, he has been taken up to his
" Father. Abgarus then said: I have believed in him, and in his
" Father. And thereupon said Thaddeus: Therefore I put my hand
" upon thee in the name of the Lord Jesus. And upon his so do-
" ing Abgarus was healed of his distemper. And Abgarus wonder-
" ed, that as it had been reported concerning Jesus, so it had been
" done by his disciple and apostle Thaddeus: insomuch as he had
" healed him without herbs, or other medicines. Nor did he heal
" him alone, but also Abdas, son of Abdas, who had the gout. For
" he came to him, and fell down upon his knees before him, and by
" the laying on of his hands with prayer he was healed. The same
" Apostle healed many other citizens of the same place, and wrought
" many and great miracles, as he preached the word. After which
" Abgarus spoke to this purpose: Thou Thaddeus doest these things
" by the power of God, and we admire thee. But I beseech thee
" to inform me about the coming of Jesus, how it was, and of his
" power, and by what power he did all those things, which we have
" heard of. To which Thaddeus answered: Now I forbear, though
" I am sent to preach the word. But to-morrow gather together
" all the citizens. And then in their hearing I will preach the word
" and sow in them the word of life, and will inform them of the
" coming of Christ, how it was, and concerning his mission, and
" for what cause he was sent by the Father, and concerning the
" power of his works, and the mysteries, which he spoke in the
" world, and by what power he did these things: and concerning his
" new doctrine, and the mysteries, which he spoke in the world: and
" about the meannesse and despicablenesse of his outward appearance,
" and how he humbled himself, and died, and (f) lessened his deity:
" how

(f) ᾗ ἐσμίκρυνεν αὐτοῦ τὴν θεότητα. p. 35. A.

"how many things he suffered from the Jews, and how he was
"crucified, and defcended into hell, and rent afunder the enclofure
"never before feparated, and arofe, and raifed up the dead, who
"had been buried many ages: and how he defcended alone, but
"afcended to his Father with a great multitude: and how he is fet
"down on the right hand of the Father with glorie in the heavens:
"and how he will come again with glorie and power to judge the
"living and the dead. Abgarus therefore iffued out orders, that all
"the citizens fhould come together early the next morning to hear
"the preaching of Thaddeus. And after that he commanded, that
"gold and filver fhould be given to him. But he did not receive it,
"faying: When we have left our own things, how fhould we re-
"ceive thofe things which belong to others? This was done in the
"four hundred and thirtieth year. Thefe things tranflated from the
"Syriac language word for word, we have placed here, as we think,
"not improperly."

Thus I have now tranflated this whole hiftorie from Eufebius at large, thinking that to be the fhorteft way to a good conclufion: and that all my readers may be the better able to judge of the remarks that fhall be made.

Various are the opinions of learned men concerning this hiftorie, fome receiving it as true, or at leaft (g) being favorable to it: others rejecting it, as (h) falfe and fabulous. I fhall put down here the following obfervations.

1. In

(g) Cav. H. L. Grabe Spic. Affem. Bib. Or. T. i. p. 554. ABp. Wake's Introduction to his tranflation of the Apoftolical Fathers. ch. ix. Tillem. Mem. Ecc. St. Thomas. T. i. p. 360. Addifon of the Chriftian Religion Section i. num. viii. p. 280.

(h) Ja. Bafnage. Hift. de l'Eglife. l. 21. ch. ii. p. 1312. Hift. des Juifs. Vol. i. p. 200. S. Bafnag. Ann. 29. n. xxxvii.. xlii. Fr. Spanh. H. E. T. i. p. 578. et 794. Pagi. ann. 244. n. vii. Cleric. H. E.

Ch. I. *with our Saviour's Refcript.*

A. D. 33.

1. In the firſt place, then, I think, we are not to make any doubt of the truth of what Euſebius ſays, that all this was recorded in the archives of the city Edeſſa in the Syriac language, and was thence tranſlated into Greek. Euſebius has been ſuppoſed by ſome to ſay, that himſelf tranſlated it from the Syriac. But that is not clear. Nor is it certain, that he underſtood Syriac. Much leſs have we any reaſon to ſay, that he was at Edeſſa, and took this account from the archives himſelf.

2. This hiſtorie is not mentioned by any before (*i*) Euſebius: not by *Juſtin Martyr*, nor *Tatian*, nor *Clement of Alexandria*, nor *Origen*, nor by any other. Nor does Euſebius give any hint of that kind. He had it from *Edeſſa*. It was unheard of among the Greeks, till his time. But having received it, he thought it might be not improperly tranſcribed into his Eccleſiaſtical Hiſtorie.

3. It is not much taken notice of by ſucceding writers. It is not mentioned, I think, by *Athanaſius*, nor *Gregorie Nyſſen*, or *Nazianzen*, nor *Epiphanius*, nor *Chryſoſtom*. *Jerome* has once mentioned it, and will be cited by and by. But he has not inſerted in his catalogue of Eccleſiaſtical writers, either *Jeſus*, or *Abgarus*: neither of whom would have been omitted, if he had any reſpect for the epiſtles here produced by Euſebius. This affair is indeed mentioned, or referred to by *Ephraim the Syrian*, in his Teſtament. But that is not a work of ſo much authority, as has been ſuppoſed by

E. p. 332. *et Bib. ch. T. xvi. p.* 99. *Fabr. Cod. Apocr. N. T. T. i. p.* 319. &c. *Philip. Jacob. Sklerandr. H. Antiq. Ec. Chr. cap. vii. not.* 65. J *Jones upon the canon of the N. T. Vol.* 2. *p.* 1. &c. *Du Pin Diſſ. Prelim. Tom. ii. Vid. et Valeſ. Annot. in Euſeb. Colonia La Religion Chrét. authoriſée par les Payens. T.* 2. *p.* 339. &c.

(*i*) Tous les ecrivains Eccleſiaſtiques, qui ont eſté depuis J. C. juſqu'au temps d'Euſebe, ne nous parlent ni près ni loin de cette Hiſtoire, ni de ces Epitres. Et qui croira, qu'ils n'en euſſent rien dit, ſi elle leur euſt eſté connuë? &c. *Sueur. Hiſtoire de l'Egliſe, et de l'Empire. A. J. C.* 31. *T. i. p.* 103. &c.

by some. And it is interpolated in several places, both in the Greek and Syriac copies of it: as was observed (k) formerly.

4. This whole affair was unknown to Christ's Apostles, and to the believers, their contemporaries, both Jews and Gentils: as is manifest from the early disputes about the method of receiving Gentil converts into the Church. If Jesus Christ had himself writ a letter to a Heathen Prince, and had promised to send to him one of his disciples, and if that disciple had accordingly gone to Edessa, and there received the King and his subjects into communion with the church, without circumcision; there could have been no room for any doubt or dispute about the method of receiving Gentil converts to Christianity. Or if any dispute had arisen, would not this historie of the visit of *Thaddeus* have been alleged? Which would have been sufficient to put all to silence. Nor is there any room to say, that this visit of Thaddeus at Edessa was after St. Peter's going to the house of Cornelius, or after the Council of Jerusalem. For it is dated in the 340. year, that is, of the aera of the Seleucidae, or of the Edessens. Which is computed to be the 15. or 16. year of the reign of Tiberius, and the year of Christ 29. when, according to many ancient Christians, our Lord died, and rose again, and ascended to heaven. Indeed, I think, it is impossible to reconcile this account with the historie in the Acts of the Apostles.

5. If Jesus Christ had writ a letter to King Abgarus, it would have been a part of sacred scripture, and would have been placed at the head of all the books of the New Testament. But it was never so respected by any ancient Christian Writers. It does not appear in any catalogues of canonical books, which we have in ancient authors, or in Councils. In the Decree of the Council of Rome, in the time of Pope *Gelasius*, in the year 496. the Epistle of Christ to Abgarus is

(k) *See the Credibility, &c.* P. 2. *vol.* ix. *p.* 183. 184.

Ch. I. *with our Saviour's Rescript.*

is expressly called *(l)* apocryphal. Nor does Eusebius himself upon any occasion reckon it up among canonical scriptures, received by those before him. The titles of the chapters of his Ecclesiastical Historie are allowed to be his own. The title of the chapter, which has been just transcribed from him is this : *A Historie concerning the Prince of the Edessens.* It was a storie, which he had received. And he afterwards tells us particularly, where he had it. And in the first chapter of the second book of the same work, having mentioned the choice of Matthias in the room of Judas, and the choice of the seven Deacons, and the death of St. Stephen from the Acts, he recites again briefly the historie before told concerning Abgarus, and says : *This (m) we have learned from the historie of the ancients. Now we return to the sacred Scripture.* Where he proceeds to relate from the Acts what followed after the martyrdom of St. Stephen. In short, though Eusebius would not pass over this affair without notice, he seems not to have placed any great weight upon it. And succeeding writers have better understood his meaning, than some of late times, who have shewn so much regard to this relation.

6. It was the opinion of many of the most learned and ancient Christians, that our Lord wrote nothing. Therefore this epistle was unknown to them, or they did not suppose it to be genuine. To this purpose speak (*n*) Origen, (*o*) *Jerome,* and *(p) Augustin.*

7. There are several things in this epistle to Abgarus, which are liable to exception.

1.) At the begining of the epistle our Lord is made to say : *Abgarus, thou art happy, forasmuch as thou hast believed in me, though*

(l) Epistola Jesus ad Abgarum Regem apocrypha.

(*m*) Καὶ ταῦτα μὲν ὡς ἐξ ἀρχαίων ἱστορίας εἰρήσθω. Μετίωμεν δ' αὖθις ἐπὶ τὴν θείαν γραφήν. L. 2. c. 1. p. 39. B.

(*n*) *Contr. Celf. l. i.* §. 45. *p.* 34.
(*o*) *Hieron. in Ezech. cap. xliv. T. iii.* p. 1034.
(*p*) *De Consens. Evang. l. i. cap.* 7. *et Retract. l.* 2. *cap.* 16.

A. D. 33.

thou hast not seen me. *For it is written concerning me, that they who have seen me should not believe in me, that they who have not seen me might believe in me, and live.* Says *Du Pin*, and to the like purpose say others: " Where *(q)* are those words written? Does not one see, " that he who made this letter, alludes to the words of Jesus Christ " to St. Thomas: *Blessed are they, who have not seen, and yet have* " *believed.* John xx. 29. Words which were not spoken by Jesus " Christ untill after his resurrection, and which were not writ, untill " long afterwards. Which manifestly shews the forgerie of this " epistle."

2.) Our Lord here seems to speak more clearly of his resurrection, or being *taken up to heaven*, than he does to the disciples in the Gospels.

3.) Christ here defers to cure Abgarus of his distemper. He tells him, *that some time hereafter he would send one of his disciples to him, who should heal him.* Which is altogether unworthie of the Lord Jesus, and different from his usual and well known conduct, who never refused to grant the requests of those who sought to him, and expressed faith in his power. Instead of what is here said to Abgarus, after commending his faith, our Lord would have added, and said: *Henceforth thou art healed of thy distemper.* Or *be it unto thee according to thy faith.* Or, *as thou hast believed, so be it done unto thee.* This we can conclude from similar cases, recorded by authentic witnesses. Matt. viii. 13. xv. 28. Mark vii. 29.

8. There are several other things in this historie, which are very liable to exception.

1.) It is said, that after our Lord's resurrection and ascension, Thomas sent to Edessa Thaddeus, *one of Christ's seventy disciples.* But Thaddeus was an Apostle, as we learn from Matt. x. 3. and Mark iii. 8. It is likewise here said, that *Judas called also Thomas,*

sent

(q) Diss. Prelim. liv. 2. ch. vi. §. 1.

Ch. I. *with our Saviour's Refcript.* 307

fent Thaddeus. Upon which *Valefius (r)* obferves: "Thomas, who A. D. 33.
" was one of the twelve, was alfo called Didymus, as we learn from
" St. John. But that he was alfo called Judas, is no where faid,
" but in this place. For which caufe this ftorie is juftly fufpected."
Jerome fpeaking of this matter (*t*) fays, " Ecclefiaftical Hiftorie informs us, that the Apoftle Thaddeus was fent to Edeffa, to Abgarus king of Ofrhoëne, who by the Evangelift Luke is called Judas
brother of James. Luke vi. 16. and Acts i. 13. and elfewhere is
called Lebbeus. Matt. x. 3. So that he had three names."

2.) When Thaddeus comes to Edeffa, he does not go immediatly to the King, to whom he was fent, as might be reafonably expected. But he goes to the houfe of *Tobias*, where he ftays fome
while, and works many miracles: which being noifed abroad, the
King hears of him, and fends for him. All this is very abfurd. If
Thaddeus, a difciple of Jefus, had been fent to the King of Edeffa,
he ought, and would have gone to him directly, or would have
made application to one of the courtiers to introduce him to the
prince. This therefore cannot be true hiftorie, but muft be the
invention of fome ignorant, though conceited perfon.

3.) " It looks not a little fabulous, fays Mr. *Jones*, that upon
" Thaddeus's appearing before the King, he fhould fee fomewhat
" extraordinarie in his countenance, which none of the company elfe
" could perceive. Eufebius calls it ὅραμα μέγα, a great vifion: Va-
" lefius renders it *divinum nefcio quid,* fome divine appearance."

R r 2   4.) "The

(*r*) Thomas quidem, qui fuit unus ex duodecim, dicebatur Didymus, tefte Jo-anne. Evangelifta. Sed eundem Judam effe cognominatum, alibi quod fciam non reperitur. Itaque et hoc nomine narratio ifta merito in fufpicionem venit. *Valef.* in loc. p. 21.
(*t*) Thaddacum Apoftolum, Ecclefiaf-
tica tradit hiftoria miffum Edeffam ad Ab-garum regem Ofroënae, qui ab Evange-lifta Luca Judas Jacobi dicitur: et alibi appellatur Lebbaeus, quod interpretatur corculus. Credendumque eft eum fuiffe trinomium. *Hieron. in Matt. x. 3. Tom.* 4. *P. i. p.* 35.

4.) "The account in the history, says the same laborious author, "that Abgarus designed to make war upon the Jews for crucifying "Christ, seems very unlikely: because it is plain he was prince only "of a small city, and that at a vast distance from Judea: and there- "fore could never be so extravagant, as to imagine himself able to "destroy so powerfull a nation, as the Jews then were."

5.) Abgarus is said to have had a grievous and incurable distemper, for which he desired relief of Jesus. This is said over and over. But what the distemper was, is not said. Learned moderns, (*u*) who are not wanting in invention for supplying the defects of ancient historie, say, some of them, that it was *the gout*, others *the leprosie*. However, presently after the cure of the prince, we are told of one *Abdus* son of *Abdus*, whom Thaddeus cured of the gout.

6.) We read not of any other city or countrey, in the first three centuries, where the people were all at once converted to the Christian faith. If the people of Edessa had been all Christians from the days of the Apostles, it would have been known before the time of Eusebius. And I may add, that if this storie, told by our Ecclesiastical Historian, had been esteemed credible, it would have been much more taken notice of by succeeding writers, than it is (*x*).

7.) I forbear to remark, as I might, upon that expression of Thaddeus in his discourse with Abgarus: *Jesus Christ, our Lord and God fulfilled the will of the Father:* or upon what is here said of Christ's *descent into hell*.

(*u*) Cet Abgare est qualifié tantôt Toparque, ou Prince, et tantôt Roy. Procope en dit bien des choses, qui sont agreables, mais qui sentent fort la fable.

Ce prince estoit travaillé d' une maladie fascheuse et incurable, (ce que Procope entend de la gout, et les nouveaux Grecs de la lepre) &c. *Tillem, as before.* M. E. T. i. p. 361.

(*x*) The conversion of the whole city is implied in what is above transcribed, and so Eusebius understood it, for he says, in the first chapter of the second book, p. 39. A. Ἐισέτι τε νῦν ἐξ ἐκείνυ ἡ πᾶσα τῶν ἐδεσσηνῶν πόλις τῇ τῦ χριςῦ πρӧανάκειται προσηγορίᾳ.

9. The obfervations, which have been already made, are fufficient to fhew, that the Letter of Abgarus to Jefus Chrift, and our Lord's Refcript, cannot be reckoned genuine. The whole hiftorie is the fiction of fome Chriftian at Edeffa, in the time of Eufebius, or not long before. The people of Edeffa were then, generally, Chriftians, and they valued themfelves upon it. And they were willing to do themfelves the honour of a very early converfion to the Chriftian Faith. By fome one, or more of them, united together, this hiftorie was formed, and was fo far received by *Eufebius*, as to be thought by him not improper to be inferted in his Ecclefiaftical Hiftory. Nor could I omit to take fome notice of it, as great regard has been fhewn to it by fome. But all my readers may perceive, that I bring not in this thing as a teftimonie, of the firft antiquity: though it may afford good proof of the Chriftianity of the people of *Edeffa*, at the begining of the fourth centurie, when Eufebius flourifhed, or before.

CHAP.

CHAP. II.

Of the Knowledge, which the Emperour Tiberius had of our Saviour, Jesus Christ.

§. I. *The Acts of Pontius Pilate, and his Letter to Tiberius.* II. *The Storie of Thamus, in Plutarch, concerning the Death of Pan, considered.*

A. D. 33.

Acts of Pilate, and his Letter to Tiberius.

I. JUSTIN MARTYR, in his first Apologie, which was presented to the Emperour Antonin the Pious, and the Senate of Rome about the year 140. having mentioned our Saviour's crucifixion, and some of the circumstances of it, adds. " And (*a*) that these things were so done, you may know from the Acts made in the time of Pontius Pilate."

Afterwards in the same Apologie, having mentioned some of our Lord's miracles, such as healing diseases, and raising the dead, he adds : " And *(b)* that these things were done by him, you may know from the Acts made in the time of Pontius Pilate."

Ter-

(*a*) Καὶ ταῦτα ὅτι γέγονε, δύνασθε μαθεῖν ἐκ τῶν ἐπὶ Ποντίου Πιλάτου γενομένων ἄκτων. *J. M. Ap. i. p.* 76. *C. Paris.* 1636. *num.* 35. *p.* 65. *Bened.*

(*b*) Ὅτι δὲ κ̣ ταῦτα ἐποίησεν, ἐκ τῶν ἐπὶ Ποντίου Πιλάτου γενομένων ἄκτων μαθεῖν δύνασθε. *Ib. p.* 84. *C. Paris. num.* 48. *p.* 72. *Bened.*

Ch. II. Acts of Pontius Pilate, &c.

Tertullian, in his Apologie about the year 200. having spoken of our Saviour's crucifixion, and resurrection, and his appearances to the disciples, and his ascension to heaven in the sight of the same disciples, who were ordained by him to preach the gospel over the world, goes on. " Of (c) all these things relating to Christ, Pilate " in his conscience a Christian, sent an account to the Emperour " Tiberius, then Emperour."

A. D. 33.

In another chapter, or section of the same Apologie, nearer the begining, he speaks to this purpose. " There (d) was an ancient " decree, that no one should be received for a deity, unless he was " first approved of by the Senate. Tiberius, in whose time the Chri- " stian Religion had it's rise, having received from Palestine in Sy- " ria an account of such things as manifested our Saviour's divinity, " proposed to the Senate, and giving his own vote as first in his fa- " vour, that he should be placed among the gods. The Senate re- " fused, because he had himself declined that honour. Nevertheless " the Emperour persisted in his own opinion, and ordered, that if " any accused the Christians, they should be punished." And then adds.

(c) Dehinc ordinatis eis ad officium praedicandi per orbem, circumfusa nube in coelum est creptus, multo melius quam apud vos asseverare de Romulis Procculi solent. Ea omnia super Christo Pilatus, et ipse jam pro sua conscientia Christianus, Caesari tunc Tiberio nuntiavit. *Tertull. Ap. cap.* 21. p. 22. C.

(d) Ut de origine aliquid retractemus ejusmodi legum. Vetus erat decretum, ne qui deus ab Imperatore consecraretur, nisi a Senatu probatus. Scit M. Aemilius de deo suo Alburno. Facit et hoc ad caussam nostram, quod apud vos de humano arbitratu divinitas pensitatur. Nisi homini deus placuerit, deus non erit. Homo jam deo propitius esse debebit. Tiberius ergo, cujus tempore nomen Christianum in seculum intravit, annuntiata sibi ex Syria Palaestina, quae illic veritatem istius divinitatis revelarant, detulit ad Senatum cum praerogativa suffragii sui. Senatus, quia non ipse probaverat, respuit. Caesar in sententia mansit, comminatus periculum accusatoribus Christianorum. Consulite commentarios vestros. Illic reperietis, primum Neronem in hac sectam cum maxime Romae orientem Caesariano gladio ferocisse. *Ib. cap.* 5. p. 6.

Acts of Pontius Pilate,

A. D. 33.

adds. " Search, says he, Your own writings. And you will there find, that Nero was the first Emperour who exercised any acts of severity toward the Christians, because they were then very numerous at Rome."

It is fit, we should now observe what notice *Eusebius* takes of these things in his Ecclesiastical Historie. It is to this effect.

" When (*e*) the wonderfull resurrection of our Saviour, and his
" ascension to heaven, were in the mouths of all men, it being an
" ancient custom for the Governours of provinces, to write to the
" Emperour, and give him an account of new and remarkable oc-
" currences, that he might not be ignorant of any thing, our Savi-
" our's resurrection being much talked of throughout all Palestine,
" Pilate informed the Emperour of it, as likewise of his miracles,
" which he had heard of: and that being raised up after he had
" been put to death, he was already believed by many to be a god.
" And it is said, that Tiberius referred the matter to the Senate, but
" that they refused their consent under a pretense, that it had not
" been first approved of by them: there being an ancient law, that
" no one should be deified among the Romans, without an order of
" the Senate: but indeed because the saving and divine doctrine of
" the gospel needed not to be confirmed by human judgement and
" authority. However, Tiberius persisted in his former sentiment,
" and allowed not any thing to be done that was prejudicial to the
" doctrine of Christ. These things are related by Tertullian, a man
" famous on other accounts, and particularly for his skill in the Ro-
" man laws. I say, he speaks thus in his Apologie for the Christi-
" ans, writ by him in the Roman tongue, but since translated into
" Greek. His words are these: *There was an ancient decree, that
" no one should be consecrated as a deity by the Emperour, unless he was
" first*

(*e*) *Euseb. H. E. l. 2. cap. 2.*

"first approved of by the Senate. Marcus Aemilius knows this by his A. D.
' god Alburnus. This is to our purpose, forasmuch as among you di- 33.
" vinity is bestowed by human judgement. And if God does not please
" man, he shall not be God. And according to this way of thinking,
" man must be propitious to God. Tiberius therefore, in whose time the
" Christian name was first known in the world, having received an ac-
" count of this doctrine out of Palestine, where it began, communicated
" that account to the Senate: giving (f) in at the same time his own
" suffrage in favour of it. But the Senate rejected it, because it had
" not been approved by themselves. Nevertheless the Emperour persist-
" ed in his judgement, and threatened death to such as should accuse the
" Christians." " Which, adds Eusebius, could be no other than a
" disposal of Divine Providence, that the doctrine of the gospel,
" which was then in it's begining, might be preached all over the
" world without molestation." So *Eusebius*. I forbear as yet to
take particular notice of what is said of this matter by later writers.

Divers exceptions have been made by learned moderns to the original testimonies of Justin Martyr, and Tertullian. " Is there any
" likelihood, say they, that Pilate should write such things to Tibe-
" rius concerning a man, whom he had condemned to death? And
" if he had writ them, is it probable, that Tiberius should propose
" to the Senate to have a man put among the number of the gods
" upon the bare relation of a Governour of a province? And if he
" had proposed it, who can make a doubt, that the Senate would not
" have immediatly complied? So that though we dare not say, that
" this narration is absolutly false, yet it must be reckoned at the lest
" doubtfull." So says *(g)* Du Pin.
These and other difficulties shall be considered.

(f) δῆλος ὢν ἐκείνοις, ὡς τῷ δόγματι ἀ-   (g) Bib. des Aut. Ec. T. i. p. 24. a.
ρίσκεται. Ἡ δὲ σύγκλητος ἐπεὶ οὐκ αὐτῇ
δεδοκιμάκει, ἀπώσατο. P. 41. C.

Now therefore I shall mention some observations.

In the *first* place I observe, that *Justin Martyr* and *Tertullian* are early writers of good repute. That is an observation of Bp. (*h*) *Pearson*. These testimonies are taken from the most public writings, Apologies for the Christian Religion, presented, or at least proposed and recommended to the Emperour and Senate of Rome, or to Magistrates of high authority and great distinction in the Roman Empire.

Secondly, it certainly was the custom of the Governours of provinces to compose acts, or memoirs, or commentaries of the remarkable occurrences in the places where they presided.

In the time of the first Roman Emperours there were Acts of the Senate, Acts of the City, or People of Rome, Acts of other cities, and Acts of Governours of provinces. Of all these we can discern clear proofs, and frequent mention, in ancient writers of the best credit.

Julius Caesar ordered, that (*i*) Acts of the Senate, as well as daily Acts of the People, should be published.

Augustus.(*k*) forbad publishing the Acts of the Senate.

There (*l*) was an officer, himself a Senator, whose province it was to compose those Acts.

The

(*h*) Nihil igitur est, quod in hac historia refelli possit. Et cum Tertullianus adeo gravis, adeo antiquus auctor, adeo rerum Romanarum peritus fuerit, tutius multo est istam Tiberii ad Senatum de Divinitate Christi relationem amplecti. *Pearson. Lection. in Acta Apost. iv. §. xv. p.* 65.

(*i*) Inito honore, primus omnium instituit, ut tam Senatus quam populi diurna acta conficerentur. *Sueton. Jul. Caes. cap.* 20.

(*k*) Auctor et aliarum rerum fuit: in queis ne acta Senatus publicarentur. *Sueton. Aug. cap.* 36.

(*l*) Fuit in Senatu Junius Rusticus, componendis patrum actis delectus a Caesare, eoque meditationes ejus introspicere creditur. *Tacit. Ann. l.* 5. *cap.* 4.

Ch. II.   *and his Letter to Tiberius.*

The Acts of the Senate must have been large and voluminous, containing (*m*) not only the question proposed, or referred to the Senate by the Consul, or the Emperour, but also the debates and speeches of the Senators.

The (*n*) Acts of the People, or City, were journals or registers of remarkable births, marriages, divorces, deaths, proceedings in Courts of judicature, and other interesting affairs, and some other things, below the dignity of historic:

To (*o*) these Acts, of each kind, Roman authors frequently had recourse for information.

There were such Acts or registers at other places, beside Rome, particularly at *Antium*. From them (*p*) *Suetonius* learned the day and place of the birth of Caligula, about which there were other uncertain reports. And he speaks of those Acts (*q*) as public authorities, and therefore more decisive and satisfactorie, than some other accounts.

(*m*) Nescio an venerint in manus vestras haec vetera, quae et antiquorum bibliothecis adhuc manent, et nunc maxime a Minucio contrahuntur: ac jam undecim, ut opinor, Actorum libris, et tribus Epistolarum composita, et edita sunt. Ex his intelligi potest, Cn. Pompejum et Marcum Crassum, non viribus modo et armis, sed ingenio quoque et oratione valuisse. &c. *Tacit. seu quis alius, in Dialog. de Orator. cap.* 37.

Acta Senatus vocabant commentarios, Graece ὑπομνήματα, quibus breviter inscriptum quicquid apud Patres diceretur, agereturque.... Venio ad populi. &c. *Lipsii Excurs. ad Taciti libr. v. annal. cap.* 4.

(*n*) Nerone secundum et Lucio Pisone Consulibus, pauca memoria digna evenere: nisi cui libeat, laudandis fundamentis et trabibus, quis molem amphitheatri apud Campum Martis Caesar adstruxerat, volumina implere: cum ex dignitate populi Romani repertum sit, res illustres annalibus, talia diurnis actis mandare. *Tacit. Ann. l.* 13. *cap.* 31.

(*o*) Matrem Antoniam non apud auctores rerum, non diurna Actorum scriptura, reperio ullo insigni officio functam. *Tacit. Ann. l.* 3. *cap.* 3.

(*p*) Ubi natus sit, incertum diversitas tradentium facit. ... Ego in Actis Antii invenio editum. *Sueton. Cal. cap.* 8. *Vid. et Tiber. cap.* 5.

(*q*) Sequenda igitur est, quae sola restat, publici instrumenti auctoritas. *Id. Calig. cap.* 8.

Acts of Pontius Pilate, Ch. II.

There were also Acts of the Governors of provinces, registring all remarkable transactions and occurrences. *Justin Martyr* and *Tertullian* could not be mistaken about this. And the learned Bishop of Cesarea admits the truth of what they say. And in the time of the persecuting Emperour Maximin, in the year of Christ 307. or thereabout, the Heathen people forged Acts of Pilate, derogatorie to the honour of our Saviour, which were very diligently spread abroad, to unsettle Christians, or discourage them in the profession of their faith. Of this we are informed by Eusebius in his Ecclesiastical Historie (*r*).

Thirdly, it was customary for Governours of provinces to send to the Emperour an account of remarkable transactions in the places where they presided (*s*).

So thought the learned Eusebius, as we have seen. And Pliny's letters to Trajan, still exstant, are a proof of it. Philo (*t*) speaks of the Acts or Memoirs of Alexandria, sent to Caligula, which that Emperour read with more eagernesse and satisfaction, than any thing else.

The (*u*) Acts of Pontius Pilate, and his Letter to Tiberius, which we now have, are not genuine, but manifestly spurious. Neverthelesse it must be allowed by all, that (*x*) Pontius Pilate composed some memoirs.

(*r*) Vid. H. E. l. 1. cap. ix. et l. 9. cap. v.

(*s*) Omnino igitur credendum est aliqua fuisse Pilati acta, ipsius auctoritate confecta, et ad Tiberium transmissa. *Pearson. Lect. iii. in Act. Ap. §. iv.*

(*t*) ... τῇ μὲν ταῖς ὑπομνηματικαῖς ἐφημερίσιν, ὃς ἀπὸ τῆς Ἀλεξανδρείας διεπέμποντο τινες, προσέχων· ἥδιστα γὰρ ἦν ἀνάγνωσμα τὸ τοῦ αὐτῷ, ὡς τὰ ἄλλων συγγραφέων κ᾿ ποιητῶν ἀνδράσατα συγκρίσει τῆς ἐν τούτοις χάριτος.νομίζεσθαι. κ. λ. *Philo de Legat. ad Caium. p.* 1016. *A.*

(*u*) *Vid. Fabric. Cod. Apocr. N. T. p.* 298. *et p.* 972. &c.

(*x*) Imo non potuit Pilatus officii sui rationem tantopere negligere, ut tantae rei in sua provincia gestae notitiam Imperatori non impartiretur. *Pearson. ubi supr. Lect. iv. n. xiv. Vid. et Tob. Eckard. cap. iv. n. xi. p.* 126.

Ch. II. *and his Letter to Tiberius.*

memoirs concerning our Saviour, and fent them to the Emperour, whether Juftin Martyr and Tertullian have given a juft account of them, or not.

A. D. 33.

Fourthly, It (y) is faid to be very unlikely, that Pilate fhould write fuch things to Tiberius, concerning a man, whom he had condemned to death.

To which it is eafie to reply, that if he wrote to Tiberius at all, it is very likely, that he fhould fpeak favorably, and honorably of our Saviour. That (z) Pilate paft fentence of condemnation upon our Lord very unwillingly, and not without a fort of compulfion, appears from the hiftorie of the Evangelifts. Matt. xxvii. 11. 26. 62. ... 65. Mark xv. 1. ... 15. Luke xxiii. 1. ... 25. John xvii. 28. ... 40. xix 1... 13. Pilate was hard preffed. The rulers of the Jews *vehemently accufed* our Lord to him. They faid, *they had found him perverting the nation, and forbidding to give tribute to Cefar, faying, that himfelf is Chrift,* a King, and the like. And all without effect for a great while. Pilate ftill fought for expedients to fet Jefus at liberty. As his reluctance had been very manifeft and public in a court of judicature, in the chief city of the nation, at the time of one of their great feftivals: it is highly probable, that when he fent to Rome, he fhould make fome apologie for this conduct. Nor could any thing be more proper, than to allege fome of our Saviour's miracles, which he had heard of, and to give an account of the zeal of thofe who profeffed faith in him, after his ignominious crucifixion,

---

(y) Negare interim minime velim, Pilatum aliquid fuper tali ac tanto negotio fcripfiffe: at incertum effe quid ac quale id fuerit, atque ideo prudentiores, Eufebium, Hieronymum, fimilefque, talia cautius prodidiffe. *Ant. Vandale Diff. de Actis Pilati. p.* 615. *Amft.* 1700.

(z) ... cujus et Pilatus, qui nolens compulfus eft, contra Dominum ferre fententiam. *Hieron. adv. Jovin. l.* 2. *p.* 218. *Tom.* 4.

cifixion, and openly afferted, that he was rifen from the dead, and afcended up to heaven.

If Pilate fent any letter to Tiberius, (as very probably he did,) he would not dare to write falfhood, nor to conceal the moft material circumftances of the cafe, about which he was writing. At the trial of Jefus, he publicly declared his innocence: and told the Jews feveral times, *that he found in him no fault at all*. And when he was going to pronounce the fentence of condemnation, *he took water and wafhed his hands before the multitude, faying: I am innocent of the bloud of this juft perfon.* See ye to it. Matt. xxvii. 24. When he wrote to Tiberius, he would be very naturally led to fay fomething of our Lord's wonderfull refurrection and afcenfion, which were much talked of, and believed by many, with which he could not poffibly be unacquainted. The mention of thefe things would be the beft vindication of his inward perfuafion, and repeated declarations of our Lord's innocence upon the trial, notwithftanding the loud clamours, and united accufations of the Jewifh people, and their rulers.

Pilate, as has been faid feveral times, paffed condemnation upon Jefus, very unwillingly, and not till after a long trial. When he paffed fentence upon him, he gave orders, that this title, or infcription fhould be put upon the croffe: *Jefus of Nazareth, the King of the Jews*. When he had expired, application was made to Pilate, by Jofeph of Arimathea, an honourable Counfellor, that the body might be taken down and buried. To which he confented, but not till after affurance received from the Centurion, that he had been fome time dead. The next day fome of the *Priefts and Pharifees* came to him, faying: *Sir, we remember that that deceiver faid, while he was yet alive, After three days I will rife again. Command therefore, that the fepulchre be made fure; untill the third day, leaft his difciples come by night, and fteal him away, and fay unto the people, He*

is

is risen from the dead. So the last errour shall be worse than the first. Pilate said unto them. Ye have a watch. Go your way, make it as sure as ye can. So they went, and made the sepulchre sure, sealing the stone, and setting a watch. Whilst they were at the sepulchre, there was a great earthquake, the stone was rolled away by an angel, *whose countenance was like lightening, and for fear of whom the guards did shake and became as dead men. Some of the guards went down into the city, and shewed unto the chief priests, all the things that were done.* Nor can there be any doubt, that those things came also to `*⁎*` the Governour's ears. Pilate therefore was furnished with many materials of great importance relating to this case, very proper to be sent to the Emperour. And very probably he did send them. For he could do no otherwise.

Fifthly, It is said, that (*a*) if Pilate had sent such things to Tiberius, it is nevertheless very unlikely, that Tiberius should propose to the Senate, that our Saviour might be put among the number of the Gods. For that Emperour had little or no regard to things of religion.

But it is easie to answer, that such observations are of little or no importance. Few princes are able to preserve uniformity in the whole of their conduct. And it is certain, that Tiberius varied from himself upon many occasions, and in different parts of his life.

Sixthly,

(`*⁎*`) Illud certe dubitare non possumus, Pilatum vocasse ad se hos milites, ex iisque rem vere gestam cognovisse. *Heumann. Testimonium militum de Resurrectione Christi. p.* 100. *ap. Primitias Gotting.*

(*a*) Mihi certe, . . . haud facile persuaserim, Tiberium Caesarem, cujus mores ab omni religionum omnium cultu per quam fuisse alienissimos, comperior, de

Christo Dom. et Christiana religione, tantopere curasse, ut de illa retulerit ad Senatum, . . . Tota hominis vita nil aliud praedicat, quam quod dico. Et Suetonio dictum est expresse et signanter. *Circa deos ac religiones negligentior, quippe addictus mathematicae, persuasicuisque plenus cuncta fato agi. Tan. Fab. l. 2. Ep.* 12. *p.* 35.

Sixthly, It is farther urged, that *(b)* if Tiberius had propoſed the thing to the Senate, there can be no doubt, that the Senate would have immediatly complied.

But neither is this difficulty inſuperable. For we are aſſured by Suetonius, that *(c)* Tiberius let ſeveral things be decided by the Senate, contrarie to his own opinion, without ſhewing much uneaſineſſe.

And when he had determined to remove and deſtroy Sejanus, who had long been his favourite, he was far from being certain of the Senate's compliance. He *(d)* employed the utmoſt art and ſkill, and yet was for ſome while anxious and doubtfull of the iſſue.

Seventhly, The right interpretation of the words of Tertullian will be of uſe to remove difficulties, and to confirm the truth of the account.

I have tranſlated them in this manner. *When Tiberius referred the matter to the Senate, that our Lord ſhould be placed in the number of the gods, the Senate refuſed, becauſe he had himſelf declined that honour.* The words are underſtood to the like purpoſe by *(e) Pearſon*.

There is another ſenſe, which is that of the Greek tranſlation of Ter-

---

(b) Hem! Reſpuit Senatus, quod Tiberio placuit. *T. Faber. ibid.*

(c) Quaedam adverſus ſententiam ſuam decerni ne queſtus quidem eſt... Cum ſenatuſconſultum per diſceſſionem forte fieret, tranſeuntem eum in alteram partem, in qua pauciores erant, ſecutus eſt nemo. .. &c. *Sueton. Tiber. cap. 31.*

(d) Sejanum res novas molientem... vix tandem, et aſtu magis ac dolo, quam principali auctoritate ſubvertit. *Sueton. ib. cap. 65.*

(e) Senatus, inquit Tertullianus, *quia in ſe non probaverat.* Ubi optima facti ratio redditur. Senatus antea Tiberio divinitatem obtulerat, quam ille ſibi oblatam reſpuit. Templa, Flamines, ſacerdotes decerni ſibi prohibuit... ut refert Suetonius. Quia igitur divinitatem in ſe non probaverat Tiberius, ſed oblatam rejecerat, tutiſſimum putabat Senatus alium neminem in deos ſuos referre, ne eum Tiberio majorem efficere viderentur. *Pearſon. Lect. 4. num. xiv.*

Ch. II.   *and his Letter to Tiberius.*

Tertullian's Apologie, made ufe of by Eufebius. *The Senate refufed, becaufe it had not itfelf approved of it.* But that fenfe, if it be any fenfe at all, is abfurd, and therefore unlikely. If none befide the Senate had a right to confecrate any for a deity, yet certainly the Conful, or the Emperour, might refer fuch a thing to that venerable body. According to Tertullian's account, the whole is in a fair way of legal proceeding. By virtue of an ancient law, no one might be reckoned a god (at left by the Romans,) without the approbation of the Senate. Tiberius having been informed of fome extraordinarie things concerning Jefus, referred it to the Senate, that he alfo might be placed in the number of the deities. Was it poffible, after this, that the Senate fhould refufe it, under a pretenfe, that Tiberius had beftowed divinity upon Jefus, without their confent, when he had done no fuch thing, and at that very time was referring it to their judgement in the old legal way?

Le Clerc objects, that *(f)* the true reading in Tertullian is not, *quia in fe non probaverat,* but *quia non ipfe probaverat.* Be it fo. The meaning is the fame. *Ipfe* muft intend the Emperour, not the Senate. The other fenfe is abfurd, and next to a contradiction, and therefore not likely to be right. And at the fame time it is a rude and needlefs affront. The other interpretation reprefents a handfome compliment, and a compliment not without foundation. For it is very true, that *(g)* Tiberius had himfelf declined receiving divine honours.

Eighthly, It has been objected, that Tiberius was unfriendly, to the Jewifh people, and therefore it muft be reckoned very impro-

---

(f) Cleric. H. E. an. 29. *n.* 97.
(g) Templa, flamines, facerdotes, decerni fibi prohibuit: etiam ftatuas, atque imagines, nifi permittente fe, poni: permifitque ea fola conditione, ne inter fimulachra deorum, fed inter ornamenta aedium ponerentur. *Sueton. Tiber. cap.* 26.

bable, that he should be willing to put a man, who was a Jew, among the number of the gods.

But there is little or no ground for this objection. It was obviated long ago in the first part of this work, where, beside other things, it is said. " In the *(h)* reign of Tiberius the Jewish people
" were generally well used. They were indeed banished out of Ita-
" lie, by an edict: but it was for a misdemeanour, committed by
" some villains of that nation. The great hardship was, that many
" innocent persons suffered beside the guilty. Upon other occasi-
" ons, Tiberius shewed the Jews all the favour they could desire,
" especially after the death of Sejanus, and is much applauded for
" it by (*i*) Philo." And what there follows.

Ninthly, Still it is urged, " Nothing *(k)* can be more absurd than
" to suppose, that Tiberius would receive for a deity a man, who
" taught the worship of one God only, and whose religion decried
" all other deities, as mere fictions."

Upon which I must say: Nothing can be more absurd, than this objection. Tertullian does not suppose Tiberius to be well acquainted with the Christian Religion, or our Saviour's doctrine. All he says is, that having heard of some extraordinarie things concerning him, he had a desire to put him among the Roman deities.

Tenthly, Tertullian proceeds. " Neverthelefs the Emperour per-
" sisted in his opinion, and ordered, that if any accused the Christi-
" ans, they should be punished."

This

(*h*) See the *Credib. P. i. B. i. ch. viii. p.* 394.

(*i*) *De Legat. ad Caium. p.* 1015. C. D.

(*k*) Noverat Jesum fuisse hominem Judaeum, uniusque Dei cultorem, et qui omnes alios deos, quasi hominum commenta rejiceret: ac proinde religionem, qua cum iis conjungeretur, summopere improbaturum, si in coelo viveret: et tamen eum una cum Romanis diis coli voluisset. Quo nihil absurdius fingi poterat. *Cleric. H. E. an.* 29. *n.* 96.

Ch. II. *and his Letter to Tiberius.*

This was very natural. Though the Senate would not put Jesus in the number of the deities, the Emperour was still of opinion, that it might have been done. And he determined to provide by an edict for the safety of those, who professed a high regard for Jesus Christ. Which edict, as Eusebius reasonably supposes, was of use for securing the free preaching of the gospel in many places. But the authority of that edict would cease at the Emperour's demise, if not sooner. Undoubtedly, it could not be in force, or have any great effect, for a long season.

Nor need we to consider the ordering such an edict as this, in favour of the Christians as an incredible thing: if we observe what Philo says, who assures us, " that (*l*) Tiberius gave orders to all the " Governours of provinces, to protect the Jews in the cities where " they lived, in the observation of their own rites and customs: and " that they should bear hard upon none of them, but such as were " unpeaceable, and transgressed the laws of the state."

Nor is it improbable, that the Christians should partake of the like civilities, they being considered as a sect of the Jews. And it is allowed that the Roman Emperour's did not openly persecute the Christians, till they became so numerous, that the Heathen people were apprehensive of the total overthrow of their religion.

In the *eleventh* place. Says a learned and judicious (*m*) writer:
" It is probable, that Pilate, who had no enmity toward Christ, and
" accounted him a man justly accused, and an extraordinarie person,
" might be moved by the wonderfull circumstances attending and
" following his death, to hold him in veneration, and perhaps to
" think him a Hero, and the son of some Deity. It is possible, that
" he might send a narrative, such as he thought most convenient, of
" these transactions to Tiberius: but it is not at all likely, that Ti-
" berius

(*l*) ... ἀλλ' ἐπὶ μόνοις τοῖς αἰτίοις. De *Legat. ad Caium*, p. 1015. C.

(*m*) Dr. *Jortin's Remarks upon Ecclesiastical Historie*. vol. i. p. 2. ... 4.

A. D. 33.

"berius propofed to the Senate, that Chrift fhould be deified, and
"that the Senate rejected it, and that Tiberius continued favour-
"ably difpofed toward Chrift, and that he threatened to punifh
"thofe, who fhould moleft, and accufe the Chriftians." "Obferve
"alfo, *fays the fame learned writer*, that the Jews perfecuted the A-
"poftles, and flew Stephen, and that Saul made havock of the
"Church, entering into every houfe, and haling men and women,
"committed them to prifon, and that Pilate connived at all this vi-
"olence, and was not afraid of the refentment of Tiberius on that
"account."

Admitting the truth of all thefe particulars juft mentioned, it does not follow, that no orders were given by Tiberius for the protection of the followers of Jefus. For no commands of Princes are obeyed by all men every where. They are oftentimes tranfgreffed. Nor was any place more likely than Judea, where the enmity of many againft the difciples of Jefus was fo great. Nor need it to be fuppofed, that Tiberius was very intent to have this order ftrictly regarded. For he was upon many occafions very indolent and dilatorie. And he was well known to be fo. Moreover the death of Stephen was tumultuous, and not an act of the Jewifh Council. And farther the influence of Pilate in that countrey was not now, in it's full height. We perceive, from the Hiftorie of our Lord's trial before him, as recorded in the Gofpels, that he ftood in fear of the (*n*) Jews. "He (*o*) was apprehenfive, that if he did not gratify them
"in that point, they might draw up a long lift of mal-adminiftra-
"tions for the Emperour's view. His condemnation of Jefus at the
"importunity of the Jews, contrarie to his own judgement and in-
"clination, declared to them more than once, was a point gained:
"and his government muft have been ever after much weakened by
"fo.

(*n*) See particularly *John* xix. 12. *p.* 195. *Comp.* B. 2. *ch.* iii. §. iii. *p.*
(*o*) *Credib. &c.* P. i. B. i. *ch.* 2. §. *xii.* 841.

"so mean a condescension. And that Pilate's influence in the province continued to decline, is manifest, in that the people of it prevailed at last to have him removed in a very ignominious manner, by Vitellius President of Syria."

A. D. 33.

Pilate was removed from his government before the Passover in the year of Christ 36. After which *(p)* there was no Procurator, or other person with power of life and death, in Judea, before the accession of Herod Agrippa, in the year 41. In that space of time, the Jews would take an unusual licence, and gratify their own malicious dispositions, beyond what they could have otherwise done, without controlle.

Twelfthly, Some have objected, that Tertullian is so absurd, as to speak of *Christians*, in the time of Tiberius: though it be certain, that the followers of Jesus were not known by that denomination, till some time afterwards.

But that is a trifling objection. Tertullian intends no more by *Christians* than followers of Jesus, by whatever name they were known and distinguished: whether that of *Nazareans*, or *Galikans*, or *Disciples*. And it is undoubted, that the Christian Religion had it's rise in the reign of Tiberius: though they who professed to believe in Jesus, as risen from the dead, and ascended to heaven, were not called *Christians*, till some while afterwards. So at the begining of the paragraph he says, *There was an ancient law, that no god should be consecrated by the Emperour, unless it was first approved by the Senate.* Nevertheless Tertullian was not so ignorant, as not to know, that there were not any Emperours, when that ancient decree was passed. His meaning is, that no one should be deified by any man, no not by a Consul or Emperour, without the approbation of the Senate.

Finally,

(p) See Credib. as before, p. 196.

Finally, We do not suppose, that Tiberius understood the doctrine of our Saviour, or that he was at all inclined to be a Christian. Nor did Tertullian intend to say any such thing. For immediatly after the passage first cited from him, he adds. "But *(q)* the Ce- "sars themselves would have believed in Jesus Christ, if they had "not been necessarie for the world, or if Christians could have been "Cesars."

Grotius (*r*) appears to have rightly understood the importance of these passages of Tertullian. Whose note therefore upon Matthew xxiv. 11. I have transcribed below.

Admit then the right interpretation of *Tertullian*, and it may be allowed, that what he says, is not incredible, nor improbable. The Romans had almost innumerable deities, and yet they frequently added to that number, and adopted new. As deifications were very frequent, Tiberius might indulge a thought of placing Jesus among the established deities, without (*s*) intending to derogate from the worship or honour of those who were already received. But the Senate was not in the humour to gratify him. And the reason assigned is, because the Emperour himself had declined that honour. Which is so plausible a pretense, and so fine a compliment, that we

cannot

(*q*) Sed et Caesares credidissent super Christo, si aut Caesares non essent seculo necessarii, aut si et Christiani potuissent esse Caesares. *Apol. cap.* 21. *p.* 22. C.

(*r*) Cum Paganismo Christianam religionem miscere aggressus est omnium primus Simon Magus, Claudio imperante. Nam et ipse pro deo haberi voluit. Credibile est, pervenisse ad eum famam consilii ejus, quod a Tiberio datum Senatui Romano legimus, ut Christus adderetur deorum numero. Qualem rerum plane

insociabilium mixturam postea quoque Adrianus, Severus, Heliogabalus, sed frustra, efficere conati sunt. *Grot. ad Matt.* xxiv. in.

(*s*) Tiberius autem non ita Christum voluit deum recipi, ut suetus Romanorum cultus abrogaretur, sed ut juxta coleretur, uti Julium Caesarem Augustum, et Augustum ipse Tiberius consecraverat, et coli secundum ceteros deos volebat. &c. *Tob..Echard. cap.* 4. *n.* 8. *p.* 122.

cannot eafily fuppofe it to be *Tertullian*'s own invention. Which therefore gives credibility to the account.

Eufebius, though he acknowledgeth the overruling Providence of God in the favorable difpofition of Tiberius toward the firft followers of Jefus, by which means the Chriftian Religion in it's infance was propagated over the world with lefs moleftation, does alfo fay, at the begining of the chapter before quoted: " the Senate refufed " their confent to the Emperour's propofal, under a pretenfe, that " they had not been firft afked, there being an ancient law, that no " one fhould be deified without the approbation of the Senate. But " indeed, adds he, becaufe the faving and divine doctrine of the " gofpel needed not to be ratified by human judgement and autho- " rity."

Chryfoftom's obfervation is to the like purpofe, but with fome inaccuracies. It is likely, that he was not at all acquainted with Tertullian. And he was no admirer of Eufebius. Perhaps he builds upon general tradition only. " The (*t*) Roman Senate, fays he, had " the power of nominating, and decreeing, who fhould be Gods. " When therefore all things concerning Chrift had been publifhed, " he who was the Governour of the Jewifh nation, fent to them, to " know, if they would be pleafed to appoint him alfo to be a God. " But they refufed, being offended and provoked, that before their " decree and judgement had been obtained, the power of the cru- " cified man had fhined out, and had attracted all the world to the " worfhip of him. But (*u*) by the overruling Providence of God, " this was brought to pafs againft their will, that the divinity of Chrift " might not be eftablifhed by human appointment, and that he " might not be reckoned one of the many, who were deified by
" them."

(*t*) *Chryf. hom.* 26. *in* 2 *Cor. T. x. p.* ὥςε μὴ ἐξ ἀνθρωπίνε ψήφε τὴν θεότητα ἀναχυ-
624. *A.* ρυχθῆναι τῦ Χριςῦ. κ. λ.
(*u*) Τῦτο δὲ ὠκονομεῖτο κ̣ ἀκόντων αὐτῶν,

"them." Some of which, as he proceeds to shew, had been of infamous characters.

I shall now transcribe below (x) in his own words what *Orosius*, in the fifth centurie, says of this matter, that all my readers may have it at once before them, without looking farther for it.

And I refer to *Zonaras* (y) and (z) *Nicephorus*. The former only quotes Eusebius, and transcribes into his Annals the chapter of his Ecclesiastical Historie, above quoted by me. Nor has *Nicephorus* done much more.

Upon the whole, I think, the accounts of those ancient authors, *Justin Martyr* and *Tertullian*, deserve some regard. It is upon them that I have made my comments. And my defense is confined to them. And we can perceive from Eusebius, and other later writers, that their accounts were received as true. But some make additions, or alterations in Tertullian's original narration, which diminish the credibility of the whole. *Orosius* not only says, that the Senate refused to comply with the proposal of Tiberius, but also, that *they were so provoked, as to order by an edict, that the Christians should be expelled the City.*

(x) At postquam passus est Dominus Christus, atque a mortuis resurrexit, et discipulos suos ad praedicandum dimisit, Pilatus, Praeses Palaestinae provinciae ad Tiberium Imperatorem atque Senatum retulit, de passione et resurrectione Christi, consequentibusque virtutibus, quae per ipsum palam factae fuerant, vel per discipulos ipsius in nomine ejus fiebant, et de eo quod crescente plurimorum fide Deus crederetur. Tiberius cum suffragio magni favoris retulit ad Senatum, ut Christus Deus haberetur. Senatus indignatione motus, quod non sibi prius secundum morem delatum esset, ut de suscipiendo cul- tu prius ipse decerneret, consecrationem Christi recusavit, edictoque constituit, exterminandos esse Urbe Christianos: praecipue cum et Sejanus, Praefectus Tiberii, suscipiendae religioni obstinatissime contradiceret. Tiberius tamen edicto accusatoribus Christianorum mortem comminatus est. Itaque Paullatim immutata est illa Tiberii Caesaris laudatissima modestia, in poenam contradictoris Senatus. *P. Oros. l. 7. cap. 4.*

(y) *Zonar. Ann. T. 2. p. 176.*

(z) *Niceph. l. 2. cap. 8. Conf. l. i. cap. 16.*

Ch. II.   *and his Letter to Tiberius.*   329

City. Which is loading the hiftorie with two great abfurdities. For it is very improbable, that the Chriftians fhould be fo numerous at Rome in the time of Tiberius, as to occafion any uneafinefle to the Senate. And it is equally improbable, that the Senate fhould behave fo rudely to the Emperour. Tertullian's account is free from fuch things, and ought not to be rejected, becaufe of additions made by later writers.

A. D. 33.

The truth of Tertullian's account has been contefted by divers learned moderns. I have already taken notice of what is faid by *Du Pin*, and have alfo confidered the objections of fome others. I now willingly refer to divers others *(a)* on the fame fide. Other learned men *(b)* have embraced it, as true, and have taken a good deal of pains to vindicate it againft objections. *Pearfon (c)* in particular, is very favorable to this hiftorie. And in the courfe of my argument I have quoted him feveral times. The late Mr. *Mofheim (d)* alfo

was

(a) Tan. Faber. l. 2. Ep. xii. Vandale de Orac. p. 455. *et Diff. de Actis Pilati. p.* 608. &c. *Amft.* 1700. *Cleric. H. E. ann.* 29. *n.* 96. &c. *Bafnag. ann.* 33. *n.* 192. ... 196. *et Exercitat. p.* 136. &c. *Sig. Havercamp. Annot. ad Tertullian. Apol. cap. v. Jortin's Remarks upon Ecclefiaftical Hiftorie. vol. i. p.* 2. ... 4.
(b) Sueur Hiftoire de l'Eglife et de l'Empire. Tom. i. p. 130. 131. *Tillem. Mem. Ecc. T. i. S. Pierre art.* 19. *et notes xvi.* ... *xix. Fr. Balduin. Comment. ad Edicta veterum Principum Roman. de Chriftianis. p.* 20. ... 24. 1727. *Tob. Eckbard. non Chriftanorum de Chrifto Teftimonia. cap. iv. J. A. Fabr. Lux Evangelii. cap. xii. p.* 220. ... 222. *La Religion Chret. autorifée par le temoignage des ancient au-*

teurs Payens. Par D. Colonia. Tom. 2. *ch. xi.* ... *Lettre de M. Ifelin Docteur et Profeffeur en Theologie à Bafle, fur le projet conçu par Tibere, de mettre N. S. J. C. au nombre des Dieux de Romae. Bib. Germanique T.* 32. *p.* 147. &c. *et T.* 33. *p.* 12. &c.
(c) Pearfon. Lection. in Act. Ap. iii. et iv.
(d) Negant hodie viri fagaces et eruditi, fidem huic narrationi habendam effe. Ego vero fuperftitiofi nomen minime formido, fi dixero, non prorfus eam mihi rejiciendam videri. *Mofhem. Inftitution. H. Chriftianae Maj. Sec. i. P. i. c.* 4. §. *ix. p.* 109. *A. D.* 1739.

Sunt quidem viri eruditi, quibus hoc alieniffimum a vero videtur: fed his alii doctri-

A. D. 33.

The Relation of Thamus concerning the Death of Pan.

was of opinion, that it ought not to be entirely rejected, and has spoken in favour of it in several of his works.

II. There is another thing, which may not be omitted here, though it appears to me to be of little or no importance.

It is a storie told by Cleombrotus, one of the speakers in Plutarch's dialogue concerning the cessation of oracles. " He (a) had it " from Epitherses, his master in grammar. He said, he was sail- " ing for Italie in a ship well freighted with merchandise, in which " also were many passengers. When they were one evening among " the islands called Echinedes in the Aegean Sea, the ship was be- " calmed. Most of the passengers were awake, and some were ca- " rousing after supper. At the same time there came a voice from " the island Paxae, which called aloud for *Thamus*. He was an " Egyptian, and the pilot, and not so much as known by name " to many of the passengers. He suffered himself to be called " twice, without making any answer. But at the third call he spoke. " The voice then with great vehemence said to him. *When you* " *come to the Palodes, declare, that the great Pan is dead.* They " were all astonished, when they heard this, and debated the mat- " ter, whether it were fit to perform the order or not. *Thamus* " determined, that, if when they were arrived at the appointed " place, there was wind enough to sail forward, he would pass by " in silence. But if the vessel was becalmed, he would publish
" what

---

doctrina non inferiores rationes opponunt haud facile destruendas. *Id. De Reb. Christian. ante Conft. M.* p. 92.

· Erudite, post Theod. Hasaeum peculiari libello *de Decreto Tiberii, quo Chriftum referre voluit in numerum Deorum. Erfurti.* 1715. 4. edito. pro veritate hujus facti militavit ven. Jac. Chriftoph. Ifellus, epiftola Gallica, quae legitur Bibliotheque Germanique. T. 32. p. 147. et T. 33. p. 12. *Mofbem. Infti. Hift. Ec.* p. 30. ed. 1755. Conf. fupra, not. (b).

(a) Plut. de Oracul. Defectu. Et vid. *Eufeb. Pr. Ev.* p. 206.

Ch. II.   concerning the Death of Pan.

"what he had heard. When they came over againſt Palodes, the
"winds and waves were all calm. *Thamus* therefore placing him-
"ſelf at the ſtern of the veſſel, with his face toward the land, de-
"clared as he had been told, *that the great Pan was dead*. Scarcely
"had he done ſpeaking, when they heard from the ſhores groans
"and lamentations, not of one, but as of a great multitude. As
"there were many in the ſhip, who were witneſſes of this affair,
"the fame of it ſpread in a ſhort time, ſo far as Rome, and *Tha-*
"*mus* was ſent for by the Emperour Tiberius. And Tiberius gave
"ſuch credit to the account, that he called together ſeveral learned
"men to inquire of them, who this Pan was. They delivered it
"as their opinion, that he was ſon of Mercurie and Penelope."

As this ſtorie is placed in the time of *Tiberius*, ſome learned men have been of opinion, that *(b)* by the *great Pan* was meant Jeſus Chriſt, the Lord of the univerſe, who ſuffered in the time of that Emperour. *Huet (c)* gives credit to this ſtorie, and ſuppoſeth, that thereby

---

(b) Ex hiſce audiamus, quaeſo, primo loco, Boiſſardum in hunc modum loquentem... *Quidam exiſtimant vocem illam locutam fuiſſe de Chriſti ſervatoris morte, cum audita ſit anno decimo nono imperii Caeſaris, quo Chriſtus crucifixus eſt. Et hunc credimus univerſae naturae et totius mundi Dominum et formatorem. Vandale de Orac. p.* 435.

Huic narrationi fidem creat circumſtantia temporis. Incidit enim haec res in tempus, quo Chriſtus mortuus eſt. Eſtque veriſimile, ejulationes daemonum inde ortas, quod ſcirent, morte Chriſti Satanae regnum concidiſſe. Eſt enim Pan vox aptiſſima ad ſignificandum Dominum univerſi, qui eſt omnia in omnibus, ut ait Paulus. 1 Cor.

xv. 28. *Petrus Mornaeus, citat. a Vandale. ib. p.* 437.

(c) Ethnicis vero ſtupendo miraculo Chriſti Jeſu ſignificata mors eſt, quod in libello de deſitis oraculis Plutarchus refert. Id quamquam a vulgo ſcriptorum tritum eſt, minime tamen ob admirabilitatem rei pigebit hic adſcribere.... Narrat id apud Plutarchum Aemilianus Rhetor, ut ſibi a patre Epitherſe, rei teſte, traditum. Atqui id convenit in tempus mortis Chriſti Jeſu, qui verus Pan eſt, rerum omnium parens, ac naturae totius auctor, quam Panos ſymbolo Mythologi ſignatam voluerunt. *Huet. Dem. Ev. Prop. ix. cap.* 136. *p.* 630. *See likewiſe Tillemont. Mem. Ec. J. C. art.* 21. *et note* 31.

thereby the death of Chrift, who is the true Pan, the parent of all things, and the author of all nature, was notified to Heathen people.

I fhall now make two or three remarks, which are referred to the confideration of my readers.

1. The whole ftorie is improbable, and has more the appearance of fiction, than of truth and credibility.
2. This ftorie is all over heathenifh. If there be any truth in the account, when it was brought to Rome, and the affair was examined by the learned philologifts at the court of Tiberius; their determination was, that the Pan, who was reported to be dead, was the fon of Mercurie and Penelope. Neither *Thamus*, nor *Epitherfes*, nor *Tiberius*, nor the learned men, whom he confulted, nor yet *Plutarch*, and his companie, who lived fome good while after the death of our Lord, and the publication of his gofpel, had any notion that this related to Jefus Chrift.

That this ftorie is throughout heathenifh, may be argued from what is faid prefently afterwards by *Demetrius*, another of the fpeakers in that dialogue of Plutarch. " That moft of the iflands near
" Britain are defert, and confecrated to demons and heroes: and
" that being fent by the Emperour to take a furvey of thofe iflands,
" he landed on one of them, which had a few inhabitants: and
" that foon after his arrival, there happened a tempeft, with terri-
" ble claps of thunder and lightening. When the tempeft was over,
" the people of the ifland gave out, that fome one of the principal
" demons was dead. A candle, faid they, when it burns, is plea-
" fant. But when it goes out, it leaves a ftink behind. Even fo
" the deaths of great fouls produce ftorms, and fometimes a pefti-
" ferous air. To which *Demetrius* added, that in one of thofe i-
" flands Saturn was bound, and guarded by Briareus, and that there
" were

Ch. II. *concerning the Death of Pan.*

" were many demons attending upon him, as his slaves and mini-
" sters." All fiction surely, but representing, as may be supposed,
the doctrine of credulous Heathens concerning demons.

All which, however, is quoted by Eusebius *(d)* from Plutarch, to prove the cessation or the declension of oracles soon after the coming of Christ.

His remark is to this purpose. " So far Plutarch. But it will
" be worth the while to observe the time, when he says, the death
" of that demon happened. It was in the time of Tiberius. At
" that time our Saviour dwelt among men, and it is written of him
" that he expelled all sorts of demons. And some of them fell
" down before him, entreating him, that he would not send them
" into the Abysse. Here then, you have the true time of the ex-
" pulsion of demons out of this world, a thing never heard of be-
" fore. Nor was there an end put to human sacrifices, so com-
" mon among the Gentils, till the evangelical doctrine had been
" preached to all men." So Eusebius.

And though (*e*) *Colonia* flourisheth mightily upon this storie, he in the end finds it prudent to content himself, with considering it, as an argument, " that (✱) the Gentils themselves acknowledged the
" general downfall or declension of their oracles, after the time of
" Tiberius, and the coming of Christ, and that two centuries before
" Eusebius." A point, about which I do not now particularly concern my-self.

Before I conclude this article, I would observe, that *(f) Baronius* did

---

(d) Praep. Evang. l. v. cap. 17. p. 206.
... 208.
(*e*) *La Religion Chrétienne, &c. Tom. i.*
p. 124 &c.
(✱) *p.* 129.

(*f*) Hactenus de Pane Eusebius ex Plutarcho. .. Sane quidem si rei gestae fidem adhibendam esse putamus, &c. *Baron.* Ann. 34. num. 130.

did not fully relye upon the truth of the ſtorie, told in Plutarch, concerning the Pilot *Thamus*: and that *(g)* the Centuriators of Magdeburg conſider it as an abſurd and ridiculous fiction. So likewiſe does *(b) Baſnage*, who has offered more reaſons in behalf of his opinion, than need to be repeated by me here.

(*g*) Ubi et de Pane mortuo ridicula narrat. *Centur. Magdeb. Sec. i. lib. 2. cap. xv.*

(*b*) Nobis vero propius eſt, hanc Epitherſis narrationem eſſe fabulis apponendam : neque Chriſti paſſionem Panis morte ſignificatam. . . . *Baſn. Ann.* 33. nkm. 124.

CHAP.

CHAP. III.

A Monumental Infcription concerning the Chriftians in the time of Nero.

WHAT offers next is an infcription of the Emperour NERO, on a monument found in Portugal (*a*).

To Nero Claudius Caefar,
Auguftus, High-Prieft,
For clearing the Province
Of Robbers, and Thofe
Who taught Mankind
A New Superftition.

None

(*a*) In ruinis pagi Marquofiae in Lufitania. Ap. Gruter. p. 238. 9.

NERONI. CL. CAIS
AUG. PONT. MAX
OB PROVINC. LATRONIB
ET. HIS. QUI. NOVAM
GENERI. HUM. SUPER
STITION. INCULCAB
PURGATAM

None can doubt, that by the *new superstition* is here intended Christianity. Some have questioned the genuinness of this inscription, because, say they, Nero's persecution extended no farther than Rome. The pretense for punishing them there was a charge of having set fire to the city. But it could not be so much as pretended, that they who dwelt in remote countreys were concerned in that fact.

If this be the only objection, the inscription may be reckoned very good. For if the Christians living at Rome were charged with so great a crime, all of that sect in any place would share in the scandal, and might be judged a vile sort of people, fit to be destroyed. And indeed the Christians at Rome were as innocent, as they at the greatest distance. Besides, it will presently appear from Tacitus, that the Christians were then much hated, and that they suffered at Rome, not barely as guilty of setting fire to the City, but also for their supposed enmity to mankind. And Suetonius, in his account of the sufferings of the Christians in this reign, says nothing of any concern in the fire: but only, that they were a *people of a new* and pernicious or *magical superstition*.

Which leads me to observe farther, that the stile of the Inscription is agreeable to that of Tacitus and Suetonius, some of the earliest Heathen writers, who have mentioned the Christians.

If the persecution in Nero's time never became universal, it might take place in some of the provinces, particularly, in that part of Spain, which is now called *Portugal*. The Christian writers, who speak of Nero's persecution, do *(b)* in effect, or expresly say, it was

(*b*) Confulite commentarios vestros. Illic reperietis, primum Neronem in hanc sectam cum maxime Romae orientem Caesareano gladio ferocisse. Sed tali dedicatore

was general: (c) that from Rome it spread into the provinces, and was authorised by public edicts.

A. D. 68.

Though there remain this monument only, there may have been others of the like kind, which have been destroyed out of aversion to the memorie of Nero, or by some of those many accidents, to which all things are liable in a long course of years.

If this inscription be genuine, it is as early an Heathen monument, as we could expect to find remaining concerning Christianity: especially so far off from Judea as Lusitania, now called Portugal. It must have been set up in the life-time of Nero, who died in June, A. D. 68. or at the utmost, before his death was publickly known. For after that no people paid him any honours.

I have shewn, that the stile of this inscription is agreeable to early antiquity. And I have answered the objection taken from the supposed narrow limits of Nero's persecution. Nevertheless it must be acknowledged, that the genuinnesse of it is not assented to by all. Joseph Scaliger *(d)* doubted. Pagi *(e)* and others, have endeavored to

---

dicatore damnationis nostrae etiam gloriamur. *Tertullian. Ap. cap.* 5.

Cum animadverteret Nero, non modo Romae, sed ubique quotidie magnam multitudinem deficere a cultu idolorum .. profiluit ad excidendum coeleste templum, delendamque justitiam, et primus omnium persecutus Dei servos, &c. *Lactant. vel Caecilius de M. P. cap.* 2.

(c) Hoc initio in Christianos saeviri coeptum. Post etiam datis legibus religio vetabatur: palamque edictis propositis Christianum esse non licebat. *Sulp. Sev. Hist. l.* 2. *cap.* 41.

Primus Romae Christianos suppliciis et mortibus affecit, ac per omnes provincias pari persecutione excruciari imperavit. *Oros. l.* 7. *c.* 7.

(d) Neque solum Romae saevitum in Christianos, sed etiam in provinciis. Exstat vetus inscriptio in Hispania loco Pisuerga vocato: in quo sine dubio haec crudelitas tangitur, siquidem vera est illa inscriptio. Nam dubito. *De Emend. Temp. p.* 471.

(e) Pagi *ann.* 64. *n. iv. J. E, I. Walchius De Persecutione Christian. Neroniana in Hispania.*

A. D. 68.

to vindicate it. Some others still (f) hesitate. This monument, they say, has been seen by few or none. And the credit of the first publisher of the inscription is not established above all suspicion of falshood and imposture.

I therefore must not insist upon it, as certainly genuine and ancient: though I could not forbear to propose it to be considered. Nor do I think, that any can dislike my placing it here before my readers.

(f) Exstat celebris haec inscriptio apud Jan. Gruter. p. 238. n. 9. Ipsi vero praestantissimi Hispanorum viri auctoritatem hujus inscriptionis tueri non audent, quippe quam nemo unquam vidit, et Cyriacus Anconitanus primus protulit, homo, quod omnes sciunt, fallax, et, si quis alius, malae fidei. &c. *J. L. Mosbem. Instit. Hist. Ec.* p. 37.

Verum magni homines post Scaligerum dubitant, quid de fide et auctoritate monumenti hujus statuendum sit: et, ut arbitror, justissimas habent dubitandi causas. Nemo enim vel Hispanorum, vel Lusitanorum, lapidem hunc unquam vidit, quod ipsi doctissimi Hispaniae viri non diffitentur. Is vero, si aliquando exstitisset, magnâ certe curâ ob insigne pretium asservatus fuisset. *Id. De Reb. Christian.* p. 109.

CHAP.

CHAP. IV.

PLINY THE ELDER.

CAIUS PLINIUS SECUNDUS, or (a) PLINY THE ELDER, was born at Verona, in the reign of Tiberius. He had divers public posts under the Emperours Vespasian, and Titus. Notwithstanding which, he redeemed a great deal of time for reading, and writing, in which he was indefatigable. He was suffocated in the smoak and ashes of Vesuvius, in the 56. year of his age, and the first year of the reign of Titus, in the year 79. His *Natural History* was published, and inscribed to Vespasian, or, as others think, to Titus, in the year of our Lord 77. before he was Emperour.

A. D. 77.

In his Historie is a chapter concerning the Origin of Magick: Where are these words: " There (b) is another sect of Magici-
" ans, depending on (or deriving from) Moses, and Jamnes, and
                X x 2   " Jotapes,

(a) *Vid. Plin. Ep. l. vi.* 16. *et* 20. *Voff. de H. L. l. i. cap.* 29. *Fabr. Bib. Lat. l.* 2. *c.* 13. *Basnag. Ann.* 77. ii. *et* 79. *v. Tillem. H. E. Tite. art. vi. Crevier's History of the Roman Emperours. B. xvii. vol.* 6. *p.* 291.

(b) Est et alia Magicis factio, a Mose et Jamne, et Jotape Judaeis pendens, sed multis millibus annorum post Zoroastrem. Tanto recentior est Cypria. *Plin. Nat. Hist. l.* 30. *cap. i, De Origine Magicae artis, quando, et a quibus ceperat. &c.*

A. D. 77. "Jotapes, who were Jews, but many thousand years since Zoroaster. Still so much later is the Cyprian."

Some have thought, that in this last Plinie refers to the blindnesse inflicted by St. Paul on Elymas the sorcerer in the presence of Sergius Paulus, Proconsul of Cyprus, and related in Acts xiii. But I do not affirm it.

CHAP.

CHAP. V.
TACITUS.

I. *His Hiſtorie, Time, and Works.* II. *Pomponia Graecina, a Roman Lady, accuſed of a foreign Superſtition in the year of Chriſt* 57. *the fourth year of Nero's Reign.* III. *His Account of Nero's Perſecution of the Chriſtians.* IV. *His Teſtimonie to the Jewiſh War, and the Deſtruction of Jeruſalem by Titus.*

I. CAIUS CORNELIUS TACITUS, (*a*) whoſe anceſtors are unknown, was *(b)* older than the younger Plinie, who was born in the year of our Lord 61. or 62. In the year 77. or 78. he married the daughter of Cnaeius Julius Agricola (*c*) famous for his conſulſhip, and government of Britain. He *(d)* enjoyed

A. D. 100.

His Hiſtorie, and Works.

(*a*) *Vid. G. J. Voſſ. de Hiſt. Lat. Liſi Vit. Tacit. Fabric. Bib. Lat. Tom. i. Bayle Dictiou. Tillemont H. E. Trajan. art.* 27.
(*b*) Equidem adoleſcentulus, quum jam tu famâ gloriâque floreres, te ſequi, tibi longo, ſed proximus, intervallo, et eſſe et haberi concupiſcebam. *Plin. l.* 7. *Ep.* 20.
(*c*) Conſul egregiae tum ſpei filiam juveni mihi deſpondit, ac poſt conſulatum collocavit, et ſtatim Britanniae praepoſitus eſt, adjecto pontificatus ſacerdotio. *Tacit. Vit. Agr. cap.* 9.
(*d*) *Vid. Tacit. Hiſt. l. i. cap.* 1.

A. D. 100. joyed divers pofts of honour and truft under Vefpafian, and the following Emperous. He was Praetor of Rome, under Domitian, in 88. and Conful, in the fhort reign of Nerva, in 97. The year was opened by *Nerva and T. Virginius Rufus*, who were then both of them the third time Confuls. *Virginius Rufus*, who was a man of great eminence, and then of a great age, died in his confulfhip. Whereupon (*e*) Tacitus was fubflituted in his room, and pronounced his panegyric.

But, as has been often obferved, his writings have gained him more honour than all his dignities. His works feem to have been publifhed by him in this order: firft his *Defcription of Germanie*, next *the Life of Agricola*, his father-in-law, after that his *Hiftorie*, begining with Galba, and ending at the death of Domitian, and laftly, his *Annals*, begining with Tiberius, and ending at the death of Nero. Both thefe works are now imperfect.

Tacitus and Plinie the Younger lived together in intimate friendfhip. They (*f*) revifed each others writings before publication. Divers of Plinie's letters are writ to him, in particular, thofe (*g*) two, wherein Plinie gives an account of the eruption of Vefuvius, and the death of his uncle. They were fent as memoirs, to be inferted by Tacitus in his Hiftories.

It is allowed, that (*h*) Tacitus flourifhed in the firft centurie. I therefore

---

(*e*) Laudatus eft a confule Cornelio Tacito. Nam hic fupremus felicitati ejus cumulus acceflit, laudator eloquentiffimus, &c. *Plin. l. i. ep.* 2.

(*f*) Librum tuum legi, et quam diligentiffime potui, annotavi quae commutanda, quae eximenda arbitrarer... Nunc a te librum meum cum annotationibus tuis exfpecto. O jucundas, o pulchras vices. *Plin. l.* 7. *ep.* 20. *Vid. et l.* 8. *ep.* 7.

(*g*) Petis, ut tibi avunculi mei exitum fcribam, quo verius tradere pofteris poffis. Gratias ago. Nam video, morti ejus, fi celebretur a te, immortalem gloriam effe propofitam. *L.* 6. *ep.* 16. *Vid. et ep.* 20.

(*h*) Tacite.... Hiftorien Romain, a fleuri dans le premier ficcle. *Bayle Diction.*

Of Pomponia Graecina.

therefore place him here in the year 100. the third of the Emperour Trajan. And though the two laſt, and principal of his works, were not publiſhed, till ſome time after, undoubtedly, he was now employed in collecting materials for them, and in compoſing them. Nor did either of them come down any lower, than the death of Domitian.

A. D. 100.

II. In his Annals, at the year of our Lord 57. he writes thus: "And *(i)* POMPONIA GRAECINA, a Lady of eminent quality, married to *Plautius*, who upon his return from Britain had the honour of an ovation, being accuſed of practiſing a foreign ſuperſtition, was referred to the cogniſance of her huſband. And he, according to ancient inſtitution, in the preſence of the familie, ſat in judgement upon the life and reputation of his wife, and pronounced her innocent. *Pomponia* lived to a great age, and in perpetual ſorrow, after the death of Julia daughter of Druſus, procured by the intrigues of Meſſalina. For the ſpace of forty years ſhe wore no habit but that of mourning, nor admitted any ſentiments, but thoſe of grief. And this behaviour, which in the reign of Claudius eſcaped with impunity, afterwards redounded to her glory."

Pomponia Graecina.

As it was about fourteen years from the death of Julia to this trial of *Pomponia*, Lipſius *(k)* ſuſpects the reading of *forty years:* and his emendation is approved by ſome, rejected by others. I rather think it

---

(i) Et Pomponia Graecina inſignis femina, Plautio, qui ovans ſe de Britanniis rettulit, nupta, ac ſuperſtitionis externae rea, mariti judicio permiſſa. Iſque priſco inſtituto, propinquis coram, de capite famaque conjugis cognovit, et inſontem nuntiavit. Longa huic Pomponiae aetas, et continua triſtitia fuit. Nam poſt Juliam Druſi filiam dolo Meſſalinae interfectam, per quadraginta annos, non cultu niſi lugubri, non animo niſi maeſto egit. Idque illi imperitante Claudio impune, mox ad gloriam vertit. *Tacit. Ann* *l.* 13. *c.* 32.

(k) Vid. Not. ad loc.

A. D.
100.

it to be right, as it is in all copies. Nor does Tacitus compute from the death of Julia to the time of this trial, but to the time of *Pomponia*'s death. She lived, he says, to a great age. *And all the time from the death of Julia to her own death, which was the space of forty years, she was a perpetual mourner.*

This *foreign*, or extraneous *superstition*, of which *Pomponia* was accused, is supposed by Lipsius, in his (*) notes, and by *(l)* others to be the Christian Religion. And we may be inclined to that opinion. But we cannot be certain of it. I have transcribed the whole account of this Lady, that every one may the better judge for himself.

Nero's Persecution of the Christians

III. After a description of the terrible fire at Rome, in the tenth of Nero, and the 64. of our Lord, in which a large part of the City was consumed, and an account of the orders given for rebuilding and beautifying it, and the methods used to appease the anger of the gods, Tacitus adds: " But (*m*) neither all human help, nor the
" liberality

(*) *Superstitionis externae rea.*] Christianismi credo accusatam, sive, ut tunc confundebant, Judaismi. *Lipsius in loc.*
Forte Christianam pietatem intelligit. Nam apparet, sanctam mulierem fuisse Pomponiam Graecinam. Tacitus loquitur ut Ethnicus. *Rhenanus in loc.*
(*l*) Christi doctrinam a Pomponia fuisse degustatam, non immerito conjicimus. *Basnag. Ann.* 57. *p. ii.* Pomponia Graecina fut accusée de suivre une superstition étrangere, dit Tacite : ce qui se peut entendre du Christianisme. *Tillem. Neron. art. v.*
(*m*) Sed non ope humana, non largitionibus Principis, aut deum placamentis decedebat infamia, quin jussum incendium credebatur. Ergo abolendo rumori Nero subdidit reos, et quaesitissimis poenis affecit, quos per flagitia invisos, vulgus Christianos appellabat. Auctor nominis ejus Christus, qui Tiberio imperante, per procuratorem Pontium Pilatum supplicio affectus erat. Repressa in praesens exitiabilis superstitio rursus erumpebat, non modo per Judaeam, originem ejus mali, sed per Urbem etiam, quo cuncta undique atrocia aut pudenda confluunt, celebranturque. Igitur primo correpti qui fatebantur, deinde indicio eorum multitudo ingens, haud perinde in crimine incendii, quam odio humani generis

Ch. V. His Testimonie to Nero's Persecution.

"liberality of the Emperour, nor all the atonements presented to
"the gods, availed to abate the infamie he lay under of having or-
"dered the City to be set on fire. To suppress therefore this com-
"mon rumour, Nero procured others to be accused, and inflicted
"exquisite punishments upon those people, who were in abhorrence
"for their crimes, and were commonly known by the name of
"Christians. They had their denomination from CHRISTUS, who
"in the reign of *Tiberius* was put to death as a criminal by the Pro-
"curator *Pontius Pilate*. This pernicious superstition, though
"checked for a while, broke out again, and spread not only over
"Judea, the source of this evil, but reached the City also: whither
"flow from all quarters all things vile and shameful, and where
"they find shelter and encouragement. At first they only were
"apprehended, who confessed themselves of that sect: afterwards a
"vast multitude, discovered by them. All which were condemned,
"not so much for the crime of burning the City, as for their en-
"mity to mankind. Their executions were so contrived, as to ex-
"pose them to derision and contempt. Some were covered over
"with the skins of wild beasts, and torn to pieces by dogs. Some
"were crucified. Others, having been daubed over with combus-
"tible materials, were set up as lights in the night-time, and thus
"burned to death. Nero made use of his own gardens as a theatre
"upon this occasion, and also exhibited the diversions of the Cir-
"cus, sometimes standing in the crowd, as a spectator, in the habit
"of a charioteer, at other times driving a chariot himself. Till at
"length these men, though really criminal, and deserving exempla-

neris convicti sunt. Et pereuntibus addita ludibria, ut ferarum tergis contecti, laniatu canum interirent, aut crucibus affixi, aut flammandi, atque ubi defecisset dies, in usum nocturni luminis urerentur. Hortos suos ei spectaculo Nero obtulerat, et Circense ludicrum edebat, habitu aurigae permixtus plebi vel circulo [curriculo legit Lipsius] insistens. Unde quamquam adversus sontes, et novissima exempla meritos, miseratio oriebatur, tanquam non utilitate publica, sed in saevitiam unius absumerentur. *Ann. l. xv. c.* 44.

"rie

"rie punishment, began to be commiserated, as people who were destroyed, not out of a regard to the public welfare, but only to gratify the cruelty of one man."

Divers facts of the evangelical historie are here attested: That our Saviour was put to death as a malefactor by *Pontius Pilate*, Procurator under *Tiberius*: That from *Christ* the people, called Christians, had their name and sentiments: That this superstition, or religion, had it's rise in Judea, where also it spread, notwithstanding the ignominious death of the founder of it, and the opposition, which his followers met with from the people of that countrey afterwards: that thence it was propagated into other parts of the world, and as far as Rome: where in the tenth, or eleventh year of Nero, and before, Christians were very numerous: and that the professors of this religion were reproached, and hated, and underwent many and grievous sufferings. Certainly, the great number of Christians at Rome, at this time, and their sufferings, are two things very observable.

And though they were so hated, and Tacitus himself is so much offended with them; he owns, the cruelty, with which they were treated, was so excessive, as to excite compassion. Nay, it seems, their destruction was looked upon by many, not as a public benefit, but an act of savage cruelty. Which shews, after all, that they were not such monsters of wickedness, as they are here represented.

And all this guilt, this enmity to mankind, which Tacitus imputes to them, could be nothing else, as has been well observed (*o*) by

---

(*o*) Tacitus libro xv. . . de Christianorum suppliciis. . . . Ubi *flagitia*, et *odium humani generis*, nihil aliud sunt, quam falsorum deorum neglectus. Quam eandem caussam etiam Judaeis maledicendi Tacitus habuit, et Plinius major, cui Judaei dicuntur *gens contumeliâ numinum insignis*. Cleric. Annot. ad Grot. de Ver. Rel. Christian. l. 2. §. ii.

by learned men, but their neglect of the ordinarie worſhip of the gods.

It will not be difagreeable to compare this article of *Tacitus*, with the account of the fire at Rome, and the enſuing perſecution of the Chriſtians, which is given by *Sulpicius Severus*, an elegant Chriſtian writer of hiſtorie, and in the Latin tongue, who flouriſhed about the year 400.

" In (*) the mean time, ſays Sulpicius, when the number of
" the Chriſtians was greatly encreaſed, there happened a fire at Rome,
" whilſt Nero was at Antium. Neverthelefs the general opinion of
" all men caſt the blame of the fire upon the Emperour. And it
" was ſuppoſed, that his aim therein was, that he might have the
" glorie of raiſing the city again in greater ſplendour. Nor could he
" by any means ſuppreſs the common rumour, that the fire was
" owing to his orders. He therefore endeavored to caſt the reproach
" of it upon the Chriſtians. And exquiſite tortures were inflicted
" upon innocent men. And moreover new kinds of death were in-
" vented. Some were tied up in the ſkins of wild-beaſts, that they
" might be worried to death by dogs. Many were crucified. Others
" were burnt to death. And they were ſet up as lights in the night-
" time.

(*) Interea, abundante jam Chriſtianorum multitudine, accidit, ut Roma incendio conflagraret, Nerone aqud Antium conſtituto. Sed opinio omnium invidiam incendii in Principem retorquebat, credebaturque Imperator gloriam innovandae urbis quaeſiſſe. Neque ulla re Nero efficiebat, quin ab eo juſſum incendium putaretur. Igitur vertit invidiam in Chriſtianos, actaeque in innoxios crudeliſſimae quaeſtiones. Quin et novae mortes excogitatae, ut ferarum tergis contecti, laniatu canum interirent. Multi crucibus affixi, aut flammâ uſti. Plerique in id reſervati, ut cum defeciſſet dies, in uſum nocturni luminis urerentur. Hoc initio in Chriſtianos faeviri coeptum. Poſt etiam, datis legibus religio vetabatur: palamque edictis propoſitis, Chriſtianum eſſe non licebat. Tum Paulus ac Petrus capitis damnati: quorum uni cervix gladio defecta, Petrus in crucem ſublatus eſt. *Sulp. Sever. Sacr. Hiſt. lib.* 2. *cap.* 41. *al. cap.* 29.

A. D. 100.

" time. This was the begining of the perfecution of the Chriftians. Afterwards the profeffion of the Chriftian Religion was prohibited by laws: and edicts were publifhed, that no man might be a Chriftian. At that time Paul and Peter were condemned to death. The former was beheaded, Peter was crucified."

So writes Sulpicius. It is not unlikely, that he had read Tacitus. However, I think, it ought alfo to be fuppofed, that he had other Memoirs befides.

Sulpicius fays, that Nero was at Antium, when the fire began. The (††) fame thing is obferved by Tacitus, who alfo fays, that Nero did not come to Rome, till the fire had approached his own palace, which at length with every thing near it was confumed.

Of the Deftruction of Jerufalem by Titus.

IV. It is not needful for me to tranflate, or tranfcribe all that Tacitus fays of the Jewifh people, of (p) whofe original he was ignorant, and writes very abfurdly, and therefore is called by Tertullian (q) a great liar. Nor need I tranflate exactly his hiftorie of the Jewifh war. I obferve however thefe following particulars.

He fays, that (r) Judea was firft brought into fubjection to the Romans by Pompey. After which he gives a fummarie account of their affairs under *Herod*, and his fons, the Emperours *Auguftus, Tiberius, Caligula, Claudius, Nero*. " He mentions (s) *Felix*, whom
" he

---

†† Eo in tempore Nero Antii agens, non ante in Urbem regreffus eft, quam domui ejus, quâ palatium et maecenatis hortos continuaverat, ignis propinquaret. Neque tamen fifti potuit, quin et palatium et domus et cuncta circum haurirentur. *Tacit. Ann. l.* 15. *cap.* 39.

(p) *Tacit. Hift. l. v. cap.* 2.

(q) Cornelius Tacitus, fane ille mendaciorum loquaciffimus. *Apol. cap.* 16. *p.* 17. *A.*

(r) Romanorum primus Cn. Pompejus Judaeos domuit, templumque jure victoriae ingreffus eft. *H. l. v. cap.* 9.

(s) Claudius defunctis regibus, aut ad modicum reductis, Judaeam provinciam equitibus Romanis aut libertis permifit, e quibus Antonius Felix, per omnem faevitiam

Ch. V. *His Testimonie to the Destruction of Jerusalem.* 349
" he represents as a bad man, and tyrannical in his government. A. D.
" However, the Jews, he says, bore the exactions of their Gover- 100.
                                            " nours

tiam ac libidinem, jus regium servili ingenio exercuit... Duravit tamen patientia Judaeis, usque ad Gessium Florum procuratorem. Sub eo bellum ortum, et comprimere coeptantem Cestium Gallum Syriae legatum, varia proelia ac saepius adversa excepere. Qui ubi fato aut taedio occidit, missu Neronis, Vespasianus fortuna famaque et egregiis ministris intra duas aestates cuncta camporum, omnesque praeter Hierosolyma urbes, victore exercitu tenebat. Proximus annus civili bello intentus, quantum ad Judaeos per otium transiit. Pace per Italiam parta, et externae curae rediere. Augebat iras, quod soli Judaei non cessissent. Simul manere apud exercitus Titum ad omnes principatus novi eventus casusve utilius videbatur. [Ejusdem anni principio Caesar Titus perdomandae Judaeae delectus a patre. [*Lib.* v. *cap. i. in.*] Igitur castris, uti diximus, ante moenia Hierosolymorum positis, instructas legiones ostentavit. Judaei sub ipsos muros struxere aciem... Mox cessere hostes, et sequentibus diebus crebra pro portis praelia ferebant, donec assiduis damnis, intra moenia pellerentur. Romani ad oppugnandum versi. Neque dignum videbatur, famem hostium opperiri. Poscebant que pericula, pars virtute, multi ferocia, et cupidine praemiorum. Ipsi Tito Roma, et opes, voluptatesque ante oculos: ac ni statim Hierosolyma conciderent, morari videbantur. Sed urbem arduam situ, opera molesque firmaverant, quis vel plana satis munirentur. Nam duos colles immensum editos claudebant

muri per artem obliqui, aut introrsus sinuati. [Conf. l. 2. cap. 4]... Alia intus moenia, regiae circumjecta. Conspicuoque fastigio turris Antonia, in honorem M. Antonii ab Herode appellata. Templum in modum arcis, propriique muri, labore et opere ante alios. Ipsae porticus, quis templum ambiebatur, egregium propugnaculum. Fons perennis aquae, cavati sub terra montes, et piscinae cisternaeque servandis imbribus ... magna colluvie, et ceterarum urbium clade avecti. Nam pervicacissimus quisque illuc perfugerat, eoque seditiosius agebant. Tres duces, totidem exercitus. Extrema et latissima moenium Simon. Mediam urbem Joannes, quem et. Bargioram vocabant. templum Eleazarus firmaverat. Multitudine et armis Joannes ac Simon, Eleazarus loco pollebat. Sed proelia, dolus, incendia, inter ipsos, et magna vis frumenti ambusta. Mox Joannes, missis per speciem sacrificandi, qui Eleazarum manumque ejus obtruncarent, templo potitur. Ita in duas factiones civitas discessit, donec propinquantibus Romanis, bellum externum concordiam pareret. Evenerant prodigia, quae neque hostiis, neque votis piare fas habet gens superstitioni obnoxia, religionibus adversa. Visae per coelum concurrere acies, rutilantia arma, et subito nubium igne collucere templum. Expassae repente delubri fores, et audita major humanà vox, *Excedere deos:* simul ingens motus excedentium. Quae pauci in metum trahebant: pluribus persuasio inerat, antiquis sacerdotium literis, contineri,

T A C I T U S. Ch. V.

A. D. 100.

" nours, till the time of their Procurator *Geſſius Florus*, under whom
" the war began. *Ceſtius Gallus*, Prefident of Syria, came to his
" affiſtance. But he being defeated, Nero ſent Vefpafian into Ju-
" dea, who was a General of great merit and reputation, and hav-
" ing alſo under him good officers, in the ſpace of two years, [*mean-*
" *ing the years* 67. *and* 68.] he reduced the open countrey, and all
" the cities of Judea, excepting Jeruſalem. The next year [69.]
" was taken up in civil wars. [*meaning the time of the ſhort reigns*
" *of Galba, Otho, Vitellius, till the acceſſion of Veſpaſian.*] The fol-
" lowing year, [and the begining of it,] Titus was appointed to at-
" tend the affairs of Judea. Who now drew near to Jeruſalem, and
" beſieged it. Tacitus ſuppoſeth, that Titus was in haſte to go to
" Rome, to enjoy the pleaſures and ſplendour of the City. He there-
" fore carried on the ſiege with the greateſt vigour. The armie
" likewiſe was intent upon plunder, and eager to gratify their revenge.
" The city however was ſtrong by ſituation, and with good walls
" and ramparts. The high tower Antonia, conſpicuous from far.
" The temple itſelf was like a citadel, well fortified. They had a
" fountain of water that ran continually, and the mountains were
" hollowed under ground. Moreover they had pools and ciſterns
" for preſerving rain-water. And there was a great confluence of
" people. For the men of the other cities that had been redu-
" ced, and in general all the turbulent and ſeditious people of the
" nation,

tineri, eo ipſo tempore fore, ut valeſceret Oriens, profectique Judaeâ rerum poti- rentur. Quae ambages Veſpaſianum ac Titum praedixerant. Sed vulgus, more humanae cupidinis ſibi tantam fatorum magnitudinem interpretati, ne adverſis quidem ad vera mutabantur. Multitudi- nem obſeſſorum, omnis aetatis, virile ac muliebre ſexus, ſexcenta millia fuiſſe ac- cepimus. Arma cunctis, qui ferre poſ- ſent: et plures quam pro numero aude- bant. Obſtinatio viris feminiſque par. Ac ſi transferre ſedes cogerentur, major vitae metus quam mortis. Hanc adver- ſus urbem gentemque Caeſar Titus, quan- do impetus et ſubita belli locus abnueret, aggeribus vineiſque certare ſtatuit. Di- viduntur legionibus munia, et quies prae- liorum fuit : donec cuncta expugnandis urbibus reperta apud veteres, aut novis ingeniis, ſtruerentur. *Tacit. Hiſt. lib. v. cap.* 9. . . . 13.

Ch. V. *His Testimonie to the Destruction of Jerusalem.*

" nation, came hither. There were three captains, [or heads of
" factions,] and as many armies, *Simon*, *John*, called also *Bargioras*,
" and *Eleazar*, who occupied several parts of the city. Among
" themselves they had fierce contentions, and therein great quantities
" of provisions were consumed. *Eleazar* being killed, they were
" reduced to two factions. These fought with each other, till the
" near approach of the Romans obliged them to agreement. There
" were many prodigies, foresignifying their ruin, which were not to
" be averted by all the sacrifices and vows of that people, supersti-
" tious in their own way of worship, though different from all o-
" thers. Armies were seen fighting in the air, with brandished wea-
" pons. A fire fell upon the temple from the clouds. The doors
" of the temple were suddenly opened. At the same time there
" was a loud voice, declaring, that the gods were removing. Which
" was accompanied with the sound as of a multitude going out.
" All which things were supposed by some to portend great cala-
" mities. But the most had a strong persuasion, that it was said in
" the ancient writings of the Priests [*that is, ancient writings in the
" custodie of the Priests*,] that at that very time the East should pre-
" vail, and that some who came from Judea should obtain the em-
" pire of the world. Which ambiguities foretold Vespasian and
" Titus. But the common people, according to the usual influence
" of human passions, having once appropriated to themselves this
" vast grandeur of the fates, could not be brought to understand the
" true meaning by all their adversities. We have been assured, that
" the number of the besieged amounted to six hundred thousand. And
" more bore arms than could have been expected from that number.
" For great was the resolution of all, both men and women. Against
" this city and people was *Titus* sent. As the city could not be ta-
" ken by assault, different posts were assigned to the several legions.
" Battering engines of all kinds were prepared. And all the me-
" thods hitherto practised in sieges by the ancients, as well as new
" inventions, were employed on this occasion."

A. D.
100.

So

So writes Tacitus, who could and might have been more particular in his hiſtorie of the Jewiſh War in the ſeveral parts of that countrey, and likewiſe of the ſiege of Jeruſalem. But his diſlike of the ſubject, as it ſeems, and his love of brevity, have made him very conciſe.

However, it is not unlikely that in the next book, which, with all the following books of that work, is loſt, there was an account of the triumph of Veſpaſian and Titus at Rome in the following year. Nor is it unreaſonable to ſuppoſe, that there were alſo ſome more particulars concerning the event of the ſiege of Jeruſalem. But what they were, we cannot now ſay.

It is alſo worth our while to obſerve, that in this fifth book of his Hiſtorie, from which the preceding article has been taken, at his entrance upon his account of the war, he ſays, " he (*t*) was going to relate the final end of the renowned city of Jeruſalem."

He likewiſe takes notice, " That (*u*) Jeruſalem was the capital city of Judea, and that the temple there had in it immenſe riches."

Nor ſhould we omit to obſerve, that in the firſt chapter of this book he has reckoned up the forces, with which Veſpaſian was furniſhed for carrying on this war, and not very diſagreeably to Joſephus. " For (*x*) he mentions the three Legions quartered in Ju-
" dea,

(*t*) Sed quia famoſae urbis ſupremum diem tradituri ſumus, &c. *Hiſtor. l.* 5. *cap.* 2. *in.*

(*u*) Magna pars Judaeae vicis diſpergitur. Habent et oppida. Hieroſolyma genti caput: Illic immenſae opulentiae templum, &c. *Ibid. cap.* 8.

(*x*) Ejuſdem anni principio, Caeſar Titus perdomandae Judaeae delectus a patre.... Tres enim in Judaea legiones, quinta et decima, et quintadecima, vetus Veſpaſiani miles excepere. Tradidit et Syria duodecimam, et adductos Alexandriâ duo et vicesimanos tertianoſque. Comitabantur,

Ch. V. *His Testimonie to the Destruction of Jerusalem.*

" dea, the twelfth brought in from Syria, and other legions from
" Alexandria, beside the armies of the Roman allies, the kings *A-*
" *grippa, Sohemus*, and *Antiochus*, and a large body of Arabians, al-
" ways averse to the Jews, and some volunteers of distinction even
" from Rome and Italie, who were willing to serve under *Titus*, a
" General of such renown, and expectation, desirous to signalize
" their valour before him, and thereby to recommend themselves to
" his favour."

And though we do not find in Tacitus every thing that we might
wish for; certainly what we have in his remaining works is a very
valuable testimonie to the accomplishment of our Lord's predictions
concerning the destruction of Jerusalem, and the overthrow of the
Jewish people.

He must have read Josephus. Many things are evidently taken
from him. However he differs from him sometimes. It is somewhat strange, that he should not compute a greater number within
Jerusalem at the time of the siege, than *six hundred thousand*. How
shall we account for this? I answer, that perhaps Tacitus had
met with some other accounts of the Jewish War, beside that of
Josephus. And I am apt to think it not unreasonable to believe,
that Tacitus never read Josephus with so much care and diligence,
as we Christians have since read him. Moreover, *six hundred thousand* may be a certain number, used for an uncertain, denoting, that the city was then very full of people, and not intending
to say, there were no more.

---

mitabantur viginti sociae cohortes, octo
equitum alae. Simul Agrippa, Sohemus-
que reges, et auxilia regisAntiochi, valida-
que et solito inter accolas odio infensa Judaeis Arabum manus. Multi, quos Urbe atque Italia suâ quemque spes accive-
rat occupandi Principem adhuc vacuum:
His cum copiis fines hostium ingressus,
composito agmine, cuncta explorans, pa-
ratusque decernere, haud procul Hierofolymis castra facit. *Tacit. Hist. l.* 5.
cap. i.

CHAP. VI.

MARTIAL.

I. *His Time, and Writings.* II. *His Testimonie to the Fortitude of Christians.*

A. D. 100.
His Time, and Writings.

I. MARTIAL, *(a)* or *M. Valerius Martialis*, author of fourteen books of Epigrams, was born at Bilbilis in Spain, in the reign of Claudius. He is suppofed to have come to Rome in the reign of Nero, when he was about twenty years of age, and to have lived there thirty years, beloved by the Emperours, especially Domitian, after whofe death he retired into his own countrey. As he lived long enough to *(b)* write fome Epigrams in commendation of Nerva and Trajan, I have placed him fo low as the laft year of the firft centurie, and *(c)* the third of Trajan. He was intimate with Juvenal, and well acquainted with Plinie the Younger. Martial

---

(a) Vid. Voff. de Poet. Lat. Tillemont H. E. Domitien. art. 23.
(b) Vid. L. 12. *Epigr. v. . . . ix. L. xi.* 4. 5. *x.* 34.
(c) . . . Domitiani, Nervae, et Traja-ni, tempora ingenio fuo illuftravit. Senex autem, Urbe relicta, patriam fuam repetens, in illa obiit fub eodem Trajano. Fabric. Bib. Lat. l. 2. *c.* 20. *De M. V. Martiali.*

tial was poor. When *(d)* he left Rome, Plinie made him a handſome preſent. And when he heard of his death, he lamented it very affectionatly.

II. This writer has been ſuppoſed to refer to the patient fortitude of Chriſtians, in voluntarily enduring the greateſt pains, rather than ſacrifice to the gods, or do any thing contrarie to the principles of their religion.

"You *(e)* have, perhaps, lately ſeen acted in the theatre Mucius, who thruſt his hand into the fire. If you think ſuch an one patient, valiant, ſtout, you are a mere ſenſleſs dotard. For it is a much greater thing, when threatened with the troubleſome coat, to ſay, I do not ſacrifice, than to obey the command, Burn the hand."

However, the two laſt verſes of the epigram may be otherwiſe rendred, after this manner: "For it is a much greater thing, when threatened with the troubleſome coat, you are commanded to burn your hand, to ſay: I will not."

But I can ſee no reaſon for bringing in the *troubleſome coat*, to oblige a man to act the part of *Mucius* in the theatre. And I much rather incline to the ſenſe given in the firſt tranſlation.

I ſhall

(d) Audio, Valerium Martialem deceſſiſſe. Et moleſte fero. Erat homo ingenioſus, acutus, acer, et qui plurimum in ſcribendo et ſalis haberet et fellis, nec candoris minus. Proſequutus eram eum viatico diſcedentem. Dederam hoc amicitiae: dederam etiam verſiculis, quos de me compoſuit. Plin. Lib. 3. Ep. 21.

(e) In matutina nuper ſpectatus arena
    Mucius, impoſuit qui ſua membra focis,
  Si patiens fortiſque tibi duruſque videtur,
    Abderitanae pectora plebis habes.
Nam cum dicatur, tunicâ praeſente moleſtâ,
  Ure manum, plus eſt dicere: Non facio.
                    Martial. l. x. Epigr. 25.

I shall therefore place below the remarks *(f)* of *Stephen Le Moyne* upon this epigram, who makes no doubt, that *Martial* refers to the Christians, and declares, that what *Mucius* did, is not comparable to the resolution of Christians under the sufferings, which they endured.

The *troublesome coat*, or shirt, here mentioned, a cruelty, which, as we have before learned from *Tacitus*, the innocent Christians unjustly suffered, was made like a sack, of paper, or coarse linen cloth. And having been first besmeared within and without, with pitch, wax, rosin, sulphur, and such like combustible materials, or dipt all over in them, was put upon the person, for whom it was appointed. And that he might be kept upright, the more to resemble a flaming torch, his chin was fastened to a stake fixed in the ground.

That this was esteemed a cruel death, is manifest from *Seneca*, who describing the greatest causes of fear, writes to this purpose. "Imagine *(g)* here, says he, a prison, crosses, and racks, and "the hook, and a stake, thrust through the body, and coming
"out

(f) Facinus Mucii, non videtur, inquit Martialis, cum fortitudine Christianorum comparandum. Ille ustulandam manum suam flammis exhibuit, ut ista constantia reliquum corpus suum servaret. Sed Christiani totum corpus igni vorandum tradunt, immo igni lento : et patiuntur se supervestiri cereo indumento, ut instar cereorum ardeant : quod tamen possent declinare, si vellent, et si religioni popularium suorum, et sacris Imperatoris, faciles se alligarent. Sed malunt in cineres et favillas redigi, et se vivos ardere, quam sacrificare, vel thura adolere : et cum ad id compelluntur, dicunt : Non facio, non sacrifico. . . . Et tunicae molestae praesens et tremendum supplicium illos a sacris suis non potest avellere, vel minimum terrere. *St. Le Moyne Varia Sacra. p.* 1041. 1042. *Vid. et Kortholt. De Persecutionib. primit. Ec. p.* 25.

(g) Cogita hoc loco carcerem, et cruces, et eculeos, et uncum, et adactum per medium hominem, qui per os emergat, stipitem, et distracta in diversum actis curribus membra, illam tunicam, alimentis ignium et illitam et intextam : quicquid aliud, praeter haec, commenta saevitia est. Non est itaque mirum, si maximus hujus rei timor est, cujus et varietas magna, et apparatus terribilis est. *Senec. Ep.* 14.

"out at the mouth, and the limbs torn by chariots pulling adverse
"ways, and that coat besmeared and interwoven with combustible
"materials, nutriment for fire, and whatever else, beside these, cru-
"elty has invented. It is no wonder, if in such a case fear riseth
"high, where the variety of evils is so great, and the preparation
"is so terrible."

It is hence apparent, that this was one of the worst punishments, which cruelty had invented.

I do not know, but some may think, I ought to have quoted this passage of *Seneca*, not only as a description of this coat, and the cruelty of it, but also as an allusion to the sufferings of the Christians, who felt it in so great numbers. For Seneca's death happened not *(h)* before April in the year 65. Whereas the fire at Rome began in July the preceding year, and the persecution of the Christians *(i)* commenced in November following. But, in my opinion, it is better not to insist upon any reference here to the sufferings of the Christians.

(h) See Tillemont. Neron. art. xxii.
(i) See the Supplement to the Credibility, &c. ch. xi. vol. 2 p. 139.

C H A P.

CHAP. VII.

JUVENAL.

I. *His Time and Writings.* II. *His Teſtimonie to Nero's Perſecution of the Chriſtians.* III. *His Teſtimonie to Domitian's Perſecution.* IV. *An Obſervation concerning Seneca, the Philoſopher.*

A. D. 100.
His Time, and Writings.

I. *D*Ecimus *Junius Juvenalis (a) or* JUVENAL, author of ſixteen Satyrs, which we ſtill have, is computed to have flouriſhed in the reigns of Domitian, Nerva, Trajan and Adrian. And as *Lipſius* well ſays, he *(b)* was contemporarie with Plinie the Younger, Tacitus, and others of that age. Nevertheleſs we do not find Juvenal at all mentioned in any of the letters of Plinie, now extant. I place him next to his friend Martial, and in the ſame year, the laſt of the firſt centurie of the Chriſtian epoch.

II. He

(*a*) *Vid. Lipſ. Epiſt. Qu. l. 4. Ep. 20. Fabr. Bib. Lat. l. 2. cap. 18. Tillem. H. E. Domitien. art. 24.*

(*b*) Ergo, meo arbitrio, compar Juvenalis Plinio juniori, Tacito, et illi claſſi fuit. *Lipſ. l. c.*

Ch. VII. *JUVENAL. &c.* 359

A. D. 100.

II. He seems to refer to Nero's persecution of the Christians in some lines (c) of his first Satyr, which are thus translated by Mr. Dryden.

His Testimonie to Nero's Persecution.

But if that honest licence now you take:
If into rogues omnipotent you rake:
Death is your doom, impaled upon a stake,
Smear'd o're with wax, and set on fire, to light
The Streets, and make a dreadful blaze by night.

Or, more literally. "Describe a great villain, such as was Tigel-
"linus: (*a corrupt Minister under Nero:*) and you shall suffer the
"same punishment with those, who stand burning in their own
"flame and smoak, their head being held up by a stake fixed to their
"chin, till they make a long stream (*of bloud and running sulphur*)
"on the ground."

It (d) is the opinion of *Joseph Scaliger*, and many other learned men, that Nero's cruelties to the Christians are here intended. And, that some punishments of men accused of magick in the reign of Nero, are here referred to, is affirmed by an (e) ancient Scholiast upon this place of Juvenal. Who (f) likewise speaks of them as exhibited

(c) Pone Tigellinum, teda lucebis in illa,
Quâ stantes ardent, qui fixo gutture fumant,
Et latum mediâ sulcum deducit arenâ.
Juven. Sat. i. ver. 155. &c.

(d) Scholia Juvenalis: *Nero maleficos homines teda et popyro et cera supervestiebat, et sic ad ignem admoveri jubebat, ut arderent.* Haec Scholiastes ille in illos versus Juvenalis, qui sine dubio de Christianis dicti sunt. *Jos. Scaliger. Animadv. in Euseb. Chron.* p. 197. *Videatur Id. De Emendat. Temp. l. v.* p. 471.

(e) *Vid. not.* (d)
(f) Idem Scholiastes: *Vivus ardebis, quemadmodum in munere Neronis vivi arserunt, de quibus ille jussit cereos fieri, ut lucerent spectatoribus, quum fixa essent guttura, ne se curvarent. Id. Scalig. l. c.* p. 197. *Et vide annot. ad Juvenalis locum.*

A. D. 100.

bited for a spectacle: as is particularly described by Tacitus. And Suetonius (as we shall presently see) calls the Christians, *men of a new and magical superstition.*

In another Satyr *(g)* Juvenal speaks of the pitched shirt, or troublesome coat, which they were covered with, who were condemned to that punishment. And I shall place below *(h)* a part of *Prateus*'s note upon that place.

His Testimonie to Domitian's Persecution.

III. In another Satyr Juvenal speaks of the death of *Domitian* in this manner. "Many *(i)* illustrious men he destroyed, who found "no avenger. At last he perished, when he became formidable to "the rabble. This ruined him, who long before was stained with "the noble bloud of the Lamiae."

The verses are thus translated by Mr. *Stepny.*

What folly this! But oh! that all the rest
Of his dire reign had thus been spent in jest!
And all that time such trifles had employed,
In which so many nobles he destroyed.
He safe, they unrevenged, to the disgrace
Of the surviving, tame, Patrician race.
But when he dreadful to the rabble grew,
Him, who so many Lords had slain, they slew!

) Aelius

(*g*) Ausi quod liceat tunicâ punire molestâ.

Sat. 8. *lin.* 235.

(*h*) Vestis erat e chartâ, cannabe, stuppâ. Illinebatur bitumine, resinâ, pice. Tum circumdabatur iis, qui grave quid- piam, et maxime, incendia moliti fuerant. Quâ demum incensâ vivi comburebantur. *Annot. in loc. ed. in usum Delphini.*

(*i*) Atque utinam his potius nugis tota illa dedisset
Tempora sevitiae, claras quibus abstulit Urbi
Illustresque animas impune, et vindice nullo.
Sed periit, postquam cerdonibus esse timendus
Caeperat. Hoc nocuit Lamiarum caede madenti.

Sat. iv. *ad fin.*

Ch. VII. *Of Domitian's Perfecution.*

A. D. 100.

Aelius Lamia, whofe death is likewife particularly mentioned by Suetonius *(k)* undoubtedly was a man of a very ancient and noble familie. And Domitian had killed many other Senators. The Chriftians were generally of the meaner rank of people, and more defpifed ftill for their religion, than their condition. But they were not all of the rabble, or coblers and taylors, as Juvenal would infinuate. And *Flavius Clement*, one of thofe, whom Domitian put to death near the end of his reign, and whofe death, as Suetonius exprefsly fays, haftened Domitian's ruin, was of the Imperial familie, and as we think, a Chriftian. However, it is obfervable, that Juvenal fays, Domitian's death foon followed after fome acts of cruelty toward mean people. Herein he agrees with, and confirms the accounts of fome Chriftian writers, particularly, that of *Caecilius*, or *Lactantius*, in his book of the deaths of Perfecutors. Who obferves, " that *(l)* Domitian had been long permitted to ex-
" ercife great cruelties upon his fubjects: But when he began to per-
" fecute the fervants of God, he was foon delivered up into the
" hands of his enemies."

IV. It may be obferved, that I do not allege among witneffes to Chriftianity, or the affairs of Chriftians, the Philofopher, *L. A. Seneca*. There is exftant a correfpondence between him and St. *Paul*, in fourteen Letters. Which may be feen, in Latin, in *(m)* Fabri-

An Advertifement concerning Seneca.

(k) Sueton. Domit. cap. x.
(l) Poft hunc, [Neronem] interjectis aliquot annis, alter, [Domitianus.] non minor tyrannus orfus eft: qui cum exerceret invifam dominationem, fubjectorum tamen cervicibus incubavit quam diutiffime, tutufque regnavit, donec impias manus adverfus Dominum tenderet. Poft-quam vero ad perfequendum juftum populum inftinctu daemonum incitatus eft, tunc traditus in manus inimicorum luit poenas. *Caec al Lact. De M. P. cap.* 3.
(m) Cod. Apocr. N. T. Tom. 2. *p.* 880. &c. *Conf. ejufd. Bibl. Lat. Tom. i. p.* 367.

A a a

cius,

cius, and in Latin and English, in Mr. (*n*) *Jones*, with remarks. They were in being in St. Jerome's time, and Seneca therefore is mentioned by him (*o*) in his catalogue of Ecclesiastical Writers. But they are manifestly spurious, and of no value. And therefore are not entitled to a place here. Nor do they deserve any regard.

I have put this advertisement here, at the end of the chapter of *Juvenal*, because he is the last author of the first centurie, who is alleged by me.

(*n*) See him *of the Canon of the N. T. Vol.* 2 *ch. x. p.* 80. &c.

(*o*) Lucius Annaeus Seneca Cordubensis, Sotionis Stoici discipulus, et patruus Lucani poetae, continentissimae vitae fuit. Quem non ponerem in Catalogo Sanctorum, nisi me illae Epistolae provocarent, quae leguntur a plurimis, Pauli ad Senecam, et Senecae ad Paulum. In quibus, cum esset Neronis magister, et illius temporis potentissimus, optare se dicit, ejus esse loci apud suos, cujus sit Paulus apud Christianos. Hic ante biennium, quam Petrus et Paulus coronarentur martyrio, a Nerone interfectus est. *Hieron. De V. I. cap. xii.*

CHAP.

CHAP. VIII.

SUETONIUS.

I. *His Hiſtorie, Time, and Works.* II. *The Jews expelled from Rome in the Reign of Claudius.* III. *His Account of Nero's Perſecution.* IV. *His Teſtimonie to the Jewiſh War, and the Overthrow of the Jewiſh People.* V. *Of Domitian's Perſecution of the Chriſtians.* VI. *The Sum of his Teſtimonie.*

I. CAIUS SUETONIUS TRANQUILLUS (*a*) ſon of *Suetonius Lenis*, (*b*) flouriſhed in the reigns of *Trajan* and *Adrian*, to the later of whom he was Secretarie. Which (*c*) place he loſt about the year 121. Plinie the Younger had a particular friendſhip for him. Several of Pliny's letters ſtill exſtant, are writ to him.

A. D. 110. His Hiſtorie.

A a a 2 And

(*a*) *Vid. Voſſ. de Hiſt. Lat. l. i. cap.* 26. *Bayle Dictian. Hiſt. et Crit. Suetone. Tillemont. H. Emp. Adrien. art.* 24.

(*b*) Interfuit huic bello pater meus Suetonius Lenis, tertiae decimae legionis tribunus anguſticlavius. *Sueton. Othon. cap. x.*

(*c*) Septicio Claro, Praefecto Praetorii, et Suetonio Tranquillo, epiſtolarum magiſtro, multiſque aliis, qui apud Sabinam uxorem, injuſſu ejus, familiarius ſe tunc egerant, quam reverentia domus aulicae poſtulabat, ſucceſſores dedit... *Spartian. in Adrian. cap. xi.*

SUETONIUS. Ch. VIII.

A. D. 110.

And he performed for him divers good offices. *Suetonius* having no children by his wife, Plinie procured for him from Trajan *jus trium liberorum*, or the privilege of those, who have three children. His recommendation of him to the Emperour is very affectionate, and exhibits a very amiable (*d*) character.

That he was born about the begining of the reign of Vespasian, is argued hence, that (*e*) about twenty years after the death of *Nero*, or in 88. he speaks of himself as a young man. It may be supposed therefore, that in the 13. of Trajan, or the year of our Lord 110. he was not less than forty years of age.

He was the author of a good number of books, of which there are now none remaining, but his *Lives of the first twelve Cesars*, and a part of a Work *concerning Illustrious Grammarians and Rhetoricians*.

The Jews banished from Rome in the Reign of Claudius.

II. Suetonius, in the Life of the Emperour *Claudius*, who reigned from the year 41. to 54. says of him: "He (*f*) banished the "Jews from Rome, who were continually making disturbances, "Chrestus being their leader."

This passage undoubtedly confirms what is said Acts xviii. 2. that *Claudius had commanded all Jews to depart from Rome* (*g*). Some learned men are not satisfied, that this relates to the Christians. But it is well known, that our Saviour was sometimes called (*h*) *Chrestus* by

---

(*d*) Suetonium Tranquillum, probissimum, honestissimum, eruditissimum virum, et mores ejus secutus et studia, jampridem, Domine, in contubernium assumpsi. &c. *Plin. l. x. ep.* 95.

(*e*) Denique cum post viginti annos, adolescente me, exstitisset conditionis incertae, qui se Neronem esse jactaret, &c. *Sueton. in Neron. cap. ult.*

(*f*) Judaeos impulsore Chresto assidue tumultuantes Româ expulit. *Claud. cap.* 25.

(*g*) See *the Credibility, &c. P. i. B. i. ch. xi. sect.* 3.

(*h*) ... Perperam Chrestianus pronunciatur a vobis, &c. *Tertull. Ap c.* 3. Sed exponenda hujus nominis ratio est, propter

Ch. VIII. *Of the Expulsion of the Jews from Rome.* by Heathen people. And it is not impossible, that the Jewish enmity against those of their own countrey, or others, who had embraced Christianity, might produce some disputes and disturbances, which came to the Emperour's knowledge. This seems to be the meaning of Suetonius, "that there were disturbances among the Jews and others at Rome upon occasion of Christ, and his followers."

A. D. 110.

If this passage were clear, we should have a testimonie from an Heathen author of good note, that there were Christians at Rome before the end of the reign of Claudius: as indeed we know there were, from an authentic writer of our own. Acts xviii 2. and 26. And compare Rom. xvi. And though it should not be reckoned clear and decisive, it has such an appearance of probability, as has satisfied many learned men of good (*i*) judgement.

This passage of Suetonius is expressly cited by (*k*) Orosius, a Christian

---

ter ignorantium errorem, qui cum immutata litera Chreſtum ſolent dicere. *Lact. Divin. Inſt. l.* 4. *c.* 7.

(*i*) Cum dixi ſupra, ſub Judaeorum nomine comprehenſos Chriſtianos, id dixi quod complures ante me, multo me eruditiores. Neque tamen id impedit quo minus durior fuerit conditio Chriſtianorum, ut etiam in Judaica religione multa novantium, pluresque homines a paganiſmo abducentium. Quo ſpectat illud Suetonii de Claudio, *Judaeos, impulſore Chreſto,* (id eſt, per Chriſtianum dogma,) *aſſidue tumultuantes, Româ expulit. &c.* Grot. App. ad Comm. de Antichriſto. p. 499. *Vid et Cellarii Diſſ. de primo principe Chriſtiano.* § *viii. et Baſnag. Ann.* 51.

num. 68. *Cleric. H. E. ann.* 29. *n. xc. Heumanni Diſſ. de Chriſto Suetonii ap. Diſſertation. Syll. T. i. p.* 536. *&c. Kortholt. De Perſecut. Ecc. p.* 4. *Tob. Eckhard. non Chriſtianorum Teſtimonia. cap. i.* S. *Havercamp. annot. ad Tertullian. Apol. cap.* 3. *p.* 42.

(*k*) Sed me magis Suetonius movet, qui ait hoc modo. *Claudius Judaeos, impulſore Chriſto aſſidue tumultuantes, Româ expulit.* Quod utrum contra Chriſtum tumultuantes Judaeos coerceri et comprimi juſſerit, an etiam Chriſtianos ſimul, velut cognatae religionis homines, voluerit expelli, nequaquam diſcernitur. *Oroſ. Hiſt. l.* 7. *cap.* 6.

A. D. stian Historian, of the fifth centurie. But he was not clear about
110. the meaning of it.

Nero's Persecution of the Christians

III. In the Life of Nero, whose reign began in 54. and ended in 68. Suetonius says: "the *(l)* Christians were punished, a sort of men of a new and magical superstition."

Suetonius here assures us, that the Christian Religion was lately arisen, and that it had already gained footing in the Empire. From his calling it *a magical superstition*, it may be argued, that (*m*) there were some things of an extraordinarie nature performed by the Christians: or that they endeavored to justify their embracing the religion of Christ, as of divine original, upon the ground of some wonderfull works, which bore testimonie to it's truth and authority.

I have translated, the word *Malefica*, used by Suetonius, *magical*, agreeably to the judgement of divers learned men. But Mr. Mosheim (*) thinks the word to be equivalent to *exitiabilis*, in Tacitus, meaning *pernicious*. The Christians were singular in their religious

---

(*l*) Afflicti suppliciis Christiani, genus hominum, superstitionis novae et maleficae. Sueton. Nero. cap. 16.

(*m*) *Maleficos* incantatores, magicis rebus studentes, venenarios, interpretatur Barth. Adv. viii. 17. x. 6. 45. 57. . . Pro talibus Christianos habuerunt deterrimis Gentiles, forte quia daemonia illis parebant, et ad illorum contestationem ejiciebantur. . . . Exinde capiendum putat Barthius, Luc. vi. 22. Καὶ ἐκβάλωσι τὸ ὄνομα ὑμῶν ὡς πονηρόν. Nec mirum. Hoc enim genere *maleficii* D. Jesum calumniabantur Gentilium accusationes. Arnob. p. 25. *Occursurus forsitan.rursus est cum aliis multis calumniosis illis, et puerilibus vocibus: Magus fuit, clandestinis artibus omnia illa perfecit.* Sed D. Jesu caussam satis accurate ibid. agit Arnobius. *Pitiscus ad Suetonii locum.*

(*) Neque Romanam solum, sed omnium etiam aliarum gentium religiones Christiani hostiliter invadebant: ex quo Romani concludebant, sectam Christianam non modo praeter omnem modum arrogantem, verum paci ac tranquillitati publicae inimicam, et ad bella civilia cienda aptam esse. Hoc illud est, si recte conjicio, quod Tacitus Christianis exprobat, *odium generis humani*. Nec aliunde rationem putem duci debere, cur idem Christianorum religionem, *superstitionem exitiabilem*, Suetonius autem *maleficam* nominet. *Mosheim. Instit. H. E. p. 33. 34.*

Ch. VIII. Of Nero's Persecution.

gious sentiment, and opposed the religions of all nations. The Romans therefore considered them, he thinks, as *enemies to all mankind,* and disposed to disturb the public peace.

In the word *new,* undoubtedly, there is a sting. For as Tacitus says of the Jews, " Whatever (*n*) might be the origin of their religion, it has the advantage of antiquity."

That the Christians were roughly handled in the reign of Nero, we have seen from Tacitus, a contemporarie writer. Nevertheless it has been observed by some learned men, that (*o*) Suetonius does not say, particularly, that they were *punished at Rome,* or for setting fire to the City. His expressions are general, and may include more extensive sufferings in the *provinces,* as well as the City. Of which we have good assurance *(p)* from divers ancient Christian writers.

Once more. It may be observed, that *Suetonius* speaks with approbation of the sufferings, which the Christians endured in this reign. For *(q)* they are mentioned together with divers other acts, ordinances, or institutions of Nero, which were entitled to some commendation: as (*r*) any one will allow, who observes the several articles in the same chapter.

IV. In

(*n*) Hi ritus, quoquo modo inducti, antiquitate defenduntur. *Tacit. Hist. l.* 5. *cap.* 5. *p.* 518.

(*o*) Nec refert, quod Tacitus de iis, quae in provinciis adversus Christianos gesta sermonem non habeat, cum Suetonius de Nerone, cap. 16. persecutionem ad urbem Romam non restringat. *Pagi ann.* 64. *n. iv.*

Et quidem Suetonius, a Nerone *afflictos suppliciis christianos* commemorans, nullam Romani incendii facit mentionem, sed eos *genus hominum superstitionis novae ac maleficae* appellat. Quae cum referat Suetonius inter ea, quae a Nerone instituta fuerant, haud dubium est, quin edictum adversus Christianos ab eo tyranno scriptum fuerit. *Ruinart. Pr. in Acta Mart. n.* 26. *p.* 32.

(*p*) ... ac per omnes provincias pari persecutione excruciari imperavit. *Orof. l.* 7. *aap.* 7.

(*q*) Id sane ita Suetonio persuasum erat, ut inter ea, quae aliqua laude digna a Nerone sancita commemorat, ait, ab ipso fuisse *afflictos suppliciis Christianos. Ruinart. Ib. n.* 25. *p.* 29.

(*r*) Adhibitus sumtibus modus. &c. *eod. cap.* 16.

A. D.
110.
Of the Jewish War, and the Desolations of Judea.

IV. In his Life of Vespasian Suetonius writes to this purpose: "When (*s*) Nero went into Achaia, Vespasian was one of the Court. But shewing a dislike of that Emperour's extravagances, he lay under his displeasure, and was apprehensive of the consequences of his resentment. Vespasian therefore retired into a private place at some distance, where an honorable province, with a powerfull armie, was assigned him. There had been for a long time, all over the East, a prevailing opinion, that it was in the fates, [*in the decrees, or books of the fates,*] that at that time some one from Judea should obtain the empire of the world. By the event it appeared, that a Roman Emperour was meant by that prediction. The Jews applying it to themselves, went into a rebellion. At first they had such successe, that they not only overcame their own Governour, but also defeated the Proconsular Governour of Syria, who came to his assistance. There being now manifest occasion for a General of great reputation, and a nu- "merous

---

(*s*) Peregrinatione Achaica inter comites Neronis, cum cantante eo aut discederet saepius, aut praesens obdormisceret, gravissimam contraxit offensam: prohibitusque non contubernio modo, sed etiam publica salutatione, recessit in parvam et deviam civitatem, quoad latenti, etiamque extrema metuenti, provincia cum exercitu oblata est. Percrebuerat Oriente toto vetus et constans opinio, esse in fatis, ut eo tempore Judaea profecti rerum potirentur. Id de Imperatore R. quantum eventu postea praedictum paruit, Judaei ad se trahentes rebellarunt. Caesoque Praeposito, Legatum insuper Syriae proconsularem suppetias ferentem raptá aquilá fugaverunt. Ad hunc motum comprimendum cum exercitu ampliore, et non instrenuo duce opus esset, ipse potissimum electus est. Additis igitur ad copias duabus legionibus, octo alis, cohortibus decem, atque inter Legatos majore filio assumto, ut primum provinciam attigit, proximas quoque convertit in se. Correcta statim castrorum disciplina, uno quoque et altero praelio tam constanter inito, ut in oppugnatione castelli lapidis ictum genu, scuto sagittas aliquot exceperit. . . . Et unus ex nobilibus captivis Josephus, cum conjiceretur in vincula, constantissime asseveravit fore, ut ab eodem brevi solveretur, verum jam Imperatore. . . . Talis, tantáque cum famá in Urbem reversus, acto de Judaeis triumpho, consulatus octo veteri addidit, *Sueton. Vespasian. cap.* 4. . . . 8.

Ch. VIII. *His Testimonie to the Jewish War.*

"merous armie, Vespasian was appointed for that service: who a-
"mong other commanders under him had his eldest son Titus.
"Having put his armie into good order, he entred upon the war
"with great vigour, and not without hazard to his own person, ha-
"ving been slightly wounded in an attack made at one of their
"towns, and received several darts upon his shield. Suetonius
"proceeds to relate the accession of Vespasian to the Empire, whilst
"he was in Judea, and takes notice of what Josephus, one of the
"Jewish prisoners, had beforehand said to him relating to that mat-
"ter. And he expresly mentions Vespasian's triumph over the
"Jews at Rome."

In his Life of Titus, he says, "that (*t*) whilst he yet served un-
"der Vespasian, he took *Tarichea* and *Gamala,* two strong cities of
"Judea: and that having in an engagement lost his own horse, he
"mounted another, whose rider had been killed in fighting against
"him." And he says, "that (*u*) Titus having been left in Judea
"to compleat the reduction of that countrey, he in the last siege of
"Jerusalem, killed seven of the enemie with as many darts: and
"that he took that city on his daughter's birth-day, and was then
"saluted by the soldiers with the title of Emperour." He also says,
"that (*x*) Titus triumphed at Rome with his Father."

Suetonius is a biographer. And therefore does not write of the
Jewish

(*t*) Ex Quaesturae deinde honore legioni praepositus, Tarichaeam et Gamalam urbes validissimas Judaeae in potestatem redegit: equo quadam acie sub feminibus amisso, alteroque inscenso, cujus rector contra se dimicans occubuerat. *Tit. cap.* 4.

(*u*) ... et ad perdomandam Judaeam relictus, novissima Hierosolymorum oppugnatione vii propugnatores totidem sagittarum confecit ictibus: cepitque eam natali filiae suae, tanto militum gaudio ac favore, ut in gratulatione Imperatorem eum consalutaverint. *Ib. cap.* 5.

(*x*) Triumphavit cum patre, Censuramque gessit una. *Ib. cap.* 6.

B b b

A. D. 110.

Jewish war so particularly, as an historian of another character might do. Nevertheless he may be justly reckoned a witness to the fulfillment of our Saviour's predictions concerning the destruction of Jerusalem, and the overthrow of the Jewish people. He bears testimonie to the Jewish war, and the occasion of it. He mentions the Generals employed in it, and the issue of it in the taking of Jerusalem, and the reduction of Judea, and the triumph thereupon at Rome.

In the Life of *Domitian*, whose reign began in the year 81. and ended in 96. Suetonius says: " And *(y)* beside others, the Jewish " taxe was exacted with the greatest severity, and was demanded of " those who lived in the city according to the Jewish customs, with· " out entring themselves as Jews, or who dissembling their original, " had omitted to pay the taxe laid upon that nation."

It is well known, that after (*z*) the destruction of Jerusalem, the Jewish people, wherever they dwelled, were required by Vespasian and Titus to pay that tribute to the Capitol at Rome, which they had been wont to pay for the use of the temple at Jerusalem. Among those, of whom this taxe was now exacted, it is likely, there were divers sorts of men. Some Gentils, who had embraced Christianity, might be looked upon as Jews. These were under no obligation to pay this taxe. Beside them, some Jews, who were become Christians, might think themselves excused from paying this tribute. Whether reasonably, or not, I do not determine. For according to the letter of the law, they were obliged to pay it, as being

---

(*y*) Practer ceteros, Judaicus fiscus acerbissime actus est: ad quem deferebantur, qui vel improfessi Judaicam intra Urbem viverent vitam, vel dissimulatâ origine, imposita genti tributa non pependissent. Interfuisse me adolescentulum memini,

cum a procuratore, frequentissimoque consilio, inspiceretur nonagenarius senex, an circumsectus esset. *Domitian cap.* 12.

(*z*) *Vid. Joseph. De B. J. l. 7. cap. vi. §. 6. p. 419. Havere.*

Ch. VIII.   *His Teſtimonie to the Jewiſh War.*   371

ing circumciſed : though they might think, that in equity they had a right to plead an exemption. And beſide all theſe, there might be ſome Jews, both by nation and religion, who declined this taxe. Theſe, I ſuppoſe, will not be vindicated by any, unleſs they ſcrupled to contribute to a Heathen Temple.

A. D. 110.

To theſe ſeveral ſorts of men, probably, Suetonius here refers. Nor can it be doubted, that ſome Chriſtians met with ſufferings upon this account, under the name and character of Jews, from whom they had received their religion. And, perhaps, this ſtorie of Suetonius has a reference to *Domitian*'s perſecution of the Chriſtians, commonly called the ſecond perſecution.

This (*a*) taxe was not exacted with the ſame rigour under that good Emperour Nerva. But it was not aboliſhed, as ſome have thought.

This paſſage ought to be underſtood as another teſtimonie, from the ſame writer, to the final overthrow of the Jewiſh people by the Romans, as Jeſus had foretold.

V. Among the cruelties of the later part of *Domitian*'s reign Suetonius mentions this. " And laſtly, (*b*) he put to death his couſin

Domitian's Perſecution of the Chriſtians.

B b b 2   " fin

(*a*) ... item *fiſcus Judaicus*, ut Suetonio, Domit. 12. qui cum acerbiſſime ageretur ſub Domitiano, JUDAICI FISCI CALUMNIA SUBLATA eſt ſub Nerva, ut teſtatur nummus apud Oiſelium. . . Unde tamen plane ceſſaſſe hoc tributum non evincitur, ſicut Begerus et Spanhemius jam demonſtrarunt. *Reimar. annot. ad Dion.* C. *p.* 1082. §. 43.

(*b*) Denique Flavium Clementem pa-

truelem ſuum, contemtiſſimae inertiae, cujus filios, etiam tum parvulos ſucceſſores palam deſtinaverat : et abolito priore nomine, alterum Veſpaſianum appellari juſſerat, alterum Domitianum : repente, ex tenuiſſima ſuſpicione, tantum non in ipſo ejus Conſulatu interemit. Quo maxime facto maturavit ſibi exitium. *Domit.* *cap.* 15.

SUETONIUS. Ch. VIII.

A. D. 110.

" ſin FLAVIUS CLEMENT, a man of an indolent temper even to
" contempt, whoſe ſons, when they were as yet infants, he had
" publicly declared his ſucceſſors, and changing their former names,
" he called the one *Veſpaſian*, and the other *Domitian*. Him he
" put to death on a ſudden, upon a ſlight ſuſpicion, when he was
" but juſt out of his Conſulſhip. By which action, more than by
" any other, he haſtened his own ruin."

This happened in the year of our Lord (c) 95. Suetonius does not expreſsly ſay, that *Flavius Clement* was a Chriſtian. That may be farther cleared up (✻) hereafter. However, it may be argued from the character, here given of Clement, that he was *a man of an indolent temper, even to contempt :* that having been a reproach, frequently caſt upon the Chriſtians by Heathen people, that they were uſeleſs, and unprofitable to the publick : as we learn from (d) Tertullian, and (e) other ancient writers.

In this character of *Clement* there ſeems to be a cenſure of him for exceſſive indolence. But I think, the chief and direct intention of Suetonius is to aggravate the cruelty of Domitian, who put to death ſo near a relation, in whom there was not one ſpark of ambition, and therefore there could be no reaſon to fear any thing from him.

Before I ſhut up this article, I muſt obſerve ſome things for explaining the laſt cited paſſage of Suetonius.

Flavius

(c) *Vide Pagi. ann. 96. num. ii. et Baſ-nag. ann. 95. n. iv.*

(✻) *See the chapter of Dion Caſſius, in the third volume.*

(d) *Sed alio quoque injuriarum titulo expoſtulamur, et infructuoſi in negotiis dicimur. Tert. Ap. cap. 42.*

(e) *Cum autem hunc Flavium Clementem contemtiſſimae inertiae hominem vocat Suetonus, eo ipſo Chriſtianum fuiſſe demonſtrat. De quo injuriae in Chriſtianos titulo, quod inertes, et inutiles, et infructuoſi dicerentur, Tertull. Ap. cap. 42. Torrent. in Sueton. loc.*

Ch. VIII.   *Of Domitian's Persecution.*   373

Flavius Clement was cousin-german to Domitian. There *(f)* were two brothers, *Flavius Sabinus*, and *Flavius Clement*, sons of *Flavius Sabinus*, Vespasian's elder brother. *Sabinus*, the elder of those two brothers, had been put to death by Domitian some while before, as is related by *(g)* Suetonius. The second was put to death now, as just related. The death of *Flavius Clement* is also mentioned by *(h)* Dion Cassius, as will be more particularly observed by us hereafter. It is also mentioned by *(i)* Philostratus, in his Life of *Apollonius Tyanaeus*, and as a thing that hastened the death of Domitian himself. And we ought to recollect here what we before saw in (*) *Juvenal.*

A. D. 110.

Suetonius assures us, that *Domitian had publicly declared the sons of this Clement to be his successors, and he changed their names, calling the one Vespasian, and the other Domitian.* Undoubtedly, they are the two young persons, whom Domitian had committed to the care and institution of (*k*) *Quintilian:* who calls them *the grandchildren of Domitian's sister.* Domitian's only sister, *Domitilla*, died before Vespasian came to the Empire, as we learn from *(l)* Suetonius. But she must have left a daughter of the same name; whose

---

(f) Vid. Sueton. Vespas. cap. 12. et Vitell. cap. 15. Tacit. Hist. l. 3 cap. 65. Eutrop. l. 7. cap. 18. Victor. de Caes. cap. viii. Joseph. de B. J. l. 4. cap. x. §. 3. Conf. ib. cap. xi. §. 4.

(*g*) Flavium Sabinum alterum e patruelibus, [occidit] quod, &c. *Sueton. Domit. cap. x.*

(*h*) ... ἄλλας τε πολλὰς, ᾗ τὸν Φλάβιον Κλήμεντα ὑπατεύοντα, καίπερ ἀνεψιον ὄντα, κατέσφαξεν ὁ Δομιτιανός. *Dio. l. 67. c. 14. p. 1112. al. p. 760.*

(*i*) Εὐθὺν δὲ ἐσοὶ Δομετιανὸν ἤδη τῆς αὐ‑ θρώπων προσδοκίας. Ἔτυχε μὲν γὰρ Κλή‑ μεντα ἀπεκτονὼς, ἄνδρα ὕπατον, ᾧ τὴν ἀδελ‑ φὴν τὴν ἑαυτοῦ ἐξεδώκει. *Philost. de V. A. T. l. 8. cap. 25.*

(*) *p. 360. and 361.*

(*k*) Cum vero mihi Domitianus Augustus sororis suae nepotum delegaverit curam. *Quintil. Imp. l. 4. Pr.*

(*l*) Ex hac liberos tulit Titum, et Domitianum, et Domitillam. Uxori et filiae superstes fuit: atque utramque privatus amisit. *Sueton. Vespas. cap. 3.*

whose sons therefore were her grandsons. What became of them afterwards, we are not informed.

Finally, Dion Cassius, in the place above cited, calls Clement *Consul*. Suetonius says, *he was put to death on a sudden, when he was just out of his Consulship*. But there is no disagreement between them in this. For *(m)* the ordinarie Consuls did not then serve out the whole year, but others were substituted in their room, after a few months, or a less space. However, the year was still reckoned with the names of the ordinarie Consuls, and they preserved the title throughout the whole year. Clement therefore was still Consul, though another, or several, one after another, had been substituted. As before said, Clement was put to death in 95. the year of his Consulship.

The Sum of his Testimonie.

VI. We have seen so many things in *Suetonius*, that it may not be improper to recapitulate. For he bears witnesse to the expulsion of the Jews and Christians out of Rome in the reign of *Claudius:* to the Persecution of the Christians in the time of *Nero:* to the Jewish war, and the reduction of Judea by *Vespasian and Titus*, and therein is a witnesse to the accomplishment of our Saviour's predictions, concerning the calamities coming upon that people. He likewise mentions the death of *Flavius Clement*, which we suppose to have happened in the time of *Domitian's persecution of the Christians*.

To all these things does *Suetonius* bear testimonie, who is an historian of the best credit, and lived at the end of the first, and the beginning of the second centurie.

Our

(m) Vid. *Pagi et Basnag. ut supra. not.* (c) p. 666. *et Reimar. in Dion Cass.* p. 1112.

Ch. VIII.   *The Summ of his Teſtimonie.*   375

Our next Author will be the Younger PLINY, at the begining of the ſecond centurie.   A. D. 110.

I have placed *Suetonius* before him, and in this volume, becauſe his teſtimonie has a near affinity with the particulars mentioned by Tacitus, and the two other laſt mentioned writers.

An Alphabetical

TABLE

OF

Principal Matters in the FIRST VOLUME.

A

ABgarus, King of *Edeſſa*: His Letter to our Saviour, and our Saviour's Refcript, with remarks. 297.

Abomination ſtanding in the holy place. Explained. 49.

Acts of the Apoſtles: received by the Nazarean Chriſtians. 21.

Acts of Pontius Pilate, and his Letter to *Tiberius*. 310... 330.

Acts of the Senate of Rome, and of Governours of provinces, and other *Acts*. 314... 316.

Agrippa, and his ſon *Monbaz*: put to death at Rome by Vefpaſian, according to Joſippon. 218.

Akibas: a Jewiſh Rabbin of great note: his hiſtorie, and character. 183. 185. 186. 189.

Apollonius Tyanaeus: his letter to Titus, after the conqueſt of Judea. 139.

Arch of Titus at Rome. 125. 140. 243.

B

Bagoas, an Eunuch in the Court of Herod the Great. 173.

Barchochebas: a Jewiſh impoſtor, who ſet himſelf up for the Meſſiah, in the time of Adrian. 29. 185. 186.

Mr. Baſnage: his remarks upon the prodigies preceding the deſtruction of Jeruſalem, as related by Joſephus. 108.

D. Blondel: quoted. 144. 167.

C

Calumnies upon the firſt Chriſtians: What they were, and the origin of them. 24... 29. 183. 187.

Ceſtius Gallus, Governour of Syria: his unſucceſsful expedition into Judea. 71... 75. 265.

Chri-

Christians: how treated by the unbelieving Jews. 24. that they left Jerusalem before the siege of that place began. 50. 75. 76. 131.

Flavius Clement: a relation of Domitian, and Consul of Rome, put to death by that Emperour. 371... 374.

D. Colonia: quoted. 333.

Mr. Crevier, quoted. 90. 110.

D

DION Cassius: his testimonie to the conquest of Judea by Titus. 139.

Ph. Doddridge: His observations upon the Testimonie of Josephus. 133.

Domitian: the cruelties of his reign, and the occasion of his death. 360. 361. 373. 374.

Domitilla: a relation of Domitian. 373.

E

Ebionites: two sorts of them. 17. 18. And see *Nazareans.*

Epponnina, wife of *Sabinus,* her excellent character. 90. 91.

Eusebius: his observations upon the testimonie of Josephus. 134. the paragraph in Josephus concerning our Saviour, first quoted by him. 151. 162. how he quotes Plutarch. 333.

F

Faber, quoted. 144. 162.

The famine at the siege of Jerusalem: The distresses of it described. 95. 97. 99. 100. 102. 222. 223. 225. 226.

J. A. Fabricius: his judgement upon the value and usefulnesse of the works of Josephus. 171. quoted, and commended. 155. And see p. 38. note *(l)*

G

Gagnier: quoted. 210. 212. 214. 217. 220. 239. 241. 243.

Gamaliel, the aged: St. Paul's master. His great eminence, and that he never embraced the Christian Religion. 183. 186.

Gospel: that the gospel was preached all over the Roman Empire, before the destruction of Jerusalem. 50. 51.

The Gospel according to the Hebrews. a character of it. p. 21. note (A).

J

James, the Lord's Brother: the paragraph concerning him in Josephus not genuine. 163. the true account of his death. 165.

Jehudah, or Judah, the Holy: composer of the Mishna. his time and character. 176. 177. 178. 186.

Je-

of PRINCIPAL MATTERS. 379

Jerome: well acquainted with Jewish traditions. 184. his accounts of the Nazarean Christians. 19. 22.

Jerusalem. When taken by Pompey. 39. When the siege of it by Titus began. 48. 93. When it was taken by him. 48. 117. 12. the distresses of the city, during the Siege. See *Famine*. The numbers of people who perished there in the siege, and elsewhere in Judea. 119. 129. 236.

JESUS. his predictions of the calamities coming upon the Jewish people. 41. his miracles true, and certain, and well attested. 257. 258. that he is the Christ. 292. his nativity according to Talmudical writers. 189. his journey into Egypt, according to the same writers. 190... 193. his disciples, according to them. 194. his last sufferings, according to the same. 198.

Jesus, or Joshua, the son of Ananus. his remarkable storie. 106. 112. 232.

Early Jewish Believers: their faith a valuable testimonie to the Truth of the Christian Religion. 3. ... 23. their faith a great virtue. 13.

Jewish Unbelievers: how they treated the first Christians. 24.. : 29.

Jews: their sin in rejecting the Lord Jesus very great. 70. 280. 284... 287. crucified by the Roman soldiers, before the walls of Jerusalem. 95. 96. 228. 229. and 119. ript up for the sake of treasure. 98. 227. the numbers, that perished in the siege of Jerusalem, and elsewhere. 119. 129. 236. many compelled to fight in amphitheatres. 123. 124. 236. their circumstances a cogent argument for the truth of the Christian Religion. 287... 290. required to pay tribute to the Capitol at Rome. 127. 370.

Inscriptions: in honour of Titus, after the conquest of Judea. 141. concerning the Christians in the time of Nero. 385.

John the Baptist: how he was revered for his austere character by Josephus, and many other Jews. 148... 150. the genuineness of the paragraph concerning him in the works of Josephus, asserted. 142... 150.

John, of Gischala: how he escaped from that place, and got to Jerusalem. 82. 83. taken prisoner. 235. and condemned to perpetual imprisonment, according to Josephus. 120. the account of his death in Josippon. 235. See likewise p. 265.

J. Jones: quoted. 307. 308. 362.

Fl. Josephus: His time, works, and character. 31. how he flattered

Ves-

Vespasian and Titus. 34. 35. 61. 174. his works not much respected by the Jews. 36. 211. his historie of the Jewish War, and the siege of Jerusalem, and the conquest of Judea. 71... 129. the value of his testimonie. 129.... 135. observations upon his writings and testimonie. 168... 174. three paragraphs in his works concerning John the Baptist, Jesus, and the Lord's Brother, the genuinnesse of which is considered. 142... 168.

Joseph Ben Gorion, or Josippon: His age, work, and character. 209. 243. 245. his testimonie to the Jewish war, the siege of Jerusalem, and the destruction of the city, and the temple, by Titus. 213... 241. observations upon his work. 259. 260.

Jotapata: the siege of that place, and the event of it. 33. 34. and 213. 214.

Isidore of Pelusium: his observations upon the testimonie of Josephus. 134.

T. Ittigius: quoted, and commended. 156.

Judea: first brought into subjection to the Romans by Pompey. 39.

Justus, of Tiberias: his testimonie to the conquest of Judea by Titus. 135. 136. 137.

Juvenal: his time and works. 358. his testimonie to Nero's persecution of the Christians. 359. his testimonie to Domitian's persecution. 360.

Izates, his relations in Jerusalem: surrender to Titus, and are received by him. 114. 115. 232. 233.

L

J. *Lightfoot:* quoted, and commended. 178. 180. in the notes. 190. 194. 195. 196. 198. 200. 241.

M

M*achaerus:* John the Baptist said to have been beheaded there. 143. 144. 146. how taken by the Romans. 126.

Martial: his time, and writings, and testimonie to the fortitude of the Christians. 354... 357.

MARY, our Lord's mother: how aspersed by the Jews. 28. 29. 189.

Mary, a woman of good condition at Jerusalem, who killed her child for food in the siege. 102. 230.

Massada: the remarkable siege, and surrender of that place. 127. 128.

St. Matthew: his Gospel received by the Nazarean Christians. 21.

Meïr: an eminent Jewish Rabbi. 182. 185.

Messiah: the expectation of his coming general in the time of our Saviour.

viour. 69. 283. that Jesus is the Messiah. 292.
Mishna: the time, and author of that work. 175... 178. extracts out of it. 179.
J. L. Mosheim: quoted. 329. and 338. in the notes.

N

Nazarean Christians: received St. Paul and all the Apostles of Christ, and all the books of the New Testament. 18.... 22. and 21. note (A). Their opinion concerning the person of Jesus Christ, and the observation of the rites of the Mosaic Law. 16. 22. that they subsisted in the fourth and fifth centuries. 22.
Nero: the time of his death. 85. his persecution of the Christians testified by Tacitus. 344. by Sulpicius Severus. 347. Martial. 355. Juvenal. 359. Suetonius. 366. an inscription concerning the Christians, in his time. 335.

O

Origen: refers to a passage of Josephus concerning John the Baptist. 144. and see 149 how he quotes Josephus, as ascribing the destruction of Jerusalem to the sin of the Jews, in putting Jesus to death. 152. 153. his testimonie to our Saviour's unblamable and unblemished character, in his works against Celsus. 192. 193.

P

PAN: a fabulous storie concerning his death, in the time of the Emperour Tiberius. 330.... 334.
St. Paul: his character and historie. 10. 11. rejected by the Ebionites, or some of them. 17. but received by other Jewish believers, called Nazareans. 19... 21.
Pausanias: his testimonie to the destruction of Jerusalem by a Roman Emperour. 137.
Bishop Pearson: quoted. 314. 329.
Philostratus: his testimonie to the destruction of Jerusalem by Titus. 139.
Pliny the Elder: his time, and character, and whether he refers to the blindnesse inflicted by St. Paul upon Elymas, the sorcerer, in Cyprus. 339. 340.
Plutarch: his dialogue concerning the cessation of oracles quoted. 330. 333. quoted. 91.
Pompey: the time of his conquest of Judea, and taking Jerusalem, and his behaviour there. 39.
Pomponia Graecina: a Roman Lady, accused of a foreign superstition, (supposed to be the Christian) in the time of Nero, and the year of Christ 57. 343.

Pontius

Pontius Pilate: his Acts, and Letter to Tiberius. 310... 313.
H. Prideaux: his account of the Mishna, and Talmuds. 176. 177.
Prodigies, preceding the destruction of Jerusalem, according to Josephus. 104. according to Josippon. 231. according to Tacitus 351.
Prophets: the origin of that character, signs, whereby they may be known, and the great guilt of rejecting the messages of true Prophets. 254. 255... 257... 260.
False Prophets, in Judea, before the destruction of Jerusalem. 64.... 70. 104. and see 128. 129.

R

H. *S. Reimar:* quoted, and commended. 89.
Adrian Reland: his observations upon the Arch of Titus, and the spoils of Jerusalem. 125. 126. 243.

S

S*Abinus:* a Gallic Prince, his remarkable historie. 90. 91.
L. A. Seneca, the Philosopher: his description of cruel sufferings and punishments. 356. 357. not alleged, as a witnesse to Christianity. 361. 362.
Simon, son of Gioras: one of the Jewish Leaders in Jerusalem, taken prisoner, and reserved for the triumph. 120. led in triumph at Rome, with other prisoners, and then put to death, according to Josephus. 125. the account of his death in Josippon. 235. what Tacitus says of him, and the other Jewish Generals. 351.
Spoils of the Temple: delivered to Titus. 116. carried in triumph at Rome. 124. 125. how long preserved. 126. what Josippon says of these. 233. 234. what the Talmudists say, of their being carried to Rome by Titus. 206.
Suetonius: his time, and works. 363. his testimonie to the expulsion of the Jews and Christians out of Rome, in the time of Claudius. 364. his testimonie to Nero's persecution of the Christians. 366. 367. his testimonie to the Jewish War, and the desolations of Judea by Vespasian and Titus. 368. 369... 371. and see p. 138. his testimonie to Domitian's persecution. 371... 373. the sum of his testimonie. 374.
Suicide: practised by the Jews, that they might not come alive into the hands of the Romans. 33. 80. 81. 82. 128. 215.
Sulpicius Severus: his account of Nero's persecution of the Christians. 347.

T

T

COrnelius Tacitus: his time, and works. 341. his account of Nero's persecution of the Christians. 344... 348. his testimonie to the destruction of Jerusalem by Vespasian and Titus. 348...353. and see 139.

Talmud: the several acceptations of that word. 175. the times of the Jerusalem and Babylonish Talmuds. 177. 178. extracts out of the two Talmuds, concerning the nativity of Jesus. 189. concerning our Lord's journey into Egypt. 190... 194. concerning his disciples. 194. concerning James in particular. 197. concerning his last sufferings. 198. concerning the power of miracles in Jesus, and his disciples. 202. and 203. and see 191. 192. concerning the destruction of Jerusalem and the temple, by Vespasian and Titus. 204.... 208.

The Temple at Jerusalem: when taken by Pompey. 39. when destroyed by Titus. 48. 103. it's magnificence, and great riches. 41. 42. 103. 120. 352. how rebuilt after the return from the Babylonish captivity. 271.... 273. the times of the duration of the two temples, that built by Solomon, and that built after the return from Babylon. 274. 275.

The Temple of Onias in Egypt: demolished by orders from Vespasian. 129.

The Temple of Peace: erected at Rome by order of Vespasian, after the conquest of Judea. 125. 126.

Testaments of the twelve Patriarchs: a character of that work. 18. 19.

Thamus: an Egyptian Pilot: a storie concerning him in Plutarch. 330. .. 334.

Tiberius, the Roman Emperour: what knowledge he had of our Saviour Jesus Christ. 310... 330.

L. Tillemont: his observations upon the testimonie of Josephus to the destruction of Jerusalem. 133. upon his paragraph, relating to our Saviour. 157.

ABp. Tillotson: his observations upon the testimonie of Josephus to the destruction of Jerusalem. 132.

Titus: his remarkable speech to the chief leaders of the people at Jerusalem. 62. his good character from Josephus, and Heathen writers. 87. unwilling, that the Temple should be destroyed. 101. proclaimed Emperour by the Roman soldiers, after taking the Temple at Jerusalem. 113. his treatment of John and Simon. 113. 114. and 120. his journey from Judea to Rome. 122.... 124. his arch at Rome. 125.

125. 140. 243. did not refuse to be crowned for the conquest of Judea. 139. an inscription to his honour. 141. how he is asperfed by the Jewish Rabbins, and Talmudical writers. 206. 207. 243. commended by Josippon. 242.

Toldoth Jeschu: quoted. 190. quoted again, and the character of that work. 247. note (*a*)

V

VEspasian: appointed General in the Jewish War by Nero. 77. proclaimed Emperour in Judea, and at Alexandria. 86. 87. Miracles ascribed to him, but not really such. 87. 88. his treatment of Sabinus and Epponnina, with remarks. 90. 91. his good character. 87. and see p. 77. note (*o*)

C. *Vitringa*: his judgement concerning the passage in Josephus, relating to Jesus Christ. 162.

W

J. C. *Wagenseil*: his accounts of the time of the Mishna, and of Jehudah the composer of it. 175. 177. 187. his remarks upon a passage in the Talmud. 197. upon the Toldoth Jeschu. 247. note (*a*)

War: the time and duration of the Jewish war with the Romans. 48. events, preceding the war, and the siege of Jerusalem. 50. . . 60. the occasion of the war, according to Josephus. 60. . . . 71. the historie of the Jewish war, and the siege of Jerusalem, from Josephus. 71. . . 129. from other histories of the Jewish war, beside that of Josephus 135. . . 141.

Dr. *Warburton*, Bp. of Gloucester: quoted with respect. 163.

Dr. *Willes*: his remarks upon the prodigies preceding the destruction of Jerusalem, as related by Josephus. 107.

W. *Whiston*: quoted. 38. 94. 159. 173.

D. *Whitby*: his observations upon the testimonie of Josephus, and the Talmuds, to the destruction of Jerusalem. 134.

W. *Wotton*: his observations upon the testimonie of Josephus to the destruction of Jerusalem. 133. upon the two Talmuds. 175. 177. note (*c*)

The End of the first Volume.

www.ingramcontent.com/pod-product-compliance
Lightning Source LLC
Chambersburg PA
CBHW032009220426
43664CB00006B/185